D0793269

40$\frac{00}{x}$
1st ed.
Inscr.
Review copy

Pasó por Aquí

Para mi amigo
Jim, quien pasó
por mi vida
dejando claras
huellas, con
gran afecto

egb
1989

Pasó por Aquí

Critical Essays on the New Mexican Literary Tradition, 1542–1988

EDITED BY ERLINDA GONZALES-BERRY

UNIVERSITY OF NEW MEXICO PRESS

ALBUQUERQUE

Library of Congress Cataloging-in-Publication Data

Pasó por aquí : critical essays on the New Mexican Hispanic literary tradition, 1542–1988 / edited by Erlinda Gonzales-Berry. — 1st ed.
p. cm.
Bibliography: p.
ISBN 0–8263–1158–X
1. American literature—New Mexico—History and criticism.
2. American literature–Hispanic American authors—History and criticism.
3. Hispanic American literature (Spanish)—New Mexico—History and criticism. 4. Hispanic Americans—New Mexico—Intellectual life.
5. Hispanic Americans in literature. 6. New Mexico—Intellectual life.
7. New Mexico in literature. I. Gonzales-Berry, Erlinda, 1942–
PS283.N6P37 1989
860.9′9789—dc20 89–33819
CIP

Chapter 11 originally appeared as "A Reassessment of Fray Angelico Chavez's Fiction" in MELUS II, No. 2. Copyright MELUS (Society for the Study of Multiethnic Literature of the United States), 1984.
Chapter 13 was originally published in *Hispania* (September 1985) and is reprinted by permission.
Chapter 14 was originally published in the *New Mexico Humanities Review* (Fall 1985) and is reprinted by permission.

First edition

Contents

INTRODUCTION

ERLINDA GONZALES-BERRY

Almost one hundred years ago Walt Whitman recognized the need to acknowledge the contributions of Hispanic culture if a true syncretic portrait of American culture were ever to emerge: "To the composite American identity of the future, the Spanish character will supply some of the most needed parts." It is in the spirit of realizing Whitman's prophecy that we offer this text.

When Europeans first stumbled upon the land they later called America they found a concrete geographical entity that was overwhelming by its sheer presence. The immediate problem posed to its "discoverers" was how to share their finding with Europe; how to re-present it in a manner that would generate approval for its appropriation and domination. A preliminary step in the description of America necessitated its placement within the boundaries of previous experience. When concrete entities and events—land, animals, and weather—did not match the lived experiences of the observer, the alternative was to draw upon textual experiences. In fact, Columbus's first journey, Tzvetan Todorov reminds us, was motivated by his textual experience of a previous journey, one which had groomed Europeans for their forays into the unknown. "Did not Columbus himself set sail because he had read Marco Polo's narrative?"[1] Thus from the beginning, European knowledge of America—and knowledge is a prerequisite for domination—was placed within a textual framework, and to the texts that nourished the initial descriptions, new texts were added: letters, chronicles, epic poems, histories. It is this textualization that has led contemporary scholars to speak of "the invention of America."

The exploration of what is today the American Southwest added new chapters to that invention, initiating what was to become a rich Hispanic literary tradition in New Mexico. As early as 1542 accounts of the land and its inhabitants had appeared in print in a volume called *La relación*. Alvar Núñez Cabeza de Vaca's was the first of a prolific series of chronicles devoted to a description of the exploration and colonization of the region by Spanish adventurers and friars, among them men who cherished the Renaissance ideal of cultivating both pen and sword. Colahan's and Leal's contributions to this book demonstrate that this literature seeks to re-present New Mexico as both concrete and textual reality. Resonances of the "legitimate marvelous" espoused by European Renaissance narrators abound in the chronicles discussed by Colahan as do echoes of the oral texts of the native peoples, though the latter tend to be veiled by the overwhelming prominence of dialogues with European texts. Likewise, Villagrá's epic poem, which depicts the tangible events surrounding the defeat of the Acomas, is inspired by the text of another Spaniard: Ercilla's *La Araucana*. Villagrá's poem is an important counterpart of the chronicle. While the chronicle purportedly documents the real while drawing upon inspiration from the imagined, the poem unravels within the boundaries of a literary genre but draws heavily upon experienced reality—so much so, Leal points out, that it has served as a primary source for historians.

The postexploration period saw New Mexican Spanish colonials faced with the reality of survival in a harsh and isolated environment. Formal literary activity was generally limited to official documentation by government scribes and ecclesiastical scholars. A lone voice of creative expression from that period is to be found in the poetry of a *vecino* of Santa Cruz, Miguel de Quintana. Lomelí and Colahan's study links Quintana's poetry to the Spanish mystical literary tradition and gives some evidence of the central role of religion in the lives of eighteenth-century Hispanic colonists. Of special importance is what their essay reveals about the role of the Spanish Inquisition in New Mexico.

The fact that isolation and lack of the appropriate means of production prevented the printing of texts and the development of literacy on a grand scale does not mean that creative expression ceased to exist. The creative spirit bequeathed to New Mexicans by early chroniclers and the poet Villagrá continued over a 250 year period to encourage a rich oral tradition of folk drama, tales, and balladry. This tradition, generated in the arid landscapes of Spain, was transplanted to the equally arid landscapes of New Mexico where it was enriched by the lore of the indigenous population and vigorously continued to renew itself with each generation and to fill the void created by the scarcity of written literature. Rivera and Anderson's contributions shed light on the formal and traditional characteristics of folk verse and drama and situate them within the social contexts that generated new topics for old forms.

Political events in the nineteenth century ushered in the decline and eventual end of Spanish-Mexican dominion in the Southwest and created conditions propitious for the "reinvention" of New Mexico. Not unlike the Spaniards of the sixteenth century, the recently arrived *americanos* faced an unknown land and a foreign "other." Highly motivated to appropriate this land, they moved quickly in their observation, description, and textualization of the "unknown" in order to create a corpus of knowledge that would facilitate the process. It is not coincidental that many of the texts written by Anglo explorers echo European texts that gave shape and essence to the discourse on Orientalism in the eighteenth and nineteenth centuries. Edward Said, in his discussion of the origins of the invention of the "Orient" observes that "Many terms were used to express the relation: Balfour and Cromer, typically used several. The Orient was irrational, depraved (fallen), childlike, 'different'; thus the European is rational, virtuous, mature, 'normal'."[2] We could easily examine all the texts (historical, judicial, journalistic, creative) about the Southwest immediately before and long after its annexation to the United States and unravel therein the components of a discourse of domination that echoes the discourse of Orientalism described by Said: "Orientalism was ultimately a political vision of reality whose structure posited the difference between the familiar (Europe, the West, 'us') and the strange (the Orient, the East, 'them')."[3] A similar political vision of the Southwest clearly pointed to the need for regeneration and salvation of the area and of the foreign "other" in the interest of progress, civilization, and cultural hegemony. This political vision was inscribed in the texts of Josiah Gregg, W. W. H. Davis, the *New York Times*, and the rhetoric of politicians in Congress, who for sixty-two years denied New Mexico statehood.[4]

Ironically, it was the political machinations surrounding the statehood issue that generated the need for yet another discourse, one capable of undoing the damage created by the initial "inventors" of the American Southwest. To the texts that posited New Mexicans as inferior, immoral beings, thus unworthy of citizenship, countertexts such as the following were offered:

> Those who have opportunities of meeting socially the better classes of people will concur that a more courteous, hospitable, and chivalric social element does not exist in the land. They are fit representatives of the level of the Cid, and successors of the historic discoverers and conquerors of the soil.[5]

Thus, with one swift penstroke, Lebaron Bradford Prince, eager to see more immigration of easterners to New Mexico—he was the first director of the New Mexico Bureau of Immigration—and genuinely interested in the material and political development of the state, engraves in the discourse of domination a white legend that was to strip New Mexican culture of all traces of *mestizaje*, to affiliate Nuevo Mexicanos with an elite cadre of knights on white horses, to relegate them to the memory of a utopian past, to historicize them so that the present and the future belonged exclusively to the *americanos*.[6] The creative literature of the late nineteenth and the early twentieth centuries was to disseminate this discourse, and its most refined expression is to be found in what Carey McWilliams has called "the Spanish fantasy heritage."[7] We are inclined to view expressive literature as the product of original perceptions and interpretations arising from the creative and critical capacities of writers. But in the case of the literature of authors who found in the Southwest the enchantment of the pastoral paradise negated by their own industrialized milieu (so aptly characterized by Leo Marx with his metaphor, the machine in the garden[8]), we cannot lose sight of the fact that as cultural artifact, literature is moored in sociocultural processes. As such it tends to articulate a selectivity atuned with the needs of the dominant power structure. Edward Said's observations on the relationship between the seemingly autonomous text and sociohistorical conditions clarify the political nature of European cultural products of the nineteenth century:

> For to see the novel as cooperating with society in order to reject, what Gareth Steadman Jones has called outcast populations, is also to see how the great aesthetic achievements of the novel . . . result from a technique for representing and appropriating subjects, people, settings, and values in affiliation with specific historical and social norms of knowledge, behavior, and physical beauty. . . .
>
> . . . Apologists for the novel continue to assert the novel's accuracy, freedom of representation, and such; the implication of this is that the culture's opportunities for expression are unlimited. What such ideas mask, mystify, is precisely the network binding writers to the State and to a world-wide "metropolitan" imperialism that, at the moment they were writing, furnished them in the novelistic techniques of narration and description with implicit models of accumulation, discipline, and normalization.

Perhaps no other Southwestern novel exemplifies this process as egregiously as Willa Cather's *Death Comes for the Archbishop*. In her portrayal of Father Martínez, for example, she inscribes in the creative domain the attitudes toward the native clergy disseminated by the texts of Gregg and Davis. Cloaking New Mexican priests in habits of licentiousness and immorality, the texts of the latter facilitated the Americanization of the Mexican Catholic church and its people.

Consequently, whatever Cather's intent, her novel must be viewed as part of a larger discourse of domination.

Aware of their gradual dislodgement and of the danger posed by the newcomers to their native language and way of life, Hispanics engaged in a flurry of cultural activity, evidence of which is to be found in the proliferation of Spanish-language newspapers, particularly during the middle and late Territorial Period. One senses from a reading of the extant material that the motivating force was to affirm cultural identity by a positing of the written Spanish word as an amulet against imminent displacement. Much of the creative literature of this period does not raise the voice in blatant protest,[10] yet it establishes itself firmly and must be viewed as a response to the discourse being generated by the texts of the dominant culture, that is, as discourses that speak from a condition of subordination.

When overt examples of protest do appear in the creative literature, they tend to be veiled. For example, in Eusebio Chacón's allegorical novel a narrative mode of seemingly pure fantasy hides a caustic comment on the social chaos of his time. As Lomelí has pointed out, some of the poetry of this period demonstrates a more obvious expression of resistance. The link between this poetry and oral verse is apparent, since it is in the oral genres that response to conflict is most frequently expressed. Walter Ong, in his study of the relationship between orality and literacy, points out that oral creative expression tends to be "agonistically toned," for "by keeping knowledge embedded in the human lifeworld, orality situates knowledge within a context of struggle."[11] He adds, "Portrayal of gross physical violence, central to much oral epic and other oral genres and residual through much early literacy, gradually wanes or becomes peripheral in later literary narrative" (44). Once again, Lomelí's study on Eusebio Chacón's work exemplifies this observation for, as he points out, despite the fact that it is a highly self-conscious literary work, it is a product of residual orality. The violence depicted therein is further proof of its rootedness in the oral tradition.

The literature of Hispanic New Mexicans does not always represent the feelings of resentment generated by displacement that are more apt to be found in the oral genres. Hispanos themselves often participated in the political and economic process whereby their people were subordinated, and it is possible to encounter, in the literature of the Territorial Period, attitudes toward the mexicano population that coincide with the discourse of domination generated by Anglo texts since the secession of Texas. Though not included in this study, an examination of M. A. Otero's autobiography would reveal such attitudes.[12]

Unfortunately many of the works produced in the territorial period remain unpublished. Manuel Salazar's novella, "Gervasio y Aurora, o la historia de un caminante," 1883, and Porfirio Gonzales's "Historia de un Cautivo," 1898, are unpublished manuscripts that testify to the creative forces alive within the Hispanic community during this period but that have not yet received due attention by literary scholars precisely because they are not accessible in print. Yet a true portrait of the period, a portrait capable of balancing the prevailing discourse of dominance, will emerge only when all texts are brought to light and given the attention they deserve. Jacqueline Meketa, in her recent publication of Rafael Chacón's memoirs, *Legacy of Honor*, acknowledges the importance of incorporating the Hispanic perspective into the existing discourse: "Perhaps now the distorted portraits of New Mexico's earlier colonizers, seen through a glass darkly, will be corrected through the rare Hispanic perspective presented in Chacón's account."[13]

In the twentieth century we find that Hispanics continue to record their experiences, their dreams and aspirations, their fears and disappointments. The impact of English-language education is evident as most writers turn to English as the primary mode for expressive communication. Exceptions are Vicente Bernal's collection of poetry, *Las Primicias*, 1916, which contains a number of entries in Spanish, and Felipe Maximiliano Chacón's collection of poetry and prose, *La obra de Felipe Maximiliano Chacón "El Cantor Neomexicano": Poesí y Prosa*, published in 1924. Bernal's poetry of exile is perhaps more interesting for what it does not express than for what it does. His apparently neutral stance vis-à-vis the political events of his time does not necessarily reflect acquiescence. But neither does his work fall clearly within a discourse of resistance that was gradually being written by those who found themselves marginalized from mainstream society. Perhaps his ambivalent stance was the only one afforded Nuevo Mexicanos at a time when they were trying to prove their worth as bona fide American citizens, yet were not completely oblivious to the machinations that denied them legitimacy. F. M. Chacón clearly grapples with this issue as he extolls the patriotic virtues of his fellow Nuevo Mexicanos, urging them to be model citizens. There is, nonetheless, an awareness in his work of the damaging effects of the discourse of domination. But rather than offer a countertext, Chacón makes much of the fact that having endured and survived that discourse is precisely what, in the long run, will make Nuevo Mexicanos more worthy of a place in the new order afforded by statehood. If Chacón's work, which seems to balance precariously between two discursive modes, is to be viewed as leaning more toward a discourse of resistance, we must accept as evidence his choice to write in Spanish despite his bilingual ability.

Other pioneer writers of the twentieth century are Nina Otero-Warren, Cleofas Jaramillo, and Fabiola C. de Baca. By the time these women wrote, the "Spanish fantasy heritage" was well entrenched in the minds of both Anglos and Hispanics. Nowhere is this attitude so obvious as in Otero-Warren's campaign for Congress in 1922. It is her filiative genealogy—"Spanish Don's Daughter Among 4 Women in Race for Congress" reads the headline of one newspaper article—that aroused public interest and allowed her to affiliate with the dominant culture whose conquistador rhetoric provided a social aperture for those Hispanics who would proclaim their roots in an ahistorical past. Otero's *Spain in Our Southwest* clearly places the Nuevo Mexicano *ricos* in a medieval reality: "So, in this country, a grandee of New Spain still held court. He followed the old customs every day; his home was his court, from this he received courtly attention, his servants were his vassals and gave him submission."[14] Furthermore, "The Spanish *doñas* always sat with an air of great dignity, as of holding court" (36), from which they awaken to find that new knights have conquered their kingdom. While Otero indeed enunciates a plaintive lament against the social change that has displaced New Mexican Hispanics from the land, she eases the pain by mystifying the past. The danger of such mystification is that it creates a utopian vision that obfuscates more dynamic historical analysis. Yet that vision highlights, by contrast, the instability of the writing present and Otero's feelings of helplessness and inadequacy to alter the course of events.

Jaramillo and C. de Baca, like Otero-Warren, use the autobiographical perspective to render their memories of a way of life that was rapidly passing on, and, like her, they desire to preserve through the written word. Landscape becomes an important image whereby they attempt to contrast the instability of the moment with the memory of a less troubled and discordant past where order was imposed by tradition and by knowledge of one's place within an unthreatened cultural milieu. Jaramillo and C. de Baca's sense of loss is more authentically rendered than Otero-Warren's, for they occasionally offer glimpses of a world grounded in contradiction and conflict rather than in a static pastoral setting. In a number of ways the work of these women echoes some of the trappings of the prevailing discourse of domination; yet, as Diana Rebolledo points out, it is surprising that they wrote at all given the role of women, and specifically the role of Hispanic women, during their time. Their works fill many pockets of silence on the lives of women, providing information that male writers are apt to pass over or to trivialize.

Fray Angelico Chavez began writing in the thirties and continues to do so today. In the main, Fray Angelico has been dismissed as a writer prompted above all by religious inspiration, whose writings are of interest to a limited audience. Genaro Padilla observes, however, that, behind the seemingly idyllic religious vision, lie hidden intergroup allegories of class conflict and indictments of the aggressive American "Philistines." Chavez is not to be faulted for his cryptic renditions, for like F. M. Chacón, Otero, Jaramillo, C. de Baca, and Bernal, he wrote in a period in which the pressure to adapt to "the ways of the *americanos*," to pay perennial proof of loyalty and patriotism, left little room for public expression of discontent with their subordinate social position.

The work of Sabine Ulibarrí provides a bridge between these early pioneers and contemporary Chicano writers. Steeped in traditional life, but made wise to the ways of the world by a college education at the University of California, Ulibarrí draws upon Spanish belles lettres and the bucolic life-style of his youth to give us stories tinged with the same nostalgia that appears in the work of the pioneer writers. To preserve this past for posterity is obviously a strong motive for Ulibarrí, as is his desire to resist total change. The latter is made manifest in his use of Spanish at a time when publication possibilities for works in Spanish were virtually nonexistent. His use of Spanish links him to the contemporary Chicano generation, because for them language became central to their discourse of cultural identity, affirmation, and self-determination.

The last section of the book consists of an appraisal of the poetry and narrative of a younger generation of writers who have drawn inspiration from the pioneers, from the oral tradition, and from contemporary trends in order to offer now sweet, now bitter memories of the past and optimistic visions of the future. The primary difference between the literature of the contemporary writers and that of the pioneers is that the contemporary writer works within the context of a sociopolitical movement that self-consciously sought to respond to discourses of domination and to offer in their stead re-visions of the past. These young writers do not write alone as did the pioneers before them; the advent of university classes in which their works are read, the emergence of presses eager to print materials produced from a bilingual and bicultural perspective, the nascent interest among mainstream scholars in the cultural production of non-centralized groups, makes them aware that they are part of a new movement that encompasses more than a regional perspective. Though they continue to express regional concerns, they enter into dialogues with Chicano writers in Texas and Arizona, with critics from California and from Yale University. Thus, their work reflects a spirit that is so aptly captured in the title of Márquez's article, *Algo viejo y algo nuevo*. Rudolfo Anaya forms the link between the old and the new with his mythical vision of the past and his focus on contemporary existential issues. Well grounded in their study of the broader corpus of Chicano and Chicana literature, Lamadrid, Bruce-Novoa, and Márquez interpret what it means to write from a Hispanic perspective, the roots of which reach far back into New Mexican history, and they link that perspective to the shared cultural experience of Mexican Americans throughout the United States.

A proud literary tradition notwithstanding, New Mexican Hispanic writers have been virtually ignored in mainstream literary histories of the Southwest. There is little that might add to Lomelí's excellent attention to the matter. From his essay it becomes clear that the omission is the result of a long and complex process that generated a well-entrenched discourse of domination wherein invasion, usurpation of power, and relegation of a people were justified. In light of this problem, it is the intent of these essayists to bring the work of New Mexican Hispanic writers to the attention of a broad reading public and to illuminate the Hispanic writer's interpretation of the historical and social events that have shaped the multicultural character of the region.

NOTES

1. Tzvetan Todorov, *The Conquest of America: The Question of the Other*, trans. Richard Howard. (New York: Harper and Row Publishers, 1985), p. 13.

2. Edward Said, *Orientalism* (New York: Pantheon Books, 1978), p. 40. The tendency in Western culture to embed all knowledge within the confines of a binary system results in the creation of a hierarchical system wherein the elements associated with one end of the pole (the "known subject") are valued positively and those of the opposite (the "unknown object" or "other") are represented in the most negative of terms. Scholars of contemporary culture, among them Said, have pointed out that the discourses resulting from this process become the legitimate or received discourses whereby domination and subordination are justified. It is within this conceptual framework that many of the comments in this introduction are posited.

3. Ibid. The European need to concretize this view in order to achieve political and economic power in the Orient does not escape Said: "Orientalism is therefore not an airy European fantasy about the Orient, but a concrete body of theory and practice in which for many generations there has been a considerable 'material investment' " (p. 6).

4. See for example Josiah Gregg, *Commerce of the Prairies: The Journal of a Santa Fe Trader* (New York: Henry G. Langley, 1844; rpt. Dallas: Southwest Press, 1933), who in one of the earliest *americano* texts sets the tone for subsequent evaluations of New Mexico and her people:

> The New Mexicans appear to have inherited much of the cruelty and intolerence of their ancestors, and no small portion of their bigotry and fanaticism. Being of a high imaginative temperament and of rather accommodating moral principles—cunning, loquacious, quick of perception and psychopantic, their conversation frequently exhibits a high degree of tact—a false glue of talent eminently calculated to mislead and impose. They have no stability except in artifice; no profundity except in intrigue; qualities for which they have acquired an unenviable celebrity. Systematically cringing and subservient while out of power, as soon as the august mantle of authority falls on their shoulders, there are but little bounds of their arrogance and vindictiveness of spirit (p. 143).

Embedded in William W. H. Davis's text, *El Gringo, or New Mexico and Her People* (New York: Harper and Brothers, 1857, rpt., New York: Arno Press, 1973), are resonances of the black legend and a sense of racial and moral superiority that is in no way inferior to Gregg's:

> As would naturally be the case, a people so various in their origin as the Mexicans, and in whose veins flows the blood of three distinct races, would present a corresponding diversity of character. They possess the cunning and deceit of the Indians, the politeness and spirit of revenge of the Spaniard, and the imaginative temperament and fiery impulses of the Moor. . . . They have inherited a portion of the cruelty, bigotry, and superstition that have marked the character of Spaniards from the earliest times (p. 217).

These same racialist arguments were aggressively reiterated for years as justifications for the denial of statehood to New Mexico. In 1882, for example, a letter in the *New York Times*, 2 February 1882, carries the following attack against the women of New Mexico: "It is a patent, notorious fact, blasoning itself forward with startling boldness that in no other part of Christendom are the women of the entire community so generally without virtue, and so ready to prove their insensibility for a money consideration."

5. Lebaron Bradford Prince's response to the letter cited above in the *New York Times*, 28 February 1882.

6. For further discussion on this matter see Russel E. Saxton, "Ethnocentrism in New Mexico Historical Literature," Ph.D. diss., University of New Mexico, 1980.

7. Carey McWilliams, *North from Mexico: The Spanish Speaking People of the United States* (1948, rpt., New York: Greenwood Press, 1972). While McWilliams's discussion focuses primarily on California, evidence of the legend can be found beginning in the late territorial period in New Mexico, and it certainly remains present today. Most historians associate the Hispanic New Mexican's tendency to identify with things Spanish while denying all ties to things Mexican to the arrival of massive waves of immigrants during the Mexican Revolution. The practice, however, begins much earlier and is the result of a deliberately engineered strategy of political and economic implications. The desire to lure Eastern immigration to New Mexico, on the one hand, and the need to make the native population acceptable to a race-conscious Congress, thereby facilitating statehood, are intimately linked to the emergence of the "Spanish fantasy heritage" in New Mexico. Initially, the pressures exerted on the native population as a result of the frustrating attempts to achieve statehood and, subsequently, pressures resulting from nativist reactions to Mexican immigration led Nuevo Mexicanos to assimilate and to propagate the idea as ultimate truth. Spanish suppers, at which enchiladas and tamales are served, Spanish *caballeros* dressed in Mexican *charro* costumes, Spanish fiestas held on the Mexican holiday *Cinco de Mayo* are all ironic examples cited by McWilliams to point out the contradictions inherent in this myth. Furthermore, he discusses the origins and numerous factors that have contributed to the myth; but, more important, he makes manifest the effects of this cultural discourse:

> By emphasizing the Spanish part of the tradition and consciously repudiating the Mexican-Indian side, it has been possible to rob the Spanish-speaking minority of a heritage which is rightfully theirs. . . . The constant operation of this strategy has made it difficult for the Spanish-speaking people to organize and it has retarded their advancement. (p. 45)

8. Leo Marx, *The Machine in the Garden: Technology and the Pastoral Ideal in America* (New York: Oxford University Press, 1964).

9. Edward Said, *The World, The Text, and The Critic* (Cambridge, Mass.: Harvard University Press, 1983), p. 176.

10. Exceptions, of course, are to be found. Doris Meyer in her article "Early Mexican-American Responses to Negative Stereotyping," *The New Mexico Historical Review* 53:1 (1978), draws material from the Territorial newspapers to demonstrate that Neuvo Mexicanos did not acquiesce passively vis-à-vis the rhetoric of Anglo-American writers. The following citation from *La Voz del Pueblo*, 7 August 1897, is an example of the type of response that indeed belongs to the discourse of resistance of which I speak in this introduction:

> In the view of the people of New Mexico, in the opinion of every man who possesses a heart and soul and in whose character there exists nobility, one does not judge a whole people to be bad because they are poor or because they are ignorant, especially when the blame for their ignorance rests with government under whose protection they live. And the person or persons who make such judgments are themselves the best evidence of their own low character, of their own baseness. (p. 78)

11. Walter J. Ong, *Orality and Literature: The Technologizing of the Word* (London and New York: Methuen Press 1982), p. 44.

12. See, for example, Miguel Otero, *My Life: Nine Years as Governor of New Mexico, 1897–1906.* (Albuquerque: University of New Mexico Press, 1940, rpt., 1987).

13. Jacqueline Dorgan Meketa, *Legacy of Honor: Rafael Chacon, a Nineteenth Century New Mexican.* (Albuquerque: University of New Mexico Press, 1986), p. 9.

14. Nina Otero-Warren, *Old Spain in Our Southwest.* (New York: Harcourt Brace and Co., 1936), p. 15.

1

NORTHWARD BOUND

Literature of Discovery

1

CHRONICLES OF EXPLORATION AND DISCOVERY

The Enchantment of the Unknown

CLARK COLAHAN

Only a century separated Columbus's first voyage to the New World and the Spanish settlement of New Mexico under Oñate. During a little less than the first half of that century New Mexico and what is now the American Southwest remained unknown, unnamed, and nonexistent for Europeans. But by the fourth decade of the sixteenth century Cabeza de Vaca and three companions, helped by Indians all along their way, walked across the state from Carlsbad to Redrock in their escape from a failed expedition to Florida, an escape guided by the hope fulfilled eight years later that by following the setting sun they would reach their countrymen in Mexico. The news with which they arrived there spurred on the advance of exploration from the recently established Spanish "kingdoms" to the north of Mexico City, and the next sixty years saw several expeditions of discovery, all of which left records of what they found and did in the form of reports, letters, or chronicles. As literature they culminate in Villagrá's Renaissance epic describing Oñate's 1598 "conquest" and settlement, as discussed by Luis Leal in the following chapter.

But the earliest chronicles are literature, too, and worth reading for more than their contribution to what we know about the land and its peoples before Europeans came and about the beginnings of Spanish rule, settlement, and culture.

They easily lend themselves to being read as more than documentary, more than the unfolding of the geographic and ethnographic map of the area. They are examples of what has been called, with special reference to the exploration of America, the discovery of the "other," an experience that can take a variety of forms, but not that of pure intellectual observation.[1] Such a discovery always has an impact on the discoverer. These writers made value judgments on what they encountered, chose in some way how much they would accept or reject the image of the world held by the indigenous Americans, and obtained varying degrees of insight into the real nature of all that was different from them. Like snails, like the medieval men they still were in many ways (indeed like all of us to some extent), they carried the dome of their own sky with them, their image of the world, their own previously established way of making sense of people and places.

Their belief in the fabulous and wealthy Seven Cities of Cíbola, thought for a while to be located in New Mexico, was medieval. Earlier known as the cities of Antilia (hence the Antilles), they were believed in the Middle Ages to have been founded on an island in the Western Ocean by seven Spanish bishops fleeing from the Moorish conquest of their city.[2] On the other hand, their historical experience at Mexico City was very recent. The discovery of Mexico City's wealth and advanced civilization greatly increased the reasonableness of looking for such cities found in myth and legend. Thus the persistence with which the Spanish pursued the fabulous and legendary in New Mexico and the chronicles that record it can be read not only as uncalled-for heroics inspired by fanciful literature but as examples of a human response, daring yet rational, to the possibilities of the unknown.

Nevertheless, the form taken by these accounts is closer to literature than to social science. They bear the stamp of each writer's personality and life situation. These author-participants write in the first person and, with one or two fascinating exceptions, tell us their stories guilelessly, enabling us to perceive the circumstances and motivation behind their taking pen in hand to write. Their extraordinary undertaking—the break with the ordinary that defines exploration—calls for explanation, and each explains and justifies himself in his own particular way; they emerge as characters in their own more or less purposeful and artful creation. What distinguishes one chronicle from another is not—as one might expect if they were thought of as documents of the expanding information on file about New Mexico in the sixteenth century—at what point in the series of expeditions to the region they were written, but rather the unpredictable set of variables that come together in each author; the accounts do not evolve like a hypothesis corrected by subsequent experiments. The fact is that through viceroys' secrecy, lack of access to printing, and the spread of stories by word of mouth these chroniclers were often unaware of what their predecessors had actually done and reported, and each chronicle is primarily the record of a personal discovery of the unknown.

ALVAR NÚÑEZ CABEZA DE VACA

Probably born about two years before Columbus's first voyage, Cabeza de Vaca is in some ways the first European to have a true North American experience, yet the man who emerges from this encounter in the pages of his *Relación* has seemed to many readers to be instead the last conquistador, the closest to us in time by virtue of the quality of his response. The grandson of Pedro de Vara, cruel conqueror of the Canary Islands, he joined the Pánfilo de Narváez expedition to Florida as second in command, having been named by the crown treasurer and *alguacil mayor*, the official responsible for presenting accusations to the king regarding cruelty to the Indians. After enduring every sort of hardship, including shipwreck in improvised boats on islands off the Texas coast, he and other survivors lived enslaved there by the Indians. But possessing extraordinary intelligence and initiative, he became a trader between tribes, an occupation that gave him a degree of freedom and eventually the opportunity to escape. Slowly he and three companions worked their way west, at first supporting themselves by making combs, arrows, and other salable items, but later helped on their way by being identified by the Indians themselves as spiritual healers. In the company of an escort formed by members of one tribe after another they were received as children of the sun having power to kill or cure. One of the four was a bright Moorish slave known as Estebanico from the northwest coast of Africa. His dark complexion, which led the Spanish to refer to him as *negro*, helped convince the tribes they met of their supernatural origin, for the appearance of something so strange as both black and white men seemed clearly miraculous.

It was not until October 1535 that they entered southern New Mexico, which made a very good impression on them after the primitive living conditions on the Gulf Coast. Shortly after entering Arizona they turned south and encountered a tribe that told them the Spanish were near, and soon thereafter their extraordinary journey from the Atlantic to the Pacific was completed. In 1542, after being passed over in favor of De Soto to head another expedition to Florida, Cabeza de Vaca made his discoveries public by bringing out his account in Spain, the only one describing exploration in New Mexico to be published before Villagrá's *Historia* in the next century.[3]

Compared with that epic in verse, or Inca Garcilaso de la Vega's *Florida*, it is a straightforward, unpolished recounting of actions and observations; the writer has been so completely separated from Europe and lived so differently that the conventionally heroic, with reminiscenses of the popular romances of chivalry we find in other chronicles, is absent.[4] Instead we meet a somewhat self-effacing, direct observer offering precise yet full information, more interested in the people than the land and its resources. In his case intimate familiarity frees him to see and be fascinated. For example, he prefaces his description of how the Jumanos, a plains tribe, cooked food by heating stones and placing them in gourds full of water by saying, "to show and make known how diverse and strange are the wit and inventiveness of human beings."[5]

His perception of New Mexico is of a culture superior in every way to those he had previously encountered. He tells us that he and his companions were overjoyed and thanked God when they reached the Jumanos, who were living near El Paso with the benefits of agriculture, an abundance of buffalo meat and hides, and what he thought were fixed houses. As he crossed the state he heard stories of surprisingly advanced cultures living up the Rio Grande, of copper deposits there from which the forged rattle they showed him had come, of their cotton cloth, of their cities. And he found the tribes he saw in the south to be the most obedient and handsome he had known. Later in the San Bernardino Valley of Sonora he was given "emerald" (probably malachite) arrowheads and told by the Opatas that they came from the tall mountains in the north, where there were large towns with big buildings, and for this reason he called the Sonoran village at the site of modern Ures "The Gateway to the North."

In his own time this picture of the still mysterious yet beckoning northland was what most interested the public. In our century two different, but essentially American themes have won him readers. First is his approach to the question of how different races live together, and specifically his growing admiration and even partial identification with the peoples he meets.[6] The primary explanation for this is surely that, in spite of the label, he does not arrive among them as a conquistador. He is not traveling with a large group of armed men capable of and prepared to impose their views and desires on others. He learns and is helped by the native Americans, and without them he would never have survived nor made his way across the continent. Another reason that has been suggested for his ability to empathize is his compassion for the sick and injured who were brought to him for help at each village. Those who say that this is the story of a writer learning of "brotherhood and human kinship" are unquestionably right.[7]

But in terms of a mode of discovery, one notes that he does not give up his cultural identity. His thoughts of escape to Spanish Mexico and his Catholic religious convictions sustain him. The very acts of writing and publishing his account, and its favorable reception, are reminders, if we should need them, that his mind remained European. It seems more accurate to say that by being absent from European society and immersed in American life for so long he forgot the usual concerns that drove Europeans to undertake conquest, and he saw the true nature—the good as well as the bad—of what other conquerors typically sought to possess and change without knowing. There is truth, too, in the assertion that he was quixotic,[8] a representative of the Spanish ideal of the compassionate Christian man of arms that one hundred years later Cervantes would look back to with nostalgic humor. There were others in the New World at that time, notably De Las Casas, magnanimous defender of the Indians with whom he has been compared.[9]

In judging him as a chronicler, however, one admires most the fact that he did not go to either extreme, that just as he was not overly critical neither did his admiration for the native peoples blind him to what was unquestionably wrong by his standards; we do not feel that he overlooks or excuses, or that he in fact looks out at the world from a completely foreign cultural perspective, but rather that he has simply looked longer, more clearly, and more thoughtfully than other chroniclers. He tells us that some tribes murder, ambush, and inflict atrocities on each other. While commenting that the endurance, eyesight, and hearing of the Indians are the strongest and keenest he has ever encountered, he also says that they are horribly vengeful people. By living among them he learns something that will not, to their grief, be grasped by many subsequent explorers in the region: that the indigenous peoples were fond of inventing stories and could, if it was in their interest, be skillful liars.[10] He criticizes their stealing, failing to understand that it was thought of in different ways on the two continents he had known. But just as he is more objective about the Americans, by the end of his journey he is also capable of being so about the Spaniards. The first ones he makes contact with on reaching Mexico are slave hunters, and he condemns them immediately, warning the Indians accompanying him against them. He documents the violence reported to him:

> They brought us some of the blankets they had hidden from the Christians and gave them to us, and they went on to tell us that other times the Christians had come into their lands and had destroyed and burned the villages and carried off half the men and all the women and children, and that those who had been able to escape from their hands were fleeing.[11]

The second theme that ties him to the best of American literature is that of man isolated and tested in the wilderness, a test even more of the spirit than of the body. One of his readers has commented that, "By being stripped naked, spiritually as well as physically, the Spaniard was thrust 'into a world where nothing, if done for another, seems impossible.'"[12] This, then, would be the explanation for the faith healing. While the "psychosomatic presentation" of the ailments, "empirical hypnotism," and other such phrases have been used to question the real, organic basis of the diseases he cured, no one has called into doubt his sincerity or sanity in reporting cases as remarkable as the resuscitation of a man believed to be dead. In spite of his cultural neutrality and almost scientific objectivity, he grows spiritually in extraordinary ways, and the metaphysical materializes convincingly and intriguingly out of the palpably factual wilderness he recreates. One can almost hear ghostly footsteps of the "ultimate realities" of Latin American magic realism.

FRAY MARCOS DE NIZA

When Cabeza de Vaca burst unexpectedly into Mexico with his exciting news of a civilization to the north, Viceroy Mendoza was aware that two rivals for further exploration of North America were moving ahead in their preparations. De Soto was planning another expedition from the eastern coast and Cortés was about to advance along the northwest coast of Mexico. As a way of winning royal permission for a full-scale entrada of his own he decided to send a small group forward, obstensibly for missionary purposes, to bring back further encouraging reports. He chose Fray Marcos de Niza, *vicecomisario* of the Franciscans in Mexico, a man who had previously served in Peru and Guatemala and was recommended by church officials as a highly competent geographer. In the company of Estebanico, who led the way back over the route he had followed with Cabeza de Vaca, an escort of Indians and, for a while, another Franciscian, Fray Onorato, he walked north at a pace too slow for the Moorish slave, who went on ahead to prepare a good reception for the friar, send back reports, and doubtless to seize what he considered a golden opportunity to win freedom and fame as the discoverer of a fabulous land. After crossing the border of present-day New Mexico and reaching the small Zuñi pueblo of Hawikuh, Estebanico was killed there. The reasons for his killing have been explained in various ways: he was the messenger of a god alien to that people (per Fray Marcos), he demanded to be given turquoises and young women (the Zuñis themselves), or he tried to escape while under investigation as a scout for an unfamiliar and so possibly hostile tribe (anthropologists). Fray Marcos tells the reader that when he was brought news of Estebanico's fate his escort turned against him, but he mastered the situation and resolutely continued on, accompanied only by two Indians. He describes approaching close enough to Hawikuh, which he refers to throughout his story as Cíbola (a word of uncertain but possibly Central Mexican origin), to be able to see from a distance that it was a tall city more populous than the Mexican capital. Then he hurried back south to Spanish civilization.

Most historians now agree that Fray Marcos came no closer to New Mexico than northern Sonora, turning back when he learned of Estebanico's death, and that his account of what he did in New Mexico is fabrication. From the point of view of a literary historian, however, a better adjective would be "fictional," and therein lie the fascinating circumstances that set this New Mexico "chronicle" apart from the others. It is fiction, planned and executed to be a convincing imitation of life, and as literature of a pretended trip, something like *Gulliver's Travels*, it has had a degree of success indicative of the author's skill.

Not that all of his contemporaries were deceived. Two years later Coronado did in fact enter Hawikuh and reported that the friar had told the opposite of the truth about everything. His detractors uncovered the fact that in Peru and Guatemala he had earned a reputation for exaggeration, and they labeled him "the lying monk." While the report he wrote on returning to Mexico[13] was not immediately made public, he talked freely and was accused of having spread stories of pagan temples with altars of pure gold and a Cíbola twice as big as Seville.[14] Even an early English historian (Heylyn) reached the verdict that Fray Marcos's story was "so disguised in Lyes and wrapped up in fiction that the light was little more than darkness."[15]

But for most unsuspecting readers still unfamiliar with New Mexico, the friar's carefully chosen words have had "an undeniable air of plausability."[16] These readers have included, naturally, those who in 1540 found themselves in Mexico City eager for new worlds to conquer, but more surprisingly, distinguished American historians of the nineteenth and early twentieth centuries, although in all fairness it must be added that some did take the view that wishful thinking had led him to glimpse from afar more of Cíbola than he could really see. However, an informed reading of the text today convinces one that Cleve Hallenbeck was right, if perhaps unnecessarily indignant, in concluding in 1949 that, "there is too much of such deliberate falsehoods in his narrative to permit the charitable hypothesis that he was mentally off balance—too much 'method in his madness,' in fact."[17]

The method, the art with which he told his story, we can assume was primarily his own, but the madness behind it appears to have been the viceroy's. The Franciscan was sent to find a basis on which the king could be convinced to authorize exploration under a commander responsible to Mendoza; he tried to comply. But since what he actually encountered in his travels as far as Sonora was not sufficiently impressive he added the grand finale of reaching Cíbola, and, just as importantly, emphasized throughout his story his version of what he was *told* about the lands ahead. The contrast with Cabeza de Vaca's firsthand, detailed descriptions couldn't be more pronounced. His picture of a buffalo appears to be by someone who has never seen one. He knows what overall effect he wants it to create and is careful to limit himself to features that will confirm it, leaving most of the figure undistractingly and noncommitally blank: "It has only one horn on its forehead, and this curves down toward the chest, but ending in a straight-ahead point of such strength that—so they say—there is nothing, no matter how strong, that won't break if the horn runs into it."[18] The viceroy's purposes reveal themselves, too, in the very slight discussion by the supposedly evangelical explorer of the native people's abilities to receive Christianity and his constant references to their mineral wealth and materially advanced culture.

Once the reader becomes aware of this pattern, the pieces in the jigsaw puzzle of more or less noticeable inaccuracies begin to fall into place. Commissioned to take possession of new lands in Mendoza's name, he gives the misleading impression that he is in an area never before visited by Europeans. Although he retraces Cabeza de Vaca's route he never mentions the Indians referring to that recent previous contact with Europeans. Or again, there were in fact six Zuñi pueblos, but the legend of the Spanish bishops specified seven cities on the island of Antilia, so in all likelihood for that reason he linked the two places, claiming that the Indians told him about the wonders of the *seven* cities of Cíbola. As regards mineral wealth, of course turquoise was used in the region, but his descriptions of how much was used, even by the tribes far from Cíbola, begin hyperbolically and grow as the account continues:

> Before reaching the uninhabited region I encountered an oasis of a town with irrigation. . . . Everyone in this town goes around loaded down with turquoise hanging from their nose and ears, and they call it 'cacona'. . . . And they brought me plenty of game . . . and offered me a lot of turquoise and cowhides and very pretty cups made of gourds."[19]

Soon after he writes,

> In this town . . . I saw more than 2000 cowhides that had been exceedingly well dressed, I saw a much larger quantity of turquoise and necklaces made with it in this valley than in all the places I had left behind, and everyone says that it comes from the city of Cíbola.[20]

In the ten-story buildings of Cíbola itself turquoise is so abundant that "the main doors are artistically decorated with it."[21] In contrast, the coast, which the king had assigned to Cortés for exploration, is characterized as utterly barren and useless, and Fray Marcos takes the trouble of pretending to have made side trips there that he presents as confirmation of that evaluation. Finally, he creates the impression that Cíbola is a powerful and warlike city-state, quite the opposite of the actual nature of the pacific Zuñis. One of his informants tells him that none can withstand its might and he assures the reader that when Estebanico was killed the inhabitants senselessly slaughtered the three hundred Indians who were traveling with him. This, too, makes most sense in terms of Mendoza's plans. If any nation were so belligerent as to bloodily massacre its neighbors, the king of Spain, committed to bringing Christian justice to the world, would see his way clear to sending his representatives to control and punish (and loot) it, another excellent justification for the enterprise the viceroy had in mind. With precisely these thoughts of human rather than divine justice before him, Fray Marcos describes a solemn promise made to the kin of the supposed survivors of the massacre: "I told them that Our Lord would punish Cíbola and that as soon as the Emperor knew what was happening he would send many Christians to punish them."[22]

On his return to Mexico he saw, again from a distance, a fertile valley with a lot of smoke rising from it. He affirms (though this claim was disproved within a year) that there were seven large towns in it; perhaps he again used the number seven to suggest that the inhabitants of all the lands to the north of Mexico had prosperous groups of seven cities, Cíbola being just one among others, or perhaps it was an alternate goal held out to those insufficiently daring to venture all the way into the hostile far north. The information that he says he was given makes it, too, sound like a rich prize: "There is a lot of gold in it and the inhabitants work it to make jars and jewels for their ears and little blades with which they scrape themselves to remove sweat."[23]

Just as he shapes New Mexico to fit the image he seeks to project, likewise he uses his freedom as a literary creator—freedom from the facts, historians have insisted—to re-create himself as a character in his own work, one showing the right qualities and acting for the right motives. Regardless of what really may have sent him off to explore the unknown, the Fray Marcos who lives in his chronicle is a courageous missionary whose zeal is guided by the Holy Spirit. On leaving behind his sick companion, Fray Onorato, in a small village, he explains, "It was best for me to leave him there; and following the instructions mentioned above I continued on my journey where the Holy Spirit guided me, though I was unworthy of that."[24]

Nor is there any false modesty about his courage as he assures the reader that at all times he was ready to give his life for the cause. When news comes that Estebanico has been killed his reaction is that of an exemplary man of God and servant of a Christian king:

> I wasn't afraid so much of losing my life as of not being able to return and bring word of the land's grandeur, where Our Lord God can be so well served and His holy faith exalted and the royal estate of His Majesty be increased. . . . I began to commend

> myself to Our Lord and to ask Him to guide this matter according to His will and to shed His light in my heart.[25]

And lest one forget what that perfect response cost in human terms he adds, "God can bear witness to how much I wanted to have someone there to ask him for his advice and opinion, for I confess I didn't know what to do."[26] All alone and forced to draw on his own inner resources, he was equal to the challenge, he tells us, showing himself to be a capable and decisive student of human nature. Feeling that under those circumstances he had reason to fear that his Indian escorts might kill him, he first warned them that if they did so they would only manage to send him to Heaven as a martyr, while they would go to Hell. Moreover, other Christians would come and kill them. And in case these somewhat remote eventualities should fail to calm the passions of the moment, he distributed free trinkets and clothing among them. Then in a show of courage he called for volunteers to accompany him to Cíbola to see if he could assist any other survivors or learn more about Estebanico's death. Although all present initially refused, he persevered and finally prevailed, convincing two "important" Indians to accompany him. Days after, on coming within sight of the death-dealing fortress larger than Mexico City, he still had the temerity, he assures us, to consider entering it and so to die in the fulfillment of his mission: "because I knew I was risking only my life and it I had offered to God the day I began my journey."[27] Once again, only the thought that he would be unable to carry his report back restrained him.

But he protests too much. Even without the other discrediting evidence now available against him, an objective reader finds this self-portrait a little too heroically drawn. The fact that he cast himself in the role of a committed missionary lifted his believability rating with many later American historians, although not, as we have seen, with all his contemporaries. However, the tale gains its air of credibility not only from the perceived character of its narrator, but also from quasi-legal literary techniques with which the pieces of "evidence" are presented to the reader, and this process is somewhat less transparent.

He repeatedly reminds us that he did not believe everything that the Indians told him, a claim to skepticism taken at face value by one historian who defended him saying, "all through his narrative he is careful to distinguish between observation and hearsay."[28] Like a scholar arguing a hypothesis, he makes use of word-for-word quotes supposedly spoken by Indians he encountered. The barriers separating him from their several languages make questionable whether or not such detailed conversations could have taken place, even though the Indians who had accompanied Cabeza de Vaca and then lived in Mexico were available for translation into some languages. Still Fray Marcos, whether he invented or simply fleshed out these quotations, certainly knew the literary value of such firsthand, dramatic statements. But he doesn't leave the matter there; to a (fictional) scout and investigator of his caution and perspicuity a single incidence of direct testimony by a competent witness may still not be entirely up to standards. His refusal to be convinced too easily early in the story prepares the reader to be overwhelmed later by corroborating data that will make dramatic entrances several times farther on as the plot advances: "and he told me so many wonderful things about the land that I decided not to believe them until I had either seen them myself or received additional confirmation."[29] He conducts his cross-examinations with rigor: "We went through a lot of questions and answers, and I found his story very solid."[30] When possible, he introduces character witnesses for his informants, as when he puts the burden of credibility on Estebanico saying that "he sent word to me that he had never caught the Indians in a lie."[31]

Gradual crescendo is perhaps Fray Marcos's most sophisticated technique. As in many journeys out of literature, each new encounter on the road confirms the author's vision of the world and builds on it. Hallenbeck points out that no fewer than seven times does he state that different villages described Cíbola to him in the exact same terms,[32] although one notes that in fact each time it becomes a little grander. Even the villages themselves become progressively richer in food, clothing, buffalo hides, and, above all, turquoise as he approaches that happy Camelot of the North.

Crescendo figures also in his skillful creation of suspense. He does not immediately summarize the events surrounding Estabanico's death; rather he recounts how he learned of it, first only from incomplete information suggesting that frightening development, then later the nearly crushing blow of a detailed account confirming it. The first news comes with an escaping Indian who has indeed been with Estabanico at Cíbola, seen the beginning of the hostilities, has reason to suppose the Moor has been killed, but who has made his own escape before actually seeing it. This allows Fray Marcos to describe his painful shock and fears for the worst, along with, naturally, his courageous decision to go on. Only then do two eyewitnesses to the killing arrive, bringing dramatic and pathetic details of the Cíbolans hostile reaction, Estabanico's attempted escape, the massacre of the three hundred people in his escort, and their own nearly miraculous preservation by means of playing dead for several hours in a pile of corpses. The friar's resolve to continue his mission in spite of all this now makes an even bigger impression than before.

On balance, Fray Marcos de Niza's has been the most controversial of the New Mexican chronicles of discovery precisely because it is at once the least documentary and the most literary, the most crafted. He was not simply reporting in good faith a new world seen through the glass of his own European prejudices, as happened to many early observers, for he never physically saw New Mexico at all.

For this, recent historians have disgustedly condemned him to be pigeonholed "along with the other Munchausens of history."[33] Unlike Cabeza de Vaca's account, which was the result of both an open mind and years in the land that allowed him to see the "other" clearly, Fray Marcos's document is rather of a purely imaginative country. It describes what the Spanish hoped to find there, that in turn being a mixture of archetypal European ways of thinking—legends and myths—and what Europeans living in Mexico thought they had been told by the indigenous peoples. Fictional, but in itself historically documented proof of the power of literature to change reality, it made possible the large and tenacious expedition of Coronado that followed on its heels and first made the region known. It had an undeniable role in creating for the Spanish a persistent aura about the Southwest—an aura comparable in its functioning to that of the Wild West in the literature of ninteenth-century North America. That aura was anything but unique, as the many names like El Dorado in Peru, and Quivira, the successor to the dream of Cíbola in New Mexico, remind us, but that is not to deny its power. As fiction it was free not only from strict adherence to the facts as the author knew them, but also to appeal to the more perennial and persuasive stuff of dreams, man's basic hope in the possibilities of the unknown, the belief and enthusiasm that drives the phenomenon of quest.

PEDRO DE CASTAÑEDA

Coronado's ambitious and well-managed expedition lasted from 1540 to 1542 and produced a dozen accounts written by the participants themselves, including the leader.[34] The most important, however, is that of Pedro de Castañeda, a common soldier who joined the northbound army when it passed through the outpost of Culiacán, where he had settled after growing up in northern Spain and where he wrote his chronicle twenty years after returning from New Mexico.[35] Almost nothing is known about him beyond what he tells the reader, but he says he is writing out of a concern lest the accomplishments of a most remarkable human effort be forgotten or remembered only in confusion. Fame has accorded it insufficient recognition, he insists, and the government as well. That the nation should be more generous in its appreciation of past services seems to be the unsurprising implication; in 1554 his family had already presented a claim against the Mexican treasury on the strength of his heroic deeds.

Less predictably, historians have been practically unanimous in their agreement with his evaluation of the importance of the enterprise in which he participated and their appreciation of the way he reconstructed it. Frederick Hodge wrote that his account "bears every evidence of honesty and a sincere desire to tell all he knew of the most remarkable expedition that ever traversed American soil."[36] As a chronicler he shares many things with another enlisted man whose account has won respect and readers, Bernal Díaz de Castillo. One is his use of long ungrammatical sentences that ramble on without stopping points; the best that can be said of his style is that it has the unpolished vigor of conversation. Yet Ternaux-Compans set the tone for later historians when he wrote that Castañeda was not a complete stranger to the art of writing, and that he showed order, method, "and above all a great naiveté, without excess verbiage or exaggeration."[37]

While becomingly modest about his own skills as a writer, he energetically defends his work on two other grounds. First, he argues that a retrospective summary of events is superior to one generated in the heat of the moment; it is only human to fail to grasp the significance of the present and he compares the perspective he enjoys writing years later to that of the spectators at a bullfight, who from their vantage point in the seats are able to perceive the development of the *corrida* more surely than the matador himself in the ring. Second, he emphasizes the reliability of his statements, his participation in most of the events as an eyewitness. Fray Marcos went on Coronado's expedition, too, and the inaccuracies of what he had written became apparent; Castañeda presents him in a very unsympathetic light and makes it clear that his own account adheres strictly to the truth.

Questions of accuracy aside, the reader immediately perceives other differences in style that set his story apart from that of the fictionalizing friar. One is his interest in and development of the psychology of the characters, particularly their motives in certain situations. He includes details, for example, of a minor incident that happened before the expedition even left Mexico, explaining how and why a soldier feigned a religious vision in order to escape from the commitment he had made to participate. Or again, critical of Coronado's decision not to establish, nor even allow, a permanent Spanish settlement in New Mexico, he attributes it to the leader having left estates and a pretty wife at home.

Second, Castañeda shows a genuine curiosity and familiarity with everything related to the indigenous peoples. While he paints a balanced picture that avoids branding either the Spaniards or the Indians as all good or all bad, his attitude throughout toward both Pueblo and Plains tribes is highly positive. Although his wish to see a new colonizing expedition to the area could be used as the basis for an argument that, consciously or not, he recalled and colored his memories so as to paint a favorable picture, the number and sort of details he includes leave no doubt that the native Americans had gained his attention and his respect. He describes fully the immediately apparent aspects of the cultures he encountered—

clothing, personal adornment, food, agriculture, construction styles and techniques, their cleanliness—but also less visible features of family and society, such as the function of the kivas and marriage and funeral rituals. He considers their religious leaders highly effective in promoting behavior free from undesirable practices found elsewhere: drunkenness, sodomy, human sacrifice, cannibalism, and theft. He questions the report that they killed the friars who remained behind as missionaries when the soldiers left, maintaining "the people there are merciful and not at all cruel; rather they are . . . enemies of cruelty, loyal and true to their friends."[38]

Yet to a reader familiar with sixteenth-century literary theory and practice in Spain, the most striking feature of the entire narrative is Castañeda's apparent awareness and use of the concept known to counterreformation literary critics as "the legitimate marvelous." With the invention of printing near the turn of the sixteenth century, books of chivalry and knight-errantry became the first best-sellers, full of a multitude of amazing adventures—enchantments, prophecies, magic potions, superhuman feats of arms—that clearly, in the eyes of critical and rational church scholars, could not be true. And in the austere intellectual atmosphere produced by the Council of Trent, untruths, even seeming untruths, were equated with lies that undermined the authority of the written word. Yet the popularity of such preposterous chivalric subject matter could not be ignored, and even theorists had to recognize that the most ennobling book is ineffective if not read. It was a dilemma that the idea of the legitimate marvelous was created to solve. Writers should, it was argued, make use of material that is at the same time both astonishing *and* not obviously false, i.e., legitimately marvelous. The exotic customs and strange natural phenomena of distant and little known lands, being at once almost incredible and yet not demonstrably false, were specifically recommended by literary rule makers.[39] In his long and action-packed romance set in the mysterious lands of Europe's far north, *Los trabajos de Persiles y Sigismunda*, Cervantes heeded the precept, including sea monsters, werewolves, endless nights, ships trapped in the ice and other adventures of their ilk in abundance, although he insisted repeatedly (albeit occasionally tongue in cheek) that everything was perfectly factual.

While Castañeda recounts an actual trip, in contrast with the imaginary one invented in the *Persiles*, he discusses it in his introduction very much as though it were literature and in terms of the same question—offering the reader astonishing marvels while still being truthful—that preoccupied Cervantes:

> The truth is that whoever might undertake in this way to write down the things that happened on the journey and the things that were seen in those lands—the rituals

> and customs of the native peoples—would have more than enough subject matter to demonstrate his good judgment, and I am sure there would be at least one account that, though dealing with the truth, would be so amazing as to seem incredible.[40]

Further evidence that he was aware of the importance of presenting the amazing, yet in a convincing way, is that he sets aside an entire chapter for what he calls the Marvels of the Buffalo Plains, all of which are documented and logically explained as far as possible.

While he records a wealth of indigenous customs, he perceptibly pays special attention to ones that seem particularly strange. For example, he comments on the rationale with which his informants explained the fact that girls wore no clothes at all until married. Nor does he fail to mention a ritual use of horse sweat: "they held their peace ceremonies . . . ; going over to the horses and taking sweat off them, they would rub it on themselves and make crosses with their fingers. . . . "[41] He is surprised that the Indians knew and venerated the cross before the expedition arrived, but unlike some other early visitors to the region he does not attribute it to divine intervention; he speculates, instead, that they learned the custom from other tribes that must have been in contact with the Spanish, a response typical of his concern with finding rational explanations.

In his section on the Great Plains he says of several natural phenomena, "They were remarkable things not seen elsewhere, and I dare to write about them because I am writing at a time when many men are alive who saw it and will bear out the truth of what I write."[42] The grass, for example, was so tall and resilient that a large group of soldiers, sheep, and horses passed over it leaving no mark, and the explorers were forced to erect piles of bones to mark the way for the rear guard. Naturally created bone heaps were so large that they measured "in length a crossbow shot or just slightly less, in height almost two *estados* [i.e., 3½ yards] in places, and in width three fathoms . . . ; and what is remarkable is the number of cattle that would be necessary to leave so many bones."[43] That strange new beast that left the bones, the buffalo, is described in terms of a collection of anatomical parts resembling those of several other animals. The comparisons provide familiarity and so credibility, while the number and bizarre combination of animals used as points of reference bring out its amazingness. It has the color and shape of a Spanish calf, with the hump of a camel, the hair of a sheep, the mane of a lion; like a snake it sheds its skin, like a scorpion raises its tail when it runs. And it seems, due to the extreme flatness of the earth (Castañeda hastens to explain), as tall as the top of a pine tree.[44]

When another person has reported something remarkable happening for which he personally is not prepared to vouch, he immediately says so, yet still doesn't keep the interesting information from the reader. Everyone familiar with the expedition knew that the Indian called The Turk had been lying in the fabulous promises that he used to lure Coronado away from the Río Grande Valley and all the way to Kansas, yet Castañeda records their most fabulous elements: Brobdingnagian canoes, fish as big as horses, silver plates and bowls in common use among the people, and a king who took his siestas under a tree in which the breeze played golden bells. When a soldier assigned to guard The Turk informs his superiors that he saw him talk to the devil in a jug of water, Castañeda repeats the claim without passing judgment on its validity.

His attitude toward his fellow Spaniards, in whose honor he repeatedly says he is writing, is surprising in itself, for while at times praising their bravery, endurance, and resolve he also reveals and censures their occasional lust and violence. He dwells on an incident in which the rape of an Indian wife—followed by fighting, imprisonment, promises of safety that were not respected, and, finally, merciless slaughter—led the Indians to become unwilling to make peace treaties. Nonetheless, his point of view is typical of Renaissance Spain to the extent that he views the positive accomplishments of the men on the expedition in the heroic framework of books of chivalry, and here comparison to Bernal Díaz de Castillo and his mention of chivalric heroes can be complemented by an equally revealing reference to Don Quijote. Though laughable in defeat, Cervantes's archetypal character represents the idealism and undaunted heroism of Spain before the Armada, and his desire to imitate Amadís of Gaul and restore the Golden Age to the world is uncannily anticipated in Castañeda's seventh chapter fifty years before his creation:

> It will be quite permissible in the last chapter to have left unmentioned the heroic deeds done by the captain Juan Gallego with twenty companions he had with him so that in this chapter it may be told and in later times any who may read and then spread word of it will have a reliable author on which to base themselves and show that they are not writing made-up stories, as clearly happens with some of the things that in our time we read in books of chivalry; but if it weren't for their including those fictions about enchantments there are things being done this very day in these parts by our own Spaniards in conquests and clashes with the natives that outdo for amazing deeds not only the books already mentioned but also those written about the twelve peers of France; for when you think about and take into consideration the lethal strength the authors from those times attribute to them and the magnificent, shining arms with which they adorn them and the small stature of the men of our time and the sorry, scarce arms there are in this region, then even more amazing than what is written about the men of old are the extraordinary things that with such weapons our men undertake and accomplish this very day; for the ancient warriors also fought with barbaric, naked peoples as ours do with the Indians, among whom

there are certainly powerful, brave men who are expert archers, for we have seen them bring down birds on the wing and while running after rabbits put an arrow through them; all of this I have said so that some things held to be fictional may become true and since every day we see in our own times even greater things, such as those done by Don Fernando Cortez . . . "[45]

Of all the sixteenth-century chronicles of discovery in New Mexico, Castañeda's is the most valuable. In his years of living and wandering in Texas, Cabeza de Vaca learned to love the native peoples. But the time he spent in New Mexico was short; his story is his journey, his adventure, his escape. Castañeda relives his trip, too, but his topic is just as much New Mexico itself, a place from which he seeks not to escape but to return, something of a promised land. And he remains entirely a Spaniard, though like Cabeza de Vaca a thoughtful representative of his country's Renaissance ideal of arms and letters rather than the ruthless and driven conquistador that lives on in stereotypes of Spain's Black Legend. From a Spaniard's perspective he documents with care and sensitivity the first two years of Hispanic-Indian *convivencia* in a country he found as astonishing as the lands of enchantment out of Spanish chivalric romance.

HERNANDO GALLEGOS

Coronado's failure to make immediately profitable discoveries was discouraging to potential entrada backers and organizers in Mexico, and laws enacted in 1542–43 and again in 1573 strictly prohibited new expeditions without official sanction, so no further entries into the region, with the exception of a minor venture led by Francisco de Ibarra in 1565, materialized for forty years. Spanish settlement on Mexico's central plateau was moving north, however, drawn along by the search for slaves and mines and by 1580 had gone as far as the town of Santa Barbara near the present border of Durango and Chihuahua. Then another Franciscan friar, Agustín Ramírez, talking with a captured Indian about the lands to the north, resolved to organize a missionary expedition to New Mexico. After some two years of planning and a trip to Mexico City to obtain permission from the viceroy, he set off in June 1581 with two other friars, nine soldiers, and about fifteen Indian servants. The soldiers' main interests were not evangelical, of course, but in the more worldly gains they hoped to make through exploration.

The captain in command of the military escort was Francisco Sánchez, nicknamed El Chamuscado, who is described in the chronicle as being sixty or seventy years old. On the return leg of the trip he fell ill and died, and as the friars never returned from New Mexico, it was the party's clerk, a twenty-five-year-old soldier named Hernando Gallegos, who wrote the only extensive account of the journey. We know about him only what he writes there and in a much shorter preliminary report prepared jointly with Pedro de Bustamante, another of the soldiers.[46] In the joint report he is described as a native of Seville, having come to Mexico nine years before. The report continues:

> in all the aforesaid years his occupation has been serving His Majesty, both in Diego de Ibarra's government and in the mines at Macapil, involved in the punishment of the warring Indians that are in rebellion there, as well as in making discoveries of mines at his own cost. . . . He had made many trips into the back country beyond Santa Barbara, in pursuit of raiding Indians."[47]

He says that the expedition was guided and inspired not only by contemporary reports of New Mexico, but to a considerable extent by Cabeza de Vaca's account. As the only chronicle of exploration in the region to have been printed, it remained known later in the century, while those generated by the Coronado expedition, which naturally were incomparably more informative about the Pueblo country, remained as manuscripts whose effective contribution to knowledge of the area was soon lost. To this day Gallegos's own account has not been published in Spanish, although it is available in English translation.[48]

After leaving Santa Barbara the small party followed the Conchos River north to the Río Grande, which they named after the Guadalquivir, the river flowing through Seville, and then explored its valley as far north as Taos, which they named for Mexico's Tlascala. But the most significant name they gave was that of New Mexico itself, taking possession for the king at San Felipe on August 21. To the west they went as far as Zuñi, in the east to the beginning of the great plains, where they saw buffalo. One of the friars, who chose to return alone to Mexico to ask that more missionaries be sent immediately, was killed by Indians within two or three days after separating from the other Spaniards, although the latter did not learn of this until later. The rest of the party, with the exception of the two remaining friars, who stayed in New Mexico to teach the gospel, and Chamuscado, who fell ill and had to be carried in a litter before he died, reached Santa Barbara again on Easter Sunday the following spring. The local authorities there attempted to extract from them the news of their discoveries, but Gallegos and Bustamante escaped and presented their reports directly to the viceroy.

The chronicle is clearly the work of an observer conscious, not that all societal values are culturally conditioned, but certainly that different cultures have different customs. Gallegos often comments on differences or similarities with practices not only in Mexico but other societies as well. He notices that the women wear a blanket in the same manner as Jewish women, that the pots are as good as the ones the Portuguese make, and that the way of putting a palm cushion on their head to carry jars is similar to what is done in Old Castile. He is a comparatist, too, in that he records lists of words in several native languages for things often encountered, such as "corn," "water," and "turkey."

His description of the buffalo recalls Castañeda's in its obvious familiarity with the subject and its use of some comparisons to other animals. But there are fewer of them, and they are less graphic. Here as elsewhere, the writing is more prosaic, less elegant, and less expressive of a sense of wonder. He tells the reader more baldly that the buffalo are the same size as Mexican cattle, but humpbacked and woolly, with short, black horns and a large head. The bulls have beards like those of male goats. They run fairly quickly and in the manner of pigs. On the flat prairie they look, not as though they were as tall as pine trees, but like ships at sea or carts on land.

The presence of his avowed literary inspiration, Cabeza de Vaca, is visible in two ways, even though Gallegos is clearly a very different sort of man. First, Gallegos gives the impression that Coronado, who is never mentioned directly, hardly reached New Mexico at all, and that his own expedition is the one that fell heir to the great New Mexican discoveries of which Cabeza de Vaca had first spread the word. Second, the party's leaders apparently took from the latter's account the germ of the idea to tell the Indians that the friars with them were children of the sun come down from Heaven, and that the soldiers were in turn the children of the friars. They went on to claim also that their firearms were gifts from the sun. But there is a jarring difference between Cabeza de Vaca and Gallegos as regards this claim, for in the first case it was not a lie consciously and premeditatedly prepared for the purpose of manipulating the Indians, but rather a belief that arose within those peoples themselves on seeing and admiring the character of certain individual Europeans.

An incident that again shows this sort of manipulation in religious matters involves mock preparations for an execution of several Indians. A large chopping block was set up in the middle of a square, the prisoners were brought out fully expecting to die, the ceremony proceeded until the very moment when the blade was to fall, and then suddenly the friars rushed out in their flowing robes and saved them. While this drama was staged, Gallegos explains, to win the good will of the hoped-for converts, among whom the Franciscans were planning to stay on alone, it is also significant because the friars had convinced the soldiers to conduct this charade instead of actually carrying out their original intention, which was in fact to kill the Indians. It follows the pattern of conflict between missionaries and civil authorities that would be typical of the early years of the New Mexico colony, as elsewhere in Spanish America. Moreover, Franciscan historical sources have made it clear that Chamuscado, Gallegos, and the other soldiers were at odds with the friars from the time they reached the pueblo country, often disregarding the religious goals of the expedition and acting independently. In general the account by Gallegos, who was writing in hopes of royal reward, is designed to place the soldiers in a better light than the friars.[49]

Still, the fact that the expedition has been authorized by the viceroy for missionary purposes leads the chronicler to portray the native New Mexicans as good candidates for religious instruction. On the one hand he repeatedly insists that they are sinful in their basic nature, "born liars," and likely to murder the defenseless friars who stayed behind unless soldiers were sent again to protect them. A section of the narrative on Indian rites is labeled "the evil practices of these people," and it includes a detailed description, one of the most arresting sections of the whole work, of a dance, like those still practiced by the Hopi, in which rattlesnakes are used. Those present, he reports, gather around a "mosque" and whip one of their number until he bleeds and looks like a Spanish disciplinant. That individual then engages in dialogue with a snake as thick as a man's arm, which coils up when it wishes to speak. Another dance involving handling two rattlesnakes is also detailed. Happily, the conversion-oriented reporter doesn't completely resist the fascination of the subject matter, but rather puts his interest in the proper religious framework by affirming that the Spaniards were of the opinion that the snake was the devil, by whom the Indians were enslaved, and that it had been God's will they be discovered so that they could be freed from these errors. On the other hand, the indigenous peoples appear as appropriate recipients of evangelical efforts not only because of their sinfulness, but also because of their advanced state of civilization. Gallegos frequently points out that they are intelligent and clean, as well as accomplished craftsmen. He expresses his surprise at the orderliness of all their activities. A long account of a wedding ceremony, which complements that of the snake dances in its intrinsic cultural interest and its contrasted evaluation of the society, is presented to demonstrate the extraordinary abilities God has given them.

But as mentioned before, Gallegos was not himself a missionary, and more practical reasons for a permanent settlement in the region are mentioned at certain points in the work. He enthusiastically affirms that since the Indians are accustomed to paying tribute among themselves, it will be easy for the Spanish, too, to exact it from them. Acoma would be the strongest fortress in all of Christendom. And on their return down the Río Grande they discovered an area (probably the San Mateo Mountains) with abundant water and timber, as well as a "marvelously" large number of mineral deposits and mines. Lack of time prevented further investigation of this mineral wealth, but he assures the reader that nearly all the men were miners, and all agreed that there was every indication of very rich mines.

ANTONIO DE ESPEJO

When the Rodríguez-Chamuscado expedition returned bringing word that the friars with them had stayed behind alone, the Fransiscans on the northern frontier thought immediately of sending aid. Friar Bernaldino Beltrán, stationed in Durango, agreed to obtain official authorization for a party to enter New Mexico, and Antonio de Espejo, a wealthy Spaniard settled in Mexico City but in trouble with the law at the time, offered to pay for an escort and lead it personally.[50] By late fall of the same year, 1582, some fourteen soldiers had been signed up and the party set out from the vicinity of Santa Barbara on November 10. Following the same route taken two years before, they reached central New Mexico and learned that all three of the missionaries had been killed. But Espejo was eager to continue exploration, and did so for several months, even though Father Beltrán and a number of the soldiers returned to Mexico without him before he was willing to leave. Of particular importance for the decision made shortly thereafter to organize Oñate's colonizing expedition were his glowing descriptions of discoveries in northern Arizona. He returned to Santa Barbara in September 1583 and wrote his report there soon after.[51]

What sets Espejo apart from the previous writers about the Southwest is that he was a wealthy land owner, keenly interested in opportunities for both mining and ranching. Although he goes into considerable detail about certain specific topics, such as native clothing and ways the hair was worn, in general his descriptions are more summarized, get more quickly to the practical points that he makes, somewhat in the style of a prospectus for a business venture. Near the end he makes explicit a dislike for wasting words that the reader has already begun to sense: "and not everything that happened could be written down nor could I give a written account of it because it would go on and on, for the lands and the provinces we crossed in this journey were wide and many."[52] Plants and animals are most commonly viewed from a utilitarian point of view. For example, instead of expanding on how, why, or where the deer and the buffalo roam, he concentrates instead on what the deer and the buffalo's hide can be used for commercially:

> The Jumanos make their animal-skin clothing from deer hides that are also dressed as in Flanders. . . . The buffalos, as far as their hair goes, look like Irish cattle, and the hides of this cattle [i.e., the buffalo] are dressed by the natives as elk skins are in Flanders.[53]

He exclaims on the wide variety of breads made from the corn ground by the women, and he takes enthusiastic note of the announcement made by one friendly Indian group that they were planting extra corn that spring so that they would be able to feed all the additional Spaniards whom they hoped to see returning the following year. At Moqui he apparently showed considerable interest in cotton blankets, to judge from the fact that the Hopis made him a present of four thousand of them. He observes approvingly that the New Mexicans irrigate and cultivate like the Mexicans, work the fields from dawk to dusk like the Castilians. He remembers his homeland often, christening the region Nueva Andalucia in honor of his own native *patria chica*, and often sees the similarities between the local plants and their counterparts in Spain: roses and onions (encountered at Acoma), flax (found at Zuñi and in northern Arizona), pine nuts, walnuts, and even a parrot are described as being like those in Castile.

His mining interests were rewarded with promising results, too. Urged on by stories told him by the Zuñis and Hopis, he went west in search of "una laguna de oro," a place where a people adorned with golden jewels lived on the shores of a large lake that Pedro de Tovar had also gone on to seek. While the mirage failed to materialize, Espejo emphasizes that he actually did find ore west of Prescott, Arizona: "And with my own hands I took ore out of them, and people who know about such things say that it is very rich and contains a lot of silver."[54] The Indians there, too, fueled his imagination and that of his readers with the promise that there were yet other provinces farther on, "and in comparison with those provinces and towns, the ones along the river, the provinces where we were at that time are nothing."[55]

The fundamental importance of Espejo's account is its image of New Mexico as a bountiful land suitable for settlement. If it is true that next to more chivalric tales of discovery it sounds a little like an agribusiness report, it gave an impetus to the northward colonizing movement, helped to make the jump across the deserts of Chihuahua and southern New Mexico. His final summary describes it in a way that must have been inviting indeed:

> and in those provinces, in the majority of them, there is much game to be hunted on the ground and in the air, rabbits and hares, deer and the cattle of that country, and ducks and geese, and cranes and pheasants and other birds; good mountains with all types of woods, salt pits, and rivers with a wide diversity of fish, and in the greater part of these lands wagons and carts can be used; and there are very good pastures for the cattle, and lands from which to make farms, large gardens, and fields for both dry farming and irrigation, many rich veins, from which I brought ore to be assayed for its fineness, along with an Indian from the province of Tamos, and an Indian from the Province of Mohoce, so that if in His Majesty's service it should be necessary once again to undertake the exploration and settling of those provinces they would be able to shed some light on them and the way one should go, and for that purpose they should learn Mexican and other languages."[56]

The next Spanish party to enter the region was a group of would-be settlers led by Gaspar Castaño de Sosa in 1590. He was lieutenant governor of the province of Nuevo León, with whose played-out mines he had apparently grown dissatisfied. His expedition, which had been specifically forbidden by the viceroy, followed the Pecos River up to the area of Pecos Pueblo and somewhat beyond. After hardships resulting from snowy winter weather, shortage of food, and some conflict with the native peoples, he established the colony at Santo Domingo. However, on March 29 the settlement was reached by a band of forty soldiers under the command of a rival of Castaño, Juan Morlete, sent by the viceroy to arrest and return him and his party to Mexico as prisoners, instructions which he carried out vigorously. There Castaño was tried and found guilty, then sentenced to exile in the Philippines, where he died. The decision was appealed to the Council of Indies in Spain, which exonerated him after his death. He or perhaps someone close to him—the authorship is not clear—wrote an account characterized quite naturally by a primary concern not with the land and the people but with making his actions appear praiseworthy.[57] Another illegal entry was made three years later under the command of first Francisco Leyva de Bonilla and then Antonio Gutiérrez de Humaña, but the lone survivor was an Indian from the Mexico City area and no substantial report was ever written.

FRAY FRANCISCO DE ESCOBAR

The last firsthand New Mexico chronicle of exploration to be written before the publication of Villagrá's epic poem on the Spanish settling of the land is the diary kept by Fray Francisco de Escobar on Oñate's exploration from the Rio Grande to the mouth of the Colorado River.[58] After the colony had been established in 1598 at San Juan, Oñate was very active in his efforts to gather more information about the entire region. He not only undertook journeys of discovery himself, but also commissioned exploratory parties under the command of other captains. Places about which there was an air of mystery or great expectations were the Llanos de Cíbola, or Buffalo Plains, Gran Quivira, and the South Sea, i.e., the Pacific Coast, and he turned his attention to all three. An attempt by Vincente de Zaldívar to reach the sea fell short, and although Oñate was very interested in following up himself he was delayed by the unauthorized return of most of the settlers to Mexico while he was away in 1601 seeking Gran Quivira on the Great Plains. The following two years were made more difficult by accusations brought against him of mishandling his official charge, so when he finally did set out for the coast in June 1604 it was with the hope of making important discoveries that would reestablish his reputation. This underlying circumstance appears to have left its mark on Escobar's account, which Oñate had the author carry to the viceroy as a report on the expedition.

It could be argued that his narrative has little to do with New Mexico, in that it recounts travels primarily in Arizona, and that its most remarkable feature are stories told to the group by Indians there about fantastic human species supposedly living in Southern California. In reply it must be pointed out, first, that Escobar begins with an objective overall description of life in New Mexico, and second, that at the same time his account bears further testimony to the presence of the fabulous in the minds of many of those who first explored the Land of Enchantment. Escobar exhibits the same realistic practicality combined with unlimited imaginative hoping that had shortly before brought Oñate all the way to the Kansan Quivira, and Coronado, too, even after he had seen the reality of Fray Marcos's dream of Cíbola.

Escobar was the *comisario* of the Franciscans in New Mexico. An early historian of the region, Father Zárate Salmerón, writing only two decades later, called him a man of great learning with a special gift for languages.[59] In his introductory sketch of the people and the land he is even-handed, voicing neither hyperbolic praise of their attractions nor bitter complaints of hardships endured there. The first descriptive sentence rings much truer than the last laudatory one penned by Espejo:

> It is a very poor and cold country, with heavy snows, but is quite habitable for a small number of Spaniards if they have clothing with which to dress, and if they take from the pacified country cattle with which to sustain themselves and cultivate the soil, for the country produces none of these, although cattle taken to it multiply rapidly, though it is too barren to raise great numbers of them.[60]

Like other chroniclers he goes into the natives' foods and clothing; he mentions their trade with the plains tribes. Like other Franciscan missionaries, he expresses his disapproval of the treatment accorded his spiritual children by the secular Spaniards, protesting that the Indians cannot be converted because the tribute is too much of a burden for them. He finds them "very affable and docile" and is much impressed by the cordial hospitality of the Zuñis and Hopis.

In Arizona the tone becomes noticeably optimistic. He confirms Espejo's mineral discoveries in the north and, then, as the party breaks new ground along the lower Colorado, everything becomes quite satisfactory, even though he maintains a veneer of restraint and caution that strengthens his air of credibility. He reports that there is a dense population along the river, which is navigable, yet there is still ample space available for the Spaniards to cultivate the land; the climate is so mild, in contrast with snowy New Mexico, that the people go completely naked even in winter; the expedition discovers a harbor at the mouth of the river, which Oñate is convinced empties directly into the Pacific; the Indians tell him that there are large pearls nearby, although unfortunately none could be located to be taken along as proof.

What he has actually seen, he conscientiously reminds the reader, goes only as far as this (promising) point, but like New Mexican chroniclers before him he fleshes out his facts to paint an attractive portrait based on additional "information" gladly supplied by the local inhabitants. They report having mined a white metal at a place five days' journey to the west, and insist that it is silver, the same metal shown to them by the Spanish. Nine or ten days farther west, they tell of the same golden lake that Espejo had heard of. Escobar details his attempts to form a reliable opinion about whether the people there really have an abundance of precious metals by means of an almost scholarly comparison of the words for gold and silver in several Indian languages. His conclusion that the treasure is possible, although he must reserve weighty doubts, is presented very much in the manner of a self-conscious researcher investigating an issue of great timely concern to the public.

The reports that follow, however, are less cautious, and Zárate Salmerón says in his history that he declines to repeat them because they produced much disbelief when first made public. Escobar introduces them with the greatest of care, placing us imaginatively in a large assembly of Indians. Then he introduces a specific individual named Otata, living near the mouth of the Colorado, who made "a drawing of the country on a piece of paper, on which he indicated many nations of people so monstrous that I will make bold to affirm them with no little fear of being discredited."[61] Even with the responsibility now shifted to someone else, he still makes a formal disclaimer before getting into the wonders: "and although to some it must appear temerity for me to recount things so monstrous and never seen in our times . . . nevertheless I make bold to relate what I have heard stated to a great multitude of Indians in my presence, for since I affirm as true only what I saw with my eyes, I may dare affirm it.[62] To each of the peoples said to be living between the river and the coast is attributed one astonishing quality and a name related to that remarkable feature.

One has

> "ears so large that they dragged on the ground, and big enough to shelter five or six persons under each one . . . ; this nation was called in its own language Esmalcatatanacha, and in the language of this Bahacecha nation Esmalca, which means 'ear,' the etymology of the word indicating the characteristic of the nation."[63]

Next are mentioned a people "whose men had virile members so long, they wrapped them four times around the waist, and that in the act of generation the man and woman were far apart."[64] Some people had only one foot, like the mythical Patagones who gave their name to the south of Argentina. Another "lived on the banks of a lake in which they slept every night, entirely under the water. These people, they said, were the ones who wore handcuffs and bracelets of yellow metal, which they called *anpacha*."[65] He pauses here to assure the reader that all the Indians present verified everything Otata claimed. The list then continues with a group that "sustained themselves solely on the odor of their food, prepared for this purpose, not eating at all, since they lacked the natural means to eliminate the excrements of the body."[66] Another did not lie down to sleep but always slept standing up, bearing some burden on the head. The final astonishing nation is that of the inhabitants of the Island of California, where

> the "principal person obeyed . . . was a woman called Cinaca Cohota, which signifies or means principal woman" or "chieftainess." From all these Indians we learned that she was a giantess, and that on the island she had only a sister and no other person of her race, which must have died out with them. We learned that the men of these islands were bald, and that with them the monstrosities ended.[67]

The reaction of the modern reader might well be to suspect, if not outright fraud by either Escobar or the Indians, then a colossal straight-faced joke practiced by the latter on the gullible Europeans. The obvious absurdity of the material and its allusions to sex roles suggests a deadpan humor not unknown in later Indian-white relations. Still the descriptions may have been adapted from some body of indigenous folklore, to judge from Espejo having heard some of the same things earlier and Escobar's claim that all the Indians they encountered during the return trip to New Mexico, and even ones there, confirmed them. But assuming that the stories were in fact told him, one must understand Escobar's reaction as being in all likelihood a case of a mind educated in traditional European mythology—not radically different from mythologies elsewhere—accepting what it believes to be verification of the divinely created prodigies described in authoritative classical and medieval texts. One-legged and long-eared men abound in ancient geographers like Pliny, as Escobar himself reminds us:

> To any one who will consider the wonders which God constantly performs in the world, it will be easy to believe that since He is able to create them He may have done so, and that since so many different people, in a distance of two hundred leagues testify to them, they cannot lack foundation, being things of which these Indians are not the first inventors, for there are many books which treat of them, and of others even more monstrous and more wonderful.[68]

Besides, they were valuable additions to any report, such as Oñate's, under pressure to document some remarkable findings capable of justifying exploration:

> It appears to me doubtful that there should be so many monstrosities in so short a distance, and so near us . . . [but] if discovered, [they] would result, I believe, in glory to God and in service to the King our Lord. . . . And if they do cause wonderment, it does not seem to me that the way to their verification or to that of the other reports, of riches and of the communication of the seas, is very difficult."[69]

The contrast between the factual, objective tone Escobar uses throughout, his thoroughly recognizable and down-to-earth picture of New Mexico, and his use of preposterous yarns as the basis for requesting continued government support for the colony, is amusing if not disconcerting. One may assume there's a slight chance Oñate insisted, against the friar's better judgment, that he pull out all the stops. In any event, he overstated his case and his claims were not taken seriously, as common sense demands and Zárate Salmerón confirms. Still it can be argued that either his commander's desperation or his own gullibility merely led him to be carried away in his use of a psychological and literary principal at work in stories of discovery in general, certainly in all those from sixteenth-century New Mexico. Its application to his tale was conditioned by the fact that while by the turn of the seventeenth century the Río Grande Valley had become a known quantity, that which lay beyond still was not, and the unknown allowed the imagination room to invent, or rather to project into that new place, which was possibly radically different and extraordinary, the marvelously satisfying images out of dream and legend which in the familiar European world could exist only in the literature of enchantment.

NOTES

1. See Tzvetan Todorov, *The Conquest of America: The Question of the Other*, transl. Richard Howard (New York: Harper and Row, 1984).

2. See Cleve Hallenbeck, *The Journey of Fray Marcos de Niza* (Dallas: University Press, 1949), p. 1.

3. *La relación que dio Alvar Núñez Cabeça de Vaca de lo acaescido en las Indias en la armada donde yua por governador Pámphilo de de Narbáez, desde el año de veynte y siete hasta el año de treynta y seys que bolvio a Seuilla con tres de su compañia* (Zamora, 1542). Cabeza de Vaca published a second edition at Valladolid in 1555, of which an excellent edition was done in 1906 by Manuel Serrano y Sanz in volume 5 of his *Colección de libros y documentos referentes a la historia de America*. There are three English translations, the most recent being *Adventures in the Unknown Interior of America*, translated and annotated by Cyclone Covey, with a new epilogue by William T. Pilkington (Albuquerque: University of New Mexico Press, 1983).

4. See John E. Englekirk et al., editors, *Anthology of Spanish American Literature* (New York: Appleton-Century-Crofts, 1968), p. 25.

5. "Para que se vea y conozca cuán diversos y extraños son los ingenios e industrias de los hombres humanos." Cited in José B. Fernández, *Alvar Núñez Cabeza de Vaca: The Forgotten Chronicler* (Miami: Universal, 1975), p. 70. In this and other quotations from sixteenth-century texts I have modernized the spelling and punctuation. Translations are mine unless otherwise indicated.

6. For a typology of relations to the other, including "value judgments," "rapprochement," and "extent of knowledge," see Todorov, p. 185.

7. See Pilkington's epilogue to Covey's translation of *Adventures in the Unknown Interior*, p. 148.

8. See Covey, *Adventures in the Unknown Interior*, p. 14.

9. See Todorov, *Conquest of America*, p. 249.

10. See Covey, *Adventures in the Unknown Interior*, Chapter 43.

11. "Nos trajeron mantas de las que habían escondidas por los cristianos y nos las dieron, y aún nos contaron como otras veces habían entrado los cristianos por la tierra y habían destruido y quemado los pueblos y llevado la mitad de los hombres y todas las mujeres y muchachos, y que los [que] de sus manos se habían podido escapar andaban huyendo." (Serrano Sanz edition, p. 123).

12. Pilkington in Covey, *Adventures in the Unknown Interior*, p. 149.

13. The Spanish text of Fray Marcos' *Descubrimiento de las siete ciudadas de Cibola* is available in Joaquín Pacheco and Francisco Cárdenas, *Colección de documentos inéditos, relativos al descubrimiento, conquista* . . . , 42 Vols. (Madrid, 1864–65), 3:325–50. It was also published, along with an English translation, by Percy M. Baldwin in volume 1, Historical Society of New Mexico Publications in History (Sante Fe: El Palacio Press, 1926). There are other translations, including one by George P. Hammond and Agapito Ray in *Narratives of the Coronado Expedition*, 1540–1952 (Albuquerque: University of New Mexico Press, 1940), pp. 66–79.

14. See Hallenbeck, *Journey of Fray Marcos*, p. 90.

15. Cited in Hallenbeck, p. 77.

16. See Hallenbeck, p. 42.

17. Hallenbeck, p. 73.

18. "Tiene sólo un cuerno en la frente y que este cuerno es corvo hacia los pechos, que de allí sale una punta derecha en la cual dicen que tiene tanta fuerza que ninguna cosa por recia que sea deja de romper si topa con ella." (Baldwin edition, p. 50). Subsequent references are also to this edition.

19. "Antes de llegar al despoblado topé con un pueblo fresco de regadío . . . Todos los de este pueblo andan encacanados con turquesa que les cuelgan de las narices y orejas y a esta llaman 'cacona'. . . . Y me trajeron mucha caza . . . y me ofrecieron muchas turquesas y cueros de vaca y jícaras muy lindas." (p. 46) There is an untranslatable pun on "encacanados," 'besmeared with excrement,' and the Indian word "cacona."

20. "En este pueblo . . . vi mas de 2000 cueros de vaca extremadamente bien adobados, vi mucha más cantidad de turquesas y collares de ellas en este valle que en todo lo que había dejado atrás, y todos dicen que viene de la ciudad de Cíbola." (p. 49)

21. "De ellas están hechas labores en las puertas principales." (p. 45)

22. "Les dije que Nuestro Señor castigaría a Cíbola y que como el Emperador supiese lo que pasaba, enviaría muchos cristianos a que los castigasen." (p. 54)

23. "Hay en ella mucho oro y que lo tratan los naturales della en vasijas y joyas, para las orejas y paletillas con que se raen y quitan el sudor." (p. 56)

24. "Que me convino dejarlo allí; y conforme a la dicha instrucción, seguí mi viaje por donde me guió el Espíritu Santo, sin merecerlo yo." (p. 40)

25. "No temí tanto perder la vida, como no poder volver a dar aviso de la grandeza de la tierra, donde Dios Nuestro Señor puede ser tan servido y su santa fe ensalzada y acrecentado el patrimonio real de Su Magestad . . . [Comencé] a encomendarme a Nuestro Señor y a suplicarle guiase esta cosa como fuese servido y alumbrase mi corazón." (p. 52)

26. "Y Dios es testigo de cuánto quisiera tener a quien pedir consejo y parecer, proque confieso que a mí me faltaba." (p. 52)

27. "Porque sabía que no aventuraba sino la vida y esta ofrecí a Dios el día que comencé la jornada." (p. 55)

28. Cited in Hallenbeck, *Journey of Fray Marcos*, p. 77.

29. "Y este me dijo tantas grandezas de la tierra, que dejé de creerlas para después de haberlas visto o de tener más certificación de la cosa." (pp. 42–43).

30. "Tuvimos muchas demandas y respuestas; y le hallé de muy buena razón." (p. 43)

31. "Me envió a decir que nunca había tomado a los indios en ninguna mentira." (p. 50)

32. Hallenbeck, *Journey of Fray Marcos*, p. 88.

33. Ibid., p. 95.

34. They are listed and documented in Frederick W. Hodge, *Spanish Explorers in the Southern United States* (New York: Scribner, 1907), pp. 276–80.

35. The Spanish text, *Relación de la jornada de Cibola*, was published by George Parker Winship, "The Coronado Expedition, 1540–42," in the *14th Annual Report of the Bureau of Ethnology, 1892–93*, part 2, pp. 329–469. Winship's translation appeared with it and has been reprinted elsewhere, including Winship's subsequent book, *The Journey of Coronado, 1540–42, from the City of Mexico to the Grand Canyon of the Colorado and the Buffalo Plains of Texas, Kansas, and Nebraska as told by Himself and His Followers* (New York: Barnes, 1904).

36. Hodge, *Spanish Explorers*, p. 276. On the importance of the expedition see representative comments by Herbert E. Bolton in *Coronado: Knight of Pueblos and Plains* (Albuquerque: University of New Mexico Press, 1949), "In Perspective," and Fray Angelico Chavez, O.F.M., in *Coronado's Friars* (Washington, D.C.; Academy of American Franciscan History, 1968), p. 87.

37. "Et surtout une grande naïveté sans verbiage ni exagération," Henri Ternaux-Compans, *Voyages, Relations et Memoires Originaux pour Servir a l'Histoire de la Decouvert de l'Amérique* (Paris: Arthus Bertrand, 1838), p. iv.

38. "La gente de por allí es piadosa y ninguna cosa cruel; antes son . . . enemigos de la crueldad y guardan la fe y lealtad a los amigos." (p. 462)

39. Counterreformation literary criticism, with special reference to the books of chivalry, is discussed in Allan K. Forcione, *Cervantes, Aristotle and the Persiles* (Princeton: Princeton University Press, 1970).

40. "En verdad, quien quisiera ejercitarse en escribir así las cosas acaecidas en la jornada como las cosas [que] se vieron en aquellas tierras—los ritos y tratos de los naturales—tuviera harta materia por donde pareciera su juicio, y creo que no le faltara de quedar relación que [al] tratar de verdad fuera tan admirable que pareciera increíble." (p. 415)

41. "Hicieron sus ceremonias de paz . . . ; llegar a los caballos y tomar del sudor y untarse con él y hacer cruces con los dedos de las manos . . . " (p. 431).

42. "Eran cosas señaladas y no vistas en otras partes y atrévome a las escribir porque escribo en tiempo que son hoy vivos muchos hombres que lo vieron y harán verdadera mi escritura." (p. 466)

43. "De largo un tiro de ballesta o muy poquito menos y de alto casi dos estados en partes y en ancho tres brazas . . . ' lo que se ha de notar es qué número de ganado sería menester para tanta osamenta." (p. 466)

44. See page 467 for the complete description.

45. "Bien se sufrirá pues en el capítulo pasado pase en silencio las hazañas que el capitán Juan Gallego hizo con viente compañeros que llevábase [para que se] diga en el presente capítulo para que en los tiempos venideros los que lo leyeren y de ello dieren noticia tengan autor cierto con quien aprobar y que no escribe fábulas como algunas cosas que en nuestros tiempos leemos en los libros de caballerías; que si no fuese por llevar aquellas fábulas de encantamientos hay cosas el día de hoy acontecidas en estas partes por nuestros españoles en conquistas y recuentros habidos con los naturales que sobrepujan en hechos de admiración no sólo a los libros ya dichos sino a los que se escriben de los doce pares de Francia; porque tanteado y mirado las fatales fuerzas que los autores de aquellos tiempos les atribuyan y las lúcidas y resplandecientes armas de que los adornan y las pequeñas estaturas de que ahora son los hombres de nuestros tiempos y las pocas y ruines armas de en estas partes, más es de admirar las cosas extrañas que con tales armas los nuestros acometen y hacen el día de hoy que las que escriben de los antiguos; pues también peleaban ellos con gentes bárbaras y desnudas como los nuestros con indios, donde no deja de haber hombres que entre ellos son esforzados y valientes y muy

certeros flecheros, pues le habemos visto derribar las aves que van volando y corriendo tras las liebres flecharlas; todo esto he dicho al fin que algunas cosas que tenemos por fabulosas pueden ser verdaderas y pues cada día vemos en nuestros tiempos cosas mayores como han sido las de don Fernando Cortez . . . " (pp. 464–65)

46. The preliminary report was published in Pachecho and Cárdenas, *Colleción de documentos*, along with other documents related to the expedition. See vol. 15:80–150.

47. "En todos los dichos años se ha ocupado en servir a Su Magestad, así en la gobernación de Diego de Ibarra, como en las minas de Macapil en el castigo de los indios de guerra que allí andan alzados, como en descubrimientos de minas a su costa. . . . Había hecho muchas jornadas la tierra dentro, adelante de Santa Bárbola, en seguimiento de indios salteadores." (Pacheco and Cárdenas, *Colleción de documentos*, 15:88–89)

48. Herbert Eugene Bolton reported that the Spanish text is entitled, "Relacion y concudío de el viage y subseso que Francisco Sanchez Chamuscado con ocho soldados sus compañeros hizo en el descubrimiento del Nuevo Mexico en Junio de 1581," and is located in Seville in the Archivo General de Indias, Patronato, 1-1-3/22. See his *Spanish Exploration in the Southwest, 1542–1706* (New York: Barnes and Noble, 1946), p. 140. The English translation is by George P. Hammond and Agapito Rey, *The Gallegos Relation of the Rodriguez Expedition to New Mexico*, in the Historical Society of New Mexico Publications in History, vol. 4 (Santa Fe: El Palacio Press, 1927) and in their *Rediscovery of New Mexico 1580–1594: The Explorations of Chamuscado, Espejo, Castaño de Sosa, Morlete, and Leyva de Bonilla and Humaña*, Coronado Cuarto Centennial Publications, 1540–1940, vol. 3 (Albuquerque: University of New Mexico Press, 1966).

49. See Angelico Chavez, "The Gallegos Relación Reconsidered," in *New Mexico Historical Review* 23 (1948), 1–22.

50. It was published in Pacheco and Cárdenas, *Colleción de documentos*, 15:101–126 under the title, "Relacion del viage, que yo Antonio Espejo, ciudadano de la ciudad de México, natural de Cordoba, hize con catorce soldados y un relijioso de la orden de San Francisco, á las provincias y poblaciones de la Nueva México, a quien puse por nombre, la Nueva Andalucía, a contemplacion de mi patria, en fin del ano de mill e quinientos e ochenta e dos." Bolton published a translation in his *Spanish Exploration in the Southwest* as did Hammond and Rey in *The Rediscovery of New Mexico*. Another good account by one of its participants, considerably longer than Espejo's own report, was written by Diego Pérez de Luxán, whom Hammond and Rey considered the best and most reliable chronicler of the Espejo expedition, but it has never been published in Spanish; a copy of the manuscript is at the archives in Seville (A.G.I., Patronato, legajo 22). However it can be read in Hammond and Rey's translation appearing in *The Rediscovery of New Mexico*.

51. For Espejo's prior activities in Mexico and the probable reasons for his financing and leading the expedition, as well as problems in securing permission to depart, see Hammond and Rey, *The Rediscovery of New Mexico*, pp. 16–17.

52. "Y no todo lo que pasó se pudo escribir ni yo dar relación de ello por escrito porque sería mucha prolijidad, porque las tierras y provincias que en esta jornada anduvimos fueron muchas y largas." (Pacheco y Cárdenas, *Colleción de documentos*, p. 124)

53. "Las gamuzas [i.e., ropa de piel] hacen [los Jumanos] de cueros de venados también aderezados [i.e., curtidos] como en Flandes. . . . [Los bisontes] parecen en el pelo a las vacas de Irlanda, y los cueros de estas vacas los aderezan los naturales de la manera de las antas [i.e., pieles] en Flandes." (p. 106–07)

54. "Y por mis manos, de ellas saqué metales, que dicen los que lo entienden, son muy ricos, y que tienen mucha plata." (p. 121)

55. "Y que en comparación de aquellas provincias y poblaciones, del río, no son nada las provincias donde al presente estábamos." (p. 121)

56. "Y en aquellas provincias, en la mayor parte dellas, hay mucha caza de pie y vuelo, conejos y liebres, venados y vacas de aquella tierra, y patos y ansares, y grullas y faisanes y otras aves; buenas montañas de todo género de arboledas, salinas y ríos con mucha diversidad de pescados, y en la mayor

parte de estas tierras, pueden rodar carretas y carros; y hay pastos muy buenos para los ganados, y tierras para hacer heredades, huertas y sementeras de temporal y de regadío, muchas ánimas ricas, de las cuales truje metales para ensayar y ver la ley que tienen, y un indio de la provincia de los Tamos, y una india de la provincia de Mohoce; porque si en servicio de Su Magestad, se hubiere de volver a hacer el descubrimiento y poblazón de aquellas provincias, den alguna lumbre de ellas y del camino por donde se ha de ir, y para ello apprendan la lengua mejicana y otras lenguas." (p. 125–26)

57. "Memorial del descubrimiento que Gaspar Castaño de Sosa hizo en el Nuevo México, siendo teniente de gobernador y capitán general del Nuevo Reino de León." It was published in two versions in Pacheco and Cárdenas, *Colleción de documentos*, 4:283–354 and 15:191–261. See Hammond and Rey, *The Rediscovery of New Mexico* (p. 245, n. 1) where their translation of it also appears.

58. For the historical background and an English translation see Herbert E. Bolton, "Father Escobar's Relation of the Oñate Expedition to California," *The Catholic Historical Review*, 5 (April 1919–January 1920), pp. 19–40. The Spanish text has been published for the first time in an edition prepared by Clark Colahan and Alfred Rodríguez, *Missionalia Hispanica* (Madrid: Consejo Superior de Investigaciones Científicas) 43 (1986), pp. 373–394. Although Spanish citations are from that edition, page references are still to Bolton's translation, which I use here.

59. See Bolton, "Father Escobar's Relation," p. 22.

60. "Es tierra muy pobre y fría, de muchas nieues; pero uien auitable para no muchos españoles, teniendo rropa con que vestirsse y lleuando de tierra de paz ganado con que ssustentarse y para labrar la tierra; que nada desto tiene ella de ssu cosecha, aunque se multiplica bien el ganado que a ella se lleua, pero es muy corta para poderse criar suma del." (Bolton, p. 23)

61. "Vna discrebción de la tierra en vn papel en el qual dio noticia de muchas naciones de jente tan mostruosas que con no poco temor de ser creydo las ossaré afirmar." (Bolton, p. 36)

62. "Y aunque a algunos lo aya de parecer mi atreuimiento en contar cossas tan monstruosas, no vistas en nuestros tiempos. . . . Con todo, me atreuo a rreferir lo que a grande multitud de yndios delante de my oví afirmar, que afirmar yo la uerdad de lo, de ssólo lo que con mis ojos uí me atreueré afirmarla." (Bolton, pp. 36–37)

63. "Tan largas orejas y tan grandes que les arrastrauan en tierra y que auían cinco o seis perssonas deuajo de cada una. Esta nasción se llamaua en su lengua Esmalcatatanaaha, y en la lengua desta nación de Bahacecha "esmalca" quiere decir oreja, de modo que la etimología del bocablo significa la propiedad de la nasción." (Bolton, p. 37)

64. "Tenían los ombres della el menbrun virile tan largo que se dauan quatro bueltas con él a la cinta y para el agto de la xeneración estauan el hombre y la mujer vien distantes." (Bolton, p. 37)

65. "Uibía en las orillas de vna laguna en la qual durmían todas las noches todos deuajo del agua, y esta jente, nos dijeron, heran los que trayan manillas o brazaletes de metal amarillo que llamauan anpacha." (Bolton, p. 37)

66. "Se sustentauan de sólo el olor de la comida, aderezándola para esto; no comiéndola de ninguna manera porque carecían de la uía natural para la ebaquación de los excrementos del cuerpo." (Bolton, p. 37)

67. "La perssona principal a quien rrespetauan . . . era muger, a quien llamauan Cinoca Cohota, que significa o quiere descir muger principal o capitalna. Esta supimos de todos estos yndios era giganta y que tenía sola otra hermana en la misma ysla y no otra perssona de ssu generación, que se deuía auer acauado en ellas. Los demás hombres que bibían en esta ysla supimos que muchos destos yndios eran todos caluos. Y que tuuieron fin las monstruosidades." (Bolton, pp. 37–38)

68. "Al que considerare las marauillas que Dios siempre obra en el mundo se le hará fácil creher que, como puede Dios hacerlas, puede hauerlas hecho; y que, pues las han afirmado tanta diuerssidad y multitud de jente, y algunas en más de duscientas leguas de distancia, no deue de carecer de fundamento, siendo cossas que no sson estos yndios los primeros ynuentores dellas, pues hay muchos libros donde sse trata dellas y de otras más monstruosas y que caussan mayor admiración." (Bolton, p. 38)

69. "La duda de que cossas tan monstruosas aya en tan pequeña distancia y de nossotros ayan estado

tan uezinas y cercanas . . . que, descubiertas, creo que rresultaua gloria a Dios y al rrey, nuestro señor, servicio. Porque, aunque las cossas en ssí sean tan rraras e nunca uistas. . . . no me parece está tan ympedido el passo a su uerificación y a la de las demás noticias de rriqueças y comunicación de los mares." (Bolton, p. 38)

2

THE FIRST AMERICAN EPIC
Villagrá's History of New Mexico

LUIS LEAL

INTRODUCTION

Villagrá's *History of New Mexico* has been called "the first published history of any American commonwealth," since it appeared fourteen years before Captain John Smith's *General History of Virginia*.[1] As such it deserves the attention of historians of both Mexico and the United States, for New Mexico has belonged to both countries. But the *History* is written in endecasyllabic verse and utilizes the epic form. For that reason it has not been accepted as history by some American historians. This is unfortunate, for the poem, as recognized by one of its earliest American critics, John Gilmary Shea, is "worth study as a poem written here at such an early period on events in which the author took part. It is devoted entirely to an American theme . . . [and] as an historical work it possesses remarkable value."[2]

Before Villagrá other authors, among them Alvar Núñez Cabeza de Vaca, Fray Marcos de Niza, Pedro Castañeda Nájera, and Antonio de Espejo, had written about New Mexico. But none had done it in verse as Villagrá had. His book is not only the first history of an American commonwealth, but also, as Shea pointed out "the first epic of our land" (4).

In Mexico historians have not recognized the value of Villagrá's poem either, although the literary critics have always considered it as belonging to Mexican literature. As early as 1885 the critic Francisco Pimentel included its author among the most distinguished writers of the seventeenth century, alongside other Mexican poets such as Arias Villalobos and Carlos de Sigüenza y Góngora.[3] American critics of literature, on the other hand, have been slow in claiming the *History of New Mexico* as part of their literature. In the most recent criticism, however, this attitude is changing. Werner Sollors, in the chapter of his recent book, *Beyond Ethnicity*, dedicated to the literary forms common among minority writers, states that the epic form is associated with ethnogenesis, the emergence of a people. To illustrate that statement he mentions several American epics, among them Villagrá's *History*, an example, he says, of "the earliest Colonial writing in America."[4] Chicano critics, however, have recently seen in Villagrá's work an antecedent of their literary heritage. And in New Mexico, both historians and critics have considered it as marking the beginning of their political and literary histories, for in it Villagrá covers Juan de Oñate's expedition to New Mexico from the earliest preparations for the journey to the conquest of Acoma. "It is the only key to the early history of New Mexico. Documents of great value have been printed in Mexico and Spain . . . but a student finds himself groping blindly in his endeavor to trace the series of events till he has read the poem of Villagrá" (Shea, 5).

JUAN DE OÑATE

In Canto 6 of his *History* Villagrá tells us that Oñate was "a son of kings," since his mother was Hernán Cortés's granddaughter. His father, Cristóbal de Oñate, distinguished himself in the conquest of Nueva Galicia (what today is Jalisco) and founded Zacatecas. In 1595 he was selected by the viceroy to undertake the settlement of New Mexico and was named governor of the region. His nephew, Vicente Zaldívar, was named Sergeant Major in charge of recruiting men for the expedition.

Early in 1596, four hundred men, thirty of them with their families, in eighty-three wagons and with seven thousand head of cattle, left for New Mexico, which they did not reach until April 1598. On the thirtieth day of that month Oñate took possession of the land in the name of the King of Spain. In August of the same year he founded the village of San Juan de los Caballeros, which became his headquarters and center of operations.

From San Juan, Oñate explored the region, both north and southwest. In October 1598 he left San Juan with the intention of reaching the Pacific. Juan Zaldívar, Vicente's brother, had received orders to join Oñate in this expedition. When he reached Acoma he and his twelve companions were attacked and killed. To avenge their death Oñate named Vicente, who carried out the order by destroying the town. This event gave Villagrá, who accompanied Vicente, the subject for his poem.[5]

VILLAGRÁ'S LIFE

Gaspar Pérez de Villagrá was born in Puebla de los Angeles, México, in 1555, two years after the University of Mexico was founded. His father, Hernán Pérez de Villagrá, was a descendant of a distinguished family of the town Campos de Villagrá, in Spain. About the time of Gaspar's birth another member of the family, Francisco de Villagrá, was fighting the Araucanian Indians in Chile.[6]

Villagrá's parents sent their son to Spain to study at the University of Salamanca. In a letter dated June 10, 1596, written from the village of Llerena in the state of Zacatecas to the Holy Office in Mexico City, he notes that he received the bachelor's degree.[7] It is not known when he returned to Mexico, after having spent several years at the court of Philip II. By 1596, however, he was already in Zacatecas, and there he became acquainted with Oñate, who named him procurator general of his army. He was also commissioned a captain and appointed a member of the council of war.

Villagrá accompanied Oñate on his first expedition to New Mexico and in 1598 participated in the punitive expedition against Acoma to avenge the death of Juan de Zaldívar and twelve Spanish soldiers. The cruel extermination of the city and punishment of the surviving women and children was an act unworthy of Oñate and Villagrá. The poet justified it by mentioning the rebellious Araucanians of Chile, and by reproducing, in prose (at the end of Canto 14), the opinions of the representatives of the church regarding the characteristics of a just war. In Canto 27 he says: "If sins and crimes are not promptly repressed and punished, it is impossible that peace exist in this world. Consider the case of the Araucanians. More than fifty years ago these people stained their arms with the blood of Spaniards, yet they still continue to bid defiance to our authority simply because they were not dealt with as they deserved" (219).[8]

In 1609 in Spain, Villagrá sat down to write about his experiences in New Mexico. The result was his *Historia de la Nueva México*, published in Alcalá de Henares, Cervantes's birthplace, the following year. It was dedicated to Philip III, the monarch then ruling Spain. The poem ends with these words: "O, worthy king, if it should please your majesty that I should conclude this tale at a future date, I pray you will be patient. I have served you faithfully with the sword; the pen is a new and strange implement to wield" (267).

Around 1612 charges were made against Oñate and his lieutenants for the harsh treatment given to the survivors of Acoma. Villagrá was accused of having killed some Indians after the capture of the community, and also of having taken seven Acoma girls to the viceroy to be distributed among the convents and well-to-do families of Mexico City. Villagrá defended himself in a *Justificación* published in Madrid in 1612. As a result of the accusations, in 1614 he was banished from the provinces of New Mexico for six years and from Mexico City and its environs for two years. He spent that time in Spain, where he remained until 1620. That year he was appointed *alcalde mayor* of Zapotitlan, Guatemala, a position he never occupied since that same year he died at sea while on his way to that country.[9]

THE SPANISH EDITIONS OF THE HISTORIA

The first edition of the *Historia de la Nueva México*, which came out of the presses of Luis Martínez Grande, is a volume in small octave, with 24 preliminaries and 287 folios of text.[10] The preliminaries contain nine laudatory poems, one of them by Espinel, the author of the picaresque novel *Marcos de Obregón*. Of this first edition there are very few copies in existence today. The copy in the library of don Manuel Gómez Velasco of Madrid was loaned to the Director of the National Museum of Mexico City, Francisco del Paso y Troncoso, who during a visit to Spain obtained the permission to reproduce the poem.

The result was the second Spanish edition, in two volumes, published by the presses of the National Museum of Mexico City in 1900, with an introduction by Luis Gonzáles Obregón. If not a facsimile edition, it is an exact reproduction of the first, consisting of 182 folios and including the preliminary pieces and facsimile reproduction of the title page and photograph of the author. The first volume contains the poem, and the second includes documents relative to the book and its author, among them, those collected by the Mexican bibliographer José Fernando Ramírez.[11]

Prose excerpts from the poem appeared at the end of the book *Don Diego de Peñalosa* (Madrid, 1892) by Cesáreo Fernando Duro. The editor of the collection *Libros raros o curiosos que tratan de América* (Madrid, 1892) announced a complete edition of the poem that never appeared.

THE ENGLISH TRANSLATION

In 1933 the Quivira Society published in Los Angeles, in one volume, the English translation of Villagrá's poem, together with twenty of the documents regarding the author, taken from volume II of the 1900 Mexican edition. The translator, Gilberto Espinosa, chose prose instead of verse to render the historical poem. Since the rhyme element of the Spanish is lost, the translation acquires some characteristics of true history. The use of prose, the historical footnotes after each Canto, and the several photographs and index enhance the historical aspects of the work.

In the Foreword a clear account of the nature of the *History*, its contents, and its value as history are given by Professor F. W. Hodge. He ends his introduction by a reference to the translator: "In bringing this foreword to a close I take it upon myself to express to Señor Gilberto Espinosa, a direct descendant of the valiant Captain Marcelo Espinosa of Oñate's army, the grateful thanks of the Quivira Society for his excellent translation of a most difficult work" (33–34). We concur with Hodge's opinion, for indeed the translation is an excellent prose rendition of the original verse. Sometimes, however, some poetic, non-historical passages are omitted.

The poem opens with these verses:

Las armas y el varón heroico canto,
el ser, valor, prudencia, y alto esfuerzo,
de aquel cuya paciencia no rendida,
por un mar de disgustos arrojada
a pesar de la envidia ponzoñosa,
los hechos y proezas va encumbrando. (1:1)

[Arms I sing, and of the deeds of that
heroic son who, despite the envy of men and
unmindful of the sea of difficulties which
on every side beset him, patiently, prudently,
and bravely vanquished all and performed most
heroic deeds.] (41)

THE POEM AS HISTORY

In spite of the epic poem form, the *History* is more than anything else a detailed chronicle of Oñate's first expedition to New Mexico. Although Villagrá has been called "our New Mexico Homer," his poem is a simple historical narrative in verse, quite reliable as a source for the early history of New Mexico. The Mexican critic and editor of the 1900 Mexican edition, Luis Gonzáles Obregón, stated that Villagrá, like Saavedra Guzmán, the author of the epic poem *El peregrino indiano* (1599), was "a poet-chronicler, but more of a chronicler than a poet."[12]

The first two of the thirty-four Cantos of which the poem is composed are mostly mythical. They deal with the origin of the Aztecs, presumably having migrated south from what is now New Mexico. Villagrá is not sure about this theory and adds that perhaps they came from China. The myth about the founding of Tenochtitlan, today Mexico City, is expressed with these verses:

Viéredes una tuna estar pintada
y sobre cuyas gruesas y anchas hojas
una águila caudal bella disforme
con bravura cebando se entretiene,
en una gran culebra que a sus garras,
veréis que está revuelta y bien asida
que allí quiere se funde y se levante
la metrópoli alta y generosa. (2:6)

[a spot where you shall see a lofty rock
[and] a mighty eagle perched upon the branches
of a lofty cactus, feasting upon a serpent which she
shall hold in her talons. Here you shall build
your capital, and it is decreed that you shall
give it the name of Tenochtitlan-México.] (47)

The above message is given to the Aztecs by a witch, who is serving as the ambassador of their god. The description of this fantastic character is an excellent example of the narrative ability and imaginative faculties of Pérez de Villagrá:

Y así como a perdidos miserables,
Y de la santa iglesia divididos,
Marchando así estos pobres reprobados,
Delante se les puso aquel maldito,
En figura de vieja rebozado,
Cuya espantosa y gran desenvoltura,
Daban pavor y miedo imaginarla,
Trujo el cabello cano mal compuesto,
Y cual horrenda y fiera notomía,
El rostro descarnado macilento,
De fiera y espantosa catadura,
Desmesurados pechos, largas tetas,
Hambrientas, flacas, secas y fruncidas,
Nervudos pechos, anchos y espaciosos,
Con terribles espaldas bien trabadas,
Sumidos ojos de color de fuego,
Disforme boca desde oreja a oreja,
Por cuyos labios secos desmedidos,
Cuatro solos colmillos hacia afuera,
De un largo palmo corvos se mostraban,

[These miserable creatures, ignorant of the holy faith, were on the march when there appeared before their ranks this frightful demon in the guise of an old and withered hag. It is terrible even to describe her appearance. A mass of long, disheveled hair of ashen gray almost hid her fleshless face; long, crooked teeth peered forward from two misshapen, protruding lips which enclosed a leering, grinding mouth, extending from ear to ear. Her eyes, like glowing coals, shone forth from deep and sunken orbits. She had immense but unproportioned shoulders of prodigious strength which curiously contrasted with her monstrous but lean and flabby breasts and enormously long teats] (2:46)

Not satisfied with the above description, he adds:

Los brazos temerarios, pies y piernas,
Por cuyas espantosas coyunturas,
Una osamenta gruesa rechinaba,
De poderosos nervios bien asida,

[The most remarkable part of this strange and frightful creature was her gigantic arms and legs, long, bony, bereft of flesh; as she moved a weird and screeching sound went forth from [her] enormous joints] (2:46)

Upon her large and strong head she bore "an enormous mass of solid ore, shaped not unlike a tortoise shell" (2:46).

In Cantos III to V we find a reference to former expeditions to the Southwest, especially those of Cabeza de Vaca, Niza, Coronado, and Espejo. The information provided here, although not original, is a good summary of the subject. From Canto VI on the poem is dedicated to a detailed description of the Oñate expedition of 1598, ending with the taking and destruction of Acoma by Sergeant Major Vicente Zaldívar, in whose company was Villagrá. This firsthand information is very useful in reconstructing the events that led to the actual conquest of the community of Acoma.

From the historical point of view, Cantos XIV and XV are of interest because in them the author describes the discovery of the Río del Norte (Río Grande today), crossed by Oñate and his men near where El Paso, Texas, is today. Of importance also is the biographical information provided by Villagrá about himself, Oñate, and the Zaldívar family, as well as other officers and soldiers.

The reliability of the poem as history has been attested to by several historians. Bandelier, in his monograph about the Zunis (1892), wrote that Villagrá was an execrable poet, but a reliable historian insofar as he saw and took part in the events himself. "His narration of the tragedy of Acoma and of the recapture of the pueblo is too Homeric altogether; but in this he followed the style of the period."[13] Three years earlier Bancroft had made use of the poem to reconstruct Oñate's conquest of New Mexico. In his *History of Arizona and New Mexico* he states that "the veritable authority for the events presented in this chapter [VI] is to be found in the shape of an epic poem, written by Gaspar de Villagrá."[14] More recently, Professor Hodge, in his Foreword to the English translation of the *History*, has spoken of its extensive value "to the student of the colonization of New Mexico by Oñate, and especially of the tragedy of Acoma" (19). Hammond used the information provided in the poem to reconstruct the events of Oñate's expedition. As he says in the Preface to his book on Oñate, "Villagrá's immortal poem on early New Mexico (Alcalá, Spain, 1610) is full of information. Its importance is well known and need not again be emphasized" (iv).

THE POEM AS LITERATURE

The historians, with few exceptions, have followed González Obregón's judgment regarding the literary value of the *History*, that is, that Villagrá's book is valuable as history but poor as poetry. Among the historians who think otherwise we find Bancroft, who said that the *History*'s subject "is well enough adapted to epic narrative, and in the generally smooth-flowing endecasyllabic lines of Villagrá loses nothing of its intrinsic fascination. Occasionally the author quits the realm of poesy to give us a document in plain prose; and while enthusiastic in praise of his leader and his companions, our New Mexican Homer is modest in recounting his own exploits." (115). Bancroft's enthusiasm extended to the point where he translated, in verse form, the first forty-eight verses of the poem (114–15). For him history written in verse form is just as reliable as that written in prose, as he adds: "Not less remarkable is the historic accuracy of the Muse in this production."

On the other hand, the literary critics, with one exception, have spoken about the poor literary quality of the poem. The exception is the nineteenth-century Mexican critic Francisco Pimentel, who found Villagrá's verse to be fluid. Presumably he contradicts himself because he, as a positivist critic, disliked the style of the baroque poets who were active when Villagrá published his *History*. He therefore praises it for its clearness of expression. But, on the other hand, he criticizes it for the prosaic nature of its verse. Since this is one of the earliest appraisals of the poem, it is worth quoting in full; he tells us that he saw a copy of the poem in the library of the bibliographer Joaquín García Icazbalceta and that he came to form the following judgment:

> The *Historia de la Nueva México* has two laudable features, one in the contents, and the other in the form, to wit: the fidelity with which the facts are related, and the

> simplicity and naturalness of the style and the language. This is really remarkable in the period when gongorism predominated. Nevertheless, Villagrá did not keep the golden mean, and committed literary vices opposed to those of gongorism, his work being quite prosaic, without any poetic fictions to adorn it, and written in free verses that are very weak and which make its reading very tedious. . . . The poem can only be appreciated by those scholars who may be looking for obscure or unknown information that they may find there, as they may in any historical chronicle. (142–43)

There is no question, however, that the poem is a literary object whose contents deal with history. But so do most Spanish epic poems, from *El Cid* to *La Araucana*. And early in the nineteenth century the historical novel appeared and became popular not only in England but in all countries of the West. Its development culminates with Tolstoy's *War and Peace*, which, like Villagrá's poem, is also quoted by historians, especially the part dealing with the battle of Borodino, a historically accurate event, as is Villagrá's description of the destruction of Acoma.

When critics speak about the poor quality of Villagrá's poem, they are expressing a value judgment regarding its aesthetic nature, and not precisely denying that it is literature. Quite a number of literary works are of poor quality, a reason that does not eliminate them from the histories of literature. Also, there is no question as to the relatively few poetic images in Villagrá's poem. But there are excellent passages, as are the descriptions of the landscape and some of the characters. On the other hand, sometimes, as is characteristic of baroque literature, it is overly contrived, as when the poet takes fifteen verses to tell us that the soldiers engage the enemy in hand to hand fighting:

> *Y así la soldadesca en tanto aprieto,*
> *Cual suelen con fortuna los forzados,*
> *Bogar sobre los cabos reventando,*
> *Por no desmarrarse y desasirse,*
> *Y a fuerza de los puños y los brazos,*
> *Con roncos azezidos y gemidos,*
> *Contra el rigor del mar soberbio arfando,*
> *Embisten con las hondas y las rompen,*
> *Con sobre de coraje levantando,*
> *Al cielo espumas de agua así oprimidos,*
> *Los fuertes españoles arrancaron,*
> *Las valientes espadas rigurosas,*
> *De las gallardas cintas en que estaban,*
> *Y así revueltos, todos desenvueltos,*
> *Por medio la canalla se lanzaban. (22:120a)*

The terse translation by Espinosa brings out the differences between prose and poetry:

The soldiers, like shipwrecked sailors who, when their ship has foundered, abandon the craft and take to their boats in the raging sea, throwing aside their firearms, drew their swords and closed with the savage foe . . .] (191)

Counterbalancing the above are passages wherein the poet reaches a high point of inspiration. The introduction to Canto 22, where Villagrá begins his account of the tragic conflict between Spaniards and Acomas, is such an example:

O mundo instable de miserias lleno,
Verdugo atroz de aquel que te conoce,
Disimulado engaño no entendido,
Prodigiosa tragedia portentosa,
Maldito cáncer, solapada peste,
Mortal veneno, landre que te encubres,
Dime traidor aleve fementido,
Cuántas traiciones tienes fabricadas,
Cuántos varones tienes consumidos,
De cuanto mal enredo estás cargado,
O mundo vano, o vana y miserable
Honra con tantos daños adquirida,
O vanas esperanzas de mortales,
O vanos pensamientos engañosos,
Sujetos siempre a míseros tamores,
Y a mil sucesos tristes y accidentes . . . (22:117b)

[How miserably we mortals live in this ungrateful world!
We endure this false and untrue existence,
teeming with dangers so hid
by deceit which we can neither fathom
nor understand. Ungrateful
world, a festerous cancer; what poison
reeks within your bloody fangs!
What reason and betrayals have you in store for
those who place their trust in
earthly hopes! O, fickle hopes of mortal
man, subject always to a thousand ills and wrongs!
O, woeful day; O, fearful fate!] (189)

The quality of the free verse has been characterized as being prosaic, and there is no question that it is. A number of original images, however, give the poem here and there a poetic tone. Following the taste of the period, Villagrá draws upon classical mythology and the Bible to embellish his narrative and to enhance his poetic intent. The military men who set out on expeditions of conquest and return "in hopeless confusion, each giving a different and contradictory account"

(4:16) for not having accomplished their purpose, he compares to Nimrod and Phaeton. There are, however, no long mythological digressions, as is the case with Ercilla.

The frequent use of aphoristic expressions and the numerous shrewd observations about life and human nature are also characteristic of Villagrá's style:

Considerando que de un gran yerro
Suele salir un gran acertamiento. (3:14a)

[Considering that, from a great mistake,
the result is often a great success.][15]

Que aquel que ofende es fuerza siempre traiga
La barba sobre el hombre recatado (26:136b)

[Necessary it is, for he who causes
offense, to be prudently aware.] (My transl.)

About envy, he says:

La torpe envidia siempre busca,
veredas y ocasiones donde pueda,
vomitar su mortífera ponzoña. (6:31a)

[Envy and jealousy are always seeking
an opportunity to belch forth their
deadly poison.] (76)

Secrets, he believed, could not be kept for long:

No hay secreto tan oculto,
Que al fin no se revele y se nos muestre. (7:36b)

[There is never a secret so hidden that it
is not revealed to someone.] (p. 83)

Vanity is chided in a long passage (omitted in the translation) beginning with these verses:

O vanidad, vil tósigo sabroso,
Sujeto a cruel evidia y muerte acerba,
Qué mar de sangre vemos derramada,
Por sólo pretenderte . . . (21:116a)

[O vanity, sweet poison,
Subject to cruel envy and bitter death,
What a sea of blood we see spilled
By only courting you . . .] (My trans.)

About the character of the Spaniards he says:

Propia y común dolencia de españoles [es],
Meterse en los peligros sin recato,
Sospecha ni pasión de mal suceso, (22:118a)

[Of the Spaniards a peculiar and common ailment
[It is], to rush into danger without caution,
Suspicion, nor premonition of failing] (My trans.)

As an example of that rash spirit Villagrá cites the case of a Spanish captain who wants to face the enemy all by himself. Although the Maese has ordered a retreat, he refuses to move and wants to fight alone:

Y verse ha como solo me antepongo,	*[I shall alone face this rabble*
A toda esta canalla y la sujeto, (22:119a)	*and put them to flight.] (190)*

Of greater importance in the poem are Villagrá's descriptions of the landscape and the flora and fauna of New Mexico, since they are the first, in poetic form, to be found in the literature of the region. The bison he describes as being

Lanudos por extremo, corcobados,
De regalada carne y negros cuernos,
Lindísima manteca, y rico sebo,
Y como los chivatos tienen barbas,
Y son de una mano tan ligeros,
Que corren mucho más que los venados,
Y andan en atajos tanta suma,
Que veinte y treinta mil cabezas juntas,
Se hallan ordinarias muchas veces. (17:93ab)

[They are . . . extremely wooly, hump-backed,
black-horned, and have splendid meat. They
yield great amounts of lard and tallow. They
have beards like billy-goats, and are as
fleet of foot as deer. They go together in
great herds of as many as twenty or thirty
thousand.] (156)

The description of the prairie where the buffalo roam is etched with original images; the one comparing the prairie to the sea reminds us of the image used by the Argentinian Sarmiento in his essay *Facundo* (1845), where he compares the pampa to the sea.[16] Villagrá wrote:

Y gozan [los bisontes] de unos llanos tan tendidos,
Que por seiscientas y ochocientas leguas,
Un sosegado mar parece todo . . .
Que si por triste suerte se perdiese,

Alguno en estos llanos no sería,
Más que si perdiese y se hallase,
En medio de la mar sin esperanza. (17:93*b*)

[And they roam over such an extended area
that for six or eight hundred leagues
a calm sea it appears to be.
Unfortunate indeed is he who might
lose himself in these plains, for worse
he would fare than if he found himself
hopelessly lost in the middle of the sea.][17]

The following description of a round-up, where the word *vaquero* (cowboy) appears, is perhaps the first in the literature of the Southwest:

Queriendo pues en estos grandes llanos,
El Sargento mayor coger algunas,
De aquestas vacas sueltas y traerlas,
Al pueblo de San Juan, porque las viesen,
Mandó que una manga se hiciese,
De fuerte palizada prolongada,
La cual hicieron luego con presteza, . . .
Y luego que la manga se compuso,
Salieron para dar el aventada, . . .
Todos en buenas yeguas voladoras,
Aventando salieron el ganado
Y así como la manga descubrieron,
Cual poderoso viento arrebatado,
Que remata en un grande remolino
Así fue reparando y revolviendo,
La fuerza del ganado levantando, . . .
Los cuales vieron siempre en estos llanos
gran suma de vaqueros, que a pie matan,
Aquestas mismas vacas que decimos (17:93*b*–94*a*).

[The sergeant major, wishing to capture
a few of these buffalo to take back to
the pueblo of San Juan that the rest
might see them, ordered a great stockade
to be built . . . After the stockade had
been constructed, all the former, together
with the quartermaster . . . rode forth among
the cattle on fleet mares.
When the cattle discovered the stockade
they began to stampede, rushing about

like a raging whirlpool, raising an immense cloud of dust . . .
The men saw in these regions
many of the vaqueros who inhabit
these regions and who hunt these cattle on foot] (156–57).

Although Villagrá was prouder of being a soldier than a writer, his name has endured because of the use he made of the pen and not of the sword. To him, however, there is no question as to which of the two professions is nobler. Less subtle than his contemporary, Miguel de Cervantes, for whom the question was a vital one, Villagrá clearly favors the profession of the soldier, believing it to be superior to that of the man of letters. He wrote in his poem:

O soldados que al bélico ejercicio,
Sois con gran razón aficionados,
Advertid que es grandísima grandeza,
No ser nada muy pródigo en lengua,
Y serlo por la espada es cosa noble. (22:120b)

[O, ye who seek renown in battle, remember
it is well that ye be not too mighty with
your tongue; better yet that you wield a
sword with prowess!] (192–93)

He was not, however, blind to the fact that he was making a name for himself as a writer. His presence in his own work, not as a soldier but as a poet, is manifested in several Cantos. Since the poem is written to inform the King of Spain of the conquest of New Mexico, the author addresses him directly and excuses himself for his shortcomings as a poet:

Y vos Filipo sacro, que escuchando
Mi tosca musa habéis estado atento,
Suplicoos no os canséis, que ya he llegado,
Y al prometido puesto soy venido. (34:176a)

[O, worthy Philip, you have listened most
attentively to the song of this unworthy muse.
I pray you, bear with me but a little longer,
for I am about to reach the promised end.] (262)

Villagrá, of course, must have had literary ambitions, otherwise he would not have chosen the verse form to write his history of the conquest of New Mexico.

The laudatory poems in praise of the author accompanying the text are sufficient reward for his efforts. He died too early to have savored the praise of others, or to have decried the brickbats. His place in the histories of literature, however, is well assured, as his poem has endured the ravages of time and criticism. If as a soldier he participated in the conquest of New Mexico, as a poet he preserved the deed for posterity. As Don Gabriel Gómez says in his songs that he dedicated to the author of the *Historia de la Nueva México,*

> *No de otra suerte al nuevo Mexicano,*
> *Libras tu del olvido,*
> *Después que valeroso le has vencido. (182b)*
>
> *[After bravely conquering*
> *the New Mexican (with your sword)*
> *from oblivion you have*
> *rescued him (with your book).] (My trans.)*

NOTES

1. F. W. Hodge, Foreword to the *History of New Mexico* by Gaspar Pérez de Villagrá (Alcalá, 1610), trans. Gilberto Espinosa (Los Angeles: Quivira Society, 1933; rpt. New York: Arno Press, 1967), p. 17. All translations, except when indicated, are from the 1933 edition.

2. John Gilmary Shea, "The First Epic of Our Country. By the Poet Conquistador of New Mexico, Captain Gaspar de Villagrá," *United States Catholic Historical Magazine,* New York (April, 1887), p. 4. For a complete survey of the use that historians have made of Villagrá's poem see Hodge's Foreword.

3. Francisco Pimentel, *Historia crítica de la literatura y de las ciencias en México. Desde la Conquista hasta nuestros días. Poetas* (México: Librería de la Enseñanza, 1885), pp. 142–43. Although Pimentel saw a copy of Villagrá's *Historia* in the Library of Joaquín García Icazbalceta, he erroneously gives 1660 as the year of publication.

4. Werner Sollors, *Beyond Ethnicity* (New York: Oxford University Press, 1986), p. 239.

5. For a complete account of Oñate's expedition see George P. Hammond, *Don Juan de Oñate and the Founding of New Mexico* (Santa Fe: El Palacio Press, 1927), chapter 1.

6. The Araucanians are mentioned twice in Villagrá's poem, in Cantos 8 and 27. In documents of the period Villagrá's name is often spelled Villagrán. Alonso de Ercilla's poem, *La araucana,* dealing with the conquest of the Araucanian Indians in Chile during the middle of the sixteenth century, was published in three parts (1569; 1578; 1589). Unlike the *History,* critics and historians alike find in *La araucana* permanent values and consider it as one of the great epic poems in the Spanish language. See Charles M. Lancaster and Paul T. Manchester, eds., *The Araucaniad* (Nashville: Vanderbilt University Press, 1945).

7. This letter has been reproduced by Ernesto Mejía Sánchez in his article "Gaspar Pérez de Villagrá en la Nueva España," *Cuadernos del Centro de Estudios Literarios,* No. 1 (México: UNAM, 1970). Quotation on p. 6.

8. For a complete description of the destruction of Acoma see chapter 7 of Hammond's book.

9. Most of the documents relating to Villagrá's life were collected in volume 2 of the 1900 Spanish edition of the *Historia* (See footnote 11).

10. *Historia/de la Nueva/México, del Capitán/Gaspar de Villagrá.*/Dirigida al Rey D. Felipe/

nuestro señor Tercero deste nombre./Año 1610./Con Privilegio./En Alcalá, por Luys Martinez Grande./A costa de Baptista López mercader de libros.

11. *Historia de la Nueva México* por el Capitán Gaspar de Villagrá, 2 tomos (México: Imprenta del Museo Nacional, 1900). Introducción by Luis González Obregón, pp. iii–xi. All Spanish quotations are from this edition, with canto and page numbers in parenthesis.

12. This statement was taken from Pimentel, *Historia crítica* . . . , p. 99, who in turn took it from William H. Prescott's *History of the Conquest of Mexico* (1843).

13. A. F. Bandelier, *An Outline of the Documentary History of the Zuni Tribe* (Boston: Houghton Mifflin, 1982), p. 82, footnote 2.

14. Hubert H. Bancroft, *History of Arizona and New Mexico*. In *The Works of* . . . 24 vols. (San Francisco, 1883–1890), vol. 17 (1892), p. 112.

15. My translation, since these two verses are not in Espinosa.

16. Domingo Faustino Sarmiento published his famous book in 1845. It was translated by Mrs. Horace Mann, *Life in the Argentine in the Days of the Tyrants, or Civilization and Barbarism* (New York, 1868; rpt. 1960). In the first part of the book Sarmiento describes the pampa as an inland sea ("la pampa . . . es la imagen del mar en la tierra") (*Facundo*, Buenos Aires, 1925), p. 45.

17. My translation, as Espinosa seems to have misinterpreted this passage. His translation reads:

> they (the bisons) graze over such a great area that for six or eight hundred leagues it seems to be a regular sea of cattle. Unfortunate indeed would be the traveler who lost himself in these plains, for he would surely perish in the midst of this sea of beasts. (156)

2

SO FAR FROM THE MOTHERLAND AND SO CLOSE TO GOD

Colonial Literature

3

MIGUEL DE QUINTANA
An Eighteenth-Century New Mexico Poet Laureate?

CLARK COLAHAN
FRANCISCO A. LOMELÍ

New Mexican historian John Kessell has described the archives of the Inquisition in Mexico City as a computer memory bank pulsing with data on the social, intellectual, and emotional lives of Mexicans in the colonial period. There is perhaps no better example than the story of Miguel de Quintana, an intensely personal drama found among those numerous and still often undecoded *legajos*. Because of an investigation conducted by the Church in the 1730s, officially labeled as revolving around heresy, the poems and expressive prose of an eighteenth-century New Mexico writer were preserved as evidence in the case. They constitute highly subjective cultural artifacts, fashioned by a craftsman who lived from words and who sought self-justification and emotional release in a time of personal and social conflict. As such they stand as the only literary documents—putting aside the oral tradition—that have survived in written form from the least literate and least known century of Hispanic culture in New Mexico. Quintana's stature in the community, his mystical religious beliefs and experiences—a strong tradition among the people of the region and in Hispanic life in general—, plus the fact that he managed to support himself by the then uncommon ability to read and write, all combine to provide a unique portrait of social relations and spiritual beliefs in the area following Vargas's reconquest. His story also brings to light another illuminating circumstance: that in this case missionaries in Franciscan New Mexico used the Inquisition to bring pressure to bear outside the usual sphere of struggle with the civil authorities. That is, they used the Inquisition to gain leverage in a conflict regarding literary-spiritual life, and the pressure they applied had revealing psychological consequences in an intelligent, articulate, and sincere Catholic whose success as a writer had provoked the Church's opposition and wrath.

Quintana's work is also of particular interest as an antecedent to the distinctive form of Hispanic literature existing in what is now the Southwest of the United States. Although there are exceptions, the majority of the documents from the colonial period—predominantly chronicles, official diaries and records, accounts of journeys, letters, and other factual genres—provide details on the practical aspects of establishing a new colonial society. This does not, of course, detract from their worth as written accounts that taken together give an accurate depiction of the life and thought of that particular time and place. The topics and the manner in which they are presented offer greater insight into the settlers' view of the world. In this regard, Luis Leal has commented: "But whatever the purpose was of what they wrote, the important thing is those prose writers left us the history of the discovery, exploration and colonization of Aztlan, as well as the first Aztlanesque descriptions and images."[1] What Quintana adds to these more external, historical events is the voice of an artist and community leader who speaks with considerable skill and complexity about his personal circumstances and self-concept. His emotions become known at precisely the time when his sense of place in society and the universe is threatened by institutionalized authority. His determined and outspoken resistance, drawing strength from his neighbors' support and from traditional elements of Hispanic lore, shows an undeniable connection with the thrust of much of contemporary Chicano literature.

HIS LIFE IN NEW MEXICO

Although born in Mexico City in approximately 1670, Quintana arrived young in New Mexico in the caravan of colonists brought by Vargas in 1693, following the Pueblo Indian revolt that drove the Spanish out for twelve years. The official description of the group's members tells us that he was the "son of José, native of Mexico, twenty-two years old, able-bodied, round face, small forehead, large eyes, and a dimple in the chin." His wife, named Gertrudis de Trujillo, is referred to as "daughter of Nicolas, native of Mexico, fifteen years old, medium height, aquiline face, large eyes, and small nose."[2] He lived the remaining fifty-five years of his life in the Villa Nueva de Santa Cruz, a dispersed agricultural settlement founded in 1695 by Vargas for the new settlers.

For several years he supported his large family of six children by farming. The hardships of this rural life are poignantly sketched in a letter he wrote in 1712 in which he initiated an eventually successful suit against a neighbor for the theft of his two horses by the neighbor's Apache servants.[3] He describes his difficult situation in moving terms, at the same time demonstrating both his command of language and an ability to present himself as an innocent victim whose characteristics later become key elements in his more literary writings.

In the following two decades, his education in Mexico City—which can be inferred from the very fact that he was literate as well as from his clear, steady script—provided him another source of income. His signature as a notary appears on several documents he drew up in civil and criminal cases heard by the mayors of Santa Cruz. However, his neighbors also came to him for other services, for they saw him as a respected and intelligent individual, having competence in not only legal questions but personal and literary matters as well. He combined multiple writing functions still common in many Hispanic societies but currently distributed among two or three professions: the notary public/lawyer, the religious author, who both composes prayers for individual requests and serves as a playwright for parish and community dramatic productions, and the public scribe whose task is not so much to take down dictation from his illiterate customers as to express their thoughts in his own educated, though oftentimes conventional, words. Fray Angelico Chavez perhaps stated it best: "Miguel had become a kind of poet laureate,"[4] while John Kessell perceptively characterizes him as a *santero* working in word instead of wood.

Miguel de Quintana, then, enjoyed, at least in a certain period of his life, considerable recognition derived from his literary and legal activities. He himself recounts a crucial event he experienced in 1726 that clearly shows he was highly solicited by people on a regular basis to write Christmas plays.[5] A letter written to him in 1737 by a friend, Fray Juan Sánchez de la Cruz, characterized him as a man of importance in the town government. Even more convincing are the descriptive phrases used in 1734 by two priests whose relationship toward him was more one of hostility than of friendship. Fray Manuel de Sopeña stated that Quintana "has always worked as notary of the mayors, acting with all good judgment, that his writings have had acceptance, and that currently he is notary of the ecclesiastical jurisdiction." The other priest, Fray Joseph Irigoyen, declared that Quintana

> spends all his time writing things for his neighbors, that they make use of him for this purpose, and that this is his life and his usual activity. . . . His conversations are coherent, his advice gladly received and followed. . . . During the ten years that he

> [Irigoyen] has known him, he has seen him at the side of the mayor handling civil and ecclesiastical cases. He is the current notary of the ecclesiastical court, has continued to perform the duties of that office up to the present time, and finds acceptance in all matters. Not only the common men, but also many of the important people of this kingdom, consider him a man of integrity and good judgment.[6]

THE CONFLICT WITH SOPEÑA AND IRIGOYEN

For reasons that are not entirely clear, Quintana's success elicited opposition from the two Franciscan priests quoted. In testimony given to the Inquisition, they reported that he had stopped attending mass and was no longer participating in other religious activities, probably a reference to meetings of the Third Order of St. Francis. Irigoyen specifically accused Quintana of making excuses, such as "pain in his spleen," to avoid religious duties, while he was allegedly always in good health when it came to having a good time. Quintana himself expressed concern about withdrawing from the Third Order, reassuring himself in his writings numerous times that belonging to what he calls the confraternity of the Virgin, that is, feeling special devotion toward her, although not involved in a formal organization, is all that was necessary to be saved. Not by coincidence, a New Mexican tradition promised salvation to those who died while in good standing within the Third Order of St. Francis. Irigoyen, then, stressing the gap between Quintana's conduct and "his pretending to be so holy in his writing,"[7] condemned him as a hypocrite and, with very little basis, a heretic.

The two denouncing priests, like many who brought charges to the attention of the Inquisition throughout its history, may have had more complex motives for their actions than an "unburdening of their conscience," a standard formula given in this case as the basis for coming forward in defense of moral security. Jealousy, either professional or simply personal, of his recognition in the community as a religious writer can reasonably be suspected for more than one reason. Quintana suggests it when referring to Irigoyen as the "*celoso*" notary of the Inquisition, an adjective than can mean either "zealous" or "jealous." This telling description emerges years after he had vigorously begun his defense and seems to be a release of frustration for the prolonged attacks against him.

From an objective point of view, the variety of nonspiritual ends that were served by the Spanish Inquisition throughout its history are well documented. A political instrument from its inception, it often deteriorated into a vehicle for personal aggrandizement and aggression. In eighteenth-century Mexico the Inquisition directed much of its political vigilance against the Enlightenment's attempts to separate religion and government,[8] although in New Mexico, as John

Kessell points out, "as guardian of traditional Hispanic values against the blasphemy of the Enlightenment, it had little business on an illiterate frontier."[9] In Quintana's case of heresy—to the very limited extent that it truly existed—it was not of the French rationalist sort that the Church feared at the time, but rather of an older, mystical, and more familiar Spanish type that no longer caused special concern. This fact lends further support to Quintana's assertion that he was unduly attacked and harrassed for other than theological reasons. In addition, the existence of a power struggle with the Mexican Church (actually resembling only a mild squabble when viewed over the centuries) provides evidence to confirm this explanation.

In the 1730s, the decade during which Quintana was under investigation, Bishop Crespo of Durango, the highest ecclesiastical figure of northern Mexico, renewed the claims already made earlier by the diocese to jurisdiction over New Mexico. The Franciscan order, the bishop argued, had been granted authority and money by the Spanish crown only to carry out a mission to benefit the Indians. The spiritual care of the Spanish settlers was the responsibility of his regular clergy, and he charged that in their absence appropriate spiritual care was not being provided. Moreover, the mission to the Indians itself was being carried out inadequately. He accused the friars, among other things, of administering the sacraments incorrectly, permitting irregularities as to the requirements for confession, not learning the Indian languages, engaging in scandalous and suspicious conduct, not collecting the tithes correctly, and, in the case of some individuals, not actively dedicating themselves to their duties. Those indicted, on the other hand, defended themselves strenuously and attributed the charges to pure malice. Among those named by the bishop were Sopeña and Irigoyen, and whether or not the charges were grounded on fact, they help to explain why Quintana's two accusers were on the defensive, sensitive to any rivalry, and eager to point out that there were others in New Mexico much more deserving of the Church's censure.[10]

Another possible clue to the nature of the friction with the two priests is found in several visions Quintana claimed to have experienced of the ghost of Father Juan de Tagle, former *custos* [director] of the Franciscan order in New Mexico and a frequent visitor to Santa Cruz during the first quarter of the eighteenth century.[11] The tone and form of the document in which he reports the apparitions indicate that Quintana grieved for his friend's death, missing him even more because Sopeña became his replacement as the central figure in the parish. The insistent lamentations again suggest a conflict growing out of personal differences:

> Very happy and lighthearted, I was going to mass at the New Town very early in the morning. I found the doors of the church half open and went inside, but there was not a soul there. Genuflecting to the most Holy Virgin of Sorrows, I went into the

sacristy and there met the Reverend Father Juan de Tagle. I stopped short: "What is this?" I was seeing him just as he used to be in this world, his cowl pulled down, his hands stuck in his sleeves like a dead man's, wearing his cloak, and with his face extremely troubled. He did not say a word to me but just bent over as though he wished to speak to me. Seeing him dressed to say mass, I said to him: "Father, why does not Your Reverend say mass?" To this he answered: "I cannot say it;"—and his eyes were two fountains of tears—"he who can say it for me is the priest, Fray Manuel." My God! What is this? I looked at the church vestments, and they were red. I said to myself, "Today is not the feast of a martyr;" to which he said, as though he were reading my mind, "Do not be surprised at the red when it's not a martyr's day. It always stands for that bloody martyrdom of the cross on which God shed His most precious blood for us."[12]

In the 1726 incident mentioned above, Quintana supplies a more specific motive for his dislike of Sopeña. He relates that when asked to write a Christmas play he very much wanted to do so, but felt intense tension resulting from a prohibition against writing, apparently imposed by Sopeña. Under the pressure of this dilemma, which had been building for some time, something in his mind was triggered; it broke through from another mode of thought and offered a solution as extreme as the problem itself:

These thoughts troubled me so much that I felt I was about to faint, and so I thrust it away from me and was on the verge of throwing it [the manuscript of the play] into the fire. But in the midst of such great distress, I felt a great help and a prodigious favor encouraging and strengthening me. It seemed to take my hand and help me with the thought: "Don't burn it, don't burn it. Continue and offer your play to His Divine Majesty. Pick up the pen and continue." So much was this so that I could not restrain myself. I seized the pen again and as soon as I had taken it up and resumed writing all that storm left me. In my soul I felt such loving sentiments of sweetness, love and tranquility that my heart burned in divine love as I considered the love with which His Divine Majesty was willing to become man for our salvation.[13]

Thus, in a leap from the human to the supernatural, a voice seemingly from heaven speaks to him, clearing the way for him to write, free from heeding Sopeña's order. From that time on, moments of fear and anxiety are relieved by encouraging and strengthening words spoken primarily by a voice that Quintana characterizes as an irresistibly convincing spirit, and secondarily by the Virgin Mary and God the Father. These three voices dictated verses and prose, Quintana tells us, that he wrote down both as tokens of divine love and in obedience to their command.

While there is no reason to question Quintana's sincere belief in the authenticity of these heavenly voices, still it must be admitted that this new situation did offer two practical advantages in his struggle for freedom to write. First, he was now in possession of a higher authorization which allowed him to disregard the directives of the parish priest. The exemplary lives of Spanish mystics like St. Teresa and St. John of the Cross, including investigations by the Inquisition in which they were vindicated and which did not prevent their later canonization, were well known in New Spain. The church at Santa Cruz, for example, constructed from 1733 to 1744 and so contemporary with Quintana's writings, has had on its altar screen, very likely from the time of its original dedication, four Mexican paintings flanking the central crucifix; one of these shows St. Teresa receiving inspiration from the dove of the Holy Spirit as she writes.[14] The possibility of direct communion with God and the other heavenly personages was, and still is, a living part of Hispanic Catholicism. New Mexico folklore records the frequent intervention of the saints in daily life in a visible and talkative manner.

The second advantage of the voices lay in the fact that revelations from and even conversations with citizens from heaven were a lively and popular literary topic at the time. The life and legend of Sister María de Jesús de Agreda, abbess of a convent of Franciscan Poor Clare nuns, is a fascinating example. Best known for her detailed autobiography of the Virgin Mary, *The Mystical City of God*, reportedly dictated to her by the Virgin while the nun was in raptures, she had also become famous in the Southwest as the "Lady in Blue" for a miraculous bilocation in the seventeenth century that permitted her to preach the gospel to Indians not yet reached by her fellow Franciscan friars, while never leaving her home town in northern Spain. Her story was as familiar to eighteenth-century New Mexicans as to the rest of the Spanish-speaking world, and Vargas himself had all three volumes of *The Mystical City of God* in his library when he died in 1704. In sum, the whole subject of mystical revelations was in demand, and as it touched important beliefs of his culture, Quintana had every reason to believe—at some level of awareness—that his inspirations might win him public interest and support.

Irigoyen's testimony that Quintana had a reputation for piety in his writings leaves open the question of what other sorts of religious pieces besides *coloquios* he may have composed; but, the fact that he reports being prohibited specifically from writing Christmas plays further strengthens the argument that the Franciscans viewed him as an interloper in their professional domain. Juan Rael has documented the origin of the Mexican shepherds' plays in the missionary colleges of the central highlands.[16] They were a characteristic tool for conversion taken by the friars throughout the north of New Spain. While the evolution of the texts in New Mexico leaves no doubt that over the centuries lay persons made local changes and additions—and Quintana seems to have done complete new adaptations of his own—these plays began as performances composed and organized by Franciscans. The *pastorela* by Father Florencio Ibáñez confirms that this was still the case in the younger California missions as late as the beginning of the nineteenth century.

A native of the province of Aragón, Ibáñez worked seventeen years at the missionary college in Querétaro, and served as choirmaster at the college of San Fernando in Mexico City. Volunteering for the missions in Alta California, he directed Soledad from 1803 until his death in 1818. He enjoyed teaching the soldiers to read and write, as well as instructing the neophytes in music. Owen Francis Da Silva, O. F. M., writes:

> The welcome he gave his friend, Governor Arrellaga, with vocal and instrumental music, and with verses composed by himself, has come down in history. He is also remembered as a dramatist. His *Pastorela*, or Nativity Play, was a great favorite in Old California, and was usually performed on Christmas Eve.[17]

Hubert Howe Bancroft provides further evidence of the play's popularity:

> Pío Pico [who was the last Mexican governor of California] used to play the part of Bato, the chief shepherd, and the [wealthy] Vallejos frequently took part. But the best player, and the one who used to get more applause, was Jacinto Rodríguez, who used to go to the seashore to practice his part, uttering fearful shouts, and making all kinds of crazy gestures, to the great amusement of the boys who hid nearby and watched him.[18]

It is, then, possible to assume that Ibáñez's friendship with Governor Arrellaga and the prominence of his play was paralleled to some extent in New Mexico by the position of esteem that Quintana is said to have held. This sort of social as well as religious influence on the community by one of their parishioners, instead of one of the missionary priests, may have, indeed, been another source of anxiety to Sopeña and Irigoyen.

HIS STYLE

What kind of work could this experienced and respected writer produce while suffering under the threat of losing his place in society and while finding consolation in transcribing the words of divine voices? It was certainly uneven and not as varied or polished as he must have been capable of under different circumstances, although his command of literary language is unmistakable in places. Comparing the passages of prose and poetry, certain differences appear. He emphasizes that the voices who dictate to him do so in verse, but they are also present in his prose. In general, the poetry tends to be more insistent in its repetition of reassurances that he is on the right path, this in keeping with the primary function of the supernatural presence in his mind to authorize and direct his actions. In that way, the obsessive use of "Miguel," that is, of directly addressing himself by name, seems to be a sign for him that he personally had been chosen for attention by the heavenly court. As a result, two emotions—recurring fear followed by temporary relief—dominate. The limiting form of the four-line *redondilla* so predominant in New Mexico folk poetry combines with this restricted subject matter and style to produce repetitious poems, but ones that nonetheless are emotionally intense and that would have been easily understood if handed over for judgment to a jury composed of his neighbors and customers. For example:

Don't Fear Inquisition,
punishment, harm or disgrace,
It is God, Miguel, who encourages you
with such important inspiration.

God is in love
with your humble heart
Follow Him, for you have not erred;
your words are great.

You are not condemned, Miguel,
nor need you fear going to hell,
since God, a tender lover,
has granted you all you have written.

That inner motion
is not a fault in you, Miguel,
since God, kind and affable,
inspires, helps and encourages you.

Don't you see Him on a cross
torn into a thousand pieces for you,
opening His arms,
for you to enjoy the light?[19]

In the prose the intellectual man of affairs is in evidence. He sometimes assumes a more reasoned, theological defense, as when insisting that God does not ask impossible deeds of his creatures. He makes confident, even threatening assertions that eventually he will be vindicated and his enemies dismayed. It is here where his vocabulary broadens and becomes more abstract, his sentences filled with typical baroque intricacy and *retruécano*—contrasts, antitheses, parallelisms, plays on words, and especially accumulation building to a climax. The following defiant and lucid passage, in which he draws on traditional moral philosophy to equate his self-serving and false accusers with the powers of darkness, exemplifies his style in prose used to good effect:

> In His immense power and wisdom, God divided the darkness from the light, giving each a nature and consistency such that neither the light can turn back from being light nor the darkness from its obscurity, and day and night are the clear consequences. And there will be no theologian, no matter how lofty, who can deny such a remarkable premise. By these two states are understood the righteous, who follow the guidance of reason, truth and justice, and on the other side those who live fallen and enmired in the gloom of vices, following injustice, impiety, excessive ambition, luxury, the desire of authority, command and presumption; and being blind they do not recognize or understood the cliff that threatens them or the many dangers their blindness brings them.[20]

In the years following 1726, Quintana experienced extreme emotional ups and downs. Through it all, including both the ecclesiastical threats and his own fears of temporal and eternal punishments, he was not deterred from making his divinely inspired verses known. Convinced that they were his best defense, he conducted a small but resolute campaign to get them into the hands of others who would, he believed, recognize their worth. In almost all the poems, he expressed the same hope that through them he would be honored and vindicated. Considering himself a devout Catholic and trusting in the Church to see the divine aid that protected him, he entrusted them to three priests: Sopeña himself, Fray Mínguez, and a Fray Pino stationed at Cochiti Pueblo.

This required courage, but confronting Sopeña or Irigoyen with his disobedience in the confessional would, one may suppose, have been too difficult, or perhaps simply pointless. As he was refusing a long-standing order to stop writing, he had reason to fear a denial of absolution. Formerly active in the parish, during these years he failed to meet the minimal requirement of yearly confession and communion. He received several warnings about his carelessness, the most significant from Irigoyen on June 19, 1732. Ten days later he replied definitively that he could not comply, handing over at the same time verses dated the day before and containing more heavenly encouragement to persevere. This step was taken bravely, perhaps desperately, since Irigoyen held the post of notary to the agent of the Inquisition in Santa Fe. Fortunately, Quintana's decisiveness with regard to defending his own way of thinking and writing has, in fact, saved his writings and his personality for posterity, something few individuals, particularly in colonial New Mexico, have accomplished.

Three months before, Sopeña had also presented a denunciation to the Inquisition, although no action was officially taken. But on receiving the complaint that his own notary filed on the first of July, the Inquisition's agent, Fray Joseph Antonio Guerrero moved, sending the two denunciations to Mexico City on the twelfth of the same month. Throughout the investigation, which lasted five years, the Holy Office compiled a lengthy file of evidence that included both poetry and prose by Quintana, as well as correspondence and testimony from others. After requesting and later assessing further statements from the two witnesses, as well as a deposition from Quintana, the Holy Office in Mexico City wrote that it was inclined to believe that the accused merely suffered from some kind of damage to the imaginative faculty, thus discarding the principal charge of heresy. The agent was instructed to warn Quintana not to communicate his supposed revelations to anyone and to stop believing in such nonsense. If he did not obey, action would then be taken against him with all the force of canonical law applicable to "a stubborn and rebellious fraud." In order to help him calm his mind, the agent was also to choose for him a "learned and prudent confessor."

This directive, issued in 1735, was not implemented until two years later. In January 1737, Irigoyen went to Quintana's house to serve an order for him to appear and to discover whether or not he still was, as he claimed, seriously ill. The defendant affirmed that he was incapable of making the trip to Santa Fe, but promised to go as soon as his health would allow. Upon hearing the news, Guerrero, apparently having resolved to comply with the duties of his post and at last impose some authority on Quintana, took Irigoyen with him the next day and personally went through heavy snow to Quintana's house. When advised of the decision that had been made in his case, the New Mexican writer expressed his acceptance of it, but in a tone of exaggerated contrition that subsequent events proved to be an indication of questionable sincerity: "That he feels regarding his revelations and writings whatever the holy tribunal feels, and that it grieves him to have done and believed this, or that he did and wrote down such nonsense." He then signed his name for the eyes of the prosecuting inquisitor in Mexico City. The pathetic scene was capped off by Guerrero naming Irigoyen as the sympathetic confessor who was to calm Quintana's troubled spirit.

One would almost expect this to have been the end of the drama, but Quintana's convictions had not, in fact, wavered and he apparently was not prepared to bridle his will to defend himself. An opportunity presented itself only two months later. Father Cruz, worried about his friend's illness, sent word that it would be wise to examine his conscience to see if he was guilty of some spiritual failing, particularly in connection with the sacrament of communion. Quintana, doubtless nursing his wounded spirit and reaffirming the justice of his cause behind the walls of what St. Teresa called the inner castle of the soul, was in no state of mind to recognize defects, and he threw himself into writing new verses in the same manner, plus a powerful passage in prose condemning his prosecutors.

They invade his home, he angrily asserts, "with frivolous pretexts and dressed in their passions" to hit him, "with a cat-o-nine-tails," and they seek to bring about his death or drive him mad. He labels as unjust, insolent, and nauseating that Guerrero has named Irigoyen to be his confessor, and it is here that he calls the latter "su celoso notario." Under the increased pressure generated by this latest confrontation, Quintana speaks out with more impassioned rebellion than ever before. He is not a heretic. He will confess with whomever he wishes, since God has given him his free will for that purpose. After all, he believes, God does not ask for impossible things, nor does He want people to get tangled up in scruples. And, thus, God will very soon send him relief because He has a sword for everyone.

This document was sent by Quintana to Father Cruz, in whose house it was discovered and copied by another priest, who gave the copy to Irigoyen, who in turn, invoking his powers as an Inquisitorial official, went to Cruz's house at six in the morning, there demanding and receiving the original. Shortly, thereafter, locating a messenger carrying the reply from Cruz, he intercepted a polite but evasive letter claiming that his friend's ideas were too difficult for him to grasp. In this situation of renewed conflict and suspense, the known documentation in the Inquisition records abruptly ends. No further sign of Quintana remains, either in the Inquisition's files or elsewhere, until his death eleven years later in Santa Cruz. The will made by his daughter Lugarda, who died the following year, indicates that he left her a small inheritance of livestock and personal possessions.

Such an unexpected break in this detailed and highly personal record is a shock. The reader has been won over to the side of this somewhat eccentric figure who, like Don Quijote, finds a place in our thoughts closer to tragedy than to comedy, and who has more of dignity than madness about him. Even though we are confronted by an open ending to the story, the protagonist's personality is compelling. And whatever conclusion we may arrive at as a fitting ending, Quintana's writings are unquestionably valuable, first for their articulate documentation of a New Mexican writer's courage to differ with a powerful and jealous authority, and for their vivid testimony of terrifying fears that courage had to subdue. Second, they provide a psychological record of an imaginative and literary solution to the fundamental problem of freedom of expression, an extreme solution certainly, but one based on traditional Hispanic beliefs very much alive in the writer's community. As a kind of poet laureate, he was necessarily also a spokesman, and his words the voice of the people for whom he spoke.

NOTES

1. Luis Leal, "Cuatro siglos de prosa aztlanense," *La Palabra*, 2, No. 1 (Spring 1980), p. 3.

2. Quoted and translated by Fray Angelico Chavez, "The Mad Poet of Santa Cruz," *New Mexico Folklore Record*, No. 3 (1948–1949), p. 11. See the *Archivo General de la Nación*, Mexico City, Inquisición, Vol. 849, ff. 446–77. Chavez first assembled the basic facts about Quintana; they appear in the article cited, together with a brief psychological interpretation of the case different from that presented here. The only other bibliography entry on him is our recent article entitled "Miguel de Quintana, Poeta Nuevomexicano Ante la Inquisición," *Revista Chicano-Riqueña*, 12, No. 2 (Summer, 1984), 51–68.

3. See the *Spanish Archives of New Mexico*, "Pleito de Miguel de Quintana contra Joseph Trujillo," August 8–October 24, 1712, Microfilm edition, frame 627 ff.

4. Chavez, "The Mad Poet of Santa Cruz," p. 11.

5. See Folio 455v, *Archivo General de la Nación*.

6. "Siempre se ha ocupado en notario de los alcaldes mayores, actualmente es notario en la judicatura eclesiástica." "Pasa su vida con hacer escritos a los vecinos y que de él se valen para este fin, y que esta es su vida y en esto se acostumbra. . . . Sus conversaciones son bien hiladas, sus consejos bien recibidos de los que se los toman. . . . Diez años ha lo conoce lo ha avisto al lado de los alcaldes mayores haciendo causas civiles y criminales. . . . Actual notario de la judicatura eclesiástica y que en este cargo se ha ejercitado hasta la presente, y que en todo tiene aceptación, que por el vulgo, muchos principales de este reino está tenido por hombre de entereza y de mucho juicio" (Folio 463v). This and the subsequent translations are ours. We have also modernized the Spanish orthography.

7. "Haciéndose tan santo en sus papeles" (Folio 463v).

8. See Richard E. Greenleaf, "The Mexican Inquisition and the Enlightenment 1763–1805, *New Mexico Historical Review*, 41, No. 3 (July 1966), 181–96.

9. John Kessell, *Kiva, Cross and Crown* (Washington, D.C.: United States Department of Interior, 1979), p. 302.

10. See Hubert H. Bancroft, *History of Arizona and New Mexico, 1530–1888*, in *The Works of Hubert Howe Bancroft*, Vol. 17 (San Francisco: The History Company, Publishers, 1889), 239–41.

11. See Fray Angelico Chavez, *Archives of the Archdiocese of Santa Fe*, 1678–1900 (Washington, D.C.: Academy of American Franciscan History, 1957), pp. 202–4, 207, 215, 217–18.

12. "Iba a misa a esa Villa Nueva muy contento y alegre, y era muy de mañana. Hallaba de par en par abiertas las puertas de la iglesia, entraba en ella, y no había alma ninguna; haciendo genuflexión a la Virgen Santísima de los Dolores entraba en la sacristía, y en ella hallaba al Reverendo Padre Fray Juan de Tagle. Quedábame parado: '¡Jesús! ¿Qué es esto?' Veíale como andaba en este siglo: la capilla calada, las manos metidas en las mangas como difunto, su manto puesto y el rostro sumamente afligido. No me hablaba palabra; sólo se inclinaba a quererme hablar. Y yo mirando puesto recado para decir misa, le decía: 'Padre, ¿por qué no dice Vuestra Paternidad misa?' A esto me respondió: 'Yo no la puedo decir;'—siendo sus ojos dos fuentes de lágrimas—'quien la puede decir por mí es el Padre Fray Manuel.' ¡Válgame Dios! ¿Qué es esto? Volvía yo a ver los ornamentos y era encarnado, y decía ya entre mí: 'Hoy no es día de mártir.' A que me decía, como penetrando mi pensamiento: 'No te haga fuerza, que aunque no sea día de mártir en lo encarnado, siempre se significa aquel cruento martirio de la cruz en que Dios derramó por nosotros su preciosísima sangre.' " (Folio 454v).

13. "Sentía que ya desfallecía según me afligían tales pensamientos, de tal manera que lo largué y me vi de precipitado a echarlo en la lumbre. Pero en medio de tan gran aflicción siento una ayuda tan grande y un favor tan estupendo que me anima y esfuerza de tal manera que sentía como que me daba la mano y me ayudaba con estos pensamientos: 'No lo quemes, no lo quemes; prosigue y ofrécele a su Divina Majestad tu coloquio; coge la pluma y prosigue.' De tal manera que no me podía dejar. Cogí la pluma y lo mismo fue cogerla y proseguir que desviarse de mí toda aquella tormenta, sintiendo en mi alma unos tan amorosos afectos de dulzura, amor y tranquilidad que se abrasaba mi corazón en fuego de su divino amor, contemplando el amor con que su Divina Majestad quiso humanarse para nuestro remedio" (Folio 456v).

14. See Scottie King, "Santa Cruz Church—A Vigorous Renewal," *New Mexico Magazine*, 58, No. 11 (November 1980), p. 49.

15. See Eleanor B. Adams, "Two Colonial New Mexico Libraries 1704, 1776," *New Mexico Historical Review*, 19 (1944), p. 139.

16. See *The Sources and Diffusion of the Mexican Shepherds' Plays* (Guadalajara: Libería la Joyita, 1965).

17. Owen Francis Da Silva, O. F. M., *Mission Music of California, A Collection of Old California Mission Hymns and Masses* (Los Angeles: Warren F. Lewis, 1941), p. 22.

18. Hubert H. Bancroft, *California Pastoral 1769–1848*, Vol. 34 of *The Works of Hubert Howe Bancroft*, p. 429.

19. *No temas inquisición,*
castigo, daño ni afrenta.
Es Dios, Miguel, quien te alienta
con tan grande inspiración.

De tu humilde corazón
está Dios enamorado.
Síguele, que no has errado;
es grande tu locución.

No estás, Miguel, condenado,
ni esperes ir al infierno,
cuando Dios, amante tierno,
cuanto has escrito te ha dado.

¿Ese interior movimiento
no es en ti, Miguel, culpable,
cuando Dios, benigno, afable,
te inspira, ayuda y da aliento.

No le ves en una cruz
hecho por ti mil pedazos,
que te ofrece los brazos
para que goces la luz? (Folio 463v)

20. "Separó Dios con su inmenso poder y sabiduría las tinieblas de la luz, dándole a cada una el ser y consistencia de suerte que ni la luz puede retroceder de ser luz, ni las tinieblas de ser oscuridad—clara consecuencia en el día y noche—y no teólogo por sublimado que sea que te pueda negar tan admirable supuesto. Con estos dos estados están entendidos los justos que siguen el dictamen de la razón, de la verdad y de la justicia, y por el contrario, los que en la lobreguez viven precipitados y encenegados en los vicios, siguiendo la injusticia, la impiedad, la ambición, el fausto, la autoridad, el mando y la soberbia, y ciegos no conocen ni alcanzan el precipicio a que están expuestos, a tantos peligros cuanto su ceguedad les ocasiona" (Folio 460v).

4

NEW MEXICAN COLONIAL POETRY
Tradition and Innovation[1]

ROWENA A. RIVERA

Spanish colonization in the New World during the sixteenth and seventeenth centuries was inextricably bound to the mother country's economy, religion, and culture and to its artistic and intellectual specialization. A study of New Mexican colonial verbal art implies, then, that one take into special consideration the musical and literary scene in Spain and in New Spain, i.e., Mexico, which as one of the first colonies, reaped the most benefits of Spain's most illuminating period. It was Mexico—and later Peru—that most fully participated in the Spanish poetic flowering of music and literature, the two art forms that most clearly revealed Spain's spirituality and aesthetic idealization, as well as its counterpart, the beginnings of disillusion that later characterized seventeenth- and eighteenth-century Spain.

The full apparatus of European classical music, specifically Gregorian Chant, unisonous vocal music of the Christian Church, and polyphony, or musical counterpoint, was transferred to New Spain within only one generation after the conquest of Tenochtitlan in 1521. Mexico was the recipient of a century of Spain's musical vitality that spanned the years 1500 to 1600, a period of time that exactly coincided with Spanish empire building. New Spain benefitted from medieval musical manuscripts, such as the ancient codices *Huelvas* and *Calixtinus*, documents that reveal that Spanish polyphony was developed by early composers who had already begun to establish a peculiarly Spanish polyphonic tradition before the sixteenth century. Mexico's early Christian tradition was also affected by such meritorious composers as Cristóbal de Morales and Francisco Guerrero, who had been influenced by the Flemings in the Spanish court of Charles V. In New Spain, reflecting their own rich musical traditions, the Mexican Indians became so proficient in polyphony, Gregorian Chant, and part-singing that very soon after the Spaniards' arrival they were composing and singing this type of music, often setting Nahuatl texts to polyphony.

This exuberant blossoming of musical art, and to a large degree, renewal of Spanish baroque music in Mexico can be explained by the fact that the Aztecs had a highly developed and rich musical culture at the time of the Spaniards' arrival. Aztec musicians were a professionalized caste and were therefore high on the social hierarchy. They were housed in religious schools and temples and rigorously trained from childhood for the specific enactment of ceremonial music, the only music recognized in that society. Indian musicians, although at first proficient only in their own musical art, quickly adjusted and adapted to European Christian music, for as Bernardino de Sahagún and Diego Durán reported, many similarities in Aztec and Spanish Christian musical traditions prevailed. Durán relates that before the arrival of Cortés each Indian temple had several musicians whose specific duties corresponded exactly to those of the Christian precentor, or choir director, the assistant choir director, and the choir singers found in the Spanish cathedrals of the sixteenth century. In the Nahuatl language these officials' names were respectively *tlapixcutzin*, *tzapotlateutlin* and *telpochtiliztli*.[2] This similarity of Indian and Christian practices explains to a great measure why only a few years after the conquest, the principle cathedrals in Mexico City, Valladolid (Morelia), Puebla, and Guadalajara soon rivalled in activity and musical quality those of the best Iberian Cathedrals of the epoch. Furthermore musical training among the Aztecs was not too different from liturgical music and doctrinal training in medieval Europe; musicians were expected to memorize to perfection all music to be enacted. They lived in or near the Aztec temples and were trained to play special instruments that called to prayer all citizens at specific times of the day, for example, at daybreak, at noon, and at night,[3] a religious Christian custom as well. Even the learning of such a different type of music, of the particularly complex part-singing required in European polyphony, did not seem to be an obstacle. Gerónimo de Mendieta observes that almost immediately after the fall of the Aztec Empire, hundreds of Indians began to hum the melodies that they continuously heard in Christian services,[4] so that by 1525, only four years after the conquest, Indians of all social classes were already familiar with much of the highly refined religious music heard in the great European cathedrals of the sixteenth and seventeenth centuries.

What in Spain was a highly cultivated form of religious devotion and musical appreciation became in New Spain a suitable means for worship among all members of that society. But less complex and less refined music was also used for religious purposes by Indians, mestizos, and Spaniards. The Franciscans and later religious orders often taught catechism, prayers, and the legendary lives of the saints by setting these oral expressions to simple melodies, frequently using the harmonic patterns of the folk *villancico*, a type of Christmas carol that became in the New World—as well as in Spain—so immensely popular as an exuberant expression of life that Philip II, known for his religious austerity, unsuccessfully attempted to ban it for other than religious purposes.[5]

As for secular music, soldiers and colonists brought with them their local songs, romances, *coplas*, *seguidillas*, *décimas*, and *endechas* as well as the popular Iberian dances of that epoch. Since a majority of these early emigrés to the New World came from Castile and Andalusia, there was, in the early years of colonization, a predominance of musical traditions from those areas. Later, however, there appeared a high level of diversity of songs and dances, for Cortés, who was known to have had a very keen interest in surrounding himself with music, brought for his and his soldiers' entertainment, the first European minstrels to arrive in the New World.[6] These *juglares* and *trobadores*, performers and composers, were accustomed to wandering throughout the many provinces of Spain, singing, reciting, and creating romances and tales in which the feats and virtues of royal and common folk were extolled. In the Americas these roving musicians and performers, accompanied by Indian acrobats and jugglers, soon spread throughout the Spanish-dominated areas of Mexico, teaching the Indians to make and play Spanish musical instruments as well as to sing villancicos, romances, *décimas*, *redondillas*, and other poem/songs.[7] Many of these, like the *décima* and *redondilla*, came from the aristocratic and elegant poetic tradition of fifteenth-century Spain. The variety of song and of the different Iberian musical practices, still strong after just a few years since the unification of the Spanish nation, was principally brought to the New World by these restless Spanish minstrels, giving to Mexico and other Spanish territories a diversity and wealth of Spanish folk music that has survived in the Americas almost up to the present. The songs and tales of the *juglares* reflected Spain's sixteenth-century spirit of idealism and spirituality. If the aristocratic polyphonic music sought to attain a mystical union of God and man, the songs of the minstrel reflected the chivalric ideal of worthy deeds, of heroes and causes, an enduring spirit that defined the colonial romance and *décima* and much later the *corrido*, one of the most popular musical forms found in contemporary Mexico and in the Hispanic Southwest.

As in music, Spanish literature of the early colonial period reflected the new spirit of the Italian Renaissance, the cult for idealized beauty, love, nature, and art as exemplified by the Spanish chivalric novel and by courtly love poetry written by Gutierre de Cetina, Juan de la Cueva, and Garcilaso de la Vega, whose exquisitely structured works described the bittersweet pangs of desire and who longed for *amor purus*, the union of hearts and mind. This pursuit of the highest ideal was especially revealed by the mystical elevation of the soul expressed by San Juan de la Cruz and Santa Teresa de Jesús, considered today to be two of Spain's most important poets. The Spanish Golden Age of Literature, brought to its highest artistry by playwrights like Pedro Calderón de la Barca, Felix Lope de Vega, and Juan del Encina expressed the unification and perfection of its medieval folk and cultured Renaissance visions. The synthesis of these two poetic elements, which so early became rooted in the New World's literary traditions, are still reflected in the colonies' love and religious poetry and its folk theater and are a testament to the profound effect of Spanish art upon all its territories. But Spain's gradual closing up to other ideologies and its concentration upon itself was soon felt in its literature, for example, in the aesthetic and hermetic quality of some of Luis de Góngora's poetry. Juxtaposed to the new Humanism, Spain's extreme nationalism and Catholicism ultimately prevailed, and its intransigent didacticism eventually began to overpower its initial spirit of exuberant adventure and creativity.

What might be considered the beginning of the end for the Mother Country was a vibrant resurgence and beginning for her colonies, particularly for Mexico. Literature and music attained a new and dynamic energy and force in the New World; appropriated by the Mexican Indians and colonists, it gained an extraordinary degree of flexibility and resiliency. Elegant and highly refined art ceased to be only for the upper classes; the folk took what it wanted from this corpus of material and gave it new life, changing it, rearranging it, and using it for different social and religious functions and in different contexts.

In Mexico the taste and appetite for Spanish Golden Age Literature was first stimulated by the clergy, who, wishing to make their doctrinal teachings more enjoyable, interspersed their sermons and teachings with verses and lines from Biblical passages and Spanish classical writings. Furthermore, learned and well-known poets and playwrights like Gutierre de Cetina and Juan de la Cueva came to Mexico to teach, reinforcing the appreciation and enthusiasm for Spanish literature already present in Mexico. This literature was at first read only by the ecclesiastics and by the few educated Spaniards. However, as the general populace began to read, isolated fragments of verses, phrases, and strophes and, at times, entire passages were soon memorized, transmitted by word of mouth or recited publicly in town plazas. Those who could read and write began composing and, following the literary fad of the times, even glossed lines from poetry written by the major Spanish playwrights and poets of the epoch, especially by Calderón de la Barca, Lope de Vega, and Góngora, who had become instant favorites in the New

World. The poets from the non-literate tradition simply took phrases and verses and transformed them into formulaic units like refrains and repetition patterns for their orally transmitted compositions.

The enthusiasm in Mexico for experimentation with poetic patterns and classical themes is reflected in documents found in Mexican convents and monasteries. These old manuscripts show a wide range of experimentation with sixteenth- and seventeenth-century poetic forms, as well as with Medieval/Renaissance themes, like the dialogues of the soul with God, characteristic of Spanish mystical poetry. Most of these manuscripts deal with the Sacred Cycle, that is, the birth, life, death, and resurrection of Jesus Christ. Each of the four stages was expressed in a different stylistic form that coincided with the Indian and pre-Christian veneration of the four stages of nature—spring, summer, autumn, and winter. These learned documents became one of the important sources of religious poetry used as hymns to be sung at home and in community ceremonies, such as rituals, processions, and festivals honoring the saints, some of which, like Our Lady of Guadalupe/Tonantzin were originally Aztec deities.

The popular non-religious literature, in the form of legends, folk tales, secular romances, *coplas*, jests, proverbs, and other folk notions always appeared side-by-side with the highly cultivated writings. Spanish soldiers, adventurers, and colonists had, in fact, been drawn to the New World by popular legends, like that of the tall and beautiful Amazonian women whose beauty and song, it was told, lured Spanish soldiers and sailors onto the shores only to be seduced by these strange creatures. Equally tantalizing to the young, adventurous Spaniard were the many variants of the tale of El Dorado, the king who daily bathed his gold-covered body in lakes, leaving the waters saturated with the precious metal. Whether deliberately circulated by the Spanish government or whether it was a product of the mentality of that epoch, such fantastic narration soon became the most popular form of oral literature of the Americas, a place where fact and fantasy were so indistinguishable that frequently the reality of the New World, embedded with Indian animism and surrealism, was at times more fabulous than many European fables or tales. The Franciscans were also important in the dissemination of this verbal art. Considering themselves minstrels of God ministering to the poor, they flavored their teachings not only with classical literature but with native folk beliefs that viewed life with a sense of magic realism.

All classical and oral literature was acceptable as long as it was in accordance with the dogma or had been rewritten to fit the religious ideology. Of special benefit, it was thought, were the accounts of the legendary lives of the saints, filled with mystery and magic, with supernatural feats, with miracles and hope, and yet rooted in the reality of everyday living. In fact, what gave resiliency and flexibility to Spanish/Mexican colonial oral poetry was precisely its bond to the reality of the common folk. As such it was therefore always suitable to be used in any way that it was needed, so long as it adhered to the community's religious ideology, its code of ethics, its sense of aesthetics, and its own literary canons.

It was this oral poetry, this religious and secular music and literature, now imbued with the Mexican experience, that moved northward to New Mexico from the viceroyalty of New Spain. This wealth of art arrived in New Mexico with the first Franciscans and Juan de Oñate's 129 colonists on January 8, 1598. Still largely dominated by religious themes and writings, it again adjusted and adapted to a different geographical and social setting. Within a more limited ecclesiastical vigilance due to the necessities of frontier life, this verbal art began a transformation determined principally by changes of function and context, by the establishment and reenforcement of value systems and behavioral codes, and by the creation and preservation of the community's artistic conventions of composition and performance.

What had usually been sung and recited in a sacred context and in a church related setting, might become for the New Mexican Indians and colonists, part of the general corpus of folk material to be used in any aspect of everyday life. For example, the highly ecclesiastical seven Canonical Hours, appointed for the offices of prayer during the day and usually indicated by the ringing of church bells, might be prayed at home, in the fields or in oratorios while on the road. The observation of these specific moments of the day were used not only for meditation and devotion, for a much-needed respite from the tasks at hand, but also as a time for the singing of the different transitions of day and night. The following refrain of "Ya viene el alba" ("Dawn is approaching"), sung as a simple hymn, is a surviving text used in this ancient New Mexico custom:

Ya viene el alba;
ya viene el día.
Cantemos todos,
el Ave María.[9]

[Dawn is approaching;[8]
Day is near.
Together let's sing
The Ave Maria.]

The *trovo*, a type of song duel performed by famous and legendary *puetas* like El Viejo Vilmas (Vilma, Belma), Gracia, and El Negrito Pueta on the nineteenth-century caravans that took sheep and sheep products from New Mexico to Chihuahua, had similar religious and courtly antecedents. This genre of colonial New Mexican song/poetry was related to the sacred riddle song rituals in medieval Europe and Asia, in which esoteric and obscure points in religion were asked and answered by competing professional poets. In Spanish and Portuguese courts, these song duels, known as *tientos*, *justas*, or *contrapuntos*, were performed before the king by recognized poets, who strived to display their ability to spontaneously compose on the spot. In the following fragment of this *trovo*, many of which may have as many as two hundred verses, the wise and masterful poet El Viejo Vilmas, competing with Gracia, asks him, in metrical verse, a series of questions dealing with folk religion:

En el nombre de María
ahora les pregunto yo,
poetas y compositores:
¿Cuántos fueron los colores
que Dios a su gloria dió?
¿Cuántos jardines plantó,
cuando su muerte notaria?
¿A cuál es la sagrada historia
de su ser immaculado?
¿En qué modo fue formado?
Hoy Pregunto a su memoria
¿Cuántos sonores violines
deliciosos acordan?
¿Cuántos ángeles vendrán
a acompañar los jardines?
¿Cuántos son los cirubines
que alaban su melodía?

[In the name of Mary,
I now ask you,
Poets and composers:
How many were the colors
That God to his glory gave?
How many gardens did he create
When he sensed that death was near?
And what is the sacred account
Of that most purest soul?
How was He created?
Today I address your memory:
How many sonorous violins
Can be heard in delicious harmony?
And how many angels will appear
To guard earth's gardens?
How many are the cherubim
Who praise this melody?]

After several more questions of this nature, as indicated in this variant, Gracia who is losing, answers:

Maestro, ¿cómo quisiere que cante
si vengo todo turbado?
¿Cómo quiere que adivine
un punto tan encumbrado?[10]

[Master, how can you expect me to sing
If I'm all upset?
How do you expect me to speculate
On such lofty matters?][10]

The reverse situation might also take place; ordinary secular poetry and narrations could become highly ritualistic and sacred. Such is the case of the poem "El Verdadero Jesus" ("The True God"). This New Mexican Penitente prayer is one of the Hermit's dialogues in an old Mexican and Texan variant of *Los Pastores*, the Christmas Shepherds' Play, and is considered by the Brotherhood to be one of the most solemn and impressive recitations in their repertoire of religious poetry. Perhaps learned by New Mexicans through oral transmission, through deliberate memorization, or through frequent presentation of this *Pastores* variant, the poem has been used up to the present as part of the highly ritualistic initiation ceremony in many of the New Mexican Brotherhoods' *moradas*, or chapel houses. The following first and last stanzas of "El Verdadero Jesus" briefly illustrates how the

Penitentes have created an exact correlation of the poem's content, enactment, and function, for in this prayer of initiation, of beginning and end, the Brothers collectively recite each stanza, making the sign of the cross, a circular gesture in which the forehead, the heart, two shoulders, and mouth are touched.[11]

El verdadero Jesus *Nos libre de todo mal* *Vanandonos con su lus* *diciendo por la Senal* *tambien de la Santa Cruz.*	*[May the true Jesus (God)* *Deliver us from all evil,* *Bathing us with his light* *Speaking through the sign* *Of the Holy Cross.*
Siempre me percinare *Con la Santisima Crus* *a Dios me encomendare* *pues que digo amen Jesus* *yunto con M(ari)a y Jose.*[12]	*I will always sign myself* *With the most Holy Cross,* *Entrusting myself to God* *Since I say, "Amen, Jesus,"* *And also, "Mary and Joseph."]*

The unadorned and unaffected poems and songs, as well as the highly baroque poetic language of the *Los Pastores*, well-known by most New Mexicans—even memorized by many—served as a source of lines and phrases for colonial New Mexican poets in the creation of original poetry or, as seen above, in the adaptation of known poetry to new settings of context and function. These familiar verses served to artistically enhance compositions and helped listeners and readers to form a comfortable and familiar relationship to new poetic works. The most important function of *Los Pastores*, however, known also as *La Pastorela*, *Pastores chiquitos*, *Coloquio de los Pastores*, and *La Estrella*, was to venerate and recreate the birth of Jesus and to provide the community with an opportunity for a yearly theatrical experience. Most New Mexican neighborhoods and communities had a ready-made cast of stock actors and singers, many of whom inherited their roles from relatives. The director frequently was the only one possessing a manuscript, usually a highly valued family document.

The Shepherds' Play dates back to as early as the eleventh century when preliminary to the Christmas Mass, the *Officium Pastorum* was performed. In this European rite a manger was prepared at the side of the altar and images of the Virgin Mary and the Christ Child were placed on it. Then a boy, dressed to represent an angel, sang the "Annunciation" from a lofty place while shepherds entered the main aisle and went to pay homage to the newborn at the manger. The framework of this ancient drama, its characters, the minimum plot, and even the stage settings are present in the many variants of *Los Pastores*, a play that survived as a community activity in New Mexico, southern Colorado, Texas, Arizona, and California up to the 1960s. While the strict adherence to the fundamental plot and dramatic structure respected the religious significance of the original, the dialogues, monologues, and songs in the many variants are not of Iberian origin (as pointed out by Juan B. Rael[13]) but are compositions written by Franciscans and other religious orders that arrived in the early years after the conquest of Tenochtitlan.

As a folk play, usually performed in community halls, town plazas, school buildings, and even private homes, this drama has almost always had a delicate and tenuous relationship with the official church, for community theater groups have often had a tendency to go beyond what the church has considered religious discretion in their performance. While strictly adhering to the sacred content of the work, actors and directors have at times injected off-color or irreverent comments and asides, appealing to the folks' taste in theater rather than following a precise observance of the original mood of the play. This tendency toward freedom in dramatic performance was already present in sixteenth-century Spain when well-known playwrights of the epoch tried their hand in the composition of this very popular dramatic work. For example, Antonio Mira de Amescua, a follower of Lope de Vega's ideas on what theatre should emphasize, opens a scene in his *Auto del Nacimiento de Nuestro Señor* in which Joseph, upon seeing the pregnant Mary, speaks to the audience wondering whether, indeed, Mary should still be considered a virgin. His speech undoubtedly caused the clergy to raise their eyebrows and the *mosqueteros*, the noisy lower classes who occupied the *corrales*, to chuckle or laugh.

A study of these texts reveals the extraordinary folk quality of this dramatic work. In most manuscripts the conversations of the shepherds, as they circle the scene, lend an anachronistic vision of the Sacred Cycle, for their initial dialogues and monologues revolve around the Crucifixion. The discussions progressively move backward in time to relate the biblical episodes of Jesus' life until they reach the manger where they are in the process of relating his birth. This antedating of the Crucifixion of the newborn child responds to oral memory and reveals the complexity of artistic techniques sometimes employed in many examples of folk verbal and visual art. Furthermore, the play is characterized by surrealistic imagery and by the personification of objects and elements of nature. The roles of stars, the sun, the moon, and the night are, in some variants, acted out, as illustrated in the following verse in which the guiding star, usually played by a child or a woman, opens the play, singing these words:

Yo soy la Estrea Oriental *que rebente del Firmamento* *para giar alos Pastores* *Llevarlos al nasimiento.*[14]	*[I am the Eastern Star* *That burst from the heavens* *To guide the shepherds,* *To take them to the holy birth.]*

In the following verses from "Cielo soberano," the shepherds sing of the obstacles that they are encountering in their pilgrimmage toward Bethlehem, personifying the elements of nature that surround them:

Cielo soberano
Tenednos piedad
que ya no sofremos
la nieve que cai
Sospende tus iras
cesen los quebrantos
que ya estan poblados
de nieve los campos.
. . . .
Las estreas vuelan
y el cielo estreado y
asortos se quedan
de ver tan nevao.[15]

[Omnipotent heavens,
Take pity upon us
For we can no longer endure
The falling snow.
Cease your ire;
And may all troubles vanish
For all fields
Are now covered with snow.
. . . .
The stars fly
Upon a blinking sky
And both are struck with amazement
To see so much snow.]

The songs are highly lyrical and lend themselves to varied interpretations of their symbology. Many are characterized by images of transition or movement and space, expressed through the rising and the setting of the sun and moon, alluding not only to the birth of Jesus, but to his death, as well. One of the best known of these Pastorela songs is the following known as "Cuando por el oriente," and "Caminaba la Virgen." The following fragment of this composition that relates Mary's journey to Bethlehem to await the birth of her son recalls the ancient mythology of the Moon Goddess that travels forward as the sun rises behind her in the East:

Cuando por el oriente
sale la aurora
caminaba la Virgen
Nuestra Senora.
Ay, que dicha.
Ay, que alegria.
Pues, alma mia,
lo que granjeas.
Oh, reina de la luna,
bendita seas.[16]

[When from the Orient
Dawn approaches,
The Virgin, Our Lady,
Travels with this light.
Oh, such joy!
Oh, such happiness
That soothes
This soul of mine,
Oh, Queen of the Moon,
May you be forever blessed.]

The *Pastorela* effectively combines folk literary aesthetics with classical and erudite literature, for it may include verses written by major Spanish poets and playwrights of the Spanish Golden Age of literature. The survival of some of these lines from classical literature illustrates how the folk may retain for long periods of time those lines, whether from the oral or written tradition, that are artistically satisfying and that impart its wisdom and philosophical visions. The following quatrain, present in almost all New Mexican texts, was written by the seventeenth-century baroque poet, Luis de Góngora. It reminds all of the changes of fate that life may bring, of the impermanence of life itself:

Aprended flores de mi *lo que va de ayer a hoy* *que ayer maravilla fui* *y ahoy sombra de mi no soy.*[17]	*[Flowers, learn from me who knows the* *Difference between yesterday and today,* *For yesterday I was a wonderous being,* *And today I'm not even a shadow.]*

This strophe that appears in other colonial New Mexican compositions is believed to have circulated in the oral tradition in Mexico and in the Hispanic Southwest since early colonial times.[18] In a slightly changed form it becomes a refrain in "La Llorona," a popular contemporary Mexican song.

Like the equally ancient drama *Los reyes magos, (The Magi)*, still presented in Santa Fe, New Mexico the first week of January, *La Pastorela* is a work whose multiple literary levels begin to reveal important aspects of the processes of composition and performance of folk music and literature in New Mexico. Equally important is this work's disclosure of fundamental artistic and philosophical visions that have served as bases in New Mexican artistic productions.

Aesthetic concerns were of importance in all genres of New Mexican verbal art, as is the case in all communities with a strong oral tradition. Early New Mexican musical and literary items, found in handwritten historical documents, reveal that composers and writers were already aware of their own standards of excellence in their artistic compositions. Using inherited traditional models, these early artists recreated or rearranged elements such as stock themes, narrative cores, images, and structures as well as formulaic units like repetition patterns, metaphorical expression, and other prosodic features that were pleasing to their audiences. Building on these elements, colonial musicians and poets began to create original work within closely adhered to cultural patterns, a process that has continued to the present.

These aesthetic concerns were of special significance in works that dealt specifically with the community's religious and philosophical contemplations, such as questions on man's destiny and earthly situation, the meaning of his life and death, his relationship to past and future, to other men, and to God. A favorite topic of early New Mexican composers and writers was that of time and mutability, a theme inherited from courtly Spanish poetry of the Renaissance period and Mexican colonial literature. The articulating of the society's philosophy, which sometimes acquired satirical, humorous, or political tones, was always couched in fairly elegant phrases and structures. A clear example is the New Mexican *décima*, an intricate poetic form consisting of an introductory quatrain, the *planta*, followed by four ten-line stanzas, each of which ends with a line of the *planta*, respectively. The form is a direct descendent of the classic "mirror" or *espinela décima*, which has a rhyme pattern of ABBAACCDDC and was named for Vicente Espinel, the Spanish seventeenth-century poet who perfected this poetic structure. The *décima*, previously found throughout the Hispanic world, is also related to the *valona*, a form popular during the nineteenth-century in Mexico. Highly prized by the most talented folksingers, the New Mexican *décima* is an example of this area's most refined and graceful folk poetry, as the following passage from "Qué largas las horas son," illustrates:

Planta

Qué largas las horas son
en el reloj de mi afán
y que poco a poco dan
alivio a mi corazón.

. . . .

Para mí no hay sol ni luna,
no hay tarde, noche, no hay día.
Tan sólo estoy, vida mía,
pensando en ti desde la una,
que en ti ha quedado mi fortuna.
A las dos con atención
se aflije mi corazón.
A las tres diciendo suerte,
así mi vida para verte.
Qué largas las horas son.[19]

Planta

[How slowly the hours pass
By the clock of my anxiety.
Yet little by little they bring
A soothing calmness to my heart.

. . . .

For me there is neither sun nor moon.
There is no evening, night or day.
There is only the thought of you,
My love, my treasure, since
The moment the clock strikes one.
At two I'm fully awake,
And anguished is my heart.
At three, hoping,
My love, to see you.
How slowly the hours pass.]

In northern New Mexico and southern Colorado, one can still find a few surviving fragmented texts representing the fullest traditional form of the secular *décima* or the religious *décima-a-lo-divino*. And occasionally, one also finds, especially in southern Colorado, an older poet who can chant the *planta* and a few stanzas. Given the usual erosion and reshaping of songs transmitted in the oral tradition, this intricate and tightly structured form has miraculously survived in New Mexico and in Texas up to the 1960s. A closer study of the *décima* and the traditional context in which it was performed reveals, however, that its survivability is due not only to the strength of its structure, but also to the close relationship of form and function that characterized this genre. In New Mexico the folk viewed this form as the only one possible with which to express special religious and philosophical intuitions. Changes of culture and points of view, brought about by contemporary life, began to erode previously accepted visions in regard to life and death, causing the traditional *décima* to change to a more narrative genre, as has been the case in Texas, Colorado, and northern New Mexico, or weaken and disappear, as it has done in Mexico and many other areas.

Folk art continuously readjusts to new contexts. The northern Spanish frontier challenged the early colonists with a new setting and different cultural and economic circumstances. The need for survival, then, required the establishment of an appropriate value system with specific codes of individual and collective behavior. The community's music and literature served the purpose of continuously reinforcing accepted behavioral codes. Narratives, in the form of legends, tales, and memorate related the lives of saintly figures, many of whom had previously lived immoral lives and then had been touched by the hand of God, imbued with a new faith, and thereby transformed into the community's most suitable and admirable role models. Many of these New Mexican legends which became musical and literary compositions, were recreated accounts taken from ancient hagiographies. All contained the important messages to be heeded by the faithful. For example the legend of the Santo Niño de Atocha, beloved by farming communities in northern New Mexico, served to reinforce the faith in divine guidance and providence; that of San Isidro, the figure that had come to the New World as the patron saint of Madrid, Spain, became in northern New Mexico the patron saint of farmers. The legend, song, and poem that bear his name emphasize the necessity of working hard during the week but keeping the Sabbath as a day of rest and worship. Secular legends and tales served also to reinforce the community's code of ethics. The Llorona narrative, a pre-Hispanic Aztec legend, can be interpreted on many levels. It can serve, for example, as a warning to mothers who mistreat, abandon, or forget their children; it also reflects the group's disapproval and censuring of women who roam about at night and of men who attempt to pick up strange female companions in dark, isolated places.

Sung narratives, romances, were particularly popular, for they usually told a good story in a catchy melodic line. But these old Iberian ballads, are in essence, one of the most traditional genres in New Mexican folklore. They caution the community of the dangers inherent in not fulfilling community and family obligations, of neglecting aging parents and others in need, of abandoning wives and children to go in search of adventure, of the inevitable sorrow caused by unresolved family problems. These popular songs, distinguished by the ease with which they can be learned, emphasized the adherence to the group's customs and mores. Women figures in these songs were particularly bound to suffer the consequences of their misconduct, like the unfortunate Elena or Catalina or Isabel in the many variants of "La esposa infiel" ("The Unfaithful Wife") who is either killed, thrown out of her house, or returned to her parents' home by her indignant husband. There are ballads that more subtly present male and female characters whose lack of maturity and wisdom leads them astray. One of the best examples of these is the old variant of "Rosita Alvires" or "Rosita Alvidres," which now more frequently appears in the form of a *corrido*, the musical and literary descendent of the romance. This song, still popular today, relates a community tragedy in which the arrogant Rosita is shot to death by an ugly-tempered and insecure suitor when she refuses to dance with him. Both Rosita and Hipólito are depicted as figures with serious flaws in their characters, who are therefore directly responsible for their tragic end. The phrase "su mama se lo decía," ["her mother kept telling her,"] is a constant motif that transmits the warning and becomes a subtle element of this Mexican song's black humor, a reflection of the narrator's indifference to the final consequence of the actions of these immature characters:

. . . .

Su mama se lo decía:
Rosa, esta nochi no sales.
Mama, no tengo la culpa
que a mí me gusten los bailes.

. . . .

Llegó Hipólito a ese baile
y a Rosa se dirigió.
Como era la más bonita,
Rosita lo desairó.

. . . .

Echó mano a su cintura
y una pistola sacó,
y a la pobre de Rosita
nomás tres tiros le dió.
Y en esa nochi afamada
Rosita iba de suerte.
De los tres tiros que le dieron
nomás uno era de muerte.

. . . .

Su mama se lo decía:
Por andar de pizpireta
se te ha de llegar el día
en que te toquen tu fiesta.[20]

. . . .

. . . .

[Her mother kept telling her:
Rosa, you do not go out tonight.
But, mom, it's not my fault
That I like to go out dancing.

. . . .

Hipólito attended that dance
And immediately went to Rosa.
But since she was the prettiest,
Rosa refused to dance with him.

. . . .

He reached toward his belt
And took out a gun,
And poor Rosa was shot
Only three times.
But on that fateful night
Rosa was actually lucky.
Of the three shots she got,
Only one was fatal.

. . . .

Her mother kept telling her:
One of these days your flirting
and running around will bring about
Your own day of celebration.]

. . . .

Another modern descendent of the romance is the *indita*, which is structurally and thematically a specific variant of the *corrido*, the genre illustrated above. The *indita*, however, differentiates itself by its Indian rhythmic patterns, by the frequent use of drums in the performance of these narrative songs, and by the participants' dancing between the sung verses. This type of *corrido*, which also exists in Mexico, is usually employed for the praising of saints and for the narration of important events that transpired between Hispanics and Indians, including the many captives' stories that abound in New Mexico. Inditas are also used for singing and dancing in special ritualistic ceremonies, for example, the healing rites in which the oldest women and youngest girls in the Spanish/Mexican communities enacted a composition in honor of a special saint. Scholars are particularly interested in the different types of *inditas* composed by sheepherders. These narrative songs and poems have, for long periods of time, circulated anonymously within the oral tradition of New Mexican *borregueros*, reflecting the sheepherders' special language and the musical and literary style with which they interpret *inditas*. The following composition, which has lost some of its narrative quality, is reminiscent of the fifteenth century Spanish playwright, Juan del Encina, who had a predilection for writing dialogues between shepherds in which they, by means of their rustic, satirical, and vibrant language criticize, parody, and make fun of institutions. In this old New Mexican *indita*, probably rearranged within this century, the poet/singer satirically uses Spanglish in the refrain to speak of his condition as a sheepherder:

Pos hay un dicho vulgare *ques proverbio verdadero:* *que no hay trabajo en el mundo* *yugare, yugare, yugare,* *como andar de borreguero.*	*[Well, there's a common saying,* *A saying that's true as true can be,* *That there isn't any calling* *You gotta do this; you gotta do that;* *Like herding as many will agree.*
Que nohai hoy que manana. *No hay ni un santo a quien rezarle,* *y para tender la cama,* *yugare, yugare, yugare,* *no hay lugar que le cuadre.*	*Today and tomorrow are the same.* *There's no saint to whom to pray.* *And as far as making your bed,* *You gotta do this; you gotta do that;* *There's no soft spot your head to lay.*
Pos es una vida triste, *ay, andando de llano en cerro.* *No hay que disviarse,* *yugare, yugare, yugare,* *aunque uno traiga buen perro.*	*Well, it's truly a sad life,* *Trudging over mountain and plain.* *One's always careful not to stray,* *You gotta do this; you gotta do that;* *No matter how well your dog you train.*
Pos la vida del pastore *es una vida pesada.* *con su salea y colchon,* *yugare, yugare, yugare,* *y su chaqueta de almohada.*	*Yes, the life of a shepherd* *Is difficult and sad.* *His jacket's his pillow; a sheepskin,* *You gotta do this; you gotta do that;* *The only bed he's ever had.*

Gorrita achucharrada,	*A shapeless cap, all tattered and torn,*
toda rota y descosida.	*That well reveals the misery and strife*
De ese modo va pasando	*For this is the way*
yugare, yugare, yugare,	*You gotta do this; you gotta do that;*
el pobre pastore su vida.	*The poor shepherd spends his life.*
En la plasa llega a bajare	*If ever he comes down to town,*
con sus burros por delante.	*His burros leading the way,*
Unos lo tratan de trampe,	*Some people treat him like a tramp,*
yugare, yugare, yugare,	*You gotta do this; you gotta do that.*
otros lo tratan de animal.[21]	*Others, like an animal gone astray.]*

Many of the ancient Spanish ballads and the narrative and quasi-narrative forms like the *corrido* and *indita* that have modulated from these *romances tradicionales* have survived for many generations because they express the on-going value systems, the ideas and symbols that hold a society together. Scholars have documented one of the oldest New Mexican romances, "La aparición" ("The Apparition") as a fifteenth-century romance whose variants are occasionally still heard in New Mexico and in the Hispanic Southwest.[22] This song narrates a bereaved husband's encounter with his wife's ghost, who encourages him to adjust to a new life, marry again, and seek happiness and tranquility in another family setting. What distinguishes this ballad and what has made it survive, is the commonsense response it offers to death, tragedy, and grief and the advice that life, in the aftermath of ill fortune, has to be recreated all over again. Stylistically it is exceptional. It is characterized by a lyric ambiguity produced by changes of perspective, narrators, and space and time, as seen in the following verses from a variant found in the J. D. Robb Collection of folk music:

Onde bas, caballerito,	*[Where are you going, my saddened knight*
alejandote de mi?	*Where are you going, away from me?*
Boy en busca de mi esposa,	*I'm in search of my wife,*
que ase tiempo que no la bi.	*Who for some time I have not seen.*
. . . .	. . . .
Lla tu esposa lla esta muerta.	*Your wife, she no longer lives.*
Muy sierto es que yo la bi;	*That is a truth, a truth I've seen.*
cuatro duques la llebaban	*Four nobles bore her casket*
en la suida de Madri.	*In the city of Madrid.*
Los abrazos que le daba yo	*The embraces that I once gave you*
a la tierra se los di;	*To the earth I now bequeath,*
la boquita que besaba	*And the red mouth that I kissed,*
un gusano enberdesi.	*A worm I now do feed.*
. . . .	. . . .

Casate, caballerito,	*Take another wife, young man;*
casate, no estes asi;	*Saddened no longer be,*
ial primer nino que tengas,	*And the first child born to you,*
ponle el nombre como a mi.	*Name it after me.*
. . . .	. . . .
Rebento la flor de mayo,	*May's flower has bloomed.*
se seco la flor de abril.	*April's blossom no longer breathes.*
Se acabo la que reinaba	*And gone, too, is the lady who ruled*
en la suida de Madri.[23]	*In the city of Madrid.]*

The first singers of these romances, collected in Latin America, throughout the Hispanic Southwest, and wherever Sephardic Jews settled after their expulsion from Spain in 1492, were the travelling *juglares*, men and women who made their living by public performance of poetry, music, and dance, as well as by jugglery and acrobatics. They performed sometimes in public squares and sometimes in the royal courts. While Galician minstrels sang their exquisite love songs and Provençal musicians displayed their carefully turned *tensos*, the Castilian minstrels sang of heroic feats and adventures related in the *chansons de gestes*, the oral historical narratives, which early chroniclers listened to and afterwards included in their histories as a true account of what had taken place. These highly appreciated musicians, who constantly moved from one area to another, are credited for having internationalized European music and literature. They also generated, in Spain, an enormous enthusiasm and appreciation of folk speech and music, particularly the *romance* that subsequently began to develop parallel to the most elegant and aristocratic forms of poetry. This process created the synthesis of *lo popular* and *lo culto*, a characteristic that has marked Spanish and Latin American literature ever since.

Some of the oldest examples of romances, characterized as brief compositions consisting of sixteen syllables divided in two eight-syllable lines and considered by Ramon Menéndez Pidal to be fragments of the *chansons de gestes*, have been collected in New Mexico by Arthur L. Campa, Rubén M. Cobos, John D. Robb and, previously, in the 1920s, by the distinguished New Mexican scholar Aurelio M. Espinosa. Among the oldest Iberian ballads collected in New Mexico is "El Romance de Gerineldo," a ballad that according to Menéndez Pidal, the foremost Spanish scholar of romances, belongs to the Carolingian and Arthurian classification of romances, popular in the Iberian Peninsula during the thirteenth century.[24] This ballad, occasionally sung in Spain and in Mexico, was an important song in the musical repertoire of older New Mexican folksingers in the 1950s. Its survivability is due to the endurance of traditional and nationalistic values that characterize Spanish literature after the seventeenth century, but also to the sensuality and earthiness found in Spain's early medieval works. In "El Romance de Gerineldo," the princess is the aggressive partner in courtship; she invites the young Gerineldo, the king's valet, to come spend the night in her quarters:

Gerineldo, Gerineldo,
recamarero aguerrido.
¡Quién te pescara esta noche
tres horas en mi servicio!

[Gerineldo, Gerineldo,
Brave and experienced page!
If only I could get you
To serve me three hours tonight!]

To which the young lad, enthusiastic over that possibility, yet incredulous, answers:

Como dice que son tres,
que deveras fueran cinco.
Si porque de niño me han creado,
se quiere burlar de mí.

[You say three?
I wish it were five.
Or is it because I've been raised here
That you want to make fun of me?]

The king finds the couple in bed and placing his sword between the two young lovers, resolves the dramatic situation in the nonviolent manner that characterizes many of the early medieval ballads:

Levántate, Gerineldo,
recamarero aguerrido,
que mi hija, la infanta, dice
que te estima por marido.[25]

[Get up, Gerineldo,
My brave little page,
For my daughter, the princess
Wants you for her husband.]

The corpus of New Mexican oral poetry includes the major classifications of the *trovo*, folk theater, *décima*, *corrido*, *indita*, and romance, as well as many other types such as panegyric and love poetry, proverbs, riddles, and lore. Of these, the *alabado*, the religious hymn frequently associated with the Penitente Brotherhoods, is perhaps the most interesting to scholars. Often compared to European plainchant, Spanish Gypsy flamenco music, and arabic religious chanting, this type of prayer/poem has had a long history in New Mexico and has, in fact, developed its own melodic patterns and thematic content to fit its specific function. In New Mexico it is a ritualistic meditation upon the different phases of the life, death, and resurrection of Jesus and, from the eighteenth century to the present, has been sung in high ceremonial context, like the Brotherhood's services or in more informal circumstances like community religious events, wakes, funerals, and services held during Holy Week. The texts may be attributed to medieval poetic forms, to prayers written down by Franciscans and other religious orders, to compositions written by the faithful, and to the sequences of the Mass, like the *Stabat Mater*, the *Salve Regina*, and the *Miserere*, originally set to polyphony by well-known European composers like Josquin des Près and Giov Pierluigi da Palestrina. Since the content of the hymn, that is, the dialogue of God and the soul, is the essential core of the composition, many *alabados* are sung responsorially, and like the *décima*, many of these texts—although not all—may be sung to the same chant or melodic line, emphasizing, in this way, not the music but the important and magic qualities of the word of God. The following strophes from the well-known *alabado* "Mi Dios y mi Redentor," or "La Pasión," is a simple religious song in Mexico also known as "La Pasión." They briefly illustrate the type of textual phrasing by which Penitentes attempt to meditate and elevate themselves in a mystical experience. The phrase "abrazadme en vuestro amor," ("embrace me within your love"), is continuously repeated in this ceremony in which more than one hundred verses of this hymn may be sung.

Mi Dios y mi Redentor
en quien espero y confío;
por tu pasión, Jesús mío,
abrazadme en vuestro amor.

Escucha con atención
lo que padeció Jesús
desde el huerto hasta la cruz
en su sagrada pasión.

. . . .

Por tu pasión, Jesús mío,
abrazadme en vuestro amor.

. . . .

Lágrimas de devoción
nos dé a todos el Señor.
Por tu pasión, Jesús mío,
abrazadme en vuestro amor.[26]

[My God and my Redeemer, on whom
I've placed my hope and trust.
By your passion, my Jesus,
Embrace me within your love.

Take heed of
How Jesus suffered
From the Garden to the Cross
In his most holy passion.

. . . .

By your passion, my Jesus,
Embrace me within your love.

. . . .

Tears of devotion
Grant us, our Lord,
By your passion, my Jesus,
Embrace me within your love.]

Religious music and writings and secular material existed in both the oral and written traditions. Penitente documents, manuscripts, and *cuadernos* that contained poetry, song texts, and ritualistic prayers are only a partial reflection of the literate tradition in New Mexico and in the other Spanish northern territories. Church records and family papers have also preserved drama, poetry, and narratives as have missals, *novenarios*, and even ledgers where composers sometimes kept their original writings and those that were in the oral tradition. In New Mexico, early newspapers, like that established by the radical priest of the nineteenth century, Fr. Antonio José Martínez, frequently published compositions in the form of *coplas*, riddles, proverbs, protest verses, and praise poems to revered saints like La Conquistadora, Our Lady of Guadalupe, San Isidro Labrador, and the Santo Niño de Atocha. The most common and frequently the most artistically finished of these newspaper verses were those written by colonists who wished to create personal expressions to celebrate the birth and baptism of a child, the engagement and wedding of a young couple, or the community's bereavement upon the death of a relative or friend.

Although most verbal art was performed in an oral context, and performers were known to have astounding memories, it remained a cultivated art in which many formulaic units were constantly repeated and the written page was sometimes used as an aid to their recollection. There was always an overlapping and fusion, in varying degrees, of the oral and written traditions, although in the early years of colonization, writing most frequently appeared merely as an adjunct to the oral performance and enactment of song and poetry.

The study of New Mexican colonial poetry, much of which was a highly vital and extensive verbal art up to 1945, is the study of the survivability and originality of the New Mexican Hispanic culture. It reveals how a group's art endures by means of a balance of innovation and tradition. In the analysis of this art, some of which is now available only in documents and in folksingers' personal notebooks and some of which is still in the oral tradition, the two following salient points can be made.

First, New Mexican oral poetry, as in all oral traditions, is distinguished by its variability, by the absence of a single correct version. Even though memorization is almost always a direct or indirect aspect of performance, verbal art always undergoes constant transformations. Performers, like the medieval minstrels, have always changed words, phrases, sequence of episodes, omitting elements no longer popular and adding those that may more accurately reflect the concerns of their day. The performance of oral literature is therefore characterized by the uniqueness of each performance. A folk singer, poet, or storyteller, either from ancient or contemporary times, depends upon traditional art for his repertoire. This is particularly so if he is considered professional by his community. During the presentation he uses his originality, creativity, and ability to improvise spontaneously on the spot, sometimes in order to please his audiences. However a certain criterion is adhered to. With the exception of folk theater, singers and poets have always been careful to omit crude and profane words from their romances, *corridos*, and *décimas* in a family-oriented performance. And audiences, as indicated in many Penitente notebooks, are always able to note the skill and beauty, or lack thereof, with which an oral poet is able to rearrange artistic material, usually well-known to his listeners. For master performers, like the legendary Vilmas or El Negrito Pueta or Chicoria, their musical and poetic stature grew with each of their irrepeatable performances.

Second, the function of a musical or literary item determines its survivability or its disappearance. Works whose basic message still reflected the traditions of the community, continued to exist, undergoing the necessary adjustments that new times required. Examples of these enduring works are some of the old Iberian romances, those that became *corridos* and a few classic *décimas*. On the other hand those compositions that no longer mirrored the community's religious and artistic concerns, like the *trovo*, and to a certain extent, the *Pastorela*, tended to lose their relevance. Many of these works are occasionally retrieved and presented; they, however, no longer reflect the original and traditional function of the work, but become a "folkloric" and an old example of a community's artistic culture.

The fluid and ever-changing aspect of New Mexico colonial oral poetry has its own underlying mythological patterns, the sources of its dynamic energy. This mythical energy, present in all traditional communities, as well, gives rise to many of the themes and motifs that nourish all literatures. These myths in which man reflects upon his relationship with the universe, with his heroes, and his own self give much of this oral literature its permanence and originality.

NOTES

1. This article is an excerpt of the introductory chapter of a study on New Mexican folk music by Rowena A. Rivera in preparation for the University of New Mexico Press. It includes the translated and annotated manuscript *Estudio y clasificación de la música tradicional hispánica de Nuevo Mexico*, written by Vicente T. Mendoza.

2. Diego Durán, *Historia de las indias de Nueva-España y Islas de Tierra Firme* (México, D.F.: J. M. Andrade y F. Escalante, 1867) Vol. 1, p. 160. Diego Durán (1537–1588) who with Bernardino de Sahagún (1500–1590) and Juan de Torquemada (1564–1624) are some of the early missionaries who provide the most detailed information on the musical practices and festivals of the Indians in Tenochtitlan.

3. Gabriel de Rojas, "Descripción de Cholula," *Revista Mexicana de Estudio Históricos* (Nov.-Dic., 1927), p. 162.

4. Gerónimo de Mendieta, *Historia Eclesiástica Indiana* (México, D.F.: Antigua Librería, 1870) Vol. 3, Chapter 19, p. 225.

5. Robert Stevenson, *Music in Mexico*, (New York: Thomas Y. Crowell Company, 1952) p. 138.

6. *Ibid.*, p. 94. Stevenson, in his discussion of Bernal Díaz del Castillo's comments on the use of music during the early years of the conquest, states that,

> In several places Díaz dwells on Cortés's fondness for music. At a banquet given in Cortés's honor by the first viceroy, for instance, singers at each seat of honor, and trumpetry and all sorts of instruments, harps, guitars, violas, flutes, dulcimers, and oboes provided music which rivaled the best any of the guests had ever heard at home in Spain.

7. Antonio de Cibdad Real, *Relación breve y verdadera de algunas cosas de las muchas que sucedieron al padre fray Alonso Ponce en las provincias de la Nueva España* (Madrid: Viuda de Calero, 1872–1873), pp. 532–38.

8. All translations are by the author of this study.

9. Sung by Edwin Berry, interview with Rowena A. Rivera, Adelino, 10 August 1979.

10. From the notebook of F. Vigil, Wagonmound.

11. Thomas J. Steele and Rowena A. Rivera, *Penitente Self-Government: Brotherhoods and Councils, 1797–1947* (Santa Fe: Ancient City Press, 1985) pp. 184–90.

12. Recited by Cosme Trujillo from his notebook, interview with Thomas J. Steele and Rowena A. Rivera, Albuquerque, 24 May 1984. Spelling and omission of accents and other diacritical marks correspond exactly to text of variant used for this study. Untranscribed texts generally reflect the writing style of the folk.

13. Juan B. Rael, *The Sources and Diffusion of the Mexican Shepherds' Plays* (Guadalajara, Mexico: Librería La Joyita, 1965), p. 315.

14. *La Pastorela del nascimiento de Nuestro Señor*, Alamosa, Colorado.

15. *Auto del nacimiento de Nuestro Señor Jesucristo*, Las Palomas.

16. *Auto de los Pastores*, Arroyo Hondo.

17. *Auto de los Pastores*, Valdés.

18. Fernández de Lizardi, *Periquillo Sarniento* (Mexico: Ediciones Cicerón, no date of publication given) vol. 2, p. 215.

19. Próspero S. Baca, Bernalillo, 1945; from *Hispanic Folk Music of New Mexico and the Southwest*, John D. Robb (Norman, Oklahoma: University of Oklahoma Press, 1980), pp. 377–78.

20. Sung by Macedonio L. Luján, interview with Rowena A. Rivera, Las Cruces, 19 July 1981.

21. Sung by José Trujillo, interview by Rowena A. Rivera, Mountainair, 10 May, 1980.

22. Rowena A. Rivera, "A Fifteenth-Century Spanish Romance in New Mexico," *The New Mexico Folklore Record*, Vol. 15, (1980–81), pp. 8–12.

23. From the notebook of Clemente Chávez, Galisteo, and included in J. D. Robb Collection of Folk Music, no. 2009.

24. Ramon Menéndez Pidal, *Flor nueva de romances viejos* (Madrid: Espasa-Calpe, S.A., 16th edition, 1959) p. 72.

25. Sung by José de Moya, Canjilón, 1962, music and text recorded by Rubén M. Cobos. A similar variant collected by Aurelio M. Espinosa in 1915 appears in *Hispanic Folk Music of New Mexico and the Southwest*, John D. Robb, p. 74.

26. Sung by Edwin Berry, Adelino, 1981.

5

EARLY SECULAR THEATER IN NEW MEXICO[1]

REED ANDERSON

New Mexico's history as recorded since the arrival of the Europeans has been that of a frontier and a crossroads, beginning quite literally as a place in the imagination of a few who sought wealth, continuing as a sparsely settled region on the periphery of two empires (the Spanish-Mexican and the Anglo-American), and always as the site of a complex intersection of national and racial groups. The myth of the seven golden cities of Cíbola may no longer have been foremost in the minds of the settlers who set out from El Paso del Norte with Juan de Oñate at the close of the sixteenth century, but Gaspar de Villagrá's epic poem of the exploration and conquest of La Nueva México constructs a new reality to take the myth's place, not for the members of the expedition itself, but for those Spaniards in the Old World whose decisions would affect the future of this new territory.[2] Given the stark isolation and the physical hardship of life in the New Mexican territory, there was, in fact, a constant need to construct a historical and ideological reality that would make the settlers' reasons for coming there and, perhaps more importantly, for remaining there both intelligible and admirable. There was also an equally constant and pressing need for the construction of a political identity that would somehow define the territory's strategic value and its material and formal relationship to the center of governmental authority, first in Spain, then in Mexico, and finally in Washington. In examining the vestiges of the early secular drama in New Mexico it should become apparent that this drama is fully engaged in just such a process of ideological and political definition and consolidation; and in that respect, the dramatic texts that have survived ("Los moros y cristianos"; *Los Comanches*, late eighteenth century; and *Los Tejanos*, late nineteenth century) provide unique and important ways of looking at the cultural past of the region.

Villagrá's epic poem, *La conquista de la Nueva México* (1610) portrays a New Mexico of astounding contrasts, juxtaposing infernal and unforgivingly harsh landscapes (La Jornada del Muerto, for instance), populated in some places by hostile native peoples, with natural settings of almost paradisiacal beauty, populated by heathens who seemed to have eagerly awaited the blessing of Christian baptism. It is, in fact, in this latter setting, as the Oñate expedition of 1598 emerged from the desert into the flood plain of the Río Grande, that Villagrá's record tells of the first drama to be performed by Europeans on this northern frontier of the Spanish empire, and probably the earliest on the entire North American continent as well:

Y luego que acabaron los oficios
Representaron una gran comedia,
Que el noble Capitan Farfan conpuso,
Cuio argumento solo fue mostrarnos,
El gran recibimiento que a la Iglesia
Toda la Nueva Mexico hazia. . . .
(*Villagrá 2:76*)

[And when they had finished celebrating Mass, a fine drama was enacted which had been written by the noble Captain Farfán and whose principal purpose was to show us the tremendous welcome with which all of New Mexico greeted the arrival of the Church. . . .]

As far back as 1598, when the members of the Oñate party felt themselves to have been delivered from the torture of their desert trek, the moment was marked and consecrated with the double ceremony of a Mass and an original drama. We have no details about the play that was written and performed for the occasion, but it was undoubtedly a solemn piece, following as it did the first Mass to be celebrated in this new territory, and preceding the official pronouncement by which the land they had just begun to explore was claimed for the Spanish Crown. The Indians whom the Oñate party had encountered at this point were not hostile, and, in fact, Villagrá tells us that some of them formed part of the audience that witnessed these events. There is also some reason to believe that Capitán Farfán's play was in the style of an allegory insofar as Villagrá's own description of it is based on a figure of speech suggesting that the newly discovered land itself, along with its people, were welcoming the arrival of Christianity, and in fact this dramatic performance is said to have led up to the baptism of "muchos bárbaros" who were in attendance.

When the expedition had travelled several days farther to the north, it arrived at a Tewa pueblo that seemed to be ideally situated on the west bank of the Rio del Norte. Thus, the Spanish promptly took possession of the village, renamed it San Juan de los Caballeros, and "allowed" its original inhabitants to relocate on the opposite shore. The festivities at this new settlement that are described in Villagrá's epic were not held in honor of the founding of a new village, but rather to celebrate the clemency that Oñate had demonstrated in not punishing a group of soldiers who had attempted a mutiny. These circumstances would suggest that there may have been a need at this time for Oñate to reassert his leadership, and create or rekindle by means of this week-long festival a sense of solidarity among the expedition members, many of whom quickly became discouraged and disillusioned when the prospects of finding deposits of precious metals seemed increasingly remote:

> *. . . se ordenaron*
> *Unas solemnes fiestas que duraron*
> *Una semana entera, donde ubo*
> *Iuego de canas, toros, y sortija,*
> *Y una alegre comedia bien conpuesta,*
> *Regozijos de moros y Cristianos,*
> *Con mucha artilleria, cuio estruendo,*
> *Causo notable espanto y maravilla,*
> *A muchos bravos barbaros que auian,*
> *Venido por espias a espiarnos . . .*
> (*Villagrá* 2:88)

> . . . (to celebrate this event) a week of solemn festivals was organized; there were jousting matches, bull fights, the performance of a gay and well-written comedy that was composed especially for the occasion, and Moors and Christians plays which were enacted with such a thunder of artillery that they inspired remarkable fear and awe among the many barbarian braves who had come as spies to watch us. . . .

Again, dramatic performances formed part of the celebrations. In fact, there were two theatrical events. One was the unnamed "alegre comedia bien conpuesta," which may have been a more or less conventional theatrical piece written especially for this occasion, but about which we know nothing; and the other, referred to somewhat generically as "regocijos de moros y Cristianos," a kind of dramatic pageant that can take many different forms and whose tradition can be traced back to medieval Spain. Regardless of whether they all believed in it or not, the Spanish-Mexican soldiers and settlers in the Oñate expedition cannot have failed to recognize the symbolic value of the *moros y cristianos* spectacle: this expedition was meant to have a goal more transcendant than the mere discovery of wealth, and the play gave historical and ideological coherence to the "civilizing" enterprise of Christianity among the *bárbaros* of this new territory. On the other hand, its message and its function as part of a more general "culture of conquest" (Warman 69) were probably not lost on those natives of the region who witnessed this spectacle of European military and moral superiority. Similarly, both *Los Comanches* and *Los Tejanos* represent "real" historical events, from the eighteenth and nineteenth centuries respectively, and they include certain details that can be agreed upon by most scholars as having actually taken place. But even with such a starting point in corroborated events, each play writes its own history and suggests its own major lines for the interpretation of that history.

Although we know next to nothing about the first two "comedias" that were specifically composed and presented during the Oñate expedition in what is now the Southwest of the United States, we know considerably more about the plays and dances commonly known as *moros y cristianos* due to their long history in both Spain and the New World. These dramas, whose most basic common denominator is the representation of the triumph of Christianity over barbarism and heathenism, probably date from the twelfth century in Aragón. George M. Foster first, and Arturo Warman after him, have concluded that the primitive versions of this spectacle must then have spread throughout Spain accompanying the advance of the Christian reconquest. They were then consolidated as part of the festivities surrounding Corpus Christi observances during the fourteenth and fifteenth centuries. (Foster 221–25; Warman 18) These dramatic events included mounted skirmishes between Christian and Moorish forces, accompanied by an elaborate symbolism that attributed the inevitable Christian victory in the face of overwhelming odds to the intervention of the hand of God, most often represented by the visitation of archangels and the Apostle Santiago, who was known as "Matamoros" in Spain, and later became "Mataindios" in the Americas (Winter; Warman). These pageants evolved into increasingly elaborate events, some of them being performed over the course of several days, and involving huge structures that served as castles to be assaulted and destroyed, and ships that were burned and sunk, sometimes on artificial lakes during simulated naval combats (Warman 28–34). The importance of these extravagant dramatizations during the sixteenth century in Spain must be understood in historical and political terms. The reiterated performance of victories of church and state over the forces of barbarism and chaos were important symbols in the context of the consolidation of royal power in Spain after the unification of the Peninsula under Fernando and Isabela, and such performances played an integral part as well in the organization of national resources (both spiritual and material) for the vast imperial enterprise that was being undertaken in the New World (Warman 25).

Significantly, the *moros y cristianos* productions evolved into increasingly sophisticated and elaborate events during the late sixteenth and seventeenth centuries in Spain where they were transformed into colorful cavalcades or costumed pageants minus the mock battles. At the same time, in its New World manifestations, the drama recuperated all the original religious fervor and military display of its medieval Iberian antecedents. In a similar fashion, while the festivals of Corpus Christi in Spain evolved into an affirmation of Catholic dogma in the face of the threat of European Protestantism and Spanish reformism, in La Nueva España, they maintained their original ideological orientation wherein the enemy of the true faith was barbarism. This revival in the New World of the older reconquest versions of the Corpus Christi celebrations worked hand in hand with the return of the *moros y cristianos* plays to their early roots in the Spanish *Reconquista*, and with the revival of the cult of Santiago. The plays came to constitute a regular feature of the Corpus Christi observances. All of these celebratory activities came to form a very important ideological constellation in the overall culture of conquest in the New World. As Warman has written:

> . . . la península era ya el centro de un imperio. La danza de moros y cristianos pasó a ser producto de exportación, y no uno ocasional, sino uno de los más constantes y frecuentes. Este hecho se justifica en el carácter etnocentrista que siempre tuvo el tema de la danza. A donde llegara el soldado español plantaba su estandarte y realizaba un festejo de moros y cristianos, como una afirmación de su estado de gracia, pues no era sólo el elegido, sino la mano armada, el socio del Señor. (42–43)
>
> [. . . the [Iberian] peninsula was already the center of an empire. The Moors and Christians dances came to be an item for exportation, and not just on a sporadic basis, but one of the most frequent and constant of all. Such a phenomenon is understandable given the ethnocentrism that had characterized the dances from their very origins. Wherever the Spanish soldier went he raised his banner and celebrated by enacting a Moors and Christians festival. This gesture was an affirmation of the Spaniard's state of grace, for not only was he among the chosen of God, but he was also the scourge of God and His closest ally.]

Probably the most dramatic adaptation of the *moros y cristianos* plays to the imperial enterprise of conquest and conversion in Mexico during the sixteenth and seventeenth centuries was the incorporation of indigenous actors. From the very beginning, according to Motolinía, *moros y cristianos* plays formed an integral part of the "teatro edificante," and the indigenous actors were assigned the roles of Christian warriors, not Moors, in order to increase their sense of integration with and fealty toward the church (Warman 73). During the Mexican colonial period, as Warman points out, the plays evolved from being dramatic events imposed upon the indigenous population by the colonizers, and became the nearly exclusive cultural property of the colonized (123). Whether or not this process that Warman ascribes to the area of central Mexico was duplicated elsewhere in the Northern Provinces, and especially in New Mexico, is very difficult to ascertain. That the church and the crown had at least as difficult a task in continually reiterating the ideology and supremacy of church and state in this isolated frontier, there can be no doubt. The *moros y cristianos* play would certainly have been a familiar and effective vehicle for promoting the cultural and religious ideology of conquest and empire among settlers and Indians alike, but the fact is that the first notice that we have of a *moros y cristianos* performance in New Mexico (Villagrá, 1610) is also the last notice that we have before modern times. The Franciscans' widespread use of the *moros y cristianos* plays in central Mexico as part of the cultural apparatus of religious conversion and as a regular feature of the Corpus Christi festivals, would also lend some credence to the theory that the drama and spectacle were carried north with the seventeenth-century missionaries and settlers who came to New Mexico.[3] Moreover, it seems unlikely that these dramas of military triumph and conversion would not have constituted an important element in the ideology that accompanied the 1693 Vargas "reconquest" of New Mexico, with all its real and imagined parallels to the Spanish experience of the late Middle Ages on the Iberian Peninsula.[4] The probability seems high that the drama of *Los moros y cristianos*, an institution of both the Medieval Iberian frontier and of the early conquest of La Nueva España, would have accompanied this recolonization of late seventeenth-century New Mexico and become part of the popular secular culture of the region. In the absence of documentary evidence, however, we may for the time being have to agree with the cautious conclusion that John Englekirk draws in his provocative study of the New Mexican folktheater:

> There are few facts with which to support any valid consideration of the fate of . . . the Medieval European [and perhaps Englekirk should have added here, sixteenth and seventeenth-century Mexican] Moros y Cristianos . . . (although) it cannot be denied that the heroic pageant . . . may have had an uninterrupted history of performances ever since that first celebration in San Juan de los Caballeros on September 8, 1598. . . . (1957, 239)

The only published version of a New Mexican *moros y cristianos* play is the one in Aurora Lucero-White Lea's *Literary Folklore of the Hispanic Southwest* Although she gives no details about where she obtained this version, and several passages seem to be garbled, this would appear to be the same play that Lea collected at Santa Cruz de la Cañada in 1937.[5] Nevertheless, this manuscript is certainly adequate for us to gain some idea of the basic outlines of the *moros y cristianos* plays. Aside from the fact that this play may be a vestige of a long tradition of popular performances in New Mexico, it is an important text as well due to its position as an ancestor of *Los Comanches*. Such a lineage has been mentioned before (Campa 5–6; Roeder 213; A. M. Espinosa 1985, 219) and even a brief comparison will serve to show the fundamental characteristics that the two plays have in common.

At the most global level, both plays represent Spanish (or in *Los Comanches*, Nuevo Mexicano) military forces with elaborately expressed loyalties to the Spanish crown and the Catholic church, engaged in armed conflict with heathens—*moros* in one case, and *indios bárbaros* in the other. Likewise, both plays call for the staging of an elaborate simulacrum in the style of a pageant, with mock skirmishes taking place between mounted warriors, and interludes during which horses may be paraded in formation and general preparations made for battle scenes. In the case of *Los Comanches*, such preparations call for the staging of indigenous war dances. Both dramas, needless to say, have as their outcome the victory of the Christian Spanish or Nuevo Mexicano forces over the barbarous heathens. As we shall see, there are other important points of similarity, but the two plays differ significantly in their endings. In the case of the *moros y cristianos* play, the Sultan's dramatic conversion to Christianity is the culmination of all the action that goes before. In *Los Comanches*, the emphasis remains squarely on the military victory of the Nuevo Mexicanos. In the Campa (1942) edition, Cuerno Verde dies in battle, with not even a reiteration of religious motifs introduced earlier in the play. The final speech by the *Capitán* is, in fact, a paean to the Spanish flag.

In both plays, the most important speeches by the antagonists consist of boastful challenges issued to one another, which serve to define the elements of the patriotic and ideological clash that underlies the military confrontation about to be staged. At the same time, an important difference between this particular version of the *moros y cristianos* play and *Los Comanches* has to do with the characterization of the antagonists in each. *Los Comanches* devotes much more attention to the depiction of the Comanche leader, Cuerno Verde, as a character of some dignity and stature, whereas the portrayal of El Sultán in the *moros y cristianos* play is the altogether conventional and formulaic one of the scheming heathen who, although having superior numbers of soldiers, would gladly avoid armed battle in exchange for ransom. *Los Comanches* is, of course, representing a historical event that was more specific and closer in time to its audience's own personal experience than the *moros y cristianos*. The characters in *Los Comanches* can be associated with historical figures who took part in similar campaigns

(Roeder 1976, 218n16; Campa 1942), a feature that locates this play in one respect at least, closer to the Castilian epic and the *romance fronterizo* or *noticioso* than to the more allegorical *moros y cristianos*.

In both plays as well, the capture and rescue of hostages or of a sacred object is a motivating factor for the action. In the *moros y cristianos* dramas it is generally the Holy Cross or an image of the Virgin; in *Los Comanches*, two Christian children (called "*Las Pecas*") have sometime in the past been captured and raised as Indians by Cabeza Negra. As a result of the first skirmish in this play, the Spaniards recapture these two children from the Comanches. Cabeza Negra vows to recover the children whom he regards as his own. In the *moros y cristianos* play edited by Lea, the Cross has been stolen from the Christians and is being held for ransom. And while the possession of the hostage children or of the Holy Cross may appear to be sufficient motive for the Christians to go to battle with the enemy, it is not the only one. The conflict, and some of the drama of each of these plays, is clearly based on a much more transcendent clash of cultures, values, and even for added interest, personalities, depicted in the broadest terms.

An essential element in the *moros y cristianos* tradition in fact is the series of speeches by combatants from both sides who, in high and serious rhetoric, proclaim their own valor and their loyalty to their just cause. In the *moros y cristianos* play, these speeches immediately precede the actual simulacrum of warfare between the two sides and serve as rallying cries for the Christian soldiers. For example, Don Alfonso, the Christian leader makes this mocking speech when the Sultán offers to ransom the Holy Cross for money:

> *"Vuelve (al Sultán) y dile que la Cruz*
> *En valor no tiene precio;*
> *que al impulso de mis armas*
> *le daré mucho dinero". (Lea 110)*

> [Go back (to the Sultán) and tell him that the value of the Cross cannot be measured in terms of money; he must meet me on the battlefield if he wishes to take my gold.]

The structure of *Los Comanches* is significantly different from the *moros y cristianos* in this respect: the sequence of challenging speeches by the principal combatants on both sides leads to the call to arms by Don Carlos, and a brief armed clash ensues, resulting in the recapture by the Comanches of the two young children who are being kept in the Nuevo Mexicano's castle. It is immediately after this recapture that the emissary from the Comanches, Tabaco Chupa Janche, approaches Don Carlos with a flag of truce. The particular sequence of events in *Los Comanches*, then, provides the occasion for the conventional exchange of defiant speeches, leading to a brief skirmish prior to the principal one at the end of the play where Cuerno Verde is finally defeated. In some *moros y cristianos* plays the combatants would engage in this first clash (which the Moors customarily win) and then issue challenges to resume the battle on the following day, thus extending the performances over two days.

One of the most persistent elements in the *moros y cristianos* plays is the confrontation, not only between the military leaders and armies of the two sides, but also (implicitly) between the divinities or the sacred figures whose powers are invoked in order to guarantee the victory of one side or the other. The New Mexico *moros y cristianos* play we are considering here is notably formulaic where such invocations are concerned. The Christian leader, Don Alfonso, dedicates the battle "en el nombre de la Cruz y del Humano Verbo" [In the name of the Cross and the Word made Flesh]; and Federico, one of his lieutenants, shouts, "¡Viva, viva nuestra Divina Patrona!" [Long live our Holy Patroness] as he charges into battle (Lea 111), but these are the only instances of such invocations, even by the Christians. As for the Moors, the Sultán swears once by Mahoma ("y les juro por Mahoma"), and Selín, before taking the field of battle, says rather simply, "Que con el favor de Mahoma hemos de ganar el triunfo" [For with the help of Mohamed we shall be victorious] (Lea 111).

The absence of lengthy invocations of divine or sacred beings for help in the battle is consistent with this version's rather restrained rhetorical quality; these characteristics are consistent in turn with the rather schematic nature of the plot. It is a script for an action-filled and choreographed pageant, with the only real moment of intense religiosity coming at the end where the Sultán prostrates himself before the Cross and accepts the Christian God as the only true one. In *Los Comanches*, Cuerno Verde of course dies unrepentant, and this is perhaps the most important discrepancy between the traditional *moros y cristianos* structure and the structure of *Los Comanches*. Religious fervor in the latter play is overshadowed by the patriotic crusade to defeat the *indios bárbaros*, and the possibility of Cuerno Verde's conversion is never even remotely suggested. The missionary goal of the sixteenth and seventeenth century antecedents has now given way to the goal of physical defeat and subjugation, with the survival of the New Mexican settler community as the historic context.

On the other hand, the *moros y cristianos* tradition of presenting the "edifying spectacle" of the clash of opposing cultures and faiths is much stronger in *Los Comanches*. The "barbarism" (that is, the absence of anything that the imperial Church would have recognized as religious practice or belief) of Cuerno Verde and the Comanches is not only made absolutely clear, but Cuerno Verde's utter contempt for the Christians is also unmistakable in much of what he says. In this drama, written for a Mexican-Spanish audience in the traditional Spanish octosyllabic verse, Cuerno Verde's failure to invoke any divinity whatsoever at the beginning of battle, or to dedicate his cause to any higher motives than those of revenge and further personal aggrandizement, serve to foreground for this particular audience the vast moral differences between the Comanches and the Christian soldiers of the King and Cross.

The Nuevo Mexicanos, on the other hand, emphatically and repeatedly identify their cause with the greater glory of God, the Virgin, and the Crown of Spain, calling on the saints and the archangels Gabriel and Miguel to guide and protect them in their righteous struggle, as in this speech by Don Carlos Fernández:

Por Dios and por nuestra patria
Y la corona del rey,
Porque confío en María
Y en el patriarca José,
Que nos han de dar victoria
Piedad concesión divina,
Consebido (a) sin pecado;
Tan limpia y de gracia llena.
El arcángel San Gabriel
De aquellas tropas escelsas.
Preciso es tocar el arma,
Marche el campo a la batalla
Y todo el campo aprevenga.
. . .
El Apóstol Santiago
Y concepción de María
Contra esta gente cobarde
Me sirva de norte y guía.
(*Campa* 39)

[(We must fight) for the sake of God and of our fatherland, and for the royal crown. Because my faith is in Mary and in the Patriarch Joseph who will assure us the victory, a sacred gift from Heaven, as was She who conceived without sin, pure and full of grace. Let the Archangel Gabriel now sound the trumpet to call these noble troops to prepare to take the field of battle.
May the Apostle Santiago and the Holy Son of Mary serve me now as guides and protectors against this cowardly enemy.]

Clearly *Los Comanches* was built around a model (the *moros y cristianos* plays) that by the end of the eighteenth century had a long and vigorous tradition in the lower provinces of *La Nueva España*, and was probably known as well in the *Provincias Interiores*. The historical situations that are alluded to are similar insofar as both the *moros y cristianos* plays and *Los Comanches* have as their context the violent clash of cultures and individuals in the historical circumstances of an ill-defined frontier, lacking formal boundaries, and complicated in the case of Nuevo México by a network of complex and volatile treaty arrangements among the various bands of indigenous people and the Spanish-Mexicans who were occupying and trying to maintain their hegemony in the territory. It is difficult to say whether the Lucero-White Lea manuscript of the New Mexico *moros y cristianos* drama is typical of a genre that proliferated in New Mexico in general, or whether it is a unique artifact; at this point, we simply do not have the documentary evidence by which to make a judgment. This play may have become as terse and schematic as it is through having survived over a period of purely oral transmission. But there is abundant evidence of very elaborate and almost literary versions of *moros y cristianos* plays in Mexico in the eighteenth century whose overall conception appears to resemble that of *Los Comanches* at least as much, if not more than the New Mexico version (Warman). The possibility cannot be dismissed that the more direct inspiration for *Los Comanches* were the Mexican rather than New Mexican *moros y cristianos* plays; alternatively, it is altogether possible that at one time the New Mexican play was a somewhat more elaborate drama than the one whose manuscript we now have. In any case, even the structural similarities between these two New Mexican plays are numerous and substantial enough for us to place *Los Comanches* squarely in the *moros y cristianos* tradition.

What can be said about the more specific circumstances that would have inspired the writing of a play modeled on the *Moros y cristianos* dramas in the late eighteenth century? The historical background of the Comanche campaigns of the eighteenth century is fairly well known. As early as 1705, nomadic Comanche bands began appearing around Taos, seeking to barter with the Mexicans and the Pueblos alike (Kenner 29). As they became increasingly successful in obtaining horses and firearms the Comanches' ability to raid settlements and sometimes to prevail in outright combat with presidial troops and militia developed into a serious and constant threat. The very self-sufficiency of the province of Nuevo México, which had been the primary goal of the Vargas reconquest and occupation, had also resulted in patterns of widely scattered settlement that made any kind of consistent military protection from Indian raids virtually impossible. During the eighteenth century, a small group of wealthy "*estancieros*" and government officials came to constitute a political, social, and economic elite (often referred to as *los ricos*), while the vast majority of the population lived outside of the villages and towns as independent smallholders and/or laborers on the larger *estancias*. This decentralization of the population not only constituted a problem concerning physical safety from Indian raiding, but it led to the formation of an individualistic class of small property owners, and a large number of free laborers, *peones*, servants and artisans, all of whom had little contact with or need for the colonial government apparatus (Swadesh; Jones; Ramírez; Tjarks). This was a population that was living virtually at the outer limits of Spanish colonial hegemony, in a frontier area that throughout the eighteenth century was subject to constant hostilities. Simmons (1977) quotes Antonio de Bonilla's report on New Mexico of 1776:

> The settlements of Spaniards are scattered and badly defended . . . and quite exposed to entire ruin. Because the greater number of them are scattered ranches, among which the force of the settlers is divided, they can neither protect themselves nor contribute to the general defense of the country. This, in consequence, results in the abandonment of their weak homes and the terror of seeing themselves incessantly beset by the enemy. (65)

Simmons also mentions here that the Miera y Pacheco 1779 map of New Mexico (the same year of the De Anza Comanche campaign) shows more abandoned towns in New Mexico than inhabited ones (65). This precarious situation seems hardly consistent with the geopolitical importance that was being claimed for the region by Comandante Teodoro de Criox in his report of 1781 wherein he asserts that the "conservation (of Nuevo México) is so important that if we should lose (the territory) a second time, we should have upon Vizcaya, Sonora, and Coahuila all the enemies that now invade that province" (Thomas 1941, 105–06).

Two particular moments in the New Mexico Comanche campaigns of the 1770s are of particular relevance for our consideration of the drama, *Los Comanches*. In 1774 after several dramatically successful Comanche raids against Albuquerque and smaller settlements, Governor Pedro Fermín de Mendinueta responded by commissioning a veteran Indian fighter, Don Carlos Fernández, to retaliate with force. In September 1774 Don Carlos's expedition, consisting of six hundred poorly equipped troops, settler militia, and Indians, set out from Santa Fe. They came upon a Comanche ranchería east of Santa Fe and immediately launched a surprise attack. Governor Mendinueta's report to Viceroy Bucarelli, says that about one hundred people managed to escape before the attack, and that out of those who did not, only one hundred and fifteen "women and children" survived to be taken prisoner. In all, more than four hundred Comanches were killed or taken captive in this encounter (Thomas 1940).

Now while this retaliatory victory was a dramatic one in terms of the numbers of casualties inflicted and prisoners taken, by all accounts it not only failed to stop Comanche raids on New Mexican settlements, but it may have caused them to intensify. By 1775 a widespread depopulation of the countryside up and down the Río Grande was taking place due to the Comanche threat (Simmons 86–87).

Kenner, in fact, says that the ratio of New Mexican settlers killed as compared to Comanches during the summer 1775, just one year after the Fernández expedition, was six to one (126). Thus, while Don Carlos's campaign may have been judged a success in terms of the immediate punishment it inflicted on the *indios bárbaros*, it seems to have had only negative consequences for the settler population of Nuevo México. With Don Carlos Fernández as the protagonist of *Los Comanches*, it is reasonable to conclude that the battle that is dramatized in the play, is in fact this 1774 victory of Don Carlos Fernández at Antón Chico as documented by Thomas and later by Kenner. But there may be some doubt as to whether or not Don Carlos actually engaged the Comanche chief, Cuerno Verde, in this battle. The account of Don Carlos's victory may be found in Governor Mendinueta's report to Viceroy Bucarelli, but there is not a single mention there of Cuerno Verde's having been at the head of the Comanches who were attacked and defeated (Thomas 1940; Bobb 1962). While the battle of September 1774 is a matter of historical record, it would seem strange that the most notorious of Comanche leaders would not be mentioned by name in Mendinueta's report, if indeed he had actually led the Comanche band that was defeated by Don Carlos Fernández.

By 1777 the Spanish Crown finally realized the seriousness of the situation for its colonial enterprise in the north, and created a special office, that of the Commandancy General of the Interior Provinces, appointing Teodoro de Croix to address the problems of defending Spanish hegemony in the northern regions. One of Croix's first actions was to name Don Juan Bautista de Anza as Governor of the Province of Nuevo México and to assign to him the organization of security for the settlers in the north of the province and the prosecution of a military campaign against the Comanches. De Anza's assessment of his troops as he prepared to mount his major offensive is indicative of the relative state of neglect in which the financially pressed Spanish Crown had left Nuevo México. His regular soldiers were well prepared, but as for the settlers' militia and the Indians, De Anza's report says that, "because of their well-known poverty and wretchedness, the best equipped presented themselves with two riding beasts, the most of them almost useless; their guns were the same, very few of them having three charges of powder; in everything else the proportion was similar" (Thomas 1932, 123). Nevertheless, De Anza's pursuit of the Comanches was notably successful. The New Mexicans mounted a devastating surprise attack on a Comanche encampment in southern Colorado in late August, and a few days later, they caught up with a party of raiders who were being led by Cuerno Verde on an expedition against New Mexican settlements. In the ensuing battle Cuerno Verde was killed along with his eldest son, his medicine man, and his four principal chiefs (Thomas 1932, 69–70).

De Anza's own account of the 1779 Comanche campaign is extremely revealing for what it tells us about this encounter between two seasoned and determined military leaders. De Anza's fascination with Cuerno Verde is the most intriguing element in this otherwise businesslike communication to Commander General de Croix. And as for the actual armed confrontation between the two warriors, De Anza describes the killing of Cuerno Verde quite obliquely, preferring to reiterate with a mixture of admiration and censure, the fatal defect that he sees in the Comanche leader's character; De Anza attributes Cuerno Verde's death to the "arrogance, presumption and pride which characterized this barbarian, and which he manifested until the last moment in various ways"—character flaws whose discussion then begins to occupy considerable space in De Anza's letter as in this description of his first vision of Cuerno Verde:

> In this way was recognized from his own insignia and devices the famous Cuerno Verde, who, his spirit proud and superior to all his followers, left them and came ahead, his horse curvetting spiritedly. Accordingly, I determined to have his life, and his pride and arrogance precipitated him to this end. (Thomas 1932, 133–134)

De Anza clearly recognized the significance of this leader's death, explaining, "I determined, although the time was propitious for my return, to see if fortune would grant me an encounter with him (Cuerno Verde)," and adding by way of justification, "a larger number (of Comanches) might have been killed, but I preferred the death of this chief even to more of those who escaped, because of his being constantly in this region the cruel scourge of this kingdom" (Thomas 1932, 135).

Finally, in the "carta de relación" that accompanied his diary-report to Commander Croix, De Anza turns once more to an assessment of "the haughtiness and pride of this (the Comanche) nation," concluding that Cuerno Verde's own "valor was the cause of his ruin, or the disdain which he wished to show toward our arms, puffed up over his victories. To these I am not resolved to give entire decision" (Thomas 1932, 141). De Anza himself brings the drama of this most important of military victories for the Nuevo Mexicanos down to an intensely personal level. De Anza's diary of this campaign becomes at once the account of a dramatic personal confrontation between two powerful and implacable leaders and a kind of window (from the standpoint of a veteran Mexican Indian campaigner) into the psychology of his enemy. There is no question that De Anza recognized in a profound way the great transcendence of this victory for the beleaguered Nuevo Mexicanos, both as a symbol, and as a blow to the Comanches under Cuerno Verde's leadership. The intensity of feeling that comes through the De Anza narrative on several levels is also a fundamental quality of the drama, *Los Comanches*. All of the physical action and movement which is part of a performance of *Los Comanches* does not detract from the fact that at the dramatic heart of the play is the confrontation between two leaders of opposing cultures and the values that they represent. While the rhetoric of the play's script and the final victory of the Nuevo Mexicanos makes manifest the superiority of those who devote themselves to the cross and the crown of Spain, there is in the play another dimension that is quite clearly present in De Anza's report as well. That element is a certain awe and admiration for the pride and courage of the Comanche nation, although this same feeling stands in constant contradiction to the fact that these are precisely the qualities which, when allowed to cloud his judgement, led Cuerno Verde to his certain death.

The elements of high romantic drama are already imbedded in the text of De Anza's remarkable *carta de relación*, then, and the fact that he chose to communicate to his commander, Teodoro de Croix, this dramatic elaboration of his encounter with Cuerno Verde is an indication of the significance that this particular framing and interpretation of events held for De Anza himself. The dramatic structure for *Los Comanches* is already given in the tradition of the *moros y cristianos* plays; the vision of these events that de Anza conveys in his diary and letters underscores the importance of those events for New Mexico in the late eighteenth century under his governorship.

What is most surprising in the light of all of this, however, is the fact that De Anza is absent from the very play that dramatizes the most significant military victory of the century over the Comanches. It is an absence that must be explained in terms of the historical context in which the play must have been originally composed, and it is a peculiarity that has been commented upon in passing by practically all who have studied this text.[6] The question of the fusion of the two significant New Mexican victories over the Comanches is just one of a number of intriguing problems that still surround the play, but I will bring this part of the discussion to a close by looking at the matter of the drama's protagonist, Don Carlos Fernández.

There is ample reason to believe that after the 1774 campaign Don Carlos Fernández would have been the Comanches' most formidable enemy among the New Mexican military; such circumstances would seem to argue convincingly for Don Carlos's place as the drama's protagonist. But evidence also points to the fact that New Mexicans suffered terrible retributive raids by Comanche bands subsequent to the devastation inflicted on them by Fernández at Antón Chico in 1774. In one of his footnotes to the 1942 edition of the play, Arturo Campa states that a portion of Cuerno Verde's lengthy speech challenging Don Carlos to battle refers to the Comanche leader's previous victories over the New Mexicans (26n14), which would be in keeping with the historical situation that prompted Don

Carlos's commission to punish the Comanches. In fact, this reading essentially reverses the meaning of the speech and obscures a crucial historical dimension of the play. Rather than boasting about his victories, as Campa's reading would have it, Cuerno Verde was actually referring to a devastating and deadly defeat that had been inflicted by the Nuevo Mexicanos on the Comanches, involving men, women and children as victims—a defeat not at all unlike the one that Don Carlos Fernández had carried out against the vast ranchería east of Santa Fe in September 1774. Cuerno Verde's speech actually ends with a direct challenge to Don Carlos and the motive is clearly revenge for a past humiliation:

Es tanta mi fuerza y brío
Que entrando osado y altivo
Buscando a ese general
Que con locos desvaríos
Usó de tanta fiereza,
Destruyó como he dicho.
Lo llamo en campal batalla,
Lo reto y lo desafío.
¿Quién es, y cómo se llama?
(*Campa* 27)

> [So great are my strength and spirit that proudly and boldly I have come seeking that general whom I have already accused of destroying (my people) with such insane and savage fury. I call this man forth to take the field of battle, I challenge and defy him. Who can he be? What is his name?]

This reading would certainly support the presence of Don Carlos Fernández as protagonist of the play, rather than De Anza. Then, the drama could no longer be seen in the somewhat schematic framework of a terrorized population of settlers avenging themselves against savage but valiant *indios bárbaros*. By giving Cuerno Verde this motivation for revenge for the slaughter and dispersal of his people several years before, and by depicting Don Carlos Fernández as having met Cuerno Verde face to face in this definitive battle, the playwright has composed history in such a way as to make even higher drama than the actual historical facts would have yielded by themselves. Had De Anza appeared as the protagonist there would have been a much closer correspondence with the historical events of the 1779 campaign, ending with Cuerno Verde's death. But the drama would have lost something as well. What would have been missing is the fiction that Cuerno Verde actually met Don Carlos sometime *after* the Nuevo Mexicano's bloody expedition of 1774, and that the Comanche chief was thereby confronted with the very opportunity for revenge against this man for which he had waited so long. Clearly, De Anza's role in the history of these campaigns is that of the ultimate victor over Cuerno Verde in 1779. But in terms of high melodrama, the compelling motive for revenge on Cuerno Verde's part and the irony of this encounter would be almost entirely dissipated were he to meet De Anza instead of Don Carlos. De Anza might have been known to Cuerno Verde by the time they actually clashed in 1779, but there was not likely to have existed the kind of personal animosity that the dramatist was able to conjure up by confronting Cuerno Verde with Don Carlos Fernández, the author of one of the cruelest defeats to have been inflicted on the Comanches during the Comanche campaigns of the 1770s.[7] On the other hand, when one reads De Anza's detailed and analytical account of his meeting with the great Comanche leader, it is extremely tempting to theorize that the author of *Los Comanches* must have had some knowledge of the dramatic and definitive confrontation between these two men. There is much that remains to be done in the interest of clearing up the true origins and history of this intriguing drama.[8]

Los tejanos is the title given to the manuscript of a play that was collected by Aurelio M. and José M. Espinosa in 1931. Like *Los Comanches* this drama represents an important historical moment (the "defeat" of the Texas-Santa Fe Expedition of 1841), and it projects through its particular version of events a distinctive ideological perspective. Also like *Los Comanches, Los tejanos* focuses on an event in which the frontier character of New Mexico is a crucial factor and where the preservation of the province's geographic integrity and even the physical safety of its citizens seem to be the issue. During the governorship of De Anza, there can be little doubt about the reality of the bloody clashes that were being experienced between nomadic bands of Indians and the New Mexican settlers. The extent to which the Texas-Santa Fe Expedition represented a real and grave threat to New Mexico is at least questionable.

Certainly the way in which the two dramas create their historical reality is substantially different. Unlike *Los Comanches*, for instance, the element of military pageantry that we have traced to the *moros y cristianos* plays is entirely absent from *Los tejanos*. Also missing is the high rhetorical tone of *Los Comanches* whereby the ideals of the state and its religion are projected as fundamental patriotic principles to be defended. In contrast, *Los tejanos* depicts the humiliation of the Texan military leader McLeod (Menclaude, in the play) and his aide, Navarro, through an intricate deception on the part of the Nuevo Mexicanos, culminating in a relatively brief declaration of the principles of New Mexican sovereignty and patriotism at the end of the play.

Very little is known about the history of this play. According to its editor, Aurelio M. Espinosa, this manuscript is probably not the original, and the date of composition is assumed to be relatively soon after the events it depicts. As to the play's performance, there is no concrete evidence that it was ever staged, aside from Espinosa's observation that the manuscript he collected (which he dates tentatively from anywhere between 1850 and 1880) showed signs of considerable handling and thus may have served as an acting script. Nevertheless, basing our discussion on what the play reveals of itself and what we know of the circumstances of the Texas-Santa Fe Expedition, we can gain an understanding of the play's importance as a historical and cultural artifact.

Los comanches and "Los moros y Cristianos" reflect the conflict between the Spanish or Mexican Christian and the Native American, with the *moro* becoming the figuration of the *indio* in the New World. *Los tejanos* introduces the Anglo-American, the citizen of the Republic of Texas, a state which had only recently broken violently away from Mexico. The *tejano* now is seen as a threat to the Mexican province of Nuevo México. With the booming trade over the Santa Fe Trail, New Mexico, and especially Santa Fe, was becoming a place of business for an increasing number of "outsiders." Texas President, Mirabeau Lamar, had received reports that the majority of New Mexicans (Americans, Mexicans, and Pueblo Indians) favored an intervention from Texas that would lead New Mexico toward its own independence from Mexico, even though that might mean annexation to Texas (McClure). President Lamar was also motivated by the need to remedy the economic depression that Texas was suffering and he dreamed of an overland trade route that would connect the gulf coast of his republic with the Pacific ports of Mexico. Such a route would challenge the monopoly that was then held over westward commerce by the Santa Fe traders. Moreover, it had long been the contention in Texas that the Treaty of Velasco (1836) in effect had granted to Texas all the territory bounded by the Río Grande, which would include Santa Fe and virtually the whole eastern one-third of New Mexico. New Mexican Governor Manuel Armijo was still having to defend the province from hostile Indian raids, and he had defended the interests of the landowning and mercantile class of *ricos* in putting down the popular rebellion of 1837. American merchants in New Mexico had never felt that Armijo would protect their interests or their property in a crisis, and Armijo, on the other hand, was profoundly suspicious of the motives of the increasing number of American traders and businessmen who were coming into his province with the commerce of the Santa Fe Trail. The historic precedent of the Texas rebellion and independence from Mexico cannot ever have been far from Armijo's mind under these circumstances, and when the perceived threat of an outright invasion from Texas came to his attention in 1841, he took action on several different fronts to combat it (Tyler). Consistent with the relative neglect that had been demonstrated historically toward New Mexico by central governments, first in Spain and then in

Mexico, Armijo's requests to Mexico City for aid in this crisis of multiple threats (Indian, on the one hand, and Texan, on the other) went largely unanswered until the very last minute. Anticipating invasion from without and rebellious collusion from within, the governor placed heavy restrictions on the Americans who were living in Santa Fe, and began an extensive propaganda campaign that aimed at arousing the patriotism of the Nuevo Mexicanos in the face of an armed attempt by Texas to seize the New Mexican capital (Sánchez Lamego, 1, 2). Meanwhile, Santa Anna's administration ordered the governor of Chihuahua to help by sending troops and money to New Mexico, and a well-organized plan of defense of the province was finally designed. So while some commentators have accused Armijo of grossly exaggerating the gravity of the Texas threat (most of all in the retrospective light of the almost pathetic weakness and disorganization of the expedition when it arrived in New Mexican territory), Armijo could also be seen as having taken many drastic but necessary preparatory steps to rally Santa Anna's government to the defense of New Mexico, and, needless to say, to the defense of his own interests and those of the mercantile and landowning class (Tyler; McClure).

The drama *Los tejanos* depicts the capture of Texas General Hugh McLeod and his party by General Armijo's soldiers after they have been led into a trap by two New Mexican spies, one a Pecos Indian (referred to only as "*Indio*" in the script), and the other, Don Jorge Ramírez, an "*andaluz*." Both of these individuals are "outsiders," not only from the standpoint of the Texans but from that of the New Mexicans as well. What would this Indian and this Spaniard stand to loose or gain from allegiance to one side or the other? Both Menclaude and his aide, Navarro, are perplexed by the stories they tell to explain how they fell into Texan hands as prisoners, and the two men disagree about whether to trust them or not. Throughout the script, the play's author deftly exploits this situation for its ironic and comic potential. In the first place, after they have seized the Indian, the Texan Navarro declares that he knows exactly what "*esta clase*" (meaning Indians) needs so that they will talk:

> *Bien, hijo. Siéntate aquí.*
> *Y tráiganle que chupar*
> *que a todos los de esta clase*
> *les cuadra parlamentar*
> *con el chacuaco en la mano.*
> (A. *Espinosa* 308)

[I'm fine, my friend. Sit down here. Bring him a smoke; I know that these people love to talk with a pipe in their hand.]

The *Indio* immediately responds that he doesn't want a smoke but a good meal instead. When Navarro (due to the depletion of the expedition's food supplies) cannot give him this, the *Indio* simply answers with useless information. Finally, Navarro must give him one of his own best suits of clothes in order to elicit what he knows. The *Indio* makes a great deal of this bribe, subtly mocking Navarro's gullibility and joking about the way his new clothes will transform his life:

> *¡Agora sí, muy contento!*
> *¿No ves ya yo engalaná?*
> *Quizás (agora) fiscal,*
> *quizás gobernadorcillo,*
> *quizás capitán la guerra,*
> *mi pueblo me eligirá.*
> *Agora voy empezando.*
> (A. *Espinosa* 309)

> [Now me very happy!
> Look, me very well dressed.
> Maybe now my people elect me attorney, governor or military chieftan. Now I am beginning.]
> [Note: the Spanish imitates the ungrammatical speech of the Indian]

The *Indio* then tells of the fate of the other Texans who have been captured by the New Mexicans and warns them against resisting Manuel Armijo, "(a quien) todo el mundo lo conoce/ y le tiembla. Es muy verdad./ Es muy rico y no le cuadra/ por que la gente robá". And although Navarro counsels caution, Menclaude boldly (and, of course, foolishly in retrospect) wants battle:

> *Y yo le quiero probar*
> *que en Tejas hay hombres que*
> *(muy pronto lo vencerán),*
> *de destreza y de valor,*
> *y táctica militar.*
> (A. *Espinosa* 309–10)

> [And I want to prove to him that in Texas there are men who will soon defeat him with their bravery and their military skill.]

In order to further gain the Texans' confidence, the *Indio* pretends to betray another spy in the Texan camp, Don Jorge Ramírez. Menclaude threatens Ramírez if he does not cooperate, and offers him a lavish reward if he does:

Como también si se porta
con decencia y probidad
le hago la merced de la vida.
Y a más (usted) se conducirá
a mis expensas a Tejas,
y allí se le propondrá
un destino muy lucroso,
donde usté pueda pasar
a sus anchuras la vida
haciéndose nacional.
(A. Espinosa 312)

[And in addition, if you behave yourself with integrity and decency, I will grant to you your life. And further, you will be taken to Texas at my expense, and there you will be given a job with a good salary, and you will be able to live there comfortably and become a citizen of the Republic.]

Ramírez professes to be overwhelmed by such an irresistible offer and readily agrees to cooperate:

(Pues,) Señor, traía otro intento,
pero la casualidad
le abre la puerta a mi fortuna,
y es la que yo he de buscar
. . . ahora he pensado que mi fortuna tan cabal
me abre puerta que yo pueda
el hacerme nacional
de Tejas, patria adorada.
(A. Espinosa 312–13)

[(Well,) Sir, I came here with an altogether different purpose, but fortune has opened another door for me, and I must take advantage of it . . . now I realize that my great good fortune has opened that door for me to become a citizen of that beloved country, Texas.]

Having succeeded extravagantly in his confidence game, Ramírez's advice is eagerly heeded by Menclaude whose declared goal, according to this version of events, is to capture Armijo and take over New Mexico for the Republic of Texas:

¡Vengan los brazos, amigo,
pues yo he de recompensar
a usté todos los servicios
que me haga en particular!
. . .

Y yo lo haré mi segundo.
Y a más lo voy a premiar
con el caudal de los Chávez.
Y también le voy a dar
todo lo que en el día tiene
Don Antonio Sandoval.
(A. *Espinosa* 313)

[Let me embrace you, my friend! I will surely reward you for any and all the help that you may give to me! And I will make you my second in command. And beyond that, I will repay you with all the wealth of the Chávezes and all the wealth that now belongs to Don Antonio Sandoval.]

The satire of the Texan leaders was obviously irresistible to this play's author. They are filled with false confidence by the New Mexican spies who cleverly exploit the Texans' ambitions for conquest and power in order to lead them into a humiliating defeat. Naturally, the playwright uses a broad, comic depiction of the nationalistic bravado of General McLeod and highlights his disdainful attitude toward New Mexicans as he promises to distribute the wealth of certain *rico* families to his faithful informants as plunder. With the capture of the entire Texas expedition as an historical fact, a New Mexican audience could have been counted on to revel in the kind of arrogance displayed by the Texans, and especially in the irony of Menclaude's promise that well-known families (he mentions the specific names of Chávez and Sandoval) would have their fortunes taken away under Texan rule.

The play's final speeches, however, carry the discourse to a somewhat more elevated rhetorical plane in order to project the patriotic message. The satire and the comic irony of the play's plot are entirely congruent with the celebrations occasioned by the New Mexican victory;[8] and yet, the ideological lesson to be drawn from all of this is not merely left to the imagination of the audience at the end. Thus, the Mexican officer who captures Menclaude declares:

¡Ah, tejanos atrevidos!
¿Se atreven a profanar
las tierras del mejicano?
Ahora su temeridad
le pondrá freno a su orgullo,
¡Y a todos he de acabar!

[Ah, you insolent Texans! How dare you profane the territory of the New Mexicans? Now your recklessness will put your pride in check. And I will put an end to all of you!]

And the spy Don Jorge delivers the final ratification of loyalty to General Armijo and declaration of solidarity of the New Mexicans against any foreign incursion:

> *¡Muere, perro! ¡Has de pagar*
> *todo lo que has proyectado*
> *en contra (de) mi general!*
> *Te servirá de escarmiento*
> *que no te vuelvas a fiar*
> *de los nuevomejicanos.*
> *Pues si tú los ves ladrar*
> *siempre al extranjero muerden.*
> (A. *Espinosa* 1944, 314)

> [Die, you dog! You are going to pay for all the evil that you have plotted against my general! This will be a lesson to you never again to trust the New Mexicans. For whenever you hear them bark, then will they also surely bite the foreigners.]

The manuscript shows the word *Menclaude* at the bottom of its last page, indicating that perhaps there was another speech or speeches yet to come. If the play does in fact contain additional material in its original version, it is interesting to speculate about whether or not this new tone of seriousness and fervor would have been sustained. It is conceivable that instead of continuing with more patriotic speeches, the play might have followed the style of some Golden Age Spanish antecedents and ended with a general celebration of the event that had just been dramatized.

This is not the place to try to resolve the long-standing problem of whether or not the Texans actually were—or saw themselves as potentially being—the force that would liberate a grateful New Mexican population from the yoke of Mexican rule. Nor can we resolve the debate over Governor Armijo's possible exploitation of the circumstances in order to bolster his political position, enhance his reputation as a leader and protect the interests of *los ricos*. The fact is that the New Mexicans who held political power and controlled the wealth could hardly have afforded to underestimate the threat posed by the Texas-Santa Fe Expedition. Even if the threat was discovered not to have been as serious as it might have seemed, there was a further advantage to be gained by maintaining through propaganda a level of general alarm that would enable the government and military later to take credit for a "victory" that had been assured virtually from the beginning and accomplished without risk or loss. Under these circumstances, a play such as *Los tejanos* would have performed a necessary function in the context of a public celebration or commemoration of such a victory by erasing ambiguities, by invalidating doubts about the gravity of the menace to New Mexico's political and territorial integrity, and by not only depicting events but also by showing how they should be interpreted. And while a play such as "Los moros y los cristianos" or *Los Comanches* may survive in the folk vernacular due to their attractive and colorful patriotic pageantry, the comic and satirical view of *Los tejanos* toward the triumph of the resourceful New Mexican people over the pompous and chauvinistic Texans could certainly survive on the fundamental appeal of its "trickster" plot, even after the particulars of the expedition and of Armijo's administration had been forgotten. The lack of any kind of performance history is particularly unfortunate in this case, and something that needs to be resolved by further investigation.

Each of these three plays, which together comprise the only vestiges we have of New Mexico's early secular theater, celebrates an event, both in specifically historical terms and in terms of its ideological import. Perhaps it is only an accident of history that these are the only three plays that have survived in manuscript form; perhaps other events in New Mexican history were commemorated and interpreted in similar ways but we have simply lost the evidence of their existence. And if it is only due to chance that these three plays rather than others have come down to us, then it is even more remarkable that they seem to mark significant moments in the consolidation of a geographic, cultural, and ideological (patriotic) identity: the extension of a Euro-Christian empire into the far north of *Nueva España*, the reassertion of that hegemony in the face of armed resistance by native peoples, and the defense of Mexican sovereignty against the incursions of an expansionist Anglo-American republic. There is much more to be known about these plays and their tradition in New Mexico, and we can continue to hope that even more vestiges of a history of secular folk theater may come to light in the future.

NOTES

1. Research for this project was begun during a National Endowment for the Humanities Summer Seminar at the University of California, Santa Barbara, under the direction of Prof. Luis Leal, Summer 1986.

2. Villagrá, Gaspar Pérez de, *Historia de la Nueva México* 2 vols. (México: Imprenta del Museo Nacional, 1900). The narrative poem was originally published at Alcalá de Henares, Spain, in 1610 having been written during Villagrá's return to Spain after accompanying the Oñate expedition of 1598. George P. Hammond points out that one of the poem's purposes was to help persuade Spanish authorities of the wisdom of supporting the New Mexico colonization.

3. While making this point, however, it is necessary to acknowledge that the fierce independence of the clergy in New Mexico, and their constant battles with the civil authorities may argue against drawing too many parallels between the practices of missionaries in Mexico and in the Provincias Interiores. See, Charles R. Cutter, *El Protector de Indios in Colonial New Mexico, 1659–1821*

(Albuquerque: UNM Press, 1986) for a summary of the struggles between civil and religious authority in colonial New Mexico.

4. Certainly the ideological importance of this historical antecedent was not lost on the Franciscans who in 1693 reinstituted the cult of *Nuestra Señora, Reina de Nueva México y de su Villa de Santa Fé*, but changed her name to *La Conquistadora* in honor of the renewal of Spanish hegemony in the province of New Mexico (Chavez, p. 32ff.).

5. The files of the New Mexico Writers' Project contain a typescript, "Los Moros (danza y pieza)," prepared by Aurora Lucero White. There is an introduction suggesting (without detail) the possible connections between the *moros y cristianos* dances and the New Mexican Matachines, and between the *moros y cristianos* play and *Los Comanches*. The typewritten text is similar to the one that was published later in her book, *Literary Folklore of the Hispanic Southwest*, except that here it is transcribed in prose form, and it contains many gaps which seem to have been filled in with text for the 1953 book. Other unpublished typescripts in the same archive (both in Spanish and English) seem to be versions of this same fundamental text. In 1980 Frank M. Bond donated to the Museum of International Folk Art a typescript containing his introduction and edition of two *moros y cristianos* texts which are printed in parallel columns. One text is that which Lea published in 1953; the other is attributed to Ricardo Archuleta, Cerro, New Mexico. There are substantial differences between the texts, but I have not had time to analyze them in detail.

6. A. M. Espinosa (1907) speculates that the play was written after Don Carlos Fernández's victory (which Espinosa mistakenly places in 1777) and possibly after De Anza's 1779 victory as well, with the playwright simply combining events from the two battles; Gilberto Espinosa (1931) has Governor De Anza sending Don Carlos Fernández into battle against the Comanches in 1777, and does not mention the possible fusion of two historical events into the play; A. Campa (1942) corrects the date of the Don Carlos Fernández battle to 1774, adding that "this was undoubtedly the battle described in the drama" (p. 10); B. Roeder (1976) suggests that the play may have been written sometime after the Fernández campaign but before De Anza's victory, and that the ending was subsequently revised to reflect the 1779 death of Cuerno Verde, since one of the versions that Campa was using has Cuerno Verde surviving the battle, and another depicts his death; A. M. Espinosa (1985) also sees the possibility of the two separate events figuring into the author's conception of the play, whose composition Espinosa now places "sometime after 1779" (p. 217).

7. There are numerous other irregularities of detail surrounding this play that warrant further investigation, and I will simply list them here: 1. I by no means consider the issue of the play's apparent combination of the 1774 and the 1779 Comanche campaigns into a single event as having been definitively resolved or explained; there is an intriguing note, in fact, which I have not yet been able to corroborate, concerning an eyewitness account of a *Los Comanches* performance in southern Colorado with De Anza, not Carlos Fernández, as protagonist (Roeder p. 291n14). 2. A Campa (1942) cites the "various manuscripts (of *Los comanches*) now known," and mentions without any detail that he used "four copies" to make his edition. How many manuscripts are there now in existence? What are the similarities and differences among them, and what can we learn from them about the date of the play's composition, about its historical context, and possibly about its author? 3. What kind of performance history could be established for *Los Comanches*, and how might it relate to the manuscripts that we have of the play? Care must be taken to distinguish among several distinct dramatic performances loosely referred to as "los Comanches"; they include the *genízaro* dances that depict the kidnapping and recapture of the image of the Christ Child (King; Campa), and at least two versions of the secular *Los Comanches* (Bond p. 7–9).

8. In the preface to his 1907 edition of *Los Comanches*, Aurelio Espinosa reports that the owner of the play's manuscript, Don Amado Cháves, had claimed that Don Pedro Bautista Pino was the original author. Pino, born in Santa Fe in 1750, is best known for his role as the emissary from the province of Nuevo México to the constitutional convention at Cádiz, Spain, in 1812, and as the author of a lengthy report on the conditions in early nineteenth century New Mexico. Twitchell (1963) and Espinosa (1907) both place Pino with Don Carlos Fernáñdez in the 1774 campaign against the

Comanches in which the Nuevo Mexicanos enjoyed a substantial victory. John Englekirk (1957), while acknowledging the plausibility of Pino's authorship, maintains nonetheless, that there is not even enough evidence to be able to assert (as do Espinosa 1907, Campa, and Roeder) that the play was written close to the time of the events it depicts. Moreover, Englekirk theorizes that the relatively elaborate and flawless manuscript versions of the play used by Espinosa and Campa for their editions could not have had their origins in an almost century-long tradition of oral transmission, folk performances, and final written transcription. Englekirk maintains (as he does in the case of the New Mexican religious folk drama as well) that the 1864 manuscript version of *Los Comanches* used by Campa, was only "one or two steps removed from a printed Mexican edition of a mid-nineteenth century romantic historical vintage" (1957 p. 238n7). The question of the play's authorship is still a matter of speculation, and Englekirk's skepticism constitutes an important challenge to the generally held views.

9. There are at least three references to public festivals that were held to celebrate Armijo's triumph over the invading Texans. Stanley describes the scene in Santa Fe, mentioning dances, sermons, and "rhymes of praise for the men who conquered the terrifying Texans" (187); Simmons (1973) cites the celebrations in Las Vegas when Armijo himself returned from the field after leading the capture of the Texas Expedition, specifying that the proclamations carried by the Texans calling for the annexation of New Mexico were publicly burned, and that Armijo himself praised the heroism of the Nuevo Mexicanos (p. 75); and McClure states that "Armijo's success prompted public celebrations throughout New Mexico" (p. 53). It would be interesting to know whether the play *Los tejanos* might have been composed and performed specifically for such festivities. Certainly the comic and satirical tone of the play would have been altogether appropriate for such an occasion.

WORKS CITED

Bond, Frank M. "Los Moros y Cristianos." Unpublished edition and introduction, 1971.

———, "Los Comanches." Unpublished edition and introduction, 1972.

Campa, Arthur L., ed. "*Los Comanches*: A New Mexican Folk Drama." *University of New Mexico Bulletin* 7 (1942).

Chavez, Fray Angelico. *Our Lady of the Conquest*. Santa Fe: The Historical Society of New Mexico, 1948.

Englekirk, John E. "The Source and Dating of New Mexican Spanish Folktheater." *Western Folklore* 16 (1957): 232–55.

Espinosa, Aurelio M., ed. "*Los Comanches*." *University of New Mexico Bulletin* 45 (1907).

Espinosa, Aurelio M. *The Folklore of Spain in the American Southwest*. Ed. J. Manuel Espinosa. Norman: University of Oklahoma P, 1985.

Foster, George M. *Culture and Conquest*. New York: Wenner-Gren Foundation, 1960.

Hammond, George P. "The Search for the Fabulous in the Settlement of the Southwest." *New Spain's Far Northern Frontier: Essays on Spain in the American West, 1540–1821*. Ed. David J. Weber. Albuquerque: University of New Mexico Press, 1979.

Jones, Okah L. *Los Paisanos*. Norman: Oklahoma University Press, 1979.

Kenner, Charles L. A *History of New Mexico-Plains Indian Relations*. Norman: University of Oklahoma Press, 1969.

King, Scottie. "Los Comanches de la Serna." *New Mexico Magazine* Jan. 1979: 25–7, 42.

Lea, Aurora Lucero-White. *Literary Folklore of the Hispanic Southwest*. San Antonio: Naylor, 1953.

McClure, Charles R. "The Texas-Santa Fe Expedition of 1841." *New Mexico Historical Review* 48 (1973): 45–56.

Motolinía, Fray Toribio de. *Historia de los indios de la Nueva España*. Ed. Claudio Esteva. Madrid: Historia 16, 1985.

Ramírez, Carlos B. "The Hispanic Political Elite in Territorial New Mexico." 2 vols. PhD. Diss. University of California, Santa Barbara, 1979.

Roeder, Beatrice A. "*Los Comanches*: A Bicentennial Folk Play." *Bilingual Review/Revista Bilingüe* 3 (1976): 213–220.

Sánchez Lamego, General M. A. *The Second Mexican-Texas War 1841–1843*. Hillsboro TX: Hill Jr. College, 1972.

Simmons, Marc. *The Little Lion of the Southwest*. Chicago: Swallow Press, 1973.

———. *New Mexico: A Bicentennial History*. New York: Norton, 1977.

Stanley, Francis. *Ciudad Santa Fe*. vol. 2. Pampa TX: Pampa Print Shop, 1958.

Swadesh, Frances L. *Los Primeros Pobladores: Hispanic Americans on the Ute Frontier*. Notre Dame: University of Notre Dame Press, 1974.

(Thomas) ———. *The Plains Indians and New Mexico*. Albuquerque: University of New Mexico Press, 1940.

(Thomas) ———. *Teodoro Croix and the Northern Frontier of New Spain: 1776–83*. Norman: Oklahoma University Press, 1941.

Tjarks, Alicia V. "Demographic, Ethnic and Occupational Structure of New Mexico, 1790." *The Americas* 35, 1 (1978): 45–88.

Twitchell, Ralph Emerson. *The Leading Facts of New Mexican History*. Albuquerque: Horn and Wallace, 1963.

Tyler, Daniel. "Gringo Views of Governor Manuel Armijo." *New Mexico Historical Review* 45 (1970): 23–46.

Villagrá, Capitán Gaspar Pérez de. *Historia de la Nueva México* 2 vols. Mexico: Imprenta del Museo Nacional, 1900.

Warman, Arturo. *La danza de moros y cristianos*. Mexico: Secretaría de Educación Pública, 1972.

Winter, Joseph. "Santiago," *New Mexico Magazine* Mar. 1986: 53–57.

3

CONFLICT, RESISTANCE, AND ADAPTATION

Literature of the Nineteenth Century

6

A LITERARY PORTRAIT OF HISPANIC NEW MEXICO
Dialectics of Perception

FRANCISCO A. LOMELÍ

Nuevo México insolente
Entre los cíbolos criado;
¿Dime, quién te ha hecho letrado
para hablar entre la gente?

—TAVERAS

A LITERARY HISTORY, ACCORDING TO WHOM?

The complete restoration of the literary history of Hispanic literature in the Southwest is indeed a challenge. A thorough examination of a myriad of sources from and about the nineteenth century provides a confused and fractured history at best. It does not, as one would hope, furnish the necessary evidence with which to retrace the literary legacy as it developed. Investigations often lead the researcher into a series of labyrinthine paths with infinite dead ends. Any inquiry resembles the meticulous work of the archaeologist who collects potsherds that will some day contribute to a significant discovery. Reflections on the subject tend to lead to one central question: What data permit the reassessment of a Hispanic literary tradition as it unfolded in nineteenth-century New Mexico? And, like the archaeologist, we must ask which remains are significant. This is the case because, as archaeologists understand, significance must be determined by the society in which the remains are found.

One of the obstacles that has hampered the study of literary history of nineteenth-century New Mexico is the difficulty in locating published works by Hispanic writers of the past century. Established Southwest historians have taken publication as indication of significance. As we shall see later, that may well prove to be an ill-fitting criterion. A careful perusal of the principal works dedicated to

Southwestern letters allows us to concur with Gerald W. Haslam's premise in a seminal work titled *Forgotten Pages of American Literature* (1970), where he suggests that literature by minority groups has been—intentionally or unintentionally—excluded from mainstream consideration:

> The potential symbolic and intellectual flexibility inherent in a multi-cultural nation is unwittingly obscured in countless classrooms where a course in European-American literature is substituted for one reflecting more accurately the cultural amalgam that is in the United States.[1]

It is no coincidence that the notion of a "forgotten people"[2] emerges frequently among critics in the twentieth century to describe the positions Hispanics occupy in the annals of "official" literary history. An in-depth review of critical works that claim to represent literary history from the Southwest unveils the obliviousness exercised to exclude writers of Mexican descent. The act of forgetting is designed in this case to dismiss, to relegate significance, or simply to ignore. The overriding intent can perhaps be summarized by the circumstances described in the title of David J. Weber's work *Foreigners in Their Native Land* (1973). If the act of forgetting is not at issue, then omission becomes the next concern. A general blackout is prevalent in virtually all bibliographies, literary histories, anthologies, and critical collections. The only works to escape this trend are what might be termed the unquestionable Aztlán or Southwest classics, such as Alvar Núñez Cabeza de Vaca's *Relaciones* (1542), Gaspar Pérez de Villagrá's *Historia de la Nueva México* (1610), certain colonial plays like *Los Comanches* (1777?) and *Los Texanos* (1850?), and numerous *pastorelas* (shepherd plays). Secondary sources would have us believe that mexicanos somehow quit writing with the arrival of Anglo-Americans and that the desire to creatively express the human condition became less important for them. J. Frank Dobie, considered the first Texas man of letters, appears (with his special flair for provocation) more categorical in his judgment about the entire Southwest: "No informed person would hold that the Southwest can claim any considerable body of *pure literature* as its own."[3]

Since proponents of "pure literature" have traditionally had an Eastern U.S. perspective, particular Hispanic strains would automatically fall outside of this canon. It becomes expedient and perhaps necessary to discard or at least to ignore literature written in a language other than English. The literary modes from England or continental Europe are given strong preference over literature by racial minorities, the latter often being criticized and stigmatized for its lack of universality and breadth. The arguments for their exclusion from the American literary canon usually encompass a wide range of reasons, but the logical backdrop essentially returns to the issue of perspective and bias.

These trends and biases manifest themselves in the following instances: out of the 600 titles listed by Mabel Major and T. M. Pearce in the selected bibliography from 1938, only 7 works by Hispanic writers are mentioned; and in their revised edition of 1972 they include 21 works out of approximately 850 titles for the entire four hundred-year history of New Mexico.[4] While relying on questionable criteria with which to evaluate the mexicano's role and contributions between 1800 and 1900, Major and Pearce do not make reference to a single writer of Hispanic origin. As two of the most respected authorities on the Southwest literary heritage, they corroborate what others posit throughout the region. For example, Florence E. Barns includes only one author of Hispanic origin in her collection of approximately one thousand names in *Texas Writers of Today* (1935).[5] Lester Raines, in *Writers and Writings of New Mexico* (1934), also fails to point out any specific examples of Hispanic writers from the nineteenth century, although he does include numerous anonymous works of folklore.[6]

As early as 1917 a critic from Spain, Miguel Romera-Navarro, made the pungent observation about this apparent neglect: "La historia y exposición del hispanismo literario en Norte-América están por escribir[se]. Ni un solo estudio, comprensivo o superficial, popular o erudito, se le ha dedicado."[7] [The history and exposition of the Hispanic literary tradition in North America are yet to be written. Not even a single study has been dedicated to it, be it comprehensive or superficial, popular or erudite.] More recently in 1961 Edwin W. Gaston, in *The Early Novel of the Southwest*, analyzes thirty-one novels by Anglos, nine by European immigrants, and none by Hispanics. Generally unimpressed by the literary production of the region, he downplays the "amateur belletristic efforts" of the writers and offers an indirect explanation regarding the fate of Hispanic writings and authors: "The emphasis upon the Spaniards and Mexicans in novels coincides with Spanish dominance in the region; and the neglect of this character type in Southwestern fiction accompanies their decline."[8] Even though Stanley T. Williams, in the *The Spanish Background of American Literature* (1955), recognizes some noticeable Spanish strand in American letters, he alludes to vague points of contact that apply for the sake of specious coloring and not much else. By background he means linguistic borrowings, toponymy, and social types but not literary forms; besides, the cultural inheritance from folklore seems to him relatively ill-developed, and he labels its manifestations "subliterary patterns."[9] Lawrence Clark Powell's *Southwest Classics: The Creative Literature of the Arid Land: Essays on the Books and Their Writers* (1974) is equally remiss; of the twenty-six classics he presents, none are Hispanic with the exception of the lesser-known eighteenth-century Franciscan monk, Francisco Garcés, who is credited with a diary.[10] If the accomplishments are in fact as limited as those diverse sources suggest, then Philip D. Ortego is correct in proposing that the second half of the nineteenth century parallels the "Dark Ages" of American historiography, as was originally argued by Clarence E. Carter.[11]

Our first task, therefore, in unravelling the literary history of the Southwest, is to examine the notion that the nineteenth century was a dark age for people of Mexican descent. If there is repeated evidence of neglect and exclusion, it behooves us to ask: Why? Historically speaking, many examples can be unearthed to document prejudice and discrimination in the denigration of the mexicano. Numerous colorful characters can be mentioned, such as Judge Roy Bean or Hanging Judge Parker, whose unforgettable derogatory comments appear in the pages of popular lore.[12] The real tragedy lies in the concerted efforts to subconsciously exercise censorship in the name of serious scholarship. Perhaps the most disheartening case involves the authors of *Southwest Heritage*, who in the introduction to the first edition in 1938 plainly reveal their true sentiments. The rhetoric of exclusion is sophisticated enough in its cautious presentation; however, the ingredients of the following editors' justifications—supposedly pragmatism and expediency—are not acceptable to those who would seek a broader-based definition of the American experience, and subsequently the documentation of that experience through literature:

> Most Americans . . . have read only books made in the traditions of Europe and written in the English language. It would be desirable and profitable to include in this guide to the literature and life of the Southwest all the works, oral and recorded, in Indian, Spanish, English, and other tongues, that have sprung from the section. Some day we shall attain that breadth of vision. (2)

The open admission is of particular interest here because their next argument makes the assumption that discussion is closed; for these authors, it is imperative that Anglo-American creativity be considered *the* legitimate voice of New Mexico due to the forces of historical inevitability and determinism:

> Moreover, we shall frankly relate all other cultures in the Southwestern scene to our contemporary American life. There are good reasons besides expediency for our doing this. While civilization here is greatly enriched by contacts with other cultures and languages, today the dominant strain seems clearly to be Anglo-American, with its ever increasing tendency to spread its influence and to absorb its competitors. (p. 2)

This not-so-camouflaged ethnocentrism has become the measuring stick with which to judge a people's literature. Failing to pass muster, it remains relegated to the margins of American literary history and its omission from mainstream criticism gives credence to the displacement alluded to in 1951 by Erna Fergusson: "Much as New Mexico has been written about, its writers are few compared with its painters, and its best books have been the work of outsiders."[13] In fact, the creative abilities of mexicanos as writers still elicit so little recognition that even sympathizers such as Edward Simmen, as recently as 1971, have reverted to commonly held views from the nineteenth century that " . . . neither the upper-class Mexican-American nor the lower-class laborers has produced literature: The former is not inclined; the latter is not equipped."[14]

THE CONQUEST: TAKEOVER OR MOVE OVER

A process of disenfranchisement and relegation has been in effect for the New Mexican since the nineteenth century when the Southwest was annexed to the United States. Although Hispanics greatly outnumbered the Anglo until the middle of the twentieth century, the expansionist motives of the newcomers compelled them to carry out the charter of conquest in a sometimes subtle but usually tendentious manner. A trend was established to supplant a relatively pastoral society by waging a carefully orchestrated war of images: slothful and backward Mexicans were in need of salvation and redemption by the industrious and visionary newcomers. They thus enhanced their encroachment by giving the idea that it was prudent and judiciously accomplished; others would even claim it to be necessary, as if predestined.

Effective tactics were created to minimize the achievements and importance of Hispanics in order to alter the region's character into new Anglo molds in the areas of social suprastructures, such as law and politics. Soon the infrastructures were affected, as were attitudes, beliefs, world view, and customs. As the social, political, economic, and cultural conquest of New Mexico gained full force in the second half of the nineteenth century, the conqueror's view of history was appropriately put into motion and submitted in writing as empirical data. Although their perceptions of mexicanos varied in degrees of negativism, historians such as Ralph E. Twitchell, Josiah Gregg, Lebaron Bradford Prince, and Hubert Howe Bancroft proceeded to put Manifest Destiny into practice through their interpretation and presentation of facts.[15] When jingoism did not produce the desired results or when outright prejudice seemed too obvious, other innovative methods of displacement were devised. One was to promote biographies of outstanding civilians—almost exclusively Anglo-American—to highlight one social sector at the expense of the other. Thus, the conquest on a daily basis took on the qualities of a moral crusade against barbarism and backwardness within a justified self-righteous framework.

The process of disenfranchisement crept into the domain of literature. First was the usurpation of typically Southwestern social types, characters, and motifs. Integration of native features by Anglo-Americans generated a discriminating selection in order to make them palatable to the newcomers' tastes. A case in point: the *vaquero's* (cowboy) valor and dexterity were transferred to the cowboy as Anglo-American writers elevated the cowboy to the stature of an appealing symbol in the myth of frontier freedom, while they chose to ignore his real source of origin. This sort of cultural borrowing has resulted in a transformation of the original element while blunting or obscuring the Mexicanness of the model. Whereas for the mexicano, the *vaquero* typified hard labor and survival, the cowboy represented individualistic perseverance and a relentless urge to reach new horizons. While the Mexican *vaquero* was inclined to colonize and conquer nature, the American cowboy rebelled against society, thus seeking refuge in nature for and by himself. A symbol of permanence and tradition became radically changed to signify the American ideal of individualism and self-promoted achievement.

This system of substituting one Southwestern type for another became a device with which to put to rest previous heroic figures from the Colonial period: Indian leaders were frowned upon as dangerous ruffians, and certain Hispanic personages (i.e., conquerors, adventurers, *pícaros* (rogues), chroniclers, and even priests) were carefully deflated to acquire secondary status. In their place emerged an onslaught of trail blazers, trappers, military men, sharpshooters, hunters, and homesteaders. The Indohispanic elements, while safe in a distant time frame, passed into a mytho-legendary place beyond the realm of the flesh-and-blood. Symbolically, this act marks an honorable death to the native legacy, and at the same time announces the advent and foundation of a new cultural force. By depicting a colonial past in a Romantic mode, the assumption is that Anglo-American iconography represents a regenerative component that injects vigor and vitality into a traditional and static pastoral society. The dichotomy is consequently established between what Hispanic peoples were and what they might have been. Rarely does the inquiry raise the question, "What might they become?" Thus, things of Hispanic origin now leave the foreground to become a part of the background, usually as decorative pieces to be appreciated from afar. The tendency then is to observe Hispanic elements as quaint, simpático or overcharged with simplicity. As a result, there emerges what Franklin Walker terms "cultural hydroponics",[16] in which the original culture is enveloped to the point of obscurity and irrelevance.

By reading only Anglo-American recorded sources, we are led to believe that New Mexico could just as well have become Anglicized overnight in 1848. History clearly challenges this interpretation. A more accurate version of the

Territorial period from 1848 until 1912 (the latter being when New Mexico achieved statehood) posits different stages of transition and interaction between the two peoples struggling simultaneously for social adjustment. As new settlers arrived from the East, the divergence in literary history became more pronounced: Anglo Americans imported a northern European-based focus in their pursuit of a regional literature; Hispanics continued to cultivate their distinctively long legacy from Spain, which was expressed in a language that had grown to incorporate the Hispanic and indigenous experiences into a *mestizo* or Mexican mold.[17] Contact between the two cultures that is, *mestizo* and Anglo American, often led to conflict. For example, Edwin S. Fussell in *Frontier: American Literature and the West* (1965), ignores this legacy by implying that Southwestern literature had its beginnings with the arrival of the Anglo American.[18] This view has been amply refuted with concrete evidence to the contrary by such critics as Luis Leal, who in his two seminal studies "Cuatro siglos de prosa aztlanense" [Four Centuries of Aztlanense Prose] and "Hispanic-Mexican Literature in the Southwest, 1521–1848"[19] lays the foundation of a literary heritage that precedes any other in the region by three hundred years with the exception of the Native American voice. The year 1848 does not mark an interruption when it concerns the well-entrenched oral tradition and the inscribed creative legacy of Hispanics.

A PARALLEL LITERARY TRADITION: AUTONOMY VERSUS ISOLATION

The crux of the matter, then, is this: If we are to successfully examine the literary history of the Southwest, we must resume our work as archaeologists. The remains must be placed in the context of the existence of a society strikingly different from Anglo-American society and of a culture characterized as foreign and different that was not infrequently misinterpreted and misrepresented by the new, official records and literature. The crucial difference is as follows: The Hispanic community of the American Southwest—much like other societies in Latin America—is one in which the dichotomy between oral and written literature has never existed. Too often historians have overlooked this keystone of Hispanic culture in order to interpret Hispanic literary tradition in terms of their own choosing. Now, it seems imperative that those fabricated values be set aside and that Hispanic literature be examined in its autochthonous context. To the people who concern us here, literature is more the mode of expression than the form used to present it. Minimal publishing outlets simply reflected the social conditions of limited accessibility, but folk expression does not see publication as an indispensable vehicle for its propagation. For this reason a wide range of popular forms have endured since the Colonial period. Certain specific forms, like the *corrido* [ballads], have even flourished in the second half of the nineteenth century as have *décimas* [ten-versed poem], *inditas* [songs or poems that use the capture of women by Indians as their central motif], *versos* (verses), *pastorelas* (shepherd plays), *adivinanzas* (guessing word games), *alabados* (religious chants), *romances* (epic stories like ballads), *canciones* (songs), *autos* (brief religious plays), *cuentos* (short stories), and *cuandos* (poetic forms using "when" as their point of departure).[20] Contact with Anglo-American lore created two divergent trends: some of the forms diminished in usage, or underwent modifications, while others gained popularity because of Hispanic tenacity and indulgence.

Hispanic literature in the latter half of the nineteenth century was not, we must conclude, the literary desert that conventional historians and literary critics would have us believe. When seen in its proper context, the perception that the Hispanic voice was dormant simply does not hold up. What then prevailed was the existence of two literary foci segregated from each other; and, the situation was aggravated by the fact that the Anglo-American literary circles failed to acknowledge Spanish-language literature, both oral and written. The Hispanic community found itself in internal literary exile and that burden became harder and harder to bear. Thus, the price of cultural survival gradually increased, leaving the Hispanic community with only two media available to it: newspapers and oral tradition.[21] Sporadic attempts to maintain the newspapers as vehicles of information and mirrors of the territory's daily life drew on hard times. Newspapers in New Mexico, like *El Crepúsculo de la Libertad*, founded in 1834 by Father José Antonio Martínez, did not fare as business ventures.

These circumstances forced the mexicano to juggle the creative spirit between the performance (or live oral literature) and the opportunity to present it in written form. In light of the scarcity of stable newspapers between 1850 and 1878, much of Hispanic expression from this period is oral. As folklore, it becomes the object of inquiry by later collectors and scholars, such as Aurelio M. Espinosa, Juan B. Rael, Aurora Lucero White-Lea, and Arturo L. Campa.[22] What they salvaged is the literary background that must be recognized as authentically Southwestern. The collected stories and verses have become to the actual folklore expression of the nineteenth century what the romance was to the epics; that is, anonymous fragments that survive through word of mouth.

THE NEWSPAPER: VEHICLE OF CROSS-CULTURAL DIALOGUE

Perhaps the most obvious exception to the dismal picture of the newspaper industry between 1848 and 1878 is *The New Mexican*, which lasted from 1849 to 1950.[23] Most newspapers utilized an English language format and many included translations into Spanish. The literary samples found during this period indicate a direct transference from Colonial and Mexican periods, with a strong emphasis on forms from oral tradition, such as *décimas*, but segments of memoirs and diaries were also included. The literary pieces published in *The New Mexican* record the impact of the Anglo American's abrupt entrance into the region, as is vividly evident in the following historical-narrative *décima*:

'Jariru, Jari, camón'
dis' el vulgu americano;
comprende pero no quiere
el imperio mejicano.
. . .

Todos los indios de pueblo
se han hechu a la banda d'eos.
Disen qu'es nueva conquista
la ley d'estos fariseos.

Varios no semos con eos
peru hemos jurau em bano;
no "más no digan", fulano
nu ha prestado su atensión
porqu'en cualesquier rasón
dise'el pueblu americano,
'Jariru, Jari, camón.'[24]

['How'd you do, howdy, c'mon,'
say the American folks;
they understand but don't
care for the Mexican folks.
. . .

All the pueblo Indians
have gone o'er to their side.
They claim it's just another conquest
the law of these pharisees.

But we've sworn in vain;
don't just say it, so-and-so,
that you haven't heard
because to any situation
so says the American folks,
'How'd you do, howdy, c'mon.']

Echoing this sense of loss is another *décima* believed to have been composed in 1866 by an unknown writer whom Arturo L. Campa calls a "folk poet." In it the writer summarizes the sentiment of disillusion of the newly conquered people:

Nuevo Méjico mentado,
has perdido ya tu fama,
adonde yo jui por lana
y me vine tresquilado.[25]

[New Mexico so acclaimed
too bad you've lost your fame,
don't matter where I gone for fleece
a good shearing's what I git.]

Aside from these signs of contact, influence, or reaction to the Anglo American, much of the other writings, principally poetry and short stories written mainly in Spanish, reflected the country-within-a-country syndrome and depicted the common folk as dealing with daily living in contact with a foreign culture. A whole gamut of experiential episodes filled certain sections of newspapers: commemoration of deaths, heroic deeds, birthdays, military skirmishes, outbursts of love, and topics that dealt with the conflict generated by coexistence with Anglo-American settlers. Other writings were borrowed from Spain and Latin America or appeared in the literary sections thanks to translations. According to Porter A. Stratton, by 1879 only fifteen newspapers were in operation, seven of which were stable, suggesting that much of the popular expression was transmitted and diffused by word of mouth.[26]

Coinciding with the economic boom of the 1880s, the year 1879 marks a clear landmark in the resurgence of newspapers. The result of the railroad expansion, this period of relative prosperity had an impact of such proportions that the proliferation of newspapers extended into 1900. In this twenty-one-year period, 283 newspapers were launched[27] as a direct result of the availability of educational facilities that produced a burgeoning readership. In the decade of the 1880s, 16 bilingual and 13 Spanish-language newspapers were published; and in the 1890s, 35 Spanish-language and 11 bilingual journals appeared. The city of Las Vegas functioned as a hub in this modest renaissance with a total of 44 newspapers between 1879 and 1900.[28] Consequently, the literary resurgence spawned increased space dedicated to creative writings. As this vehicle became available, Hispanic writers spoke through newspapers to provide testimony to a variegated reservoir of literary voices. On the one hand, their writings gave proof of their participation as witnesses of their time; and, on the other hand, they acted as contributors to a long-standing literary tradition. Despite the quantity and quality of Hispanic literature produced at the time, two parallel versions of literary history developed. One version, perhaps called "official," embarked on acknowledging only Anglo-American writings; the other, a Hispanic version, made the effort to emphasize literature written in Spanish. A definite split occurred and reconciliation became impossible as social tensions arose, thus heightening the rift between the two peoples. The impact of these social conditions was such that lyrical poetry and sentimental prose showed a dramatic decrease. Issues that aroused stronger emotions were now at stake, although much frivolous writing, the sole purpose of which was to entertain or exhibit clever dexterity with the language, still appeared regularly. Much of the literature produced by Hispanics during this period, it must be said, contains a direct or indirect allusion to current events through which we can observe history unfolding. The wider issues include the concerns with land grants, the desire to maintain the Spanish language as equal to English, cultural conflict, religion, outlawry, and problems pertaining to self-determination. Two parallel trends became apparent: Anglo Americans rediscovered the Southwest, according to Cecil Robinson,[29] and they responded by romanticizing it with works such as *Ramona* (1884) by Helen Hunt Jackson; the mexicano rediscovered the region as he assessed the prospects of losing his cultural identity.

While it is true that much of the writing between 1879 and 1900 consists of emotive outbursts related to patriotism, love, death, acts of bravery, remembrances, personal dedications, and so on,[30] a sizeable portion is dedicated to political issues. Proliferation of Hispanic journalism, created the following situation, as described by Anselmo F. Arellano:

> La gente ya tenía una tradición antigua de componer versos en forma de romances y corridos, pero el periodismo ayudó [a] ampliar este ramo de la literatura nativa, junto con el desarrollo de la poesía.[31]
>
> [These people already had an old tradition of composing verses in the form of epic stories and ballads, but the newspapers helped to expand this branch of native literature in conjunction with the development of poetry.]

Consequently, the renewed written tradition often became a sort of forum to vent feelings of anguish, powerlessness, or social indigestion. In 1889 Jesús María H. Alarid presents in his poem "El idioma" [The Language] a version of the language conflict that was in vogue at that time. Obviously a controversial and highly charged issue, it forced Hispanics to reconsider the price they had to pay on the road to assimilation. As an expected reaction, many Hispanics embraced with a great deal of pride a defense of their maternal language, Spanish, as a viable and legitimate means of communication within an English-speaking country:

Hermoso idioma español
¿Qué te quieren proscribir?
Yo creo que no hay razón
Que tú dejes de existir

Afirmo yo que el inglés
Como idioma nacional
No[s] es de sumo interés
Que lo aprendamos [a] hablar
Pues se debe de enseñar
Como patriotas amantes
Y no quedar ignorantes
Mas, no por eso dejar
Que el idioma de Cervantes
Se deje de practicar.[32]

[Beautiful Spanish language
What do they want to proscribe in you?
I don't believe there is a reason
Why you should cease to exist.

I affirm that English
As a national language
Is of essential interest
That we learn to speak it;
After all, it should be taught and
As ardent patriots
Not remain ignorant of it,
But, in so doing
Neither should we cease to practice
The language of Cervantes.]

A copious list of the different poetic forms could be provided to demonstrate the variety and imaginative exposé of feelings and concerns of the period. For the time being, it is even more significant to present some of the persons whose writings appear with certain regularity in newspapers: Higinio V. Gonzales, José Manuel Arellano, Jesús María H. Alarid, Manuel M. Salazar, Eleuterio Baca, Urbano

Chacón, Florencio Trujillo, Ezequiel Cabeza de Baca, Jesús Gonzales, Antonio Lucero, Enrique Salazar, Severino Trujillo, Antonio B. Trujillo, and many more.[33]

The area of literature less mentioned in the second half of the nineteenth century is prose, specifically cuentos [short narrative pieces] and novels. Their rate of frequency is considerably less than poetry, but the actual newspaper space they occupy is not much less. In his doctoral dissertation, "Antología histórica del cuento literario Chicano (1877–1950)"[34] (Historical Anthology of the Chicano Short Story), Armando Miguélez confirms an analogous literary production in Arizona with what is found in New Mexico. He proposes that the short story in early newspapers not only appears regularly but actually comprises a high percentage of the writings presented. In other words, poetry predominates in quantitative terms, but the short story also receives considerable attention in the pages of early newspapers. In another dissertation, "Del siglo XIX al XX: La novela aztlanense escrita en español" (From the Nineteenth to the Twentieth Century: The Novel From Aztlán Written in Spanish), Cosme Zaragoza focuses on the novel, its origins and development;[35] he insists on the literary sophistication and maturity of a people commonly described as illiterate and underdeveloped. Both critics allude to narrative forms as a basis for a well-entrenched literary tradition that deserves recognition as a viable vehicle for the appreciation of the Southwest experience and history.

A BOOM: REASSESSING RELATIONS OF CO-EXISTENCE

A modest movement in Hispanic letters between 1880 and 1900 showed signs of diversity, breadth, and experimentation. Part of the reason for the upsurge was directly attributed to the creation of organizations called *sociedades* [societies] that led a regional vanguard in fusing intellectual pursuits with social action. In the first thorough analysis of these societies, Anselmo F. Arellano points out their broad objective: "to investigate and debate questions and subjects of social, literary and moral character."[36] Also, part of their charter sets forth the philanthropic task of fostering education and the facilities to achieve it. They often served as mutual aid labor unions or protective bodies for community members. They in fact offered other alternatives to Anglo-American institutions within a cultural context and so assumed responsibility for the social well-being of Hispanics. Some of these societies were: *La Sociedad Social, Literaria y de Devates de Agua Negra, Nuevo México* (established in 1898); *Sociedad Literaria y de Ayuda Mutua de Las Vegas* (1892); *Sociedad Protectora* (1895); *Sociedad Dramática Hispano-Americana* (1891); *Casino Hispano-Americano* (1891); and *Sociedad Filantrópica*

Latino-Americana (1892).[37] It is safe to assert that the varied functions of these organizations reflect a conquered people in the process of regrouping, while gaining historical consciousness and intellectual maturity.[38]

Without the activity and fervor that was generated by these *sociedades*, interest in literature and in its respective place in overall society would probably have lagged. To ascertain the impact on Hispanics of the region, we cite one of the founders of *Sociedad Hispano-Americana*, who on March 12, 1892 stated:

> Societies are like the seedling of the most progressive ideas. They are like the sun whose luminous rays of faith reach all minds and give strength, vigor and a new life to people so that they may confront the overflow of privileged classes and the preponderance of corrupt governments. All ideas of philanthropic benefit to poor people have emerged from societies, and they have served to educate him through the schools which have been established throughout—from the prairies to the most remote mountains. The most difficult questions of public interest have developed in the bosom of societies, and the best laws have been projected which today are the guarantee of all and the pride of modern civilization. All institutions in general have provided great services to the world's progress. What would humanity be without the existence of these societies? Without them we would be living in the middle ages.[39]

This scenario of unbound activity was conducive to the cultivation of prose and the narrative, particularly the novel. A readership was almost instantaneously created and the vehicle for publication was greatly facilitated by newspapers that published the novel in serial form. It was probably during the period of 1880 and 1900 when New Mexicans dramatically sought to increase personal library collections,[40] thereby establishing, from their perspective, a more international selection in their readings. They were determined to bring their reading, as well as their writing, up to standards beyond the literary tradition of their milieu. In their minds, they were simply becoming a part of the fashion dictated by the times. In actuality, they linked themselves with a belated Romantic movement that prevailed in Mexico, Spain, and Latin America at a time when a hybrid Realism and Naturalism were in vogue. A degree of eclecticism was in evidence as they combined these newer influences with traditional models, such as the picaresque novel. It soon became obvious that their quest of a literary establishment embraced the blending of known forms into local expression.

This modest boom of 1880 to 1900 marks a key period for Hispanic literary expression in New Mexico and the Southwest in general. After the conquest, however, works written or transmitted in Spanish were relegated to a Spanish-speaking audience, which progressively had at its disposal limited publishing outlets. Works in English gained stature as English became the normative form of expression through socially sanctioned publishing ventures. Literature by Hispanics became implicitly stigmatized, viewed as literature *only* for Hispanic peoples, that is, a residual product of a conquered people. Partly couched in ethnocentricism and exoticism, the new conquest explicitly attempted to minimize what was considered Mexican or Hispanic. While oral transmission kept Hispanic literature alive, its reputation suffered because it did not exist in written form. The fact that it existed in a "foreign" language further justified the perception that it was unfit to enter the canon of regional literature.

As a consequence, the boom seemed to disappear altogether from the annals of Southwestern literature. Southwest literary historians then proceeded as if Hispanic literature or even the Hispanic influence on literature had acquiesced in its own demise. This period marked a crucial transition in the reception that Hispanic literature was to receive. It is only through the efforts of scholars devoted to revisionism and canon reconstruction that Hispanic literature continues to be rediscovered.

NOTES

1. Gerald W. Haslam, *Forgotten Pages of American Literature* (Boston: Houghton Mifflin Co., 1970), p. 1. As useful as this collection is to try to fill gaps within American literature, it is unfortunate that the concept and the examples are not further developed.

2. The person most responsible for developing this concept and popularizing it was George I. Sanchez in *Forgotten People: A Study of New Mexicans* (Albuquerque: Calvin Horn Publishers, 1947). Directly or indirectly, this expose has probably spawned a whole series of books dedicated to researching New Mexico's Hispanic past.

3. J. Frank Dobie, *Guide to Life and Literature of the Southwest* (Austin: The University of Texas Press, 1942), p. 9. Emphasis is in the original.

4. See their otherwise authoritative study *Southwest Heritage: A Literary History With Bibliographies* (Albuquerque: University of New Mexico Press, 1st edition in 1938; revised and augmented in a 3rd edition in 1972). The work contains a wealth of information other than the deficiencies described. Other citations from this work will be indicated with its corresponding pagination appearing in the body of this study.

5. Florence E. Barns, *Texas Writers of Today* (Dallas: Tardy Publishers, 1935). From the data presented, it is obvious to conclude that Hispanic representation in arts and letters in Texas is considerably less than in New Mexico.

6. This is an enigmatic source considering its field of concentration and its blatant gaps.

7. Miguel Romera-Navarro, *El hispanismo en Norte-América: Exposición y crítica de su aspecto literario* (Madrid: Renacimiento, 1917), p. 1.

8. Edwin W. Gaston, Jr., *The Early Novel of the Southwest* (Albuquerque: The University of New Mexico Press, 1961), p. 83.

9. See Stanley T. Williams, *The Spanish Background of American Literature* (New Haven: Yale University Press, 1955).

10. Lawrence Clark Powell, *Southwest Classics: The Creative Literature of the Arid Land; Essays on the Books and Their Writers* (Los Angeles: The Ward Ritchie Press, 1974).

11. See Philip D. Ortego's doctoral dissertation "Backgrounds of Mexican American Literature," University of New Mexico, 1971, pp. 50–51. To accurately determine Clarence E. Carter's original

idea about American historiography, we recommend his article "The Territorial Papers of the United States: A Review and a Commentary," *Mississippi Valley Historical Review*, 41 (1956):521–22.

12. For further information on Judge Roy Bean, "The Law West of the Pecos," consult *A Treasury of American Folklore*, edited by Benjamin A. Botin (New York: Crown Publishers, 1944) from which we include an excerpt:

> Carlos Robles, you have been tried by twelve good men, not men of yore peers, but as high above you as heaven is of hell, and they've said you're guilty of rustlin' cattle. Time will pass and seasons will soon come and go; Spring with its wavin' green grass and heaps of sweet-smellin' flowers on every hill and in every dale. Then will come sultry Summer, with her shimmerin' heat-waves on the baked horizon; and Fall, with her yeller harvest-moon and the hills grown' brown and golden under a sinkin' sun; finally Winter, with its bitin', whinin' wind, and all the land will be mantled with snow. But you won't be here to see any of 'em, Carlos Robles; not by a dam' sight, because it's the order of this court that you be took to the nearest tree and hanged by the neck till you're dead, dead, dead, you olive-colored son-of-a-billy-goat! (p. 136)

Hanging Judge Parker fares equally well to the task of slander against a Mexican for his national origin:

> And then, Jose Manuel Xavier Gonzales, I command further that such officer or officers retire quietly from your swinging, dangling corpse, that the vultures may descend from the heavens upon your filthy body and pick the putrid flesh therefrom till nothing remains but the bare, bleached bones of a cold-blooded, copper-colored, blood-thirsty, chili-eating, guilty, sheep-herding, Mexican son-of-a-bitch. (*A Treasury of American Folklore*, p. 148)

13. Erna Fergusson, *New Mexico: A Pageant of Three Peoples* (New York: Alfred Knopf, 1951), p. 380.

14. Although the quote is somewhat out of context, it is appropriate to include since much of the other information he presents seems credible. See Edward Simmen, *The Chicano: From Caricature to Self-Portrait* (Bergenfield, N.J.: The New American Library, 1971), p. 25.

15. The enlightening study by Russel Saxton uncovers much valuable information on the subject of historiography, its development and what attitudes prevailed, despite the many attempts to camouflage them. See "Ethnocentrism in the Historical Literature of Territorial New Mexico," Ph.D. diss., University of New Mexico, 1980.

16. This interesting concept is developed by Franklin Walker in his work *A Literary History of Southern California* (Berkeley: University of California, 1950).

17. It is worth noting that Stanley T. Williams in *The Spanish Background of American Literature* (New Haven: Yale University Press, 1955) does not recognize any Southwestern works per se as legitimate pieces of literature when he states:

> Ultimately all this tangled weave form a lively expression in the nineteenth and twentieth centuries, chiefly in fiction and in works which were at once historical, descriptive, and interpretative. One might wonder why the early *relaciones* or the *documentos* or the *autos* produced during the era of the missions no authentic piece of great Spanish literature in the Southwest. . . . But nonreligious writing was sometimes burned in the courts of the missions. Soon after the law of secularization in 1833 the tide of American invaders flowed through the Southwest, contemptuous of everything which might have inspired an indigenous poet, novelist, or dramatist. (p. 212)

18. See Edwin S. Fussell, *Frontier: American Literature and the American West* (Princeton: Princeton University Press, 1965).

19. The first article appears in *La Palabra*, 2, No. 1 (Spring 1980):2–15, and the second study is in

Chicano Literature: A Reference Guide (Westport, Conn.: Greenwood Press, 1985), pp. 244–60, coedited by Julio A. Martínez and Francisco A. Lomelí.

20. These constitute the most commonly known literary forms that were already prevalent during the Colonial period and maintained constant through the twentieth century. For further explanation see Luis Leal's articles "Hispanic-Mexican Literature in the Southwest, 1521–1848," as cited in footnote 19, and "Mexican American Literature, 1848–1942" (*Chicano Literature: A Reference Guide*, pp. 280–99).

21. See the introductory comments by Armando Miguélez in his Ph.D. diss., "Antología histórica del cuento literario chicano (1877–1950)," Arizona State University, 1981.

22. Aurelio M. Espinosa is particularly outstanding in his arduous collections of *corridos* and *canciones* in *Folklore nuevomejicano y cancionero nuevomejicano* and "Romancero nuevomejicano" (1915); he also excelled in his numerous studies on language from the state. On one occasion in 1915, he commented on the state of the Spanish language:

> El elemento inglés que entró en 1846 y que ya se comienza a sentir, no ha cambiado todavía el lenguaje de los descendientes de raza española, y la tradición española vive en Nuevo Méjico como en cualquier otro país español. En la nueva generación, sin embargo, ya se puede observar un nuevo desarrollo. El idioma inglés, absolutamente necesario para el comercio, las escuelas públicas, donde se enseña solamente el inglés, en fin, la vida americana con todas sus instituciones inglesas, van haciendo desaperecer poco á poco el elemento tradicional español.
>
> [The English element, which entered in 1846 and now begins to make its presence felt, has not yet changed the language of the people of Hispanic descent, and the Hispanic tradition thrives in New Mexico like in any other Hispanic country. Among the new generation, however, one can now observe a new development. The English language—absolutely necessary for commerce—and the public schools where it is taught, plus American life with all its English institutions, are making the traditional Spanish element disappear little by little.] ("Romancero nuevomejicano" in *Revue Hispanique*, 33 [1915]:446–560)

Juan B. Rael distinguishes himself for the voluminous collections of folk tales in *Cuentos españoles de Colorado y Nuevo México* (Stanford: The Stanford University Press, 1957) consisting of two volumes and an amazing 1,378 pages. Aurora Lucero White-Lea has made valuable contributions in the area of diversified compilations of folklore in *Literary Folklore of the Hispanic Southwest* (San Antonio: Naylor Co., 1953). Arturo L. Campa is well recognized for his work *Spanish Folk-Poetry in New Mexico* (Albuquerque: The University of New Mexico Press, 1946).

23. For further information on the subject, consult Anselmo F. Arellano's unpublished study "The Rise of Mutual Aid Societies Among New Mexico's Spanish-Speaking During the Territorial Period" and Peter A. Stratton's *The Territorial Press of New Mexico, 1834–1912* (Albuquerque: The University of New Mexico Press, 1969). Arellano's article is cited with his permission.

24. Extracted from Aurelio M. Espinosa's "Romancero nuevomejicano" which appears in *Revue Hispanique*, 333, (1915):446–560. As compiler of this *décima*, he states having received it in writing from Sr. Cándido Ortiz from Santa Fe.

25. *Ibid.*, p. 526. The poem, from which this is just the beginning fragment, is attributed to Simón Gutiérrez, as compiled by Aurelio M. Espinosa.

26. Stratton, *Territorial Press*, p. 5.

27. *Ibid.*, p. 24.

28. *Ibid.*, p. 25.

29. Cecil Robinson, *Mexico and the Hispanic Southwest in American Literature* (Tucson: The University of Arizona Press, 1977), p. 137. This edition represents a revision of *With the Ears of Strangers*, originally from 1963.

30. Anselmo F. Arellano is perhaps the scholar who best summarizes the types of poetry found in the newspapers of the period in an unpublished study "Historical Sketch of Culture and Society in Las

Vegas During the 1880s" as part of his forthcoming dissertation "La Merced: The Las Vegas Land Grant and Its Colonizers," which we cite with his consent.

31. See Anselmo F. Arellano's pivotal collection of poetry and personal biographies in *Los pobladores nuevo mexicanos y su poesía, 1889–1950* (Albuquerque: Pajarito Publications, 1976), p. 13.

32. Arellano, *Los pobladores nuevo mexicanos*, p. 37.

33. The list has been composed from Anselmo F. Arellano's book in conjunction with the names provided by Benjamín B. Read in *Historia ilustrada de Nuevo México* (1910). Other additions that appear after 1900, or before 1880, might be Don Jorge Ramírez, Antonio J. Martínez, Vicente Bernal, Don Pedro Bautista Pino, José Inés García, Felipe M. Chacón, Conchita Argüello, Nina Otero, Phillip N. Sánchez, Eusebio Chacón, Aurora Lucero White-Lea, José F. Fernández, Néstor Montoya, Jovita Gonzales, Josefina Escajeda, N. Faustín Gallegos, José Gonzales and Félix Martínez. Also, consult Doris L. Meyer's "Anonymous Poetry in Spanish-Language New Mexico Newspapers (1880–1900)," *The Bilingual Review/La Revista Bilingüe*, 2 (1975), 259–275.

34. See footnote 21.

35. The doctoral dissertation is from the University of Arizona, 1984.

36. Arellano, "The Rise of Mutual Aid Societies . . . ," p. 7.

37. The entire list of societies has been extracted from Anselmo F. Arellano's article "The Rise of Mutual Aid Societies . . ." To understand some of the society's inner workings, we highly recommend perusal of the constitution found and reproduced by Arellano in a special issue of *De Colores*, 1, No. 3 (1974):5–18.

38. The point deserves reiterating with the following quote that supports our contention:

> Ignorance in literature, which existed among our people during a remote period, has disappeared forever, and in its place we find a youthful generation which is growing in education, culture, and intellectual development. We believe that the palpitating question on the Castilian language should not be an obstacle, whether it be in form of a pretext, which might impede our right to statehood, although it is certain that the United States government through the present epoch has accepted the use of the Castilian language. Our beautiful language originated in Castile and our natural dialect has been used in New Mexico before and after these lands were acquired by the American government, and each day it becomes more necessary and important to use it among ourselves; and to make it disappear from the American continent shall be a major obstacle.

The quote appears in *El Combate*, a newspaper from Wagon Mound, New Mexico, on December 6, 1902, which was translated by Anselmo F. Arellano.

39. Appears in *La Voz del Pueblo* (other pertinent bibliographical information unknown) and the translation is provided by Anselmo F. Arellano.

40. Although providing lists of the books that seemed to circulate in the region might lead us into the area of erroneous speculation, we consider it worthwhile to offer the following list of authors and works that were either found in personal libraries or were mentioned in book catalogs, or book jackets, assuming they became available. From the list, we can at least begin to ascertain the literary tastes of the times that might have had an impact on the writers. We submit only the fragmented information that has been compiled, recognizing that much remains to be accomplished in this area of inquiry:

1. Spanish novelist Fernán Caballero's novel (?) *Deudas pagadas* [Paid Debts] in *La Revista Católica* (1875).
2. Carlota M. Braeme, *Por el pecado ageno o la lucha de amor* (Another's Sin or the Struggle of Love), translated by Bachiller Sansón Carrasco (Barcelona: Casa Editorial Maucci, 1900).
3. D.J.M. Ramírez, *Avelina y Gabriela* (Paris: Librería de Rosa y Bouret, 1864).
4. I.A., *Su majestad el amor* [Love, His Majesty] (Barcelona: Casa Editorial Lezcano, n.d.).
5. Possibly other works by Casa Editorial Lezcano: *Malditas sean las mujeres (Women Be Damned), Malditos sean los hombres, (Men Be Damned), Malditas sean las suegras*

(Mothers-In-Law Be Damned), Marina o la hija de las Olas (Marina or the Waves' Daughter), El hada de los mares (The Fairytale of the Seas), El paraíso de las mujeres (Women's Paradise), El infierno de los hombres (Men's Hell), El purgatorio de las solteras (The Bachelorette's Purgatory) and *La hija de las flores* (The Daughter of Flowers).

6. Carlota M. Braeme, *Dora* and also *Azucena*.
7. George Sand, *La ciudad negra* (The Black City).
8. Victor Hugo, *Noventa y tres* (Ninety-three).
9. Victor Hugo, *Los trabajadores del mar* (Workers from the Sea).
10. Victor Hugo, *El hombre que ríe* (The Man Who Laughs).
11. Chateaubriand, *Atala, René* and *El último Abencerraje* (3 novels).
12. Jorge Isaacs, *María*.
13. E.J. de Goncourt, *Sor Filomena*.
14. A. Dudet, *Fromont y Risler*.
15. A. Belot, *La Señorita Girand, mi mujer* (Miss Girand, My Wife).
16. Spanish literature of all sorts, especially some of the masterpieces from the Spanish Golden Age such as *Don Quixote*, the picaresque novel, drama, some current Modernist poetry from Latin America and *costumbrista* (relating to customs and local color) literature from Mexico (i.e. Ignacio M. Altamirano).
17. English writers such as Shakespeare, Shelley, and Byron and other classics by Greeks and Latins.
18. It is noteworthy to mention that the *Trinidad Chronicle* and *El Progreso* in Trinidad, Colorado, in 1898 reproduced for readers the Southwest classic *Historia de la Nueva México* (1610) by Villagrá in a series form which clearly attests to the sophistication among the readership and the respective literary tastes of the times.

7

EUSEBIO CHACÓN
An Early Pioneer of the New Mexican Novel

FRANCISCO LOMELÍ

In evaluating Hispanic literary productivity, some scholarly attention has been given to popular poetic forms and theatre. However, the novel has received little critical discussion before 1972, when Rudolfo A. Anaya's *Bless Me, Ultima* contributed to breaking the silence. This does not mean that the genre did not exist before 1972, but rather, it can be translated as an indictment of critics who generally responded with indifference to the novels written by Hispanics in New Mexico. In order to identify and better assess the works of early Hispanic novelists in a context proper to their social milieu, scholars interested in the topic have had to engage in a process of historical and literary reconstruction. In this context the vindication of a figure such as Eusebio Chacón acquires new meaning because he represents a pioneer of the Hispanic novel of New Mexico.

Numerous other novelists have been recently discovered, thus giving credence to the notion that the Hispanic novel in the region did enjoy a measure of respectability. At least four known authors mark different approaches within the twenty-year period of 1880 to 1900: Manuel M. Salazar is recognized as one of the first novelists, although his manuscript "La historia de un caminante, o sea, Gervacio y Aurora" from 1881 remains unpublished; Eusebio Chacón claims to be the first novelist in 1892 with his two short novels *El hijo de la tempestad* (Son of the Storm) and *Tras la tormenta la calma* (Calmness after the Storm); Manuel

C. de Baca contributed a chronicle or historical novel in 1896 titled *Historia de Vicente Silva y sus cuarenta bandidos, sus crímenes y retribuciones* (The story of Vicente Silva and His Forty Bandits, Their Crimes and Retributions); and Porfirio Gonzales wrote *Historia de un cautivo* (The Story of a Captive) in 1898.[1]

The work of Eusebio Chacón serves well to unveil a key period of literary gestation in New Mexico. Although barely acknowledged—and now only somewhat vindicated—almost one hundred years after the publication of his two novels, it is perhaps more accurate to portray him as one writer among a cluster, instead of as an exception. Part of a dynamic period, he best exemplifies his time as a writer, spokesman, participant in his community, and promoter of literature, particularly the novel. Born on December 16, 1869, in Peñasco, New Mexico, he lived his formative years in the territory of Colorado, a region still viewed as a cultural extension of Hispanic New Mexico. A highly educated man, having received his undergraduate degree at a Jesuit College in Las Vegas, New Mexico, and his law degree from Notre Dame in 1889, he gained a rapid reputation for his multiple talents.[2] He achieved early acclaim as an orator, a public defender and an interpreter-translator for the U.S. courts having to do with land grants. His prominence grew as a direct result of his civic and literary activities. Less known as a poet, his incisive flair in the essay became his trademark in numerous newspaper columns and in meetings of *sociedades* at the moment that his Hispanic pride was the object of attacks made by an influx of contemptuous Anglo-American settlers. He was generally regarded as mild-mannered and judicious. A sign of feistiness, however, is evident in his essays whenever he is witness to distortion or unfair treatment.

For example, in 1901 when a Protestant missionary, Nellie Snider, launched an inflammatory campaign against Hispanos from Las Vegas, specifically Catholics, he rose to the occasion to refute her arguments as if he were a public defender of his people and their cultural background. In a famous speech, he demonstrates a breadth of knowledge, an assertive determination, and a keen appreciation of the historical significance of the situation. His words in a meeting known as "La Junta de Indignación 1901" (The Rally of Indignation 1901) ring with vigor and purpose *à la* Clarence Darrow:

> El sentido de dicho artículo es que los Hispano-Americanos somos una gente sucia, ignorante y degradada . . . a quienes la falta de luz evangélica tiene siempre en retroceso, y a quienes la fiebre sectaria reclama para espiritualizer con sus dogmas. . . . En fin, la primera parte de dicho escrito es un extravagante derroche de fantasía, es como diría Carlyle, una diarrea de palabras. Pero como de gustos no hay nada escrito, pasemos por alto estas extravagancias y entremos en materia. . . . Pero volviendo a los disparates de nuestra escritora, después de medir puertas y ventanas con su vara pasa a nuestras cocinas, y allí penetra con evangélica institución hasta en

los misterios del chile y de las tortillas. A las tortillas las encuentra indigestas, como quien dice, la señora ha atacado una proposición teológica más abstracta que las que robaban el sueño al apóstol San Pablo. Y que hay que sospechar que a la señora se le olvidaba que ella misma muchas mañanas, ha comido tortillas americanas, es decir, esas gamuzas terribles de la zartén (sic) que llaman *pan cakes*. . . . Como queda ya indicado, no es ésta la primera vez que el pueblo de Nuevo México se hace blanco de ataques tan gratuitos como injustificados. . . . Las pocas instituciones de educación que hay entre nosotros, son obra de nuestro propio trabajo. . . . Allí no hay ni un solo centavo de nuestro gobierno nacional . . . y aunque todavía el nombre de ningún Neo-Mexicano haya llenado el orbe con su fama, no estamos tan dejados de Dios por acá como nos pintan algunos escritores que pasan por entre nosotros como caballeros apocalípticos, con la copa de hiel en una mano y la guadaña del odio en la otra. Será esto con la esperanza de que nuestra petición no sea oída, y que sigamos en el precario estado de parias nacionales? Pueblo de Nuevo México, si tu destino es solo ser bestia de carga; si has de permanecer en el triste tutelaje de gobierno que hasta ahora has tenido; si no has de tomar parte en los asuntos públicos de esta nación, que es la tuya . . . tiempo es ya que levantes tus penates, y los lleves, con los restos de tus antepasados, a otra patria más hospitalaria. No te falta talento, no te falta energía. . . . Si la patria en donde duerme tu Diego de Vargas no tiene ya esperanzas para tus hijos, mira que el mundo es grande, el mundo es bueno, el mundo es generoso. Busca un país donde puedas ser dueño de tu destino.[3]

[The sense of the aforementioned article is that we Spanish-Americans are a dirty, ignorant and degraded people . . . whose lack of evangelical light puts them in a backward motion, and whose sectarian fever clamors for spiritualization with its dogmas. . . . Finally, the first part of the mentioned article is an extravagant squandering of fantasy; it is, as Carlyle would say, a diarrhea of words. But since nothing is written about tastes, allow us to overlook these extravaganzas and may we deal with the subject at hand. . . . But returning to the nonsense of our woman writer, after measuring doors and windows with her yardstick, she has gone on to our kitchens and from there has penetrated with an evangelical practice into the mysteries of chile and tortillas. She finds the tortillas indigestible, or as they say, the lady has attacked a more abstract theological proposition than the ones that took the apostle Saint Paul's sleep away from him. And one must suspect that this lady herself has forgotten many a morning that she has eaten American tortillas, that is, those terrible leathery cakes they call "pan cakes." As already stated, this is not the first time that the people of New Mexico became the target of such gratuitous as well as unjustified attacks. . . . The few educational institutions that exist among us are a product of our own work. . . . There we find not even a single penny of our national government . . . and although as of yet no New Mexican has achieved fame in the world, we are not as abandoned by God around these parts as some writers portray us, passing among us like apocalyptic gentlemen with the cup of bile in one hand and the scythe of hate in the other. Are we to understand that our hope will not suffice to have our petition heard, and that we should continue in our precarious state as national pariahs? People of New Mexico, if your destiny is to only be a beast of burden; if you are to remain in the sad government tutelage that you have had up to now; if you are not to participate in the public matters of this nation, which is as

> much yours, . . . it is now time that you pick up your household gods, and take them, along with the remains of your ancestors, to another more hospitable nation. You neither lack talent nor energy. . . . If your country where Diego de Vargas sleeps no longer offers hope to your offspring, look around you that the world is large, the world is good, the world is generous. Seek out a country where you can be master of your destiny.]

The excerpts reveal that Chacón assumes a combative spirit when he finds himself engulfed in some of the politically sensitive issues of his region. There can remain no doubt about his convictions and the ideological stance that thrust him into public prominence as a spokesman.

TEXTS AND CONTEXT

Along with relative prosperity, a political and economic division developed between rich and poor and between Anglo Americans and Hispanic inhabitants. The year 1889 was characterized by the polarized elements of an incipient civil war. The atmosphere of boosterism attracted waves of new Anglo settlers. Racial tension was on a definite upswing as cultural differences defined interests. The Hispanic sector began to sense a creeping threat and a possible change in the balance of power. A secret organization, *Gorras Blancas* (White Caps), was created to intimidate and resist Anglo-American encroachment. Cutting fences and destroying property, they intended to instill fear. Cross-firings and confused alliances contributed to a greater volatility. According to Robert J. Rosenbaum in *Mexicano Resistance in the Southwest* (1981), the main themes aired in New Mexico newspapers around 1890 can be reduced to sentiments against despotism and monopoly.[4] Of particular relevance to Chacon's first novel, *El hijo de la tempestad* from 1892, is Rosenbaum's observation about the newspaper *La Voz del Pueblo*:

> . . . in its continual denials of any connection between the Knights [or Los Caballeros de Labor] and violence, *La Voz* [*del Pueblo*] never failed to stress that the real villains in New Mexico were not the "vandals or masked highwaymen" but the "despotic oppressors . . . hidden technically by the law. . . . "[5]

The Caballeros of Labor, an organization resembling a labor union and somewhat of an insurance company, developed during this period to defend its members, the majority of whom were Democrats. They represent one faction within a polarized society that was experiencing highly charged sentiments about a wide gamut of regional concerns. The fundamental problem lies in that all sides sought to point out someone else as responsible for such unbridled violence. What was at stake were issues of power, possible control, and future hegemony. The various conflicting interests created agendas and clouded subtle shifts in the moral fiber of a changing society. The region was suffering growth pains in a framework of struggle between coexistence and cooptation.

ARS POETICA: THE VENGEANCE OF POETIC JUSTICE

In coping with two distinct activities, Chacón was actively engaged in reflecting the makeup of his social environment as well as exercising his creative impulse. However, his central concern was not to propose dichotomies, but rather to offer conflicting entities of a bipolar nature. This dialectical interplay manifests itself in his two novels that appeared in 1892: *El hijo de la tempestad* is characterized by an overriding tension and conflict as a result of different forms of banditry, while *Tras la tormenta la calma* represents an about-face from the semi-Realist mode and indulges in literary experimentation in order to examine the concept of honor. Together, they attest to Chacón's versatility as a writer, as well as to the wide spectrum of his personal interests.

Published at the same time, the two works deliberately advance a joint purpose: they consciously set out to establish the novel as a new genre to the region and they serve to disclose political, cultural, and behavioral dilemmas of his people. He recognizes, in the Dedication (which also operates as a preface), the significance of his undertaking as the first novelist and he directly addresses literary disenfranchisement by Anglo or foreign circles, claiming his works as a product of *his own* fantasy:

> Son creación genuina de mi propia fantasía y no robadas ni prestadas de gabachos ni extranjeros. Sobre el suelo Nuevo Mexicano me atrevo á cimentar la semilla de la literatura recreativa para que si después otros autores de más feliz ingenio que el mío siguen el camino que aquí trazo, puedan volver hacia el pasado la vista y señalarme como el primero que emprendió tan áspero camino.[6]
>
> [They [the novels] are a genuine creation of my own fantasy and not stolen nor borrowed from *gabachos* [Anglos] or foreigners. I dare lay the foundations or the seed of an entertaining literature on New Mexican soil so that if other authors of a more fortunate ability later follow the road I hereby outline, may they look back on the past and single me out as the first to undertake such a rough road.]

Composed within the tradition of a literary *manifesto*, the Dedication merits close scrutiny. First, his initial comments are filled with words that reflect a restrained hostility toward outsiders even as he claims that what he writes is neither a copy nor an imitation. His emphatic statement can only mean that he wishes to declare a literary emancipation for himself and his people. Although it might seem a false presumptuousness on his part to designate himself the originator of "recreative literature"—here meaning the novel—he must have felt compelled to create the "authentic New Mexican novel," therefore defiantly contrasting his work with Anglo-American literature. He characterizes his accomplishments as having paved a rough path for others to follow. His daring attitude might invite complications, but it seems the best way to avoid outside impositions in canon. His language in the Dedication is generally metaphoric and rarely explicit, and thus obscures his true feelings. Responding as a self-aware literary pioneer, his concluding statements also offer advice on how to complete a novel and avoid superfluous characters in the story. He succinctly justifies his use of the novella form: that is, he wishes to use oral tradition as a backdrop in order to transform what he terms "literatura recreativa" into a conscious form of written literature. With his literature he strives to provide enjoyment and construct a social situation that will stimulate a judgment from the reader. "Literatura recreativa" means to Chacón all that "recreation" connoted to Miguel de Cervantes when he theorized about the novel as a genre; in other words, he saw in the novel both delight and reproduction. His underlying purpose is to transcend the obvious so that the works may be decoded and interpreted on various levels.

IN THE EYE OF THE STORM

In the first novel, *El hijo de la tempestad* (Son of the Storm), Chacón hopes to carry out the mission stated in the Dedication. His principal objective is to create a "New Mexican novel," selectively choosing from a diverse range of literary preferences. The storyline functions as a faithful mirror of the prevalent chaos in his region, and its composition gives testimony to actual events witnessed by the author. This work, then, embodies a writer's perspective on social problems, while at the same time exhibiting inspiration in fantasy. Both literature and history become fused with the purposeful design of grappling with the complexities of his times. His proximity and attachment to the events, plus his rejection of negative foreign elements, oblige him to become even more entrenched in Hispanic literary tradition. The primary source that gives impetus to, and provides a framework for, the story is the oral tradition.

El hijo de la tempestad is filled with contradictions and mixed messages. Characterized by internal conflicts and antithetical elements, most of the novel unfolds as a dynamic struggle between forces of Evil and Good. True to a

Romantic novel, triumph of Good seems secondary. It seems more vital to Chacón to critically expose the forces of Evil in operation. If the novelist's only intent had been to denounce outlaws, he would not have chosen a villain as his protagonist and used him to disapprove of an outlaw's influence or power. Chacón resorts to allegory to show the genesis of an outlaw and associates him with the underground that becomes institutionalized in a political system. In this sense, the novel's initial fantastic scenes later acquire significance as they become the setting wherein a deplorable political situation is unveiled. In short, the outlaw protagonist represents a true menace, but the petty and corrupt politicians, by comparison, are deemed far worse. The novel ceases to operate as a literary diatribe against a certain type of outlaw because its ultimate objective is to formulate a view of the origins of corruption, evil, and power. Chacón, then, has carefully structured a political allegory in a Romantic-Naturalist mode that fits literary tastes of the times in Mexico, Latin America, and Spain. As an integral part of the literature exploring the outlaw as a social outcast, the work follows trends then in vogue at the same time that it pinpoints intricacies of local phenomenon.

The novel bears witness to the breakdown of social values that Chacón perceived in his society. According to one of the principal authorities on bandits, Eric Hobsbawm, banditry is symptomatic of the tension and crisis that appeals to major social movements for change.[7] Unlike what Germans term *Rauberromantik* ("bandit romanticism"),[8] the New Mexican novelist does not pretend to portray a social bandit, nor is idealization in order. Instead, he transports the story from the realm of popular myth and ballad to the realm of historical consciousness in order to bring attention to the regional problems that breed anarchy. The confused purposes and ambivalent resolutions challenge the reader to unravel the complex set of circumstances. We are led to see the protagonist as a rebel without a cause and the symbol of a cause without rebellion. The impasse allows Chacón to situate his story within a fable that parallels contradictory perceptions of a rapidly changing society. Old patterns of traditional alliances along cultural lines were suddenly challenged as irrelevant. It was no longer easy to determine who was what, as masquerading and assuming double identities became common practices. This is illustrated by bandits involved in double-agent activities in Manuel C. de Baca's historical novel or chronicle titled *Historia de Vicente Silva y sus cuarenta bandidos, sus crímenes y retribuciones* (1896) (*The Story of Vicente Silva and His Forty Thieves, Their Crimes and Retributions*). Vicente Silva, the ring leader and also a police officer, utilized his office as a public front in Las Vegas, New Mexico, his double-dealing eventually attaining legendary proportions. It became impossible to make justice and law synonymous; as a result justice outside of the law gained popularity. Therefore, the confused nature of rampant violence and anarchy degenerated into hidden warfare. Mixed purposes contributed to the overall chaos, thus confirming that the region experienced a serious social imbalance. The situation, as described in an excerpt from Manuel C. de Baca's book, may well explain part of the *Zeitgeist* and specifically serve to better contextualize Chacón's source of inspiration for his novel:

> Around the year 1892, the County of San Miguel was terrified by these incidents. The army of bandits that Silva commanded committed every possible kind of abuse, and the garrison of police charged with keeping the peace, maintaining order and keeping respect for the law unfortunately was counted among Silva's ranks.[9]

Both Chacón and C. de Baca focus on the same phenomenon in their indictment of outlaws, except that the former attempts to express in more literary terms what is part of a local oral tradition. Chacón's work is literature trying to comment on history, while C. de Baca's is history trying to assume literary trappings.

In *El hijo de la tempestad* the text relies heavily on oral tradition for some of its conventions in developing the storyline and characterization. Filled with fanciful flairs, the descriptions have the lack of logic generally rendered in Romantic works. A freedom of associations occurs, almost whimsically, that distorts the central storyline while injecting fantastic elements in order to enhance interest. At the root of the narrative, one can detect an interplay between what the author considers an integral voice in popular lore and a narrator with literary ambitions within the written tradition. Folklore, for example, already contains numerous cases of a son who rebels against his parents, a common theme in the *romances* "El hijo desobediente" (The Disobedient Son) and "El hijo pródigo" (The Prodigal Son). In Chacón's novel, this figure is modified considerably by stating that the son's innate fierceness killed his mother at the moment of birth. Destiny, free will, and the presence of supernatural elements contribute to highlight the action more than the content of the story. In addition, Chacón has the father abandon his son, turning him over to a gypsy woman, who is also a sorceress. If the child was born with preordained violence as a natural tendency, circumstances beyond his control do not help correct his ways; on the contrary, he is predestined to act in the name of Evil. T. M. Pearce, in "The Bad Son (El Mal Hijo) in Southwestern Spanish Folklore," points out this situation as one of the motifs of Southwestern folklore.[10] The main difference in Chacón's "hijo de la tempestad" is that the deformity Pearce refers to as essential for the "Mal Hijo" syndrome is not physical but psychological. As Cain figures, both the "Mal Hijo" and Chacón's protagonist function as prototypes that are cursed from the moment they appear on earth.[11]

The bandit, especially in the nineteenth century, was an easily recognizable Romantic motif. He operated, knowingly or unknowingly, for the good of an improved society. Seen as an indomitable idealist, the bandit generally enjoyed a positive reputation in literature and was often the source of inspiration for many popular songs. From a New Mexico newspaper of 1893, the following excerpt supports the popularization of such figures and could correspond to Chacón's nameless protagonist. The innovative feature here is that the bandit explains his own situation from a personal perspective; that is, it is not an external judgment but rather a confession on why he feels compelled to fight back.

Tantos males los hombres me han hecho
Que he perdido la fe y la esperanza;
He jurado exterminio y venganza,
Y mi voto fatal cumpliré.
. . .

[Men have caused me so much harm
That I have lost both faith and hope;
Swearing extermination and vengeance,
And my fatal wish I shall fulfill.
. . .

Cuando ruge con ímpetu el trueno
Y retiembla la tierra de espanto,
Sólo se oye en las rocas mi canto,
Y a mis pies viene el rayo a morir.

When thunder roars with force
And the earth trembles with fright,
Only my song is heard among the rocks,
And the thunderbolt lands dead at my feet.

De cien bravos se forma mi banda
Y obedecen mi altiva mirada,
Sólo allá en mi cabaña apartada,
Aparece mi rostro feroz.[12]

One hundred brave ones comprise my gang
And all obey my haughty glance,
Only yonder in my faraway cabin,
Does my ferocious face show perchance.]

Even the title *El hijo de la tempestad* reveals the close affinity between the popular versions of *romances* and Chacón's work. In the novel, as in the *romances*, the protagonist has no name because the goal of this type of literature is to provide a didactic framework. The main character is not at all sure who his parents really are, except that they are identified as "un hombre y una mujer," [a man and a woman] thus reinforcing prototypical qualities. His parents are only biological; in reality, his environment and the gypsy woman act as surrogate parents. In this way, the author utilizes the character as a symbol for the pernicious effect of the social environment on the individual.

Modeled within Romantic aesthetics, the opening scene aims to establish a mournful atmosphere of suspense and danger in the midst of a terrifying storm. Charged conditions add to the drama of a couple that seeks refuge from the threatening elements, and their pursuit of refuge becomes even more urgent because the mother is about to give birth. Hyperbole abounds to make the story more enticing. Escaping from the jagged mountain peaks and the perils of the storm, the couple enters a cave. As an opening scene, it captivates the reader, much in the same way that it would captivate a listener if the story were being rendered orally. The narrative effectiveness would probably be greater if told aloud. After the predictable beginning, the storyline follows patterns preestablished by popular tradition. In a parallel situation, simultaneous to the couple's taking refuge in the cave, a gypsy woman sings a prophecy in a nearby town about a boy's birth. She warns the townspeople against taking in the child because he is destined to be evil and the terror of the region. Therefore, when the father goes to town with the child—grieved by his wife's death but happy about his son's birth—to seek help, the gypsy accepts the child. A strong sense of determinism prevails for a boy born "en una noche sin estrellas" [on a starless night] whose only influences will supposedly be of a negative and evil nature.

Various other folklore techniques are employed to inject interest in the unfolding of the story. For example, fantastic duels between the gypsy and another mysterious woman, referred to only as "Sombra de la Luz" [Shadow of Light], take place to settle who is to keep custody of the child since each claims the sole rights to him. Relying on different interpretations of scriptures, they argue their points from contrasting views: the gypsy woman believes that the evil child is not meant to die but rather to unleash his will on an impoverished people; the other woman wants to eliminate him for being a child of the devil. Although questionable in their logic, the arguments make entertaining reading; yet as a teaching device they tend to infuse fear. Other absurd figures are used to reiterate the sense of evil as something omnipresent. For example, a monkey serves as companion to the gypsy woman and it inexplicably metamorphoses into a greater devil figure who overpowers the woman "Sombra de la Luz" (Shadow of Light). The diabolical scene closes when the latter—in a typical metaphoric representation of ridding evil—is swallowed when the earth parts. The fable switches to a visual emphasis to describe the day darkening and the earth rumbling. Designating the end of the second part of the novel, this theatrical abruptness contrasts well with the dramatic series of events that are replete with free associations and poetic liberties found mainly in the oral *cuento* tradition.

The last three parts of the novel are by comparison low-key, consisting essentially of the bandit's misdeeds, the terrorism he carries out, and his enslavement of a young lady. Ignoring explanations or any cause-and-effect relationships, a shift or flash forward in time of almost twenty years is evident. The narrative simply makes the leap from the gypsy's predictions to the point where they become fulfilled: the young man does in fact become barbaric and evil. Folk myth further fuels the narrative when the protagonist surrounds himself with one hundred thieves, bringing to mind Ali Baba's forty thieves. Operating out of the cave in which he was born, the "hijo de la tempestad" has completed a circle to his origins, now using the cave as a complex system of labyrinthine paths to the underground. Urged on by insatiable greed, he leads his group in the sacking of communities. A completely amoral character, his domination seems unchallenged until he kills the young woman's father (who was also enslaved) and attempts to rush the wedding with the disapproving maiden. These two events mark his final *faux pas* and subsequently lead to his downfall. Love might have redeemed him, but his wretched nature makes him incapable of even entertaining that alternative. The bandit's indictment reaches a conclusion only after he targets his vengeance on a defenseless victim and threatens her honor. The denouement has him succumb to rescue forces who surprise the thieves and kill him.

Most of the story shows a close affinity with folklore and legendary narratives. The death of the infamous leader at the end becomes incorporated again into a realm of myth, thus serving as a moral device. Another nameless person, a captain, who is responsible for his death, serves as the center of focus at the end of the novel as the local people recall past horrors. Resembling Cervantes' *Novelas ejemplares* (Exemplary Novels), the final scene consists of the captain telling his curious audience the whereabouts of the gypsy: "Pues sabed que se la llevó el diablo, a lo más profundo de los infiernos. . . . Tiénela allí barriendo el aposento que deben ocupar ciertos politicastros que traen a la patria muy revuelta . . . " (29). [Well, knoweth that the devil took her away to the deepest part of hell. He has her there sweeping the chamber that should be occupied by certain petty politicians who have the country in upheaval.] The captain's revelation is startling in terms of its implications for a social situation characterized by rampant lawlessness. The key significance here is that the reference goes beyond the story we just read. Chacón indeed does not condone violence, thus avoiding the idealization of the bandit figure. Instead, he utilizes this despicable character to establish the grounds for a more sweeping indictment against the squandering politicians who, by comparison, are responsible for the region's plight. The author now singles out the false heroes who hide behind the lawlessness and accuses them of being the true perpetuators of social dissolution and turmoil. In sum, the novel begins as a fable or an allegory, continues with a chain of fantastic associations common in popular storytelling, and finishes with a social commentary of redeemable value for Chacón's times.

THE LAWS OF HONOR: A ROULETTE OF IRONY

Characterized by a totally different approach, Chacón's second novel, *Tras la tormenta la calma* (Calmness After the Storm), aspires more toward aesthetic ends. He again sets out to implement another facet of the literary emancipation he defended so vehemently in the introductory manifesto. His concept of writing novels acquires new meaning: the emphasis on his own "*fantasía*" (fantasy) now refers to a renewed sense of eclecticism between English and Spanish literatures as viewed from a local perspective. The literary exercise develops into a form of syncretism tempered by a bicultural experience. While openly acknowledging his two influences, and particularly relishing Hispanic tradition, Chacón links the two together and cultivates them as one that he considers New Mexican. As a writer, he is conscious of the unique situation of creating a regional novel in Spanish, and his work emerges with force and conviction. If his first work entailed a noncompromising diagnosis of social problems pertaining to his region, *Tras la tormenta la calma* presents dilemmas of the heart, emotional predicaments of the sort that feed intrigue. Whereas the first novel deals with unbridled chaos on a collective scale, the second one reflects a state of affairs on a more subjective level. Together, both works accomplish complementing ends: one anticipates a social upheaval on the magnitude of the Mexican Revolution; the other provides a vision of social disintegration and the hope of establishing new values.

Although *Tras la tormenta la calma* might be termed escapist in nature, part of its essential motive is to promote an urban *costumbrista* (local color) novel. The many models, such as Don Juan Tenorio, Bécquer, the typical themes of the Spanish Golden Age theater (i.e., honor, personal nobility versus class nobility, love versus infatuation), Espronceda, and George Byron, can be easily identified. These established literary sources account for a majority of the influences, but Chacón again incorporates one other undeniable source: oral tradition. In numerous instances, the author borrows from both oral and written tradition to give his plot and his characters a degree of popular verisimilitude. For example, he emphasizes the unique and remarkable beauty of *morena* (brown-skinned) women, which coincides perfectly with an anonymous song, "Mi gusto" (My Taste), that was in fashion in New Mexico in 1892:

No me hables por Dios! así . . .	*[Don't speak to me that way, by God . . .*
¿Por qué me hablas al revés?	*Why do you speak to me backwards?*
Di con tu boquita 'sí';	*With your little mouth, say 'sí';*
Pero no me digas 'yes'.	*But please don't tell me 'yes.'*
. . .	. . .
Que yo, a las mexicanitas,	*I myself indeed prefer*
Las aprecio muy deveras;	*Sweet little Mexican ladies;*
Trigueñitas o morenitas	*Dark or brown-skinned*
Me gustan más que las hueras.[13]	*Blondies by comparison palor.]*

The narrator, operating as a character and witness to the action, constantly admits personal involvement—vicarious in nature—in the love triangle between

Pablo, Lola, and Luciano. Through him, Chacón manipulates the narrative perspective in order to heighten sentimentality and comment on social and literary conventions. As an intermediary between readers and characters, the narrator becomes the voice that gives direction to the events, plus he adds dimension to an otherwise predictable love story. Since part of his function is that of a narrative conscience, he judges each character's failure in living out the laws of honor and romance; thus the didactic nature of the novel.

Tras la tormenta la calma can best be understood as a nineteenth-century Hispanic dime novel or *fotonovela* (a novelized soap opera with photographs) without photographs. Part of its central objective is to experiment in recreating a sentimentalist ambiance with flowery language, including the superficialities of a fantasy-filled imbroglio of love. The three protagonists, stereotypical in their respective characterizations, follow a well-known script. It is the narrator-character who often demands to appear in the foreground, frequently interrupting the action due to his uncontainable involvement in the melodrama. Fanciful and sentimental, he interjects editorial remarks about such matters as pure, abstract love. Although plagued by ulterior fantasies, and inclined to obstruct the development of the story, his principal role is to divulge information about his native Santa Fe. He contributes to the narrative by manipulating and observing his surroundings, while providing a glimpse into local gossip and amorous affectations. A typical Romantic narrator, he reveals more than is expected of him: he reports with some objectivity about the lovers' dilemmas, but his emotional outbursts confirm his attachment to the events. In other words, he is there to augment sentimentality and frivolous relationships, an activity that also shows his own affective makeup.

Although the love story appeals mainly to the sentiments of an innocent reader, Chacón is careful to incorporate other substantive elements in an apparent attempt to salvage an otherwise simplistic story. Plot lines, stock characters, intertextual allusions, linguistic nuances, and themes from Spanish literary models, especially from the Golden Age and Romanticism, are used with the intent of uplifting the novel. Actually, this imitative slant debilitates the work, for its real value derives from the portrayal of regional qualities and social patterns. On the surface, it can be argued that the story is filled with an overabundance of decorative features, at times sacrificing action for wit and humor. This reduces the storyline to a thin plot and leaves a didactic lesson short of force.

Chacón must have been aware of the attitude toward the novel as a genre during his times. At times considered frivolous, the novel was regarded by some as a moral threat to the young reader. In *La Aurora* in 1910, a translated essay by V. E. Thomann reflects the low point of the novel's reputation:

> It is well known that any book we read leaves some kind of impression in our mind. And those thoughts when developed, form almost always the destiny of the readers. Some because of their tendency to read instructive works, develop their personal faculties and become eminent men and useful women to society; however, others who read stories or novels try to imitate what they read, and as a consequence, some manage to become clever swindlers, high-strung anarquists [sic], seductors or evil-doers, who defend themselves before the law that their deeds remain exempt from punishment, blood from the innocent is shed and justice is mocked.[14]

Such perceptions perhaps did not permit Chacón to create a purely literary exercise, especially in view of his moralizing tendencies in the other novel. Part of his intent is to entertain and at the same time demonstrate his diversified literary background. With a penchant for European modes and models, he is determined to show how New Mexico is an extension of the Old World rooted in the Southwest.

Set in the idyllic colonial environment of Santa Fe, *Tras la tormenta la calma* tells of an authentic love relationship that develops between Lola and Pablo, who seem to be naturally meant for each other. Harmony abounds in much the same manner as in the Spanish Golden Age theater, a situation that conveniently serves as a challenge to the villain named Luciano. The young couple, of humble origins, represent true nobility of character as opposed to those—for example, Luciano—who inherit their upper-class status. Pablo himself fits most of the descriptions of a Lope de Vega hero. Like Peribañez, he is known for his industriousness and impeccable morality. Lola's enticing natural beauty qualifies her as a comparable heroine. Her physical looks overcome Luciano, a wealthy student who has recently returned to his native city, and he calls upon his *Donjuanesque* talents to take advantage of her vulnerability. Thus, what seemed to be an exemplary love relationship between Pablo and Lola is challenged by Luciano, who tests for possible weaknesses. Totally infatuated by Lola's beauty, this new suitor feels compelled to break the existent harmony and balance. Luciano, whose name is ironic, desires to carry out his obsessions of conquest for the sake of sport. The challenge alone makes the opportunity appealing. He then confirms the fears V. E. Thomann expresses about certain types of literature, particularly in view of the fact that Luciano's eagerness to conquer Lola is based on living out literary fantasies in real life. The process also parallels Don Quixote's avid reading, except that the effect is the opposite: instead of correcting wrongs, he imposes his impulsive will by deception. With enchanting songs and persuasive rhetoric of love, Luciano manages to captivate Lola and both are found, by Pablo and her aunt, partially dressed in a seduction scene. At this moment the narrator engages in social commentary by pausing to mention that rumor is self-generated and that the incident spreads as gossip through town. The drama of the scene is only exceeded by humor as Luciano runs throughout the city in his undergarments until Pablo catches him and physically "teaches him a lesson."

The dénouement of the novel offers various twists to some intertextual influences. Chacón engages in intertextual discourse by following similar formulas of established literary models such as "El curioso impertinente" (The Impertinent Curious One), *El celoso extremeño* (The Jealous Man of Extremadura), and of course *Don Juan Tenorio*. The main difference between these stories and Chacón's lies in the way in which the New Mexican novelist portrays the defense of Pablo's honor in the conclusion. All receive their due punishment and poetic justice is consequently served. For instance, Pablo, who feels publicly disgraced and dishonored, had not been sufficiently protective of his loved one, and had thus left her exposed to more devious pursuers. Compelled to express a judgment, Pablo demands that the priest marry Lola to Luciano because she had surrendered to him physically. Since he had only received a commitment in promises, he feels that his own claim is a weak one. Pablo thus exercises abnegation through self-induced punishment and ends up alone in a melancholic state. Lola, on the other hand, suffers by having to marry the self-made Don Juan for whom she does not feel love, only infatuation. Her chastisement is necessary because of the insincere and questionable affection she felt toward Pablo. Luciano also experiences the opposite of his true desires: his mockery of love and honor lead him into an unwanted permanent relationship.

These relationships and their motives—Chacón seems to suggest—are exaggerated and misdirected. For that reason, punishment is applied democratically to all. Irony dictates that they lose what they originally cherished. It is in this sense that *Tras la tormenta la calma* attempts to provide a new view of honor: it becomes a relative code of social behavior that is to be implemented equally. A judicious view of reality comes forth in a literary plan that depends somewhat on European masterpieces but also includes regional elements. Chacón moralizes about how humans should be held accountable and responsible for their actions. As the title implies, the novelist is seeking calmness and refuge in more authentic modes of social behavior. The term "storm" might at first bring to mind the lawlessness and chaos of the first novel. It may also refer to the inconsistencies in social values present in a changing society. Part of the author's concern might be a melancholic lamentation of the loss of a regional self that occurs as a result of imitating others. Calmness, then, is possible only when the characters are true to themselves. Chacón contributes to the creation of a new cultural identity in a new environment. Literary emancipation, to the New Mexican novelist, is understood as an enterprise based on problems and elements characteristic of the area. Literature becomes a vehicle with which to present local concerns and comment on their problematic nature.

CONCLUSION: POPULAR FORMS FUEL A WRITTEN TRADITION

The background information provided to contextualize Eusebio Chacón's writings and the analysis of his two works clearly suggest that his contributions to the novel set him apart from other nineteenth-century writers. Both his personal qualities and his literary production attest to the presence of intellectual activity in what has generally been described as a backward frontier. As a writer, participant, spokesman, and initiator of the Hispanic novel in the Southwest, he embodies one of the paramount links to a wealth of Hispanic expression that still remains untapped. It is a shame that he has been ignored in the annals[15] of "official" literary history in New Mexico and the Southwest in general; nevertheless, that relegation now adds greater significance to his works and his civic stature. The tenacious lawyer, writer, and orator will someday occupy a distinctive place as a figure who directly contributed to the foundation of a novelistic tradition in the region. To accomplish such objectives, he has consciously focused on sources outside of his milieu in order to assimilate and mold them into viable forms that are appropriate to his people. The key to his success has been to import outside influences and cultivate only what is locally suitable and compatible. Eusebio Chacón adeptly indulged in the collective voice of popular tradition. The wisdom imbedded in that tradition is converted in his novels into a narrative consciousness that reflects and comments on itself.

NOTES

1. Following the same order, Manuel M. Salazar's manuscript is being revised by Juan Estevan Arellano and Anselmo F. Arellano; Chacón's works appeared as a limited edition thanks to La Tipografía *El Boletín Popular* from Santa Fe, New Mexico; Manuel C. de Baca's novel was published by the Las Vegas Normal University in Las Vegas, New Mexico; and Porfirio Gonzales's work appears in *La Voz del Pueblo* between June 4 and September 3, 1898.

2. For further biographical information on Chacón, we suggest Anselmo F. Arellano's summary in "La Junta de Indignación 1901" which appears in *De Colores*, 2 No. 1 (1975):30–37; also, see Francisco A. Lomelí's study "Eusebio Chacón" in *Chicano Literature: A Reference Guide*, ed. Julio A. Martínez and Francisco A. Lomelí (Westport, Conn.: Greenwood Press, 1985), pp. 91–97.

3. This speech, identified as "Elocuente discurso," is reproduced by Anselmo F. Arellano (*De Colores*, 2, No. 1 [1975]:39–46) from the original in *La Voz del Pueblo* in 1901. Already on February 28, 1898, Eusebio Chacón was described in terms of admiration that confirms much of what appears in 1901. One of the persons at an organization meeting, dealing with the Union Party, declared:

. . . es uno de los mejores oradores que tiene el país. Fluido en su lenguaje y pulido en su modo de expresarse, encantó con su discurso á cuantos tuvieron la feliz suerte de oirle (sic). Combatió con toda su energía la idea de suscitar cuestion (sic) de razas, pero agregó: "si alguien quiere levantar cuestion (sic) de raza en contra de ustedes vosotros no haréis mas (sic) que bien con defenderos de la misma manera." (*La Voz del Pueblo*, p. 1)

[. . . He is one of the best orators that this country has. Fluent in his language and refined in his manner of expression, he delighted with his speech whomever had the lucky fortune to hear him. He assailed with all vigor the idea of raising the race issue, but added: "if someone wants to bring up the race issue against you, there is nothing better for you to do than to defend yourselves in the same manner."]

4. See Robert J. Rosenbaum, *Mexicano Resistance in the Southwest* (Austin: The University of Texas Press, 1981), p. 146.

5. Rosenbaum here is referring to the herein mentioned newspaper from March 28, 1891. See Rosenbaum, *Mexicano Resistance*, p. 131.

6. Chacón, *El hijo de la tempestad*, p. 2. All other citations from work will appear with their corresponding pagination in the body of the article.

7. Eric Hobsbawm, *Bandits* (New York: Dell Publishing, 1969), pp. 17–19, has also stated:

"When banditry thus emerges into a larger movement, it becomes part of a force which can and does change society. Since the horizons of social bandits are narrow and circumscribed, like those of the peasantry itself, the results of their intervention into history may not be those they expected." (p. 23)

8. Hobsbawm discusses this category at length in *Bandits*, pp. 83–85.

9. Manuel C. de Baca, *Vicente Silva y sus cuarenta bandidos*, edited by Charles Aranda is a modern translation. No known publisher appears nor a date of publication, although it was probably 1978. Numerous other translations and editions have been made of this original book from 1896. Also, the topic of banditry was much in vogue according to the critics José Timoteo López, Edgardo Núñez and Robert Lara Vialpando who, in *Breve reseña de la literatura hispana de Nuevo México y Colorado* (Brief Review of Hispanic Literature From New Mexico and Colorado) (Juárez: Imprenta Comercial, 1959), have observed:

Las novelas aparecidas en Nuevo México a fines del siglo pasado tienen como tema la vida de los bandoleros que se hicieron famosos en toda la 'salvaje frontera'. Al lado de los cuatreros "güeros" eran famosos los hispanos Vicente Silva y Elfego Baca en Nuevo México, Joaquín Murrieta en California. . . . Las novelas editadas en Nuevo México, [están] escritas en un español sencillo y casi dialectal lleno de modismos y giros propios del Suroeste (p. 17).

[The novels that appeared in New Mexico at the end of the last century have as their theme the life of outlaws who became famous in all of the "wild frontier." Next to the Anglo horse thieves and cattle rustlers, certain Hispanics were famous like Vicente Silva and Elfego Baca in New Mexico, and Joaquín Murrieta in California. . . . The novels published in New Mexico are written in a simple and almost dialectical Spanish filled with idioms and phrases native to the Southwest.]

10. T. M. Pearce, "The Bad Son (El Mal Hijo) in Southwestern Spanish Folklore," *Western Folklore*, 9, No. 4 (October 1950): 295–301.

11. *Ibid.*, p. 289.

12. *La Voz del Pueblo*, Las Vegas, New Mexico, February 4, 1893.

13. *La Voz del Pueblo*, Las Vegas, New Mexico, June 25, 1892.

14. See *La Aurora*, August 15, 1910. V. E. Thomann continues to argue that novels can break marriages and make one lose all feeling of honor and nobility. He also warns parents to keep children away from novels, otherwise they will be prematurely gray and their children will "run around incontainably through the illusion of the world." As far as he is concerned, novels distort reality and corrupt a sense of morality.

15. Francisco A. Lomelí and Donaldo W. Urioste in *Chicano Perspectives in Literature: A Critical and Annotated Bibliography* (1976) were the first critics to specifically discuss Chacón's stature as a writer of novels. As a final biographical note, Eusebio Chacón died in Trinidad, Colorado, on April 3, 1948.

8

THE WRAGGLE-TAGGLE OUTLAWS

Vicente Silva and Billy the Kid as Seen in Two Nineteenth-Century Hispanic Documents

E. A. MARES

Two outlaws, Vicente Silva and Billy the Kid, agitated the lives of New Mexicans during the later years of the last century. Vicente Silva lived in Las Vegas and operated primarily in northeastern New Mexico while Billy the Kid ranged through the southeastern part of the state, principally in Lincoln County. Vicente Silva was a far more powerful and influential figure than Billy the Kid; yet after the passage of a century, Vicente Silva has lapsed into relative obscurity as a figure of regional interest, at best, while Billy the Kid has become immortalized in legend and myth. What led to such a different historical perspective on these two outlaws? Vicente Silva was Indohispanic but cordially detested by many Hispanics. Billy the Kid, an Anglo by origin, was idolized by many Hispanics. What factors were at work in New Mexican society to bring about this historical irony? Two Hispanic documents from the late nineteenth century help to answer these questions.

After 1846 New Mexico provided a unique setting for an ethnically mixed and unsettled frontier that favored, for a brief period, the emergence of outlaws as a significant force in society. The setting was unique because New Mexico was a neglected desert frontier for two distinct cultures, in addition to the many Pueblo and nomadic Indian cultures. One of these cultures, mestizo, partially Indian, partially Hispanicized (therefore Indohispanic), was Mexican; it had survived in the northernmost and most neglected province of the Spanish Empire and then, much later, of Mexico. The other culture was Anglo-American, which arrived with the ever larger numbers of American traders and businessmen on the northern frontier of Mexico after that nation adopted a policy of free trade and opened its northern border to trade with the United States in 1821.

By 1846 the commercial conquest of what would become the American Southwest was virtually complete and the ensuing war against Mexico was brief and decisive. In the very year that war ended, 1848, gold was discovered in California and Americans rushed there to seek their fortunes. While Spain and then Mexico had neglected this northern frontier, now the United States also neglected its acquisition, newly named the Southwest, in its haste to leapfrog across the arid lands to reach California.

The Territory of New Mexico, twice neglected by its non-Indian occupiers, carried on its rural barter economy in areas that were for the most part remote from the mainstream of social and economic activity; this mainstream, of course, was in the towns and cities that were either on the Santa Fe Trail, as Las Vegas was, or were the hubs of transportation and business, as both Albuquerque and Las Vegas were. Even these "cities," however, were not much more than towns and their political, social, and economic institutions were weak. The Mexican institutions, understood by the large Indohispanic population, were now gone, and the American institutions were in disarray after the brief transitional period to American rule (1846–1861) followed immediately by the Civil War (1861–1865). All of the ingredients for violence, as outlined by Robert Utley, were present in this society—liquor, easy availability of firearms, the desire for instant wealth and political power, and above all, a code of behavior, the so-called code of the West, based on the most primitive of problem solving techniques, instant redress of wrong, real or imagined, by violence.[1]

It is interesting to speculate on how much the code of the West owed to the older Mexican tradition of *machismo*, which it closely resembled. This is not the time or place to dwell on the theme but it seems highly likely that just as Mexican farming, ranching, and mining techniques, clothing, tools, and artifacts in general, influenced the Anglo-American cowboy, so also the *macho* ingredient of Mexican society with both its positive (protection of women and family) and negative elements (instant and often irrational violent response) had an impact on the formation of Anglo-American frontier society.

In any case, New Mexico offered a maximum of personal freedom, or license, and a minimum of law and order for about half a century after 1846. Vicente Silva and Billy the Kid were two of the most celebrated outlaws of that time, although certainly not the only ones. As noted above, we have two Indohispanic accounts of these outlaws that cast a fascinating light on how Nuevo Mexicanos responded to the changing conditions they were experiencing in the latter half of the nineteenth century.

Both of these documents are historic narratives that have been heavily colored by the use of literary devices drawn from both fiction and poetry. One of these works is *Vicente Silva y Sus Cuarenta Bandidos*, written by Manuel C. de Baca in 1896. The brief narrative has had various translations into English over the years. The best translation to date is that of Lane Kaufmann that appeared in 1947.[2] The other document is *Los Bilitos*, a narrative poem in ballad meter written by Charles Frederick Rudulph, who was a member of Pat Garrett's posse that took Billy the Kid prisoner. The late Louis Leon Branch found this document among his family's possessions in 1976. He had it published, along with his extensive commentaries, interpretations, and loose translation of the document. Information on the dust jacket of this book refers to the Rudulph poem as "an aged manuscript handwritten in 1880—discovered in 1976." The book consists of two parts; the first one, in the words of Mr. Branch, "contains this author's own recounting of a well-known, oft-written story, some of it history, some of it fallacy, but whether true or not, [it] is what is universally known as the Billy the Kid story." The second part contains the Spanish verses by Charles Rudulph that narrates his encounters with Billy the Kid.[3] This narrative poem is, of course, part of the literary heritage of Nuevo Mexicanos, New Mexico's Indohispanic population. It is this poem and not Mr. Branch's commentaries (worthy of review in a different context) that are of interest here.

Las Vegas, the city of the meadows, was the last major town to be settled by Hispanics in northeastern New Mexico. Founded in 1835 on the banks of the Gallinas River, Las Vegas was a peaceful outpost of the young Mexican nation. The Conestoga wagons had already made deep ruts in the prairie land to the east of Las Vegas as they rumbled along the Santa Fe Trail. Soon after the founding of the town, the wagons were lined up around the old plaza and Las Vegas became a thriving commercial center.

Hispanics, that is, the Mexican citizens of Las Vegas, engaged in two types of peaceful trade. One type was with the Yankees who came down the Santa Fe Trail while the other, highly adventurous, was with the Comanches. Hispanic traders known as *comancheros* rode out from northern New Mexico villages and towns, like Las Vegas, onto the high plains where they traded trinkets, cloth, and foodstuffs for horses, mules, buffalo hides, and rifles, which were easier to obtain from Comanches than from their own compatriots in Mexico. This trade eventually came to an end with the extinction of the buffalo and the suppression of the Comanches by the U.S. Cavalry.[4]

Prior to 1879, however, Las Vegas remained a thriving commercial center and also, by and large, a very peaceful community. The coming of the railroad in that year shattered this state of affairs. In the aftermath of the American Civil War, as the railroads expanded into the Southwest, they hired gunslingers from the ranks of those who no longer fit into any peaceful or orderly social pattern of existence. These gunslingers were used to control the right of way against other, competing railroad companies. Once the Atchison, Topeka & Santa Fe Railroad had won the race through Raton Pass and on to Las Vegas, the gunslingers were no longer needed and they were discharged. Unemployed, these malcontents lingered in Las Vegas where they sometimes served as lawmen and at other times simply lived as outlaws.

Other factors led to the coarsening of the social fabric in Las Vegas. As some Hispanics saw their land and ranching interests threatened and diminished by the coming of the railroad and by the commercial grazing and business interests attracted by it, they formed a secret society, *Las Gorras Blancas*, and struck back by destroying the fences of offending cattle barons and tearing up the railroad tracks and turning them into "Sherman neckties" by heating the rails and bending them around trees.

Another altogether different response to the coming of the Anglos to New Mexico was exemplified by Vicente Silva. In his narrative account, which has the full title of *Historia de Vicente Silva, Sus Cuarenta Bandidos, Sus Crimenes y Retribuciones*, Manuel C. de Baca provides a brief but fairly complete overview of his subject. It might be noted that Manuel C. de Baca was a prominent and politically conservative northern New Mexican at the time he wrote his account. Since Vicente Silva could be viewed as betraying the values of a conservative mercantile and ranching class, as will be seen below, C. de Baca's account might be suspect were it not that popular folklore apparently bears out the indictment of Silva in C. de Baca's account.

Silva, to paraphrase Manuel C. de Baca's narrative account, was born about 1845 in Bernalillo[5] and thus grew up during the early period of the American occupation of the Territory of New Mexico. Although he didn't attend school, he was intelligent, good looking, and gave the appearance of respectability. C. de Baca comments on the youthful Silva in the elegant Hispanic prose of the late nineteenth century:

> Vicente Silva nació en el condado de Bernalillo, Territorio de Nuevo México, de pobre pero respetable familia, hácia el año de 1845. En su niñez no concurrió a ninguna escuela de enseñanza y de consiguiente era enteramente iliterato. Su estatura y buen cuerpo le daban una aparencia más o menos respetable; reunía en sí un aspecto grave con cierta expresion de dulce candor; era simpático, liberal y agradable, con todos, y por su aparencia y trato, nadie podía sospechar que dentro de aquel cuerpo se ocultaba el alma más perversa del mundo. (3)

[Vicente Silva was born in Bernalillo County, Territory of New Mexico, of poor but respectable parents, about the year 1845. In his youth there was no school nearby and as a result he was completely illiterate. His stature and fine build gave him a more or less dignified mien; his face was friendly, generous, and agreeable toward all. From his appearance and manner no one could suspect that within that body was hidden the most perverse soul in the world.][6]

Lane Kaufmann, a thoughtful translator of C. de Baca's book, has commented on the moralizing tendency in the prose of Manuel C. de Baca and states that "his motive for writing the book was a mixture of righteous morality and the zeal and pride of a local historian" (v). Again, Kaufmann emphasizes the need for care in reading C. de Baca's work:

There is a continuous conflict throughout the book between Don Manuel the historian and Don Manuel the moralist. The latter has frequently triumphed to the extent of coloring the narrative with melodramatic dialogue for which he could have had no source but his own imagination. (vi)

Little is known of Silva's early years but by the mid 1880s he had become a businessman. He operated a saloon and gambling hall in Las Vegas, New Mexico. About 1885 he and his wife adopted an abandoned child and raised her. Even though the saloon and gambling hall must have been as rowdy as similar establishments throughout the West, Vicente Silva apparently attracted little attention.

Although not much status could have attached to Silva's business, it was of a type that tended to be lucrative in the old West. Silva, by all appearances, had made a successful transition from Mexican to Anglo-American rule. He might very well have been on his way to becoming a pillar of the Hispanic community. He was well liked, apparently the very picture of middle-class respectability, and prosperous. Thus matters remained until about 1892:

Acompañaba tambien á Silva y esposa, Gabriél Sandoval . . . [que] . . . frizaba en los veinte años y se ocupaba generalmente en atender a todos los negocios de Silva, y principalmente como cantinero. Nadie sabia que Silva era perverso, y lo miraban á él y á su familia, como una familia feliz, hasta el tiempo del desenlace de los acontecimientos que han dado lugar á esta historia. (7–8)

[Also living with Silva and his wife was Gabriel Sandoval . . . [who] . . . was in his early twenties, mainly concerned with taking care of Silva's businesses, principally a saloon keeper. No one knew how wicked Silva was, all regarding him and his family as an ordinary happy family until the time of the conclusion of the events with which the next chapter deals. (8)

At or about that time, Silva, probably driven by his own greedy vision of the Gilded Age in America, organized a secret society of outlaws:

> Silva había sido vencido por el interés y el amor al dinero, se había hecho avaro, y comenzó desde luego á formar sus planes para acumular fortuna con poco trabajo, y para ello organizó una cuadrilla de bandidos, á la que dio por nombre, segun confesado despues por sus mismos secuaces en el crímen: "La Sociedad de Bandidos de Nuevo México. (9)
>
> [Silva had been overpowered by a fascination and lust for money; he had become avaricious and immediately began to lay his plans for gaining a fortune without having to work for it. Toward this end he organized a group of bandits which he named, according to the confessions later made by his very followers in crime, "La Sociedad de Bandidos de Nuevo México.] (8)

Silva proceeded to terrorize the Las Vegas community with a series of crimes that lasted until 1893, when he was murdered by one of the members of his own gang. Whatever he was, Vicente Silva was most definitely not a social bandit, i.e., one who robs from the rich to give to the poor, or who at least is perceived in that light in folklore, legend, and myth.[7] Manuel C. de Baca details Silva's crimes throughout his book. They fell into the following categories: (1) theft, primarily cattle and horse rustling; (2) clandestine industry and commerce based on meat production (from the stolen herds) for sale to mining camps; (3) murder, primarily of Silva's enemies, or individuals perceived as enemies, but also of close associates or even members of his own family if Silva perceived them as interfering with his desires; and (4) an assortment of crimes of arson, rape, and various levels of violence against persons and property.

Most, if not all, of Silva's criminal activity was aimed at his own Hispanic community. Here, then, was a man who had acquired the external trappings of bourgeois respectability but remained a criminal at heart. His crimes, furthermore, were clearly for personal gain.

Unlike the Gorras Blancas, Vicente Silva fought under no social banner for a general good. At least there is no evidence to this writer's knowledge linking Silva's activities to the Gorras Blancas. Did members of Silva's gang fight for the Gorras Blancas? It is possible, of course, but judging from available evidence, Silva's gang members had no more social conscience than their leader. It would be interesting, nevertheless, to research in detail the possible links, or lack of such links, of Vicente Silva and his gang to the Gorras Blancas, however unlikely that such ties might have existed. This topic, however, is clearly beyond the scope of this essay. Silva, in any case, was utterly selfish and malevolent. After one of his lieutenants murdered him, the rest of the gang fell on Silva like vultures, robbed him, distributed the booty among themselves, and tossed his body into an arroyo.[8]

Aggravated, afflicted, and deeply hurt by what one of their own community had inflicted on them, the Hispanos gave vent to their feelings of betrayal in literary expression that is embedded in Manuel C. de Baca's text. He cites, for example, a poem titled *Duerme La Justicia* composed in response to the atrocities perpetrated by Vicente Silva:

> Inumerables incendios, estupros, robos, destrucción de todo género de propiedad y otros muchos crímenes y asesinatos que seria largo enumerar, dieron lugar á la publicacion de la siguiente poesía que retrataba el estado de la opinión pública. (63–64)
>
> [Countless fires, rapes, robberies, destruction of all types of property, and many other crimes and murders which would take long to enumerate, led to the publishing of the following poetry which portrayed the state of public opinion. (E.A. Mares translation)

The opening stanza takes justice to task for ignoring the rampant criminality and the following stanzas lament the condition into which the Las Vegas area had fallen because of the activities of Vicente Silva and others like him:

En este país desgraciado
Las leyes no se ejecutan,
Los criminales disfrutan
De renombre ensangrentado;
Su crimen queda olvidado
Y el castigo merecido
Rara vez es recibido
Por el delito de muerte;
Está la justicia inerte
Y las leyes en olvido. (64)

[In this unfortunate land
The laws are not enforced,
Criminals enjoy
Their bloody fame;
Their crimes are forgotten
And the crime of murder
Seldom receives
Its merited wrath;
Justice lies in state
And the law enjoys a similar fate.]
(E.A. Mares translation)

Written in traditional ballad meter, this folk poem repeats the lament of crimes that have gone unpunished and criminals who have been set free:

¡Cuántos crímenes tapados!
De que guardamos memoria
Nos presenta nuestra historia
Por muchos años pasados.
Cuan pocos los castigados
Y cuan muchos los que han sido
Absueltos, y han merecido
Padecer la última pena
Con la aprobación más plena
Que justicia haya tenido. (65)

[How many hidden crimes
We do remember
From the history of our times
For all these many years.
How few were punished
And how many were forgiven
Who merited death,
The ultimate punishment
To which in all justice
They should have been driven.]
(E.A. Mares translation)

The poem continues in this vein for three more stanzas and then ends with moving, heart-felt nostalgia for earlier times, before the arrival of the railroad, before the conflicts of class, culture, ethnicity, and economic forces after 1846 changed forever the peaceful city on the meadows:

Cuando las leyes triunfantes
Prevalescan donde quiera,
Este país será la esfera
De paz y quietud, y cual antes
Sus tranquilos habitantes
Vivirán ya sin temor
Y el crimen aterrador
No reinará inpunemente,
Pues la justicia imponente
Será nuestro protector. (66)

[When triumphant law
Prevails far and near,
Then this country once again
Will be the sphere
Of peace and calm,
and once again
Its peaceful habitants
Will live again without fear,
And frightening crime,
will be dethroned
By justice, sharply honed,
To protect us once again.]
(E.A. Mares translation)

As noted earlier above, it is not surprising that Manuel C. de Baca, as a representative voice from the Indohispanic conservative elites of northern New Mexico, would be sharply critical of a man like Vicente Silva. Yet there is apparently no body of popular literature, of folklore, that would dispute or counterpoint C. de Baca's dark view of Silva. On the contrary, what folk literature exists seems to corroborate C. de Baca's account. Perhaps C. de Baca was aware of his vulnerability to a charge of class bias and thought it necessary to buttress his narrative with examples of popular attitudes towards Silva as found in the folk poetry examined above.

In any case, until a body of literature, folkloric or not, is found that can seriously dispute the views advanced by Manuel C. de Baca and the scraps of popular literature that have survived from that time and that refer to Silva, it is difficult to avoid the view of Silva as a scourge to his own people, an insult and a deep wound to what had been the peaceful heritage of Las Vegas. Vicente Silva stirs no positive response from our own violent times. Unloved and unmourned, he lies in an unknown grave forgotten by all except antiquarians and the occasional scholar who stirs his bones. As Lane Kaufmann notes: . . . the value of the story of Vicente Silva is essentially that of a period document—a revealing portrait of a little known part of the history of our country . . . (vi).

Billy the Kid lived and died before Vicente Silva's crimes became known in northern New Mexico. He never commanded the economic power of a Vicente Silva, nor did he have the bourgeois status of Silva. His exploits were of relatively brief duration, he died at age twenty-one, and there is very little in the historical record to distinguish him from similar outlaws at that time. How is it, then, that unlike Silva, Billy the Kid passed from history into legend and myth?

Lincoln County in the 1870s, not unlike the environs of Las Vegas to the north, was small farming and cattle country. While Las Vegas had a population of about 2400 then, there were only about 2000 people in the entire county of Lincoln. And the county was large:

> Lincoln County embraced nearly thirty thousand square miles of southeastern New Mexico Territory—about two thirds the size of all England and roughly comparable to the state of South Carolina.[9]

With so very few people scattered over such a large geographic area, there was little economic activity. Along the banks of small streams like the Ruidoso and the Hondo that eventually flowed into the Pecos River, there was a scattering of towns such as San Patricio and Lincoln. Nearby was a military post, Fort Stanton.

Socially, Lincoln County was a mirror of the rest of the Territory. There was a substantial number of Indians on the nearby Mescalero Apache Indian Agency. There was also a large resident Indohispanic population of farmers and ranchers, possibly a majority. The Indohispanics and the Anglos farmed along the mountain streams while on the Pecos plains to the east Texas cattlemen grazed their herds.[10]

Recently conquered by the Anglos and, for a number of historical reasons, disdained by the Texans, the Indohispanics formed the bottom layer, the infrastructure, of this society. Mostly small farmers and ranchers with little if any experience of a monied economy, they occupied a position of social inferiority to the Anglos and Texans. Although some Indohispanics would rise to positions of prestige and prominence in Lincoln County, this was the exception and not the rule.

The Anglos, like the Indohispanics, formed at least three layers of society in Lincoln County. At the top were the wealthiest cattlemen, like John Chisum, who dominated ranching in the lower Pecos valley. Then there were the common farmers and ranchers who, like their Indohispanic counterparts, tried to meet their own needs and earn a little extra by selling their produce and cattle to the only major business in the town of Lincoln, Murphy's store, or the L. G. Murphy & Company. Lawrence G. Murphy and his business associates in the town of Lincoln, primarily James J. Dolan, John H. Riley, W. J. Martin, and Jacob B. "Billy" Mathews, known collectively as "The House," were also part of the Anglo elite. For Anglos and Indohispanics alike, the bottom of the social ladder was occupied by those men whose lives had been traumatized by the Civil War, or by long bouts of poverty, or by social displacement, or by whatever factors that lead some men to become drifters, ne'er-do-wells, cattle rustlers, and assorted outlaws.[11]

While it is not my purpose here to recount the detailed and complex history of the Lincoln County War, at least an outline of its principle figures and main lines of contention is necessary in order to understand the emergence of Billy the Kid as both a Hispanic and a universal folk hero. I will thus briefly indicate the social context that made the phenomenon of Billy the Kid possible.

Lincoln County, again like the rest of the Territory, primarily engaged in a barter economy. The opportunities for accumulating any kind of monetary wealth in this rural and extremely remote land were by and large restricted to the trade with the Indian agency and the army post. For this reason, it became critically important for those who wanted to make money in Lincoln County to control this trade, preferably by having a monopoly on it.

A monopoly is precisely what the L. G. Murphy & Company, or "The House" had acquired. Between 1865, when he came to Fort Stanton at the close of the Civil War, and 1876, when his own incompetence and a serious drinking problem began to disrupt his power, Murphy had built the monopoly and had come to dominate the economy, and the society, of Lincoln County. The small farmers and ranchers, be they Anglo or Indohispanic, had little choice but to trade with Murphy. He, in turn, treated them with contempt and kept them perpetually in debt to his store.[12] By 1876, then, The House was powerful but slipping and it had made many enemies.

At just the right moment when the stage had been set for a possible challenge to the power of The House, John H. Tunstall, an Englishman, arrived in the town of Lincoln and quickly formed a business partnership with Alexander A. McSween, of Scotch descent. Together, they opened their own store and sought to displace The House.

Since the town of Lincoln, like Las Vegas, had only the thinnest veneer of legality during these tumultuous times, it is no wonder that The House fought back with every means at its disposal, legal or illegal. As the year 1877 advanced, The House enlisted powerful allies in its defense. It had friends in high places so that its legal moves were protected, or fostered, by the so-called Santa Fe Ring, a cabal of lawyers who, as Robert Utley writes, sought to accrue power and wealth to themselves:

> Mainly, they (the Santa Fe Ring) concentrated on amassing huge landholdings through the manipulation of Spanish land grants and the laws regulating the public domain. But wherever money was to be made, especially where facilitated by governmental action, people suspected ring involvement. Cattle, railroads, mining, and army and Indian contracts all captured the attention of the ring members. (24–25)

The House was not adverse to operating outside the law and gradually gathered together a more or less reliable gang of outlaws and small ranchers and farmers who sometimes acted as outlaws called, simply, "the Boys."

Under duress Tunstall and McSween tried to strengthen their position by attracting as much support as they could from those elements of Lincoln society who had no use for The House. Tunstall and McSween formed their own extralegal force similarly composed of dissident small farmers and ranchers, many of whom were Indohispanic, and outlaws known as "the Regulators." Prominent among the Regulators was a young man, barely out of adolescence, known at that time as Billy Bonney, or the Kid.[13]

The "Kid" was born William Henry McCarty in New York in 1859. His mother married a William Henry Antrim in Santa Fe in 1873, and the family moved to Silver City where William Bonney, or Antrim, as he sometimes called himself, grew up. There was nothing remarkable about the young William Bonney. From a fairly early age, however, he made friends with Hispanics:

> With agreeable and winning ways, he made friends easily, especially with the Hispanics, whose language he spoke fluently. He was basically a scrappy tough, seasoned by the raw life of the Silver City mining camp. He had killed at least one man, a bully at Fort Grant, Arizona, whose death could not be properly judged premeditated or cold-blooded. Like many another drifter, he gave a false name, William H. Bonney; but he also took his stepfather's surname and answered to Henry Antrim, Kid Antrim, or just Kid.[14]

The Kid was a loyal and admiring follower of John Tunstall. After Tunstall was murdered by "the Boys" in February 1878, the Kid came to play an ever larger role in the activities of "the Regulators" who continued the struggle against The House.

After a number of shootouts and pitched gun battles, legal, quasi-legal, and illegal maneuvers by both factions in the fight, the Lincoln County War gradually subsided. It was a war nobody won. Tunstall and McSween were both killed but The House also saw its monopoly destroyed as an economic boom occurred in the 1880s. Most of those who were prominent in the war, and who survived it, drifted off into obscurity. Only two men escaped such obscurity. One was the Governor of the Territory of New Mexico during the war, Lew Wallace, who went on to literary fame as the author of *Ben Hur*. The other was Billy the Kid.

Although he died in 1881 in Fort Sumner at the hands of Sheriff Pat Garrett of Lincoln County, Billy the Kid became in folklore, legend, myth, novels, and movies the most famous outlaw of all times. There are various reasons for this postmortem rise to fame:

(1) Of all the rogue's gallery of unlikable characters in the Lincoln County War, Billy the Kid was the most likeable. He had a winning personality and generally treated most people with courtesy. Whether true or not, he was perceived as being a "social bandit," one who had a genuine concern for the poor and the downtrodden.

(2) He had an obvious attachment to the Indohispanics and they responded quite positively to him. Here was an Anglo who allied himself with the popular Tunstall and McSween faction that attracted the support of many Hispanos who wanted to end the economic domination and exploitation of The House.

(3) Because he had something of a popular following, Billy the Kid was able to count on assistance when he crucially needed it; he was helped in escape attempts and protected (often by Hispanics) when he was being hunted by "the Boys" or by the law. He was, in short, a popular underdog who joined with other underdogs, i.e., Hispanos and other small farmers and ranchers as they fought against the oppression of The House. After his death, it is understandable that his considerable real life exploits would loom larger than life.

(4) Shortly after the death of Billy the Kid, the mythmaking process began, in 1882, with the publication of Pat Garrett's *The Authentic Life of Billy the Kid, etc.*[15] Somewhere along the way, the mythmaking was greatly augmented by the movie making, but that is yet another story that lies outside the scope of this essay.

Leaving aside Louis Leon Branch's comments, opinions, and translation, part two of his book, *Los Bilitos*, consists primarily of Charles Rudulph's poem of forty stanzas, written in ballad meter, that narrates the capture of Billy the Kid by Pat Garrett in the winter of 1880. Written in 1880 soon after the events narrated, Rudulph, from Puerto de Luna, was a member of Garrett's posse and obviously a very Hispanicized ancestor of Mr. Branch.

Although the poem is favorable to Pat Garrett and the enforcement of law and order, there is an undertone of great respect for Billy the Kid in many of the stanzas. The ballad begins with Pat Garrett arriving at Puerto de Luna and asking the local people to join his posse. He has difficulty recruiting them, however, as there is a great fear, or reluctance, to take part in the search. Two strangers in the town volunteer for the posse and this puts some of the local braggarts to shame:

También dos estrangeritos
Sin ser del dicho lugar
Salieron aunque atrasito
Sus vidas a peligrar.
Para que diera vergüenza
A unos ciertos prominentes
Que hablan mucho de su fuerza
Teniéndose por valientes.[16]

[Two strangers of little fame
Who were not from there
Went out but oh so slowly
To risk their lives.
They did this to shame
Some prominent men of the town
Who talk much about being brave
And therefore think they are brave.]
(E.A. Mares translation)

Eventually, Billy the Kid is captured and taken prisoner to Las Vegas, but not before Charles Rudulph expresses an implicit admiration for Billy the Kid's sense of honor. As stanza thirty-seven puts it:

La tomada de estos hombres	*[It might have been hard*
Muy deficil parecia,	*To take these men alive,*
Pues vivos no los tomaban	*Impossible to take them alive,*
Era lo que el Bill decia.	*That's what Bill said.*
Si el Bill ubiera sabido	*If Bill had known*
Que habia una recompensa,	*About the reward,*
El no se huviera rendido	*He wouldn't have surrendered*
Y hubiera hecho su defensa. (204)	*And he would've fought hard.]*
	(E.A. Mares translation)

Stanza after stanza, in an oral poetry tradition that goes all the way back to medieval Spain, dramatically narrate the events of the manhunt. The poem ends with an exhortation that young people should beware of leading reckless lives, for they might come to a sad end like Billy the Kid and his gang.

What these nineteenth-century Hispanic documents finally reveal is the contrast, as perceived by Hispanos, between a noble and an ignoble outlaw.

Vicente Silva, in Manuel C. de Baca's account is an ignoble outlaw. Silva used force to achieve selfish, materialistic ends. Furthermore, he primarily assaulted his own people. Silva's vision of the good life springs from distorted images borrowed from the Anglo conquerors; this vision includes a respectable business front, an insatiable appetite for wealth and material possessions, and the use of any means, however ruthless and murderous they might be, to achieve his ends. Note, for example, the effort made by Silva to protect his "acquisitions":

> Silva, sigiliosamente habia comprado un rancho cerca de Monte Largo. Este lugar era por su situacion natural y topográfico el más á propósito y adecuado para los fines y usos á las cuales Silva lo destinaba.
>
> El consabido Ojo del Monte Large está situado en el Condado de Santa Fé entre unas sierras fragosas y casi impenetrables: sus altas y encrespadas montañas, sus profundos cañones y lo inaccessible del lugar, ofrecian grandes ventajas para guarecer las partidas de animales que Silva transportaba al sitio, como el lugar más seguro para ocultar sus robos y las cosechas que apercibia en violación del Séptimo Mandamiento. Allí se encontraban atajos de reses y caballada, robados por Silva y su gavilla. (10)
>
> [Silva had secretly bought a ranch near the San Pedro mining camp known as the Ojo de Monte Largo. The situation and topography of this place made it ideally

> adapted to the purpose for which Silva intended it. The Monte Largo ranch lay in Santa Fe County between craggy and nearly impenetrable peaks; the lofty mountains, deep canyons, and the inaccessibility of the place offered great advantages for protecting the herds of animals which Silva brought there and the safest place for hiding their plundered booty which evidenced violation of the Seventh Commandment. There could be found fenced-in herds of cattle and horses stolen by Silva and his band of thugs.] (13)

There is not the slightest redeeming element or ennobling vision in Silva's career. Shunned by Hispanos, and ignored by Anglos, Silva is all but forgotten save as an oddity in regional history.

How different is the fate of Billy the Kid. While the conversion of an immature, rather ordinary but likeable outlaw into a heroic figure of folklore and legend is a well known story, less well known has been the deep love by some Hispanos, and the respect of many of them, for the Kid. In history and Hispanic folklore, as indicated in the ballad composed by Charles Frederick Rudulph, Billy the Kid has come to be perceived as a mythic social bandit, friend of the despised minority, and champion of the oppressed small farmers and ranchers of Lincoln County.

One final question remains to be answered. How is one to explain the continuing fascination and popularity of Billy the Kid in our own times? The fascination with the Kid is revealed not only in popular culture but also in literature. In reference to the Hispanic connection, for example, the internationally renowned Spanish novelist, Ramón Sender, wrote and published *El Bandido Adolescente* in 1965. In this account, Billy the Kid exemplifies "valores más importantes que la vida y la muerte" (values more important than life and death).[17] The ultimate value, unattainable in real life, is absolute, total freedom combined with absolute, total responsibility to oneself and to others; this, of course, is the ideal of the anarchist.

Here is the answer to our question. The ideal vision of freedom combined with noble personal qualities, real or imagined, is at the mythopoeic core of the Billy the Kid story. The fundamental idea of this vision of freedom is best captured in a few stanzas from a seventeenth-century English ballad called "The Wraggle-Taggle Gypsies, O!" It is a ballad about a newly wedded noblewoman who leaves her husband to run off with the gypsies. Her husband, the lord, pursues her and implores her to return with him as his wife. She refuses. In the words of the ballad:

"What makes you leave your house and land?
What makes you leave your money, O?
What makes you leave your new-wedded lord,
To follow the wraggle-taggle gypsies, O!

"What care I for my house and my land?
What care I for my money, O?
What care I for my new-wedded lord,
I'm off with the wraggle-taggle gypsies, O!

"Last night you slept on a goosefeather bed,
With the sheet turned down so bravely, O!
Tonight you'll sleep in a cold open field,
Along with the wraggle-taggle gypsies, O!

"What care I for a goose-feather bed,
With the sheet turned down so bravely, O!
For tonight I shall sleep in a cold open field,
Along with the wraggle-taggle gypsies, O![18]

Billy the Kid, in the sense indicated in the above stanzas, was a "wraggle-taggle Gypsy," and this sense of freedom is primarily responsible, we believe, for his enduring fame in myth and legend. The story of Vicente Silva lacks this fundamental mythopoeic appeal. Put quite simply, our two nineteenth-century documents indicate that Nuevo Mexicanos reacted negatively to a member of their own ethnic community, Vicente Silva, because he was a most negative human being, while they reacted favorably to Billy the Kid, not because he was an outlaw, but because they perceived him as a man who empathized with Hispanics and who, like them, found himself a victim of social injustice who chose to fight for what he perceived to be a just cause. Billy the Kid was a "wraggle-taggle Gypsy" while Vicente Silva was merely a common criminal and an entirely unsympathetic one at that.

NOTES

1. Robert M. Utley, *High Noon in Lincoln*, (Albuquerque: The University of New Mexico Press, 1987), pp. 176–77.

2. Manuel C. de Baca, *Vicente Silva and His Forty Bandits*, translated by Lane Kaufmann (Washington: Edward McLean, Libros Escogidos, 1947). In The Special Collections Department, The Coronado Room, The University of New Mexico General Library.

3. Louis Leon Branch, *"Los Bilitos": the Story of "Billy the Kid" and His Gang* (New York: The Carlton Press, 1980).

4. For an overview of Las Vegas and its history the best work available is Lynn Perrigo, *Gateway to Glorieta: A History of Las Vegas, New Mexico*. Original manuscript in The Special Collections Department, The Coronado Room, The University of New Mexico General Library. See also *Las Vegas, New Mexico, A Portrait*, photographs by Alex Traube, with a text by E. A. Mares (Albuquerque: The University of New Mexico Press, 1983).

5. All references to Vicente Silva come from Manuel C. de Baca, *Historia de Vicente Silva, Sus Cuarenta Bandidos, Sus Crimenes y Retribuciones* (Las Vegas, New Mexico: Imprenta, La Voz del

Pueblo, 1896). All references preserve Mr. Baca's conventions of accentuation and orthography. In Special Collections Department, The Coronado Room, The University of New Mexico General Library.

6. Manuel C. de Baca, *Vicente Silva and His Forty Bandits*, trans. Lane Kaufmann, p. 8.

7. On the theory of the social bandit see Eric J. Hobsbawn, *Social Bandits and Primitive Rebels* (Glencoe, Illinois: The Free Press, 1959).

8. Manuel C. de Baca, *Historia de Vicente Silva, . . .*, p. 62.

9. Utley, *High Noon in Lincoln*, p. 10.

10. *Ibid.*, p. 10.

11. *Ibid.*, p. 174.

12. *Ibid.*, pp. 14–16.

13. *Ibid.*, p. 43.

14. Robert M. Utley, *Four Fighters of Lincoln County* (Albuquerque: The University of New Mexico Press, 1986), p. 22.

15. See Jon Tuska, *Billy the Kid, A Handbook* (Lincoln: The University of Nebraska Press, 1983), p. 136.

16. Branch, "*Los Bilitos*," p. 187. All further references are to this edition.

17. Ramón J. Sender, *El Bandido Adolescente* (Barcelona: Ediciones Destino, 1965), p. 247.

18. Margaret Bradford Boni, ed., *Fireside Book of Folk Songs* (New York: Simon and Schuster, 1947), pp. 70–71.

4

YA NOS ES COMO ERA
Twentieth Century Pioneers

9

VICENTE BERNAL AND FELIPE M. CHACÓN
Bridging Two Cultures

ERLINDA GONZALES-BERRY

By the time New Mexico achieved statehood in 1912, Nuevo Mexicanos had begun to assimilate those aspects of the dominant culture that would ensure them participation in the mainstream social and political order. They did not, however, deem it necessary to abandon their own cultural values and traditions but rather struggled to achieve a state of biculturalism whereby they could remain faithful to the ways of their ancestors yet enjoy the promise offered by their new political status. This new consciousness finds its expression in the creative literature of two twentieth-century pioneer Hispanic writers whose works reveal, in one case overtly and in the other more subtly, an ambivalent double-edged discourse of resistance and assimilation. Felipe Maximiliano Chacón and Vicente Bernal, whose works were published within an eight year span of each other, have each left one work in which they combine poetry and short prose. Vicente Bernal's *Las primicias* (Firstfruits) was published in 1916, and Chacón's *Obras de Felipe Maximiliano Chacón, "El Canton Neomexicano": Poesía y Prosa* (Works of Felipe Maximiliano Chacon, The New Mexican Bard: Poetry and Prose) in 1924.[1]

VICENTE BERNAL, 1888–1926

Born in 1888 and spending the early part of his life with his grandparents in Costilla, New Mexico, Vicente Bernal, like many New Mexicans of his generation, worked tending sheep and farming. His education began at the Presbyterian Mission School in Costilla and in 1907 he transferred to the Menaul Presbyterian School in Albuquerque. In 1910 he was admitted to Dubuque College in Iowa and would have attended Dubuque Seminary had he not died on April 28, 1915, of a brain hemorrhage. His single collection of poetry and ten brief pieces of prose and oratory were published posthumously by the *Telegraph-Herald* of Dubuque in 1916. This work demonstrates mastery of a classic American education and of the language of that culture. He does not, however, ignore his mother tongue as half of his collection is written in Spanish. Those who commented on his life and work praised young Bernal for "his diligent and conscientious spirit of getting the best from his tasks." Robert McLean who with Vicente's brother Luis Bernal gathered and edited *Las primicias* comments further in his brief prologue to the text that Bernal "was quiet and unassuming but with a beauty of character that remains to this day strong in the memories of his classmates and teachers" (7). W. O. Rouston, Dean of the College, in an introduction to the text, adds to the minimal sketch we have of Bernal that "in his association with men, the boy showed ready wit, which made him an acceptable companion. . . . Indeed humor was one of his chief intellectual qualities and enabled him always to keep a cheerful outlook" (10).

LAS PRIMICIAS: THE FRUITS OF ASSIMILATION OR SUBLIMATION?

His early experiences in rural New Mexico obviously left a deeply imprinted love and appreciation of nature that was to surface again and again in Bernal's poetry. In fact, nature is often a source of comfort and revelation, a mediator between the secular poetic voice and the divine:

Two birds I spied on verdant hill;
Their heads were near, their breasts more near
I heard no warbling, heard no trill
But was inflamed by God's own love.
("To Miss Self and Jimmy," 24)

In addition to religiously inspired verse of this nature there are examples in *Las primicias* of metaphysical musings. A poem bearing the noncommital title "To——," reveals a contemplative posture and a highly lyrical sense of the precarious nature of human existence:

But why should I desire to scan
More thorny hills, if life's breath
Which seeks an ampler sphere;

A flickering flame, the life of man
Extinguished by the breath of death
Which lurks forever near (28)

This is but one of several poems with allusions or direct references to death and one wonders if Bernal had a premonition of his own premature death. If, in fact, he did, he does not pine away but, rather, exalts in his love of life: "Oh let me kiss thy brow and locks,/And draw thee to my side, my life" (28).

There are a number of occasional poems, some expressing admiration for unnamed young women, others dedicated to classmates. Three of the twenty-four English language poems are songs dedicated to the college, one of which was set to music and accepted as the Alma Mater of Dubuque. Bernal's sense of humor is apparent in his poetry, though it is not always goodwilled. It occasionally takes on a biting edge, thus allowing him to satirize behaviour that he finds objectionable. The following lines from a poem called "A Teacher" clearly demonstrate this side of Bernal's wit:

But years brought greater needs
and greater needs more money.
Till mother lived on weeds,
while he was saying "Honey" (25)

Humor quickly turns to satire in this poem, as Bernal chastises selfish young men who live the good life while their parents sacrifice.

An intriguing question regarding this pioneer New Mexican poet is one upon which we can only speculate for there are no answers in his creative production. Given the times in which Bernal lived, given his ethnic and class background, given the spiritual rootedness, the *querencia* of Nuevo Mexicanos to their land, one wonders whether Vicente Bernal felt alienated during his tenure at Dubuque. Bernal lived in a period in which Hispanics were feeling the increasing pressure of displacement. Beyond their social and economic marginalization, New Mexican mexicanos were severely maligned during the statehood battle. The unflattering portraits initiated as a result of early contacts by Josiah Greg, W. W. Davis. Susan Shelby Magofflin, Lewis Garrard, Phillip St. George Cook, and others became, in the eighties and nineties, full-fledged caricatures in Eastern newspapers.[2] Surely Bernal's teachers and classmates were not ignorant of the political fracas between Washington and New Mexico nor of the stigmatized images of Nuevo Mexicanos produced by the conflict. But if Bernal indeed felt like a foreigner upon his arrival in Iowa in the fall of 1910, or during any part of his six-year tenure at Dubuque, his English language texts leave no clues regarding social alienation.

It is true that Dubuque was a mission school dedicated to the education of foreigners and its primary objective was to teach "so many of strange tongue the syllables of liberty and brotherhood, guiding their first steps to higher planes of usefullness" (editor's dedicatory note of *Las primicias* to Dubuque College). This attitude may well have discouraged explicit expression of feelings of culture shock or of ethnic and cultural differences.

The fact remains that instead of giving vent, through the highly subjective genre he exercised, to feelings of alienation, Bernal's poetry demonstrates a high level of assimilation to the new cultural experiences offered by Dubuque College. The fruits of his immersion into his secular studies are apparent in his frequent intertextual dialogs with poets and writers of the English Language. "Rubyat," "To Tennyson," "To Byron," "Elvira by the Stream," "To Miss Self and Jimmy," are examples of the homage he paid to those who inspired his own muses. Bernal's response to the historical reality of his times with a serious commitment to education is not, however, out of context. Doris Meyer in her investigation of New Mexican newspapers of the Territorial period observes the following:

> The newspapers reveal a three-part reaction by Mexican-Americans to negative stereotyping—first, an awareness of being rejected on the grounds of inferiority and unfitness, especially regarding the agonizing quest for statehood; second, a strong defensive reaction critical of unfounded negative stereotyping; and third, a campaign to transform the image of Mexican-Americans through education.[3]

Did Bernal indeed write this poetry to prove his worth as an American citizen? We will never know, yet readers of his poetry must have been convinced that this young man "from the hills of New Mexico" (*Primicias*, 7), had unequivocally mastered the rules of the game and had thus become a fit candidate for acceptance to the club.

Putting aside the political issues, we turn now to examine a more personal question. Bernal was immersed in a foreign milieu far removed from his home; yet judging from his poetry, Bernal's exile was not of the sort that sharpens the vision of the homeland or engenders nostalgia for the familiar. It was rather an exile that appears to have obliterated his past. The allusions to the landscapes of New Mexico are few. One lone dark-haired girl, a poem to his mother, a short poem prompted "by a postal received from home bearing a picture of a house and the word *Bonita*" (Editor's note, 18), scant generic references to the mountain and desert landscapes of the West exhaust the inventory. There is one short story that suggests Hispanic trappings. In "The Wedding Feast," the names of the characters are Estrella, Porfirio, and Bernardo. And though a specific setting is not indicated, the description of the wedding feast and of mysterious appariations conjure the voices of New Mexico villagers spinning folk yarns of *brujería* (witchcraft) and the like. Beyond this short sketch, however, we find no other traces of New Mexican custom or tradition in the English language prose or poetry.

There remains one very clear indication that Bernal did not totally negate his Hispanic provenance, though he indeed seems to gloss over his cultural roots. About half of the poems included in the collection are written in Spanish. It is in these poems that we find some, though not insistent, expression of longing for home. The frequent mention of letters is perhaps a projection of his *tristeza*. In one poem called "Parte de una carta," (Part of a Letter) nostalgia forms the central motif of the poem. In the following lines he focuses on the strangeness of a typical Midwestern repast:

O! de papas no te decía	*[O! Had I mentioned potatoes*
Pues esas nunca faltan.	*Well there are plenty of those*
Las tengo tres veces al día	*I eat them three times daily*
Si supieras, ya me hartan (69)	*If only you knew how fed up I am]*

The final expression of being "fed up" might just be figurative as well as literal, in which case a sense of alienation may lie between the lines. The fact that the theme is handled humorously is perhaps an indication of a need to sublimate explicit negative evaluations regarding his experiences in the Midwest and his status at Dubuque College.

One poem called "Traducción: The Barefoot Boy," is the most subjective of all of Bernal's poems. In this poem the simple education of a barefoot youth under the tutelage of nature suggests Bernal's own upbringing. In fact, explicit identification of the poetic voice with the addressee of the poem occurs in the final line of the first verse: "Parabienes jovencito!/Yo también fui descalcito" (Best wishes barefoot boy/For I too was one of you) (55). This poem together with one in which Bernal calls attention to his duties as a dishwasher and with the poem in which he chastises his spendthrift classmates suggest that Bernal was not unaware of his underprivileged position at Dubuque. Rouston, upon calling attention to the fact that Bernal spent his vacations working in local establishments, suggests that Bernal's situation did not represent the norm for Dubuque students. As such, we might conclude that the young poet experienced a double dose of marginalization. Yet, he was apparently more willing to call attention to his class status than to his distinguishing mark of ethnicity. In fact, the latter would have been lost to future readers had he not written some verse in his mother tongue.

It is my perception that Bernal's Spanish language poems do not equal, either in rich intertextuality or in treatment of universal themes, those written in English. And though Rouston assures us that Bernal studied both English and Spanish literatures, his Spanish language poetry tends to be uninspired and characterized by facile rhyme. Nonetheless, it stands as testimony to Bernal's pride in being bilingual and to his willingness to call attention to the very aspect that for so long marked his people as unfit for citizenship in the United States.

Vicente Bernal intended to return to New Mexico as an ordained minister. He hoped also to write a history of the region based on his grandfather's oral histories. Unfortunately, this was not to be, for he lived only twenty-eight years. "Written on notebooks, and upon odd-sized pieces of papers" (*Las Primicias*, 14), his poetry left notice of his life and of a gift which, in the words of Dean Rouston, was "finely literary" (14). His "firstfruits" moreover stand as one more link in New Mexico's long and rich Hispanic literary tradition.

FELIPE MAXIMILIANO CHACÓN, 1873–1948

It is unfortunate that the work of Felipe Maximiliano Chacón has gone virtually unrecognized. The poetry and short prose pieces collected under the title *Obras de Felipe Maximiliano Chacón, "El Cantor Neomexicano": Poesía y Prosa*, 1924, come from the pen of a man with a sharp sense of the past and its relation to his time and a profoundly reflective and poetic sensibility. The little that we know of Chacón's life is included in the prologue of the collection written by historian and statesman Benjamin Read. The latter is generous in his praise of "the New Mexican Bard" and impressed that he wrote in a language for which there were few opportunities for formal training. Read's praise of Chacón as the first "to call attention to his country in the beautiful language of Cervantes" (5), demonstrates that the literary achievements of earlier Neuvo Mexicano writers, i.e., Eusebio Chacón, Manuel C. de Baca, Vicente Bernal were either ignored or embedded in oblivion. Whether or not Chacón's published collection received attention or acclaim in its time is not known. We do know that the collection is not mentioned in any of the early Southwestern or New Mexican bibliographies.[5] Yet Chacón was somewhat of a public figure. Like his father Urbano Chacón, who served as the Public School Superintendent for Santa Fe County in the 1880s, Felipe was involved in journalism, having edited such varied Spanish langauge newspapers as *La Voz del Pueblo, La Bandera Americana, El Eco del Norte, El Faro del Río Grande*.

Given Chacón's work in the newspaper industry, he very likely used this medium as an outlet for his poetry prior to publication of *Poesías y prosas*.[5] Read does affirm that Chacón's verse, which he began to write at the age of fourteen, was extensively celebrated in New Mexico, but he does not indicate the medium through which it reached the public. Further research may divulge that some of the anonymous satirical ditties printed in the late 1880s in *La Aurora*, a newspaper edited by Don Urbano, belong to Felipe. These bear a distinct similarity to the "Saeta política" and the "Nocturno a . . ." included in the 1924 collection. However, Anselmo Arellano's collection of New Mexican Spanish language periodical poetry includes only samples from Chacón's published collection.[6] If Chacón did indeed print some of his poetry anonymously, this gives all the more reason to believe Read's opinion regarding Chacon's modesty: "Another characteristic of Chacón is his aversion to publicity, his dislike for appearing important. . . . Chacón is a genius, and like all geniuses, he does not know how to esteem himself" (10–11, all translations of Read's prologue are mine).

Read mentions that Chacón attended public primary schools and later studied at St. Michael's College, which at that time provided only secondary training. He dropped out in order to help support the family when his father died, but he continued to educate himself on his own. That his education went beyond what he might have achieved in high school is apparent in the frequent and extensive classical and historical references in his poetry. Likewise, seven translations of poets such as Byron, Longfellow, and Dresden included in the prologue of *Poesía y prosa*, as well as references to Latin American poets, demonstrate the breadth of his exposure, in two languages, to the humanities. That he may have flaunted his knowledge is suggested by the fact that Varela maliciously refers to Chacón as "*el catedrático*" [the professor] (see note 5).

MATTERS OF THE HEART, THE SOUL, AND THE BODY POLITIC

A reader familiar with Latin American literature will be struck by occasional resonances of Spanish American Modernism in Chacón's work.[7] Especially in his more abstract poems, Chacón, in true Modernist style, avoids commonplace vocabulary and prosaic expression, deliberately stringing his lines in such a way as to capture the musicality of Modernist verse. Though he is not as adept as, let us say, a Leopoldo Lugones or a Rubén Darío, he does create original, well-wrought strophes such as the following:[8]

Y continuando ufana su carrera	*[As she pursued her haughty flight*
vino la nocha y la metió en desvelo	*Night arrived and cast its spell*
y ya en casa, en su ambición y celo	*And once at home, in greed and zeal*
Tomó el candil por flor en primavera.	*For a flower she mistook the flame]*
("La vida," 46)	

Chacón parts ways with the Modernist aesthetic in that he does not cultivate the "ivory tower" pose of the majority of Modernists. In fact, he proves himself to be solidly grounded in the concrete events of his time and not above imitating folk humor through the exploitation of oral verse forms. His stylistic eclecticism is observed in the neoclassical trapping of his heroic odes and the romantic embellishments of his novella, "Eustacio y Carlota," and of a poem called "Nocturno a . . ." In this poem Chacón demonstrates that he was familiar with at least one Latin-American poet, the Mexican Manuel Acuña, whose famous romantic "Nocturno a Rosario" is the formal model for Chacón's own nocturn in which he ridicules a political figure whom he obviously disdained. The disparity between his topic and the form and language chosen to express his sentiments renders an acerbic yet humorous attack. The subject of the poem is identified as one Oñate, though a footnote clarifies that the name is fictitious. Further probing in historical annals might reveal that the object of his barb is Territorial governor Miguel Otero. What is impressive about this poem is Chacón's fidelity in syllabication and rhyme—on occasion he copies lines verbatim from Acuña's poem only to add an unexpected humorous twist—to the original model. This sort of discipline, demonstrated throughout his verse making, tells us that Chacón took poetry seriously and was indeed a master of his craft.

Chacón's *poesía y prosa* is divided into three sections: "Cantos patrios y miscelánea" (Patriotic Verse and Miscellaneous), "Cantos del Hogar y traducciones" (Family Verse and Translations), "Saetas políticas y prosa" (Political Barbs and Prose). The first part is the most extensive and also the most interesting because of its variety. The forty-five Spanish language poems in this section can be placed in six broad categories: love, personal misfortune, philosophical musings, patriotism and homage, commemoration of special occasions, and humor. The poems of personal misfortune, together with those of a philosophical bent and with his domestic poems demonstrate his Modernist tendencies. In his poems of misfortune, the specific sources of the vicissitudes endured remain unnamed, though the poems of death, unrequited love, and betrayal by friends must certainly be taken as evidence of misfortune. We know, for example, that Chacón was touched by death on several occasions; in addition to the death of two children mentioned in the domestic poems, the nostalgic poem entitled "Santa Fe" alludes to the death of his mother and of some brothers. In the poem "Al enviudar mi madre" (Upon the Widowing of my Mother) he takes the death of his father—according to Read, Chacón was thirteen years old at the time—as the point of departure. But, rather than focusing on the father's attributes or on his own sentiments vis-à-vis the death of Don Urbano, Chacón calls attention to the mother's pain as the poetic voice assumes the mother's persona:

Sola, sola lloré	*[Alone, alone I cried*
y al tenderme la noche sus crespones	*and as night her darkness upon me cast*
mi llanto con un suspiro agoté (89)	*I spent my tears with sighs]*

A poem of equal lyrical quality is the sonnet "Devoción." Here the poet speaks of a lost loved one to whom he remains devoted and whose resting place he frequently visits. As in all the poems dedicated to his children, the garden is the key metaphor:

Oh! cielo que tesoro me ha costado	*[Oh heaven, how dear has been the price*
Ese albergue de un polvo tan querido	*Paid for that niche of dust I so deeply love*
Ese sitio de flores nacarado	*For that nectar bed of flowers*
Su cadaver precioso está dormido	*The precious cadaver sleeps*
Bajo esa bóveda que yo he regado	*Under that dome that I have showered*
Con lágrimas del alma que he vertido (74)	*With tears wrenched from my soul]*

There is no indication whatsoever who this loved-one might be. It is tempting to speculate that it is a wife. Of the ten poems dedicated to family members, not a single one mentions a mate as the object of love. Two poems speak in passing of a mother and a father, and the first person plural verbs allude to both parents, but never by name or by epithet is the wife referred to here or elsewhere. Could it be that the absence is deliberate and perhaps linked to the personal tribulations alluded to, not only in several poems but also in a conversation attributed to Chacón by Read: "I have suffered great strokes of bad luck on various occasions in my life . . . but I have not known a pain that I have not been able to conquer. I have faced my fortune, acerbic tribulations, reminding myself that they could be worse, and in that manner triumphed vis-à-vis adversity" (10). The poetry itself reveals only passing allusions to misfortune, and the tenor is one of acceptance rather than of self-pity. Related to the poems of this category are those whose theme is unrequited love. Once again the tone is not one of intense emotion but rather one of resignation. Of course it is possible that the poems of this ilk were written in adolescence, and not linked in any way to misfortune in his adult life.

Chacón's sense of acceptance in the face of adversity tends to be expressed in a number of poems in which he stirs the ashes of the most ancient and perplexing of riddles. It is not, however, twentieth-century horror of the abyss that Chacón expresses but rather tempered sorrow in view of the ephemeral nature of life. These pale sentiments of angst are further overcome by the conviction that it is through action that humans give meaning to life and inscribe themselves in immortality:

Porque sólo el hombre que lucha cada hora	*[For only he who acts each hour*
Y en eso mejora la posteridad	*Thus leaving his mark on posterity*
Transmite su nombre perene a la Historia	*Transmits forever his name to History.*
¡Jamás su memoria se aleja y se va! (82)	*And never his memory will time devour!]*

This conviction is the motivating force behind his many poems dedicated to persons whom he admired and events he held in awe. "A los heroes" (To the Heroes), "Al Obrero" (To the Working Man), "A La Señora Adelina Otero Warren," "Al explorador del Oeste" (To the Explorer of the West), "A los legisladores" (To the Lawmakers), and a poem in honor of Octaviano Larrazolo reveal a poet who admired men and women of action.[9] Together with his patriotic poems, these homages are particularly interesting for what they reveal of Chacón's attitudes toward the sociopolitical events of his time. They also allow us to glimpse the beginning of an ideology that allowed middle class Nuevo Mexicanos to balance their precarious position in a rapidly changing society and to maintain a foothold in the political arena.

Taken as a lot these poems reveal the tenor of Chacón's thought in two directions. The first is a didactic appeal to Hispanic New Mexicans to take pride in their ancestral culture. The lesson is replete with examples of the deeds of honorable and heroic fellow Nuevo Mexicanos and with warnings against the evils inherent in being mislead by "others."[10] Additional incentives are offered when he calls attention to the racial prejudice and injustices suffered by Nuevo Mexicanos particularly in the long battle for statehood. And while he speaks of burying the past and creating a new slate filled with honorable acts, in "A Nuevo Mexico" he nonetheless feels compelled to inscribe past injustices, thereby calling attention to his people's mettle. Despite decades of ignominious acts by outsiders, they have endured and survived with their integrity intact, prepared to be outstanding citizens. They must not, however, forsake their origins is his message in "A los legisladores."

The second tendency in these poems is an insistence on bearing witness to personal and collective patriotism. As proof of loyalty to the United States, Chacón recalls the participation of Nuevo Mexicanos in the Indian, Civil, and Spanish American wars. How burdened Hispanics of this period must have been with the suspicion of disloyalty! In his long panegyric dedicated to Nuevo Mexicanos who fought in World War I, Chacón attempts to set the record straight once and for all. It is not enough, however, to state merely that they fought bravely; it is the *Americanness* of their acts that ennobles the soldiers and completes the encomium.

The high point of Chacón's patriotic rhetoric is reached with a poem written in 1918 commemorating the Declaration of Independence of the United States. Six years have passed since New Mexico joined the Union and citizen Chacón has weathered the storm of change. Gone are all allusions to injustice and gone the insecurity embedded in the defensive testimonies of collective loyalty of other poems. Instead, we hear in "A la patria" (To My Country) a self-assured poet claim filial ties to his forefathers Washington, Adams, and Jefferson as he unabashedly appropriates for himself the myths of their (now his) country:

Mas al pensar bendigo yo la estrella	*[Reason leads me to bless the star*
Que dirije en la tierra mi destino	*That leads my destiny upon the earth*
Y que guía mis pasos con su huella	*And in its wake with civic equality*
De cívica igualdad por el camino (24)	*It guides my steps upon that path]*

In exchange for this privilege the poet offers his unyielding patriotism: "Recibe por lo tanto, Patria mia/Las notas de mi ardiente patriotismo" (Receive therefore sweet land of mine/ the notes of my fervent patriotism).[11]

At first glance Chacón's patriotic discourse would seem to indicate that he was under extreme pressure to demonstrate, display, or otherwise prove his loyalty and that he seizes the pen to do so. Nonetheless, we cannot ignore the fact that his verse is written in Spanish and therefore intended for a Spanish rather than an English reading public. Did his public indeed need be reminded of its own loyalty and patriotism? Probably not. How then can we reconcile Chacón's ambivalent rhetoric which, on the one hand, calls for loyalty to and pride in ancestral culture and, on the other, pledges uncompromising patriotism to the "new way" in a language *that bears testimony to his commitment to the former*? It is unlikely that Chacón was openly advocating official cultural pluralism. The struggle for statehood had proven, in a most profound manner, that cultural difference was not viewed favorably by the dominant culture. Thus, to do so when the events were still within the reach of memory might have been dangerous. Perhaps herein lies a clue to Chacón's use of Spanish. He could do, in that language, what he dared not do in English. And, yet, there remains a blatant contradiction. If Chacón's demonstration of patriotism deflates somehow what, given the times and circumstances, appears to be a radical and potentially dangerous call to cultural preservation, as I believe it does, why did he bother with this push-me-pull-me pose in the first place? Is it possible that his rhetoric on the importance of cultural identity was more symbolic than radical?[12] The appeal to ethnic identity has long been a universal ploy of the ethnic middle class to consolidate power within boundaries of dominant sociopolitical networks. Since this has been and continues to be a political modus operandi in New Mexico, what we have in Chacón's creative work is evidence of the early stages of this strategy. When Chacón exclaims in his homage to Larrazolo that it is not only the Democratic party that stood behind him, but *the people*, we can almost detect the message implicit in the rhymed endecasyllables: Together we elect one of our own; divided (into two parties) we loose out to the Bulls of the world—to the "others" of his poem "To the Lawmakers."[13] Save face but maintain (political) space is what Chacón's ambivalent rhetoric advises. The achievement of the task he laid out before himself involved a certain amount of skill and a good dosage of veiled manipulation. There is no doubt that Chacón the editor (the political persona) hid behind Chacón the poet to inspire poetry that covertly testifies to a deeply entrenched Nuevo Mexicano political ploy that for decades has nurtured cultural survival and simultaneously ensured participation in the political machine of the dominant society.

F. M. Chacón's three narrative pieces complement, each in its own way, the poetry. The first piece, "*Un baile de caretas*" ("A Masked Ball") is a humorous sketch that tells the story of the deception of a fatuous young man by his buddies, who set him up to fall for a mysterious stranger at a masquerade ball. Upon unmasking herself, Carmen Hinojosa turns out to be José Olivas. The smitten lover takes the next train out of town and does not return for many years. The highbrow style of what turns out to be a rather mundane tale places the story squarely in the Modernist vein, recalling the narrative of Rubén Darío.

Don Julio Berengana tells the sad tale of a sheepherder who splurges his money on a saloon girl with whom he falls in love. Crushed when he discovers that she has abandoned him for an *americano*, he takes solace in the memory of the night he met her, the night that "he was king." The final note expressed in this sketch is very much in keeping with Chacón's attitude of accepting one's lot as doled out by destiny.

The modern reader of the third prose piece entitled simply *Eustacio y Carlota* might be tempted to read it as a parody inasmuch as Chacón resuscitates the trappings of the by then worn-out Byzantine novel that has as its theme separation, mistaken identity, and subsequent recognition of two loved ones. However, since no motive for parody is apparent, the second choice is to dismiss the piece as a product of Chacón's romantic temperament. There are some interesting details in the story, however, which suggest the possibility of an allegorical reading. The two Quintanilla orphans, after the death of their mother in a tenement in New York City, are adopted by Anglo parents and given Anglo names. The young boy makes a name for himself in the Rough Riders batallion in the Spanish American War, the sister is educated by a wealthy family in Colorado. As fate would have it, they meet in California, fall in love, and marry only to discover, as they undress in order to consummate their marriage, the identical medals given to them by their dying mother. And just to make sure, the young girl bears the proverbial identifying birthmark. The marriage is annulled and Amanda marries her brother's childhood friend, Orlando. The two children born of this union are given the original names of the orphan siblings: Carlota and Eustacio. Despite the melodramatic tone of this romance, might it be possible to read it as a parable for the *rico* class of New Mexico? Loss of natural parents (Mexico); "legal" adoption by Anglo parents (United States) and subsequent assimilation; discovery and acceptance of true identities; affirmation and reappropriation of ancestral roots by restoring original names and bequeathing them to the new generation are the elements that suggest such a reading. There is, furthermore, a character named Melitón Gonzales, a native New Mexican who like Henry fought bravely in the Spanish American War. His popular speech, however, sets him apart, identifies him as a member of the non-elite group. Moreover, he is not fond of women (symbol of marriage, the machinery that most rapidly sets the assimilation process in motion). In the end, however, he too succumbs to the inexorable hand of destiny and he marries a distinguished woman from San Bernardino, ever acting with "nobility of heart, sanity, common sense," and fidelity to duty. And is that duty the duty of husband to wife, or the duty of citizen to country? (The same patriotic duty displayed by Melitón's participation in the Spanish American War?) Patriotic duty, we must acknowledge, oils the wheels of assimilation. If this reading is considered, the message of Chacón's ideology, hidden beneath an ambivalent rhetoric of assimilation, *and* of preservation of ethnic culture, draws to a neat closure.

The two twentieth-century New Mexican pioneer writers considered here have produced work that bears testimony to the contradictions inherent in the historical reality of their time and to their attempts to mediate those contradictions through creative literature. On the one hand, they felt pressed to prove that they were morally and intellectually fit to join the new order. On the other, there was the tug of the old ways and the desire to preserve tradition. This they did by writing in their native tongue. Is this not standard procedure in a bicultural setting, we might ask? The fact remains that Chacón and Bernal lived in an era in which demarcations between the dominant and the subordinate cultures were clearly drawn and the antagonism between members of each had not yet been buried. It would be very tidy indeed to be able to conclude categorically that, given these conditions, the writers had internalized the dominant ideology, or, on the contrary, that their work stands as a definitive discourse of resistance. In all honesty, I can only say that their writing bears a stamp of ambivalence with which they sought to bridge two disparate realities.

NOTES

1. Vicente Bernal, *Las Primicias* (Dubuque, Iowa: Dubuque Telegraph-Herald, 1916); Felipe Maximiliano Chacón, *Obras de Felipe Maximiliano Chacón el "cantor neomexicano": Poesía y Prosa* (Albuquerque, NM, 1924).

2. See note 4, Introduction.

3. Doris Meyer, "Early Mexican-American Response to Negative Stereotyping," *The New Mexico Historical Review* 53:1 (1978) 77.

4. See Mabel Major, Rebecca W. Smith, and T. M. Pearce, *Southwest Heritage: A Literary History With Bibliography*. (3rd revised edition, Albuquerque: University of New Mexico Press, 1972); and Lester Rains, *Writers and Writings of New Mexico* (Las Vegas, NM: English Department, Highlands University, 1934), bound typed manuscript in Special Collections, Zimmerman Library, University of New Mexico; Doris Meyer's article, "Felipe Maximiliano Chacón: A Forgotten Mexican-American Author," *New Directions of Chicano Scholarship* (San Diego: Chicano Studies, University of California San Diego) (pp. 111–26) is the first critical attention called to Chacón's work.

5. His political views were certainly aired in journal print. A letter, called to my attention by Francisco Lomelí, written by Colorado statesman Casimiro Varela in response to an article published by Chacón in *La Voz del Pueblo* appears in *El Independiente*, 30 January 1913. Varela accuses Chacón of betrayal, resorts to a good deal of name calling, and attributes Chacón's ill-mannered behavior to the fact that he is fatherless. Might Chacón's response to Varela be contained in a short poem called "*Ingrato*" [Ungrateful One], in which he lambasts a friend who turns his back in time of need?

6. Anselmo Arellano, *Los Probladores Neomexicanos* (Albuquerque: Pajarito Publications, 1976).

7. Modernism was a literary movement (1888–1910) that gave new life to Latin American literature. It is characterized by new and fresh language, a search for the ideal in both expression and concept, exoticism embodied in oriental and classical themes, symbolism, and musicality. Modernism allowed Latin America to forge an artistic identity independent from that of Europe and, at the same time, prompted a hearty welcome to the modern aesthetic mainstream.

8. Lugones was an Argentine Modernist and Darío, the father of Modernism, a Nicaraguan. I disagree with one critic who sees Chacón's poetry as typical of the sort of "florid verse popular in his time." I believe Chacón was much more conscious of his craft and that, on the whole, his poetry surpasses that of other poets of the period.

9. Octaviano Larrazolo, originally from Zacatecas, Mexico, is the first Hispanic to have been elected governor of the state of New Mexico.

10. The "others" are alluded to in this poem as tyrants of yesteryear. In the homage to Larrazolo, they are more explicitly identified as the Santa Fe Ring.

11. The significance of the placement of this poem within the collection must not be overlooked. It appears in the number two slot, immediately after "*A los heroes*" (To the Heroes). The first bears proof of loyalty; the second demonstrates that loyalty has borne its just deserts, that is, that Nuevo Mexicanos have earned the right to consider themselves bona fide citizens of the United States.

12. Had his or any other Hispanic's call to cultural preservation been of a politically radical nature, the Spanish language would not have disappeared from public education and the official public domain (i.e., the courts) as early and as easily as it did. Despite the fact that the framers of the state constitution set forth stipulations for the maintenance of Spanish in public education, the Hispanic community was apparently not very active in demanding adherance to the law until the late sixties.

13. Beyond alluding to the "bullish" nature of Lazarralo's opponents the poet refers to a concrete person, Richard "Bull" Andrews, who apparently was one of Chacón's least favorite politicians. The poem entitled "*Saeta política*" (Political Barb) has as its theme Andrew's political chicanery.

10

LAS ESCRITORAS
Romances and Realities

TEY DIANA REBOLLEDO

> *Without the guidance and comfort of the wives and mothers, life on the Llano would have been unbearable, and a great debt is owed to the brave, pioneer women who ventured into the cruel life of the plains, far from contact with the outside world.*
>
> FABIOLA CABEZA DE BACA[1]

Early Hispanic women writers of New Mexico are often mentioned only in passing, if at all, in the discussions of general cultural production of New Mexico and the Southwest. They are part of a "culture of silence" which, until the Chicano cultural renaissance of the late 1960s, effectively obscured those women who did write, and who, for the most part, remain unread and unpublished. Despite this exclusion, many Hispanic women were creating and writing. There are three sources that pinpoint early literary production by women writers: 1) the oral tradition (which includes the *cuentos* collected by the Public Works Administration in New Mexico in the 1930s; 2) the Spanish language literary tradition, and 3) the works written in English.

One of the earliest texts of local writers in Spanish is a poetic lament written in Chama, New Mexico, by Hirginia V. González.[2] This lament written on October 26, 1898, is a memorial dedicated to her *comadre* María Elena de Romero on the death of her husband Juan de Dios Quintana. The lament follows a carefully rhymed, perfect ballad form. In the text the author speaks of the inadequacy of her words but nevertheless wishes to extol Juan de Dios and to commemorate his life as well as to recognize the grief of his wife and children.

Another early writer and the only woman included in Anselmo Arellanos' *Los pobladores Nuevo Mexicanos y su poesía, 1889–1950*, is María Esperanza López de Padilla. In her short autobiography, López de Padilla (b. 1918) explains that as a child her father and his friends recited poems that they never wrote down.[3] Her mother also knew many verses, prayers, and sayings by heart. López de Padilla was not influenced by established writers. Her poetry is characterized by her relationship to the landscape and to the people she knew. One text, "Simplicidades" [Simple Things], sings to common ordinary objects and images that bring the lyric speaker happiness—among them are romantic images such as poppies in the breeze, the wind blowing through her hair, but also clothes drying on the line, the bathing of her children, and white curtains in the window. She documents her relationship with her mother and tells how her name, María Esperanza, was chosen. Her father chose Esperanza (Hope) but her mother and godmother wanted María (in honor of the Virgin). In "María Esperanza" she explains that her parents were from the north of New Mexico and her godparents from the north of Mexico. Both families had recently arrived in Pueblo, Colorado, to work in the steel mills. With her baptism the two families sealed their friendship forever. In this poem we receive cultural information as well as information about the patterns of migration in Southwest. Although code switching is minimal, (the only word in English is "steel works"), that word symbolizes her family's economic dependence on non-Hispanic institutions.[4]

In addition to these pieces, some women writers were able to publish in Spanish language newspapers. Many more original texts, I am sure, languish carefully guarded in family trunks and among old photographs and papers. Nevertheless in the 1930s through the 1950s at least three New Mexican writers were involved in the cultural flourishing of the Northern New Mexican writing scene. Fabiola Cabeza de Baca Gilbert, Nina Otero Warren, and Cleofas Jaramillo were not only active in their communities and in public life, but each of them produced several books that recorded the folklore and ways of Hispanic New Mexico: books that preserved recipes of native peoples, collected folk tales, and at the same time, revealed many autobiographical details of their lives and those of their families. They are also highly original works that consciously tried to preserve, in writing, the Hispanic oral tradition.[5] They were written by a first generation of New Mexican Hispanic women writers who were conscious of their heritage and cultural identity. They were writing, in part, because they wanted to communicate their sense that this culture and identity was somehow slipping away, that it was being assimilated through changing conditions and cultural domination.

These writers document their lives and the lives of Hispanic New Mexicans during the time when the land and society in New Mexico were shifting from Hispanic to Anglo control. They came from old, landed, upper-class New Mexican families. The perspectives presented in their stories therefore generally reflect these class origins. They extol the Spanish (and not the mestizo or Indian) heritage, and see the past as a utopia in the pastoral tradition where humans were integrated with nature and tied to the land. Because many of their books are first-person accounts utilizing stories of older family members (already an incorporation of the *cuento* tradition), such as aunts and grandmothers, or persons employed by the family (for example, "el cuate", the ranch cook in *We Fed Them Cactus*), the narrative accounts often extend back into the nineteenth century.

In *We Fed Them Cactus* Fabiola Cabeza de Baca tells about the arrival of Hispanic pioneers to the Llano Estacado, the establishment of ranches and communities, the arrival of Anglo settlers and homesteaders, and the gradual loss of the land by Hispanics due to drought, fencing and plowing practices of homesteaders, taxes, and other political realities. There is rich documentation of ranch life, politics, education, and recreation. By the end of the book, with her father's death marking the end of an era, the life of abundance is over, the tone is one of sadness and loss for:

> The Hispano has almost vanished from the land . . . but the names of hills, rivers, arroyos, canyons and defunct plazas linger as monuments to a people who pioneered into the land of the buffalo and the Comanche. These names have undergone many changes but are still known and repeated. Very likely many of those who pronounce them daily are unaware that they are of Spanish origin. . . . Corazon Peak took its name because its shape resembles a heart. Cuervo is the Spanish word for crow, and the creek received the name from the abundance of crows in that area. La Liendre was originally settled by a family who were small in stature, whose nickname was liendre, meaning nit. Las Salinas were the mines. Los Alamitos signifies little cottonwoods. (6)

Nina Otero Warren's *Old Spain in our Southwest* (1936) and Cleofas Jaramillo's *Romance of a Little Village Girl* (1955) also parallel the changes over the same time frame. The New Mexico landscape as well as the land is seen as an Eden where humans and animals (and Native Americans and Hispanics) lived in harmony with nature.

Their work, along with that of other New Mexican writers of the time, has been severely criticized by more recent Chicano literary critics. Raymond Paredes, in a generally perceptive study, condemns these early accounts saying that the writers had a "hacienda" mentality, that they ignored social concerns, and that in general it is difficult to take their writing seriously because they were too "sappy and genteel." Furthermore, he states;

> The Mexican American literature in English that emerged from New Mexico during the 1930s evokes a past that, while largely imaginary, is presented with rigid conviction. . . . the writers described a culture seemingly locked in time and

> barricaded against outside forces. Here the New Mexico Hispanos pass their lives in dignity and civility, confronting the harsh environment with a religiosity and resolve reminiscent of the conquistadores themselves.[6]

Paredes also notes that "there is something profoundly disturbing about this body of work. It seems a literature created out of fear and intimidation, a defensive response to racial prejudice, particularly the anglo distaste for miscegenation and ethnocentrism" (56). Paredes is one of the few male Chicano critics to even consider the early women writers in a serious way. Nevertheless, his perspective on their writing is exceedingly harsh, and he overlooks those parts of their writings that contrast with the "romantic" view. He criticizes these writers for internalizing the class, sexual, and racial attitudes of their socialization process. Nevertheless, Paredes' commentary raises some interesting questions as to what should be included in the literary canon. To ignore the writings of the middle and upper middle class is to ignore literary history as well as the origins of much women's literature.[7] The non-traditional forms of their writing and their "feminine" concerns make many male critics dismiss early efforts by women to write and to break into print. However, they usually have no problems with the "masculine" concerns of long, boring descriptions of skirmishes between natives and soldiers or with the "sappiness" of long-winded, sugar-coated love quatrains published by romanticizing male authors of the 1880s and early 1900s.

To this end, therefore, the study of the writings of early women needs serious consideration particularly when one considers that these women were confined to fairly rigid gender roles, and that writing was not considered a suitable pursuit for women (except for the occasional poem). It is a wonder that they wrote at all. The assumption implicit in many critics' writings is that "true" Mexican-American literature cannot ignore social concerns, and that the definition of Chicano/Mexican-American culture is a monolithic concept best described as a "culture of resistance." One must nevertheless define what it is they are resisting. Clearly these early women writers are not only describing the loss of their lands and culture, but also they are actively resisting culturally defined roles for themselves and for all Hispanic women. Close readings will show that the paradise depicted at the beginnings of their books becomes a land of transition and struggle (almost a purgatory) in the early twentieth century.

In Nina Otero-Warren's book most things of value are presented as an end product of Spain, evidenced by her title *Old Spain in Our Southwest*. Nevertheless, one must look at her work as an early attempt to preserve in literary images a vanishing way of life. The transition from utopia to instability is clearly delineated by Otero Warren who states, "This southwestern country, explored and settled nearly four hundred years ago by a people who loved nature, worshiped God and feared no evil, is still a region of struggles."[8] And while she concentrates on quaint folkloric vignettes praising the lost Spanish heritage, she nevertheless communicates to us her growing sense of disjunction from the landscape, illustrating her feeling of alienation and isolation in a time of transition.

She envisions the Indian as well as the traditional Hispanic shepherd as integrated with nature both in religious belief and in their understanding of the land. She, however, remains on the edge, longing for the sense of integration denied her, in part because she is a woman, but also because she represents a culture and class undergoing a profound transition.

> In the only room of my house, a melancholy candle was flickering as if gasping for breath. . . . I had a feeling of vastness, of solitude, but never of loneliness. . . . The night was alive with sounds of creatures less fearful than humans, speaking a language I couldn't understand, but could feel with every sense.
>
> In the night the storm broke, wild and dismal. The wind hissed like a rattler, and as it struck the branches of the trees, it made a weird sound like a musical instrument out of tune.
>
> At dawn, the clouds parted as if a curtain were raised, revealing the outline of the mountains. The hush following the storm was tremendous. . . . As the shepherd was extinguishing the camp fire, there appeared on the top of the hill a form with arms stretched to heaven as through offering himself to the sun. The shepherd from his camp and I from my window watched this half-clad figure that seemed to have come from the earth to greet the light. A chant, a hymn—the Indian was offering his prayer to the rising sun. The shepherd, accustomed to his Indian neighbors, went his way slowly, guiding his sheep out of the canyon. The Indian finished his offering of prayer. I, alone, seemed not in complete tune with the instruments of God. I felt a sense of loss that they were closer to nature than I, more understanding of the storm. (4–5)

The language throughout this description emphasizes her outsideness, her nostalgia, her loss. She communicates her sense of disjunction from the landscape, illustrative of her feelings of alienation and isolation in a time of change.

The romanticized class differences noted by Paredes are also abundantly clear in this text. Otero Warren says, "The Spanish descendant of the *Conquistadores* may be poor, but he takes his place in life with a noble bearing, for he can never forget that he is a descendant of the Conquerors" (9). And later, "Near the house of the patrón were the houses of the peones who were not slaves, but working people who preferred submission to the patrón rather than an independent chance alone" (10). Nonetheless, there is an awareness that the old system is not just, "The men of the village liked to hunt, and hunting was more of a necessity than a sport, as a means of obtaining food; game was plentiful. . . . There was very little money in the country and whatever there was was usually in the chests of the patrones" (50).

We also have descriptions of the work women did and we discover, for example, that they did the plastering of the walls in houses and churches: "The women did the plastering. They worked all day save for the afternoon siesta time. They protected their skin from the hot sun by a face powder which they made for this purpose. This face powder called cáscara was made of dried bones finely ground, mixed with herbs and made into a paste" (11).

We also see the incorporation of the oral tradition in the "stories" told in the text. In "The Field Crosses of the Farmers" the author tells of seeing a small cross on the stumps of trees left after the clearing of her land during planting time. When she asks Anastacio, the foreman, his reason for "planting" crosses in her fields, he answers that it is to protect her crops and tells her the following tale.

> . . . there lived in our community an old woman who was peculiar in her mind, and because of the strange things she said and her queer actions, she was called a witch. She lived alone in one small room. It was the duty of the community to see that she did not want either for food or for wood to keep her warm. . . . As you know, *señora*, there is always a concern among us for the old and the unfit.
>
> One day, in the spring of the year, this old woman went about. . . . "whispering in the shadows." There was great concern in her voice, so the people passing by stopped in to listen. The old witch told the men that there was a great storm coming. "See the white clouds on the Sandia mountains," she said. "It is God's hand laying a cloth on His high altar to receive the pure snow. The heavens will freshen the earth. But it will then turn bleak, and the raindrops that fall on your fields will turn to hail which will beat down and make cold your young plants!"
>
> They all laughed at this witch. They said that she was simple-minded, for the skies were clear and the country flooded with sunshine.
>
> Days passed and the villagers watched their crops grow bigger and stronger. They had forgotten the first warning of the simple-minded old woman. They paid little heed to her mutterings and wanderings. How she insisted that everything would be lost to them unless they planted little crosses in their fields. . . . one night a cold wind came down from the mountains. . . . the clouds parted and the skies opened. The rain came down like many knives. The hail came, and beat all growing things to the earth. The following morning, the ground looked as through a blanket of ice had been laid over it. My grandfather said, "It is a cold shroud for the young plants; the storm wished to hide its own damage."
>
> The men went silently to their fields. Their crops were frozen and beaten down to the ground. In all this valley only one field had not shared in this ruin. An old couple had listened to the witch and had believed. They had nailed little wooden crosses to their fence posts and to the stumps of trees. Their fields were green. Their corn and bean plants were refreshed by the moisture and untouched by hail or frost. Silently and greatly humbled these men returned to their homes, their faith as real as their sorrow.
>
> Since that time, patrona, when we plant seed, and before the day's work is ended, we erect small crosses (123–128).

And finally, included in the text are some indications of the growing tensions between Anglos and Hispanos as the Anglos enter the territory and populate the state in ever growing numbers.

> "Strangers do not understand our hospitality," said Don Antonio's brother-in-law. "A young attorney from the States came to the hacienda a short time ago on business. He brought his wife. My *señora* received her guest in her usual courteous manner. The shutters of the guest room had been opened, the room well aired, the sun allowed to look through the deep windows. The high bed, with its feather mattress, was made ready. A silver basket, filled with fruit, was placed beside the candle on the bedside table. On retiring for the night, my wife told the American lady: "My house, all that it contains, is yours." She did not know that this phrase, perfectly sincere, is our way of making a guest feel at ease. One hardly accepts a house and its belongings! My *señora* had left a set of jewelry, a brooch, bracelet and earrings on the dresser of the guest room. The American lady took these away with her, thinking it was a gift to her. It was her understanding of our hospitable, "My house is yours". (33)

Cleofas Jaramillo in *Shadows of the Past*, *Romance of a Little Village Girl* and *The Genuine New Mexico Tasty Recipes* (1939) parallels the concern with the disappearance of cultural traditions. Her mother was a storyteller, and in *Spanish Fairy Tales* Jaramillo translated into English and published twenty-five of her mother's stories. Jaramillo was active in trying to preserve Hispanic culture, not only through her writing but also by founding the Sociedad Folklórica. In June 1935 she saw an article in *Holland Magazine* about Spanish and Mexican food, an article which, in her opinion, was not accurate. She thought, "Now, why don't we who know our customs and dishes do something about preserving the knowledge. . . . we who know the customs and styles of our region are letting them die out."[9] In her cookbook she preserves that aspect of culture embodied in native food, encouraged no doubt by her brother Reyes Martínez who was involved with the *Federal Writers Project*. And in *Shadows of the Past* she leaves us with a series of unforgettable portraits of the women in her family. One of them is her Grandfather's spinster sister who was "quite amusing":

> She was very stately, tall and fair, with a delicate skin, for the sun or wind never touched it. She wore her long silver braids like a crown around her shapely head, which was always covered with a silk skull cap to protect it from the air. She ground roots and herbs, rubbing them on her temples and back of her head, to cure her continuous headaches, which she said were caused by *aire en la cabeza*, air in the head.
>
> At night she pushed her bed into the farthest corner, away from doors and windows, placed two chairs on the side, and spread the bed cover over them, to

> screen off the air, which she said made whirls in the corners. When not occupied with her remedies or knitting, aunt Cencionita made thin, long-necked, long-waisted, rag dolls for her nieces. When we begged her for thread to sew our doll dresses with, she would give us a long strip of muslin and show us how to pull out some strands and twist them into thread.[10]

Jaramillo's work is important, moreover, because, although influenced by "los cinco pintores" and the writer Mary Austin and although she writes in English, it is clear that the necessity of writing in English made her task more difficult. The loss of the Spanish language emphasizes what she sees as a disappearing culture, and she feels "alien" writing in English. In *Romance* she states "I feel an appalling shortage of words, not being a writer, and writing in a language almost foreign to me. May I offer an apology for my want of continued expression in some parts of my story."[11]

Romance of a Little Village Girl, an autobiography, is perhaps Jaramillo's most important contribution to documenting the past because in it she gives us the perspective of almost seventy years of her life. Framed in a *romance* (ballad) form, she narrates once again the descent from an edenic girlhood in northern New Mexico, to a more ambivalent present where she feels the loss of traditions, the loss of New Mexican Hispanic culture. Like Cabeza de Baca she traces the history of the "New Spanish Province" from the time of the early settlers (and the role of her family, the Martíns—later Martínez—and the Luceros) played in its settlement, to the present day. Here, for example, Jaramillo details the Hispanic perspective as the area became an American territory in 1848. "After existing surrounded by the struggle of life and death . . . for almost three centuries under Spanish rule, with one stroke the new colony was brought under the rule of a foreign government under a new, unknown constitution, which helplessly the Spanish population must accept" (6–7). Only slowly, according to Jaramillo, did the Hispanic *ricos* become aware that they needed to control the rapidly deteriorating situation.

> The Spanish Dons could not prevent their leisurely sons from patronizing these gambling places and squandering fortunes. Eventually it dawned on the parents that times had changed and the new generation was changing with them. The only remedy they could see was to send their sons to Eastern schools, where they could learn the English language and deal with this energetic race. Some of these boys came back from Georgetown and other schools speaking good English but still playing the part of the fine gentlemen they had been brought up to be. They would not take to work. The fortunes of the Dons soon passed out into the hands of strangers, for minimum sums. Adobe mansions began to crumble into ruins, their owners having lost their means to keep them up . . . servants were discharged and Doñas now became their own maids (8–9).

Although a somewhat simplistic analysis of the complex reasons why the Hispanics lost their fortunes and their lands, this passage reveals the frustrations and bewilderment felt during this time of loss and change. Her own father prospered over these years, however, because of his energy and his various business interests: sheep raising, farming, and mercantile. He was, moreover, a man who "kept up with the times." Her mother too was energetic; "If my father was out busy . . . and someone came who wanted something at the store, mother dropped her work and went and waited on the customer. Our store supplied the simple needs of the people, from dry goods and groceries to patent medicines, which mother would tell the people how to use" (11–12).

One chapter of interest is her account of English teaching schools. Jaramillo says that Spanish teaching schools had been established in Taos in 1721 and Padre José Antonio Martínez had his own college in Taos in 1826. Jaramillo herself attended the convent school in Taos when she was nine. As she states "We were not allowed to speak any Spanish and the first English words were, 'Put some wood in the stove'" (29). At this school there were only six boarders and fifty day students. The nuns had a hard time indeed keeping the school open. After five years Jaramillo transferred to Loretto Academy in Santa Fe where there was just one other "Spanish" girl in her class. Here, after she asked, she was allowed to formally study Spanish (52).

The book documents, in precise detail, Jaramillo's life, particularly the Spanish customs and rituals that governed it: religious ceremonies, holidays, courtship, weddings, and funerals. In 1898 she marries wealthy, good looking Venceslao Jaramillo. She relates the birth and death of two children, her travels, her husband's life in politics, and finally the birth of a third child Angelina. Still young, her husband becomes ill and dies. Jaramillo finds that their extravagant life has been lived at great cost. All their fortune has been lost and Jaramillo becomes a businesswoman in order to survive. Her strength throughout her life is clearly evident, particularly when her daughter Angelina is brutally murdered when still young.

Romance is a text, like that of the other two New Mexican writers' narratives, where the landscape underlies the narrative content. At the beginning of the narration her home was a paradise with crystal clear springs and bountiful meadows, the landscape was pure and clean with no social disorders to jar the sensibilities. Early in the book there is a passage describing her return home from boarding school:

> I climbed up on the seat by my father and rode along inhaling the fresh fragrance of the newly-awakened sage and wild flowers. The desert plain seemed turned into a fairy-land. Icy winter had given place to warm summer, melting snow and filling rivers and causing ditches to overflow. Here and there we dropped into a verdant

> little valley, the sparkling river fringed with new green plants and drooping willows. From the edge of the highest ridge we looked down into the Arroyo Hondo . . . which in its rich verdure seemed to lie asleep, the deep silence enveloping the valley broken only by the rattling of our carriage wheels or the distant barking of the dog. Happy in letting my tongue loose in my fond Spanish, I had chatted all the way. (41–42)

At the end of the narrative her perspective has completely changed. Returning to her old village, the scene is one of sadness and loss.

> After dinner, my nephew took me in his car for a visit to my old home at Arroyo Hondo. In fifteen minutes I found myself gliding down the once-steep hill now almost level, and I was surprized to see before me the little sunken green valley. What a different aspect it now presented! High pitched roofs, a new, modern-looking schoolhouse—with nothing left but memories of our once lively, happy home, now in melting ruins . . . With a sigh I turned away from this sad sight. (187)

Even the Virgin that once stood in the chapel "seemed to have a sadder and a lonelier expression that day" (188).

All three writers are remarkable for their concern and their production in a time when most Hispanic women had little education, and if they were educated, little leisure or encouragement to write. They did so against the overwhelming dominance of Anglo culture and language, against patriarchal norms. Their narratives are valuable not only because they preserve accounts of folk life but because in particular they document the customs a woman thought important to record: those accounts of private lives and duties of women not usually included in male narratives. Thus we are able to glimpse something of the experience of the female half usually left out of history.

Cabeza de Baca's *We Fed Them Cactus* is especially valuable for its historical perspective. The title itself is symbolic since the cactus stands as a central symbol not only for her but also for many of the contemporary women writers. The cactus holds water in reserve over times of draught and protects itself with thorns. The book refers, on one level, to the drought of 1918 when Hispanic farmers fed the cactus to their cattle for survival. On another level, it refers to the Hispanos themselves as survivors able to weather misfortunes. At the beginning of her narrative, once again the New Mexico landscape is a rich, nourishing, fruitful yet domesticated garden of Eden. "There are wild flowers in abundance, and when the spring comes rainy, the earth abounds in all colors imaginable. The fields of oregano and cactus, when in full bloom, can compete with the loveliest of gardens" (1). It is clear her family depends upon the land, and that the relationship of land, weather, and landscape is dominant.

> Money in our lives was not important; rain was important. . . . rain for us made history. It brought to our minds days of plenty, of happiness and security, and in recalling past events, if they fell on rainy years, we never failed to stress that fact. The droughts were as impressed on our souls as the rains. When we spoke of the Armistice of World War I, we always said, "the drought of 1918 when the Armistice was signed. (11–12)

We Fed Them Cactus is an extraordinary account of the evolution and change suffered by a people expressed through references to landscape.[12] By the end, as in Jaramillo's account, we have this description of the land as a purgatory. Bitterness over lost land and nostalgia over lost culture are implicit in the images of a barren wasteland that before had been paradise:

> The land between the years 1932–1935 became a dust bowl. The droughts, erosion of the land, the unprotected soil and over grazing of pastures had no power over the winds. The winds blew and the land became desolated and abandoned. Gradually the grass and other vegetation disappeared and the stock began to perish. There was not a day of respite from the wind . . . In the mornings upon rising from bed, one's body was imprinted on the sheets which were covered with sand. . . . The whole world around us was a thick cloud of dust. . . . The winds blew all day and they blew all night, until every plant which had survived was covered by hills of sand. (p. 177)

The tragedy of the Hispanos of New Mexico is reflected in the interrelatedness between the land and her father's life. In addition, the loss of her father's land parallels the loss of land to all Hispanos. The land is gone forever, having passed into the hands of Anglos:

> The land which he loved had sucked the last bit of strength which so long kept him enduring failures and sometime successes but never of one tenor. Life so cruel and at times so sweet is a continuous struggle for existence—yet one so uncertain of what is beyond fights and fights for survival.
>
> He is gone, but the land which he loved is there. It has come back. The grass is growing again and those living on his land are wiser. They are following practices of soil and water conservation which were not available to Papa. But each generation must profit by the trials and errors of those before them; otherwise everything would perish. (p. 178)

We Fed Them Cactus is also an account of how women functioned in this community. Throughout the narrative we get glimmers of a life contrary to typical stereotypical images of Hispanic women. Cabeza de Baca apparently had a somewhat free childhood, growing up under the supervision of her grandmother.

"As a child, I was a problem to my grandmother and was forever running away from her. She called me from morning to night trying to locate me" (84). This is in contrast to the childhood of Cleofas Jaramillo who depicts the women and children as enclosed behind the tall walls of the houses and, on a rare day, describes an excursion out in the country; "I can still see myself, like a wild bird set free of a cage, running from one berry bush to another, filling my little play basket, my heart beating with delight at the sights of beautiful mariposa lilies, blue bells, yellow daisies, feathery ferns."[13] Cabeza de Baca, nevertheless, had to learn to behave like a lady of her class, and with some nostalgia tells us;

> Each boy on Papa's ranch had from ten to twelve horses as remuda. I had my own horses, too, but they were gentle ponies. True to aristocratic rearing, I had to lead a ladylike life and should not resemble that of our uncouth neighbors whose women were able to do men's work. I always envied any woman who could ride a bronco, but in my society it was not done. How skillfully they saddled a horse! I often watched them but it was never my privilege to have to do it. When I arose each morning, my horse was already saddled and tied to a hitching post waiting for me if I cared to ride. (p. 129)

She also admires the pioneer Hispanic women and the women who lived on the ranches. As she says, "The women had to be a hardy lot in order to survive the long trips by wagon or carriage and the separation from their families . . . they had to be versed in the curative powers of plants and in midwifery, for there were no doctors within a radius of two hundred miles or more" (59). Her own grandmother was "called every day by some family in the village, or by their *empleados*, to treat a child or some other person in the family. In the fall of the year she went out to the hills and valleys to gather her supply of healing herbs" (59). This same grandmother was later able to convince the villagers to vaccinate for smallpox after terrible outbreaks of the disease. Her grandmother is the symbol of both traditional medicine associated with the *curandera* and the progress of modern medicine.

In *The Good Life* (1949), Cabeza de Baca incorporated the oral tradition (as well as her training as a home economist) in a text that combines creative tales about a mythic family, the Turrietas, living in an isolated village in New Mexico, with recipes for the preparation of traditional foods. Because this book was meant to be used as a guide to food, the most important characters in the book are the women in the family. And among these women is a singular character, Señá Martina the *curandera* of the village. Little is known about her but the following:

> The medicine woman seemed so old and wrinkled to Doña Paula and she wondered how old she was. No one remembered when she was born. She had been a slave in

> the García family for two generations and that was all any one knew. She had not wanted her freedom, yet she had always been free. She had never married, but she had several sons and daughters.[14]

Doña Paula, the mother of the family, converses with the *curandera* saying:

> "Señá Martina, you will have to tell me the names of the plants and what their uses are. I can never remember from one year to another," said Doña Paula.
>
> "You young people believe too much in doctors and you have no faith in plants," answered Señá Martina . . .
>
> "Doña Paula, why don't you put down all the prescriptions that I give you each year? You who can write need not rely on your memory only, as I have for years. I cannot live forever and when I am gone you will have no one to ask."
>
> "You are right," said Doña Paula. "I shall write them down." She had said the same thing for twenty years. (14)

Señá Martina grumbles and limps her way through the narrative, becoming by the end a thoroughly likeable character. She arrives at the house on Christmas eve limping and complaining that if she had not promised, she would not be there to help as her rheumatism is getting worse every day, while in the same breath she asks, "What do you want me to do?" And when she dies, the entire community is saddened:

> The men carried the body on a litter as there was no coffin for Señá Martina; she had asked to be given an Indian burial. She had often said to Doña Paula, "I do not want a coffin. There is no need for pomp and expense because once we are dead nothing matters anymore. The coffin rots and we return to the earth as was intended." . . . Doña Paula was the chief mourner for Señá Martina, who had been closer to her than even her own mother. She had depended on her since she came to El Alamo as a bride and theirs had been a silent friendship, deeper than words could express and only the heart could feel. (43)

For Cabeza de Baca, the *curandera* is the symbol of the old ways of healing as well as knowledge that is passing on. As these women who have stored the tradition in their memories die, the only way to preserve it is to incorporate as much as possible into the literary, written tradition. And Cabeza de Baca does so in her books, consciously attempting to capture as much of the orality of that tradition as possible, using narration as well as inner monologues prayers, songs, sayings and, yes, recipes to portray it. Thus the feminine discourse of this tradition is intimately tied into the portrayal of a female way of life, in the work they do, and in the traditions and rituals they hold dear.

Cabeza de Baca started her long distinguished career of public service (thirty years as an extension agent) as a country schoolteacher and in *We Fed Them Cactus* she has left us an account of her life during this period when she taught reading, spelling, history, grammar, arithmetic, physiology, penmanship, and geography. She had definite ideas about teaching English to Spanish-speaking children, without denying the children the value of speaking their native languages, since among other things, "We had bilingual readers for the primary grades. These were the adopted texts of that day. In this way, the English-speaking children learned Spanish and the Spanish-speaking learned English" (161). At the end of the section on her experience as a teacher she leaves us on this note, "As I look back to my first year of teaching, I know I have never been happier and I have never been among people who were more hospitable, genuine and wholesome than those who lived on the Ceja" (170).

These early writers and the oral story tellers have many things in common. There is a desire to preserve the "old ways": the traditions, the stories, the cultural history and rituals, and the foods and to do it more or less "truthfully." The strong resourceful female is an integral part of both *cuentos* and written tales. The figure of the *curandera/bruja* or healer is a cultural symbol, even an archetype, who stands out as a continuous link from the *cuentos* to the early written tradition and who continues to be an important literary symbol for contemporary writers such as Pat Mora, Carmen Tafolla, and Sandra Cisneros. Description, both realistic and imaginary, is essential because it is through these detailed images that we remember how things were. People, houses, and villages are carefully described. The perspective on landscape is recorded as evidence of a vanishing cultural scene—and we go through an edenic past to a disintegrated present: a symbolic representation of the loss of Hispanic control of the land to Anglo domination. The land reflects connectedness to culture and society. We see this same transference connected to the language issue, as the three sources that comprise our tradition show. Later writers will solve the language problem for themselves by using both English and Spanish and incorporating the oral tradition. At this early stage, however, the writers are still "explaining" things, describing and detailing. Romantic, nostalgic, yes, but at the same time complex, recording, detailing. And quite clearly we can discern that there is a "feminine" voice, for we have women working, laughing, sharing, conversing, caring for each other. These women who are captured in these pages are strong women, they are survivors. Women who used their intelligence and ingenuity to survive in a harsh land—and who did it with laughter, tenderness, and a strong sense of self. Contemporary Chicanas could not ask for better ancestors.

NOTES

1. Fabiola Cabeza de Baca, *We Fed Them Cactus* (Albuquerque: University of New Mexico Press, 1954), p. 61.

2. Hirginia V. González, poem, 1898. Special Collections, Zimmerman Library, University of New Mexico.

3. In Anselmo Arellano, *Los Pobladores Nuevo Mexicanos y su poesía, 1889–1950* (Albuquerque, N.M.: Pajarito, 1976), p. 145.

4. *Mis padres eran del norte de Nuevo Mejico*
Y mis padrinos eran del norte de Mejico
Pero las dos familias estaban recién venidas
A Pueblo, Colorado, en los Estados Unidos
Y allí en los steel works se encontraron
Y con mi baptismo su amistad para siempre cellaron.
[My parents were from the north of New Mexico
And my godparents were from the north of Mexico
But both families had recently arrived
in Pueblo, Colorado, in the United States
And there in the steel works they met
And with my baptism sealed their friendship forever]
(Arellano, 148)

5. In recent years several more books by New Mexican women have added to our knowledge of oral traditions. Moreover, they follow many of the structures of the writers mentioned here. *Enchanted Temples of Taos* (Santa Fe, N.M.: The Rydal Press, 1975) by Dora Ortiz Vásquez is an account of the history and people of Taos as told by her mother and by a Navajo Indian woman simply called "Rosario." Of interest here is the author's intent to capture truthfully the nature of these *cuentos*.

> Rosario always spoke a broken Spanish and when she told stories about Luardo, a character she hated, she used her worst Spanish to tell them. When she told the Padre's stories (Father Antonio José Martínez) she called him Tata-Padre, then she used her best Spanish. It was all very interesting to me. If I could only write them as told! I think this has been my discouragement first in translation and my way of writing might lack or change some of their deep feelings. I wrote those stories for my children in the late 30's and put them away. (xi)

Another is Josephine M. Córdova, *No lloro pero me acuerdo* [I Don't Cry But I Remember] (Dallas: Mockingbird Pub. Co., 1976). Cordova was a school teacher in Taos for many years and her book is a collection of local color, literature, customs, and personal memoires. She proudly points out that she has used no references in her book. "All the material presented here has come to me by tradition" (p. 6). "Having lived a long life, I was here to see the covered wagon and the beginning and outcome of the First World War" (p. 8).

6. Raymond A. Paredes, "The Evolution of Chicano Literature" in *Three American Literatures* ed., Houston A. Baker Jr. (New York: Modern Language Association, 1982), p. 56.

7. There is, in addition, the theoretical issue of what texts should be included in the literary canon: whereas all explorers, conquistadores, priests, and military officers, (Cabeza de Baca, Marcos de Niza, Juan de Oñate et al) are touted as the Aztlanense literature pioneers with their expository texts, the distinctly female non-fictional texts are dismissed.

8. Nina Otero Warren, *Old Spain in Our Southwest* (New York: Harcourt Brace and Co., 1936), p. 3. Further citations appear in the text.

9. *The New Mexican* (Feb. 26, 1954), p. 26.

10. Cleofas Jaramillo, "Shadows of the Past" (1941) in *The New Hispano* (New York: Arno Press, 1974), p. 29.

11. Cleofas Jaramillo, *Romance of a Little Village Girl* (San Antonio: Naylor, 1955), p. vii. All further citations appear in the text.

12. While she was sympathetic to the Hispano loss of land to Anglos, there is no corresponding sympathy about the Indian plight in relation to the Spanish conquest. This is true also of the other writers who view the Indians before the conquest (and for some time after) as barbaric savages.

13. Jaramillo, *Romance*, p. 10.

14. Fabiola Cabeza de Baca, *The Good Life*, 1949 (Santa Fe, NM: The Museum of New Mexico Press, 1982), 14. Further references appear in the text.

11

THE SOCIAL ALLEGORIES OF FRAY ANGELICO CHAVEZ

GENARO PADILLA

Fray Angelico Chavez has had a long and remarkably distinguished career as a man of letters. He has proven himself a capable historian with such scholarship as *Origins of New Mexico Families in the Spanish Colonial Period* (1954), *Archives of the Santa Fe Archdiocese* (1957), *Coronado's Friars* (1968), *My Penitente Land* (1974), and most recently, *But Time and Chance: The Story of Padre Martínez of Taos* (1981). Over a period of some forty years, Chavez has published five volumes of poetry, and for one volume, *The Virgen of Port Lligat*, was recognized for his "very commendable achievement" by T. S. Eliot.[1] And, during these many prolific decades, he has not neglected to write a good deal of short fiction. Many of Chavez's stories appear in two collections—*New Mexico Triptych* (1940) and *From an Altar Screen: Tales from New Mexico* (1957). Other stories remain hidden away in various journals, as well as in church magazines such as the *St. Anthony Messenger* and *Sodalist* where Chavez published regularly in the 1930s and 1940s. In addition to these publications, there is a wealth of miscellaneous material—historical articles, biographical profiles, contributions to other books, and scores of book reviews—for which Chavez must be credited.[2]

Yet, despite this outpouring of material about the Hispano experience in New Mexico, Chavez has been largely overlooked as one of the pioneers of Chicano writing in this century. Moreover, often charged with writing about the romantic, the wistful, the engagingly Spanish past in New Mexico, the social concerns that pervade Fray Angelico's work have been neglected by much recent criticism. Since he is a Franciscan friar, he is often thought to be too mystical, as in his poetry, or exclusively concerned with church related history instead of with what Juan Rodríguez, for instance, calls "the specifics of the Mexican American experience."[3] Other critics like Rodolfo Acuña, author of *Occupied America: A History of Chicanos*, actually dismiss Chavez's historical scholarship, saying that he "ignores history" by expounding the Spanish "fantasy heritage" and the "myth that New Mexicans peacefully joined the Anglo nation and 'became a willing enclave of the United States.'"[4]

While Chavez's poetry may shun the world because it emerges from the meditative tradition and, as he says, the "pure English lyric" form,[5] in its offering of love and service to Christ and the Blessed Mother, such otherworldliness cannot be charged to his historical studies. Unlike much of the poetry, the subject of which I leave for another article, Chavez's history is grounded in the world, even when that world is seen from a religious perspective and lyrically. Fray Angelico's Franciscan habit of mind understandably informs his interest in church related history, but that history has been conducted with painstaking archival research in such studies as *Archives of the Archdiocese of Santa Fe*, *Coronado's Friars*, and *But Time and Chance: The Story of Padre Martínez of Taos*, not to mention the volume of historical articles for various publications. The story he records from such archival material is invariably transformed from dry documents—church records, exploration chronicles, letters, wills—into a colorful narrative pastiche of New Mexico's past four centuries. One such pastiche, *Coronado's Friars*, a study of the identities of the Franciscans who accompanied the Coronado expedition of 1540, is considered the definitive word on a "seemingly unsolvable problem," which was unraveled, not through scholarly luck, but through careful collation and reexamination of sixteenth-century documents that Chavez suspected were based upon an altogether distinct and previous source.[6] That he chose to write primarily on early New Mexico history need not indict him for ignoring the more recent intercultural tensions in the state; on the contrary, his knowledge of the long-ago past often informs his understanding of events in the last century.

My Penitente Land, for instance, is written in the same spirit that early American historiographers reconstructed their people's errand into the American wilderness. Like them, he discovers parallels between life, landscape, and religious devotion in the biblical Holy Land and that in Hispanic New Mexico. Offering no notes at all, Chavez writes a sweeping profile of the Hispanic soul of New Mexico. A people's history, he insists, cannot be understood by merely "stringing out facts and dates." More meaningful is a history that seeks to record the internal dynamics of a people's "beliefs and yearnings," not a pedantic history but rather a spiritual one.[7]

Given this intention, Chavez's *My Penitente Land* is a provocative, even controversial, apologia for a unique cultural and religious climate represented not only by penitente rituals but by an entire way of life. Unless we understand the manifold forces that shaped Hispanic consciousness in New Mexico, we simply fail to touch a people's historic essence, as have so many "American newcomers." He writes from an internal or spiritual perspective, Chavez argues, precisely because so many American historians, well-meaning or not, have so consistently mangled the facts and dates.

In upholding the honor of his people, however, he does tend to over-emphasize the Spanish heritage of New Mexico. His preoccupation, for instance, with what he refers to as the "castizo" ancestory of many New Mexico families and village clans becomes offensive when he rather casually distinguishes between the refined manners of these "pure" *castizos* and the coarser, sometimes uncivil, basically "Indian" manners of the *genízaros* who resided along the fringes of many settlements. Moreover, he notes but does not elaborate upon the abuse heaped upon these people of mixed Spanish-Indian blood by the *ricos*. While he admits that these "poorer and lowlier folks were made to feel that they were an inferior class among God's children," he only mentions their exploitation by the "castizos" for whom they were forced to labor in the fields, as servants in homes, or as livestock herders.[8] But if here he has little to say about class tensions, his fiction, as we will discover, often revolves around such tensions.

As to the charge that Chavez is among those who expound the myth of the bloodless conquest of New Mexico in 1846, one can only say that he reports the fact that General Kearney's march into Santa Fe was not met by resistance, Governor Armijo and his soldiers beating a fast retreat to El Paso. He does go on to say that even though there was no bloodletting in this initial encounter, there later was, physically and certainly spiritually. While Chavez contends that, in the main, New Mexicans accepted the new flag, or at least tolerated it, he points out that there was a good deal of self-serving betrayal on the part of the ricos:

> the New Mexican leaders were of little or no help to their humbler and poorer countrymen. In what we now call "vanity biographies" appended to regional histories of the times, they falsely claimed that their immediate grandparents had come directly from Spain. It was a handy way of disassociating themselves from their less fortunate cousins bearing the same surnames. . . . This, of course, helped them in competing successfully with the newcomers . . .[9]

Finally, Chavez, drawing upon biblical allusion again, rather sardonically refers to the American invaders as cultural "philistines,"[10] crass and materially greedy that they were. Among these philistines were the new non-Hispanic clergy, starting with Jean Baptiste Lamy, a French priest appointed first Bishop of Santa Fe in 1850, who disrupted long established religious practices.

In *But Time and Chance: The Story of Padre Martínez of Taos,* Chavez returns to documentary history to assess the rift between Bishop Lamy's Church and the native Catholic clergy and populace. A full biographical study of Padre José Antonio Martínez, the influential Taos priest who was excommunicated by Bishop Lamy for alleged ecclesiastical infractions, *But Time and Chance* lauds Padre Martínez's clerical and political achievements, without romanticizing his life. On the old controversy over whether Martínez broke his vows of celibacy to sire a number of children, a contention that forms the basis of Willa Cather's vilification of Martínez in *Death Comes for the Archbishop,* Chavez deduces, on the basis of some dubious circumstances surrounding baptismal records, that Martínez may well have been the father of one Teodora Romero's four children.[11] In addition, he says that Martínez had a streak of intellectual pride, tended to boast his accomplishments, and could be manipulative. Still, he gave freely of his inherited bounty, never pressed for tithing, frequently attended the sick, and traveled a wide circuit to bestow the sacraments.

As to the ecclesiastical charges leveled against him by Archbishop Lamy and Lamy's henchman, Vicar Joseph Machebeuf, Martínez was innocent. Chavez shows that Lamy and Machebeuf arrived in New Mexico already quite decided that the native Hispanics were primitive, grossly immoral, treacherous, and stupid; the clergy, moreover, were suspected of even greater moral turpitude, drunkenness and concubinage, for instance, as well as clerical incompetence. Their concerted efforts to scandalize the native clergy, and to denigrate the populace in sermons and pastoral letters, are scrupulously exposed as little more than self-serving and hypocritical sham, not to mention un-Christian behavior.

By way of illustrating the methods American historians used in vilifying Martínez, Chavez shows how easily fragmentary information can be maliciously distorted. Since seminary days, Lamy and Machebeuf had had an *amitie particuliere* that might be considered a bit too particular, too intimate. Just as they had defamed the native clergy's morals, so also might the almost inseparable pair's morals be questioned. To wit, in the text of one Christmas Pastoral Letter warning against various forms of vice, Chavez discovers an interesting discrepancy:

> He [Lamy] warned then in all charity to avoid such scandalous occasions of sin as divorces, dances, and gambling, and ended with a quotation from I Corinthians 6;9–10: *Be not deceived, neither fornicators, nor adulterers, nor thieves, nor drunkards, nor railers, nor extortioners, shall possess the kingdom of God.* If the later detractors of the native clergy in general took this biblical citation as directed at them

> personally, which it most certainly was not, one could ask them with the same unfair reasoning why Bishop Lamy happened to leave out "nor the effeminates, nor sodomites" between the words "adulterers" and "thieves." This would be entirely reprehensible, to say the least. But to the francophile biographers, it seems, everything was fair in love when it came to their French heroes—and in war when it came to the so-called Mexican opposition.[12]

Chavez may restrain himself from uttering outright the charge, but the seed he plants is capable of growing into a mustard tree-sized suspicion. After all, everything is fair in war.

As a historian, then, Fray Angelico is hardly a humble, little brown-robed Franciscan, stooped in quiet prayer while oblivious to injustice and racial hatred, even within his own Church. If he is too *castizo* and too defensive about the labeling of his people as Mexicans, it is largely because he hears well the reverberations of that word's other meanings, its intentional meanings. Among themselves people have long called themselves mexicanos, but when called "Mexicans" by the American invaders it was the echo in the calling that grated, the slant of the quotation marks themselves that bruised—greaser! lazy! stupid! All epithets meant to dehumanize, and therefore to rationalize land grabbing, cultural pillaging, thievery and Aryan disdain. Psychological defenses, Quixotic as they might be, have played a significant role in this people's cultural endurance and distinct identity. Moreover, if non-New Mexicans chastise Chavez for his view that Hispanic New Mexicans have, up until World War II, comprised a distinct, largely insular culture, it is because they would have New Mexico be more Mexican when it simply has not been. This is not to say, as Chavez freely admits, that many people haven't come from Mexico, at least in the last century, or that Mexico has not influenced the way of life in the region. Nevertheless, three hundred years of life on that particular landscape has indelibly forged a unique regional consciousness. That is essentially what Chavez lays claim to in his history, and also in the fiction to which we now turn. For it is in the fiction that the dramatization of the Hispano's long tenure upon that landscape is best evidenced in both its concrete sociocultural realities and its spiritual nuances.

On the narrative surface, the stories in *New Mexico Triptych* and *From an Altar Screen* are genial, often pastoral, even *cuento*-like, while beneath the restrained, stylized writing manifold social tensions come into sharp relief. Read chronologically as the settings move through time from the eighteenth century all the way up to World War II, the stories and the village surroundings in which those actions take shape produce a *retablo* of interconnected panels that dramatize a people's cultural evolution.[13] Most of the stories are, to be sure, about some human relationship gone awry, some moral lapse that is set aright through a visionary experience, usually the dreamlike appearance of a village patron saint, which restores grace and the moral sight of the characters. Even so, there is more complexity to this religious aspect of Chavez's stories than has been recognized by critics who have glossed over his serious social themes while commenting upon their "great charm . . . and droll wisdom."[14] For it is in his fiction that Chavez's writing reveals a complex interplay between the artist's fictive imagination, his moral and religious perspectives, and his historian's knowledge of the troubling realities of New Mexico's intercultural conflicts. The stories subtly examine the tensions that have long existed within the Hispanic culture itself, as well as the tensions between the Chicano and what Chavez in *My Penitente Land* calls the "philistine" American culture.

In the fiction that focuses upon life before the American occupation, stories such as "The Bell That Sang Again," "The Ardent Commandant," "The Black Ewe," the tensions within the culture itself, especially between classes, are played out in isolated Hispanic settings.[15] Each of these stories pits an arrogant stranger, usually a Spanish officer sent to supervise the long established colonists, or a rich *patrón*, against simple villagers or shepherds. In "The Bell That Sang Again," Joaquín Amaya, a dark-featured *genízaro*, fights to the death with a Captain Pelayo, a red-headed soldier born in Spain, who has openly flirted with Amaya's wife. Even before their duel, the stranger has incited resentment and anger in the village men by charming their wives with tales of Spain, while briskly ordering them about and letting fall "occasional slurs about their own unlettered speech or about their humble blood" (6). An adaptation of the well-known *cuento* about a woman who keeps a secret assignation with a handsome stranger only to discover moments before she is seduced that he is the cloven-footed devil himself, "The Ardent Commandant" reveals the colonists' long distrust of the officials arbitrarily imposed upon them by the Mexican Viceroy, many of whom were regarded as equal to the devil himself in their deceit, political greed, and carelessness of the colonist's needs. Outsiders, however, are not the only ones capable of deceit. The *patrón* who owns thousands of sheep and their shepherds in "The Black Ewe" sends a certain villager out onto a distant range in order to seduce his young *genízara* wife. In this story the peonage system is exposed for its inhumanity, for even when the guilty lovers are exposed, it is the *genízara*, her dark hair mysteriously clipped to the skull, who must bear the public burden while the *patrón* returns to his hacienda untainted. Still, his sin does not go unpunished altogether, at least symbolically, since his rich grazing land turns to desert following years of severe draught. The land itself recoils against his deceit.

The misrelations between classes, characterized by the exploitation of the "lowly villagers" by Spanish snobs and self-serving *patrones*, is certainly at the core of Chavez's fiction here. Instead of ignoring history, he dramatizes the intracultural hostilities that have long brewed in New Mexico, hostilities that have, in part, shaped the consciousness of its people. Emblematic of the struggle, the two ill-fated adversaries in "The Bell That Sang Again" lie together in death, "Joaquín with a military dagger completely buried in his throat, while next to him lay the Captain with a hunter's knife pushed deep under his ribs" (12). Through such death embraces was the new world born.

As village life moves closer to the present, after the American invasion, the trials Chavez's characters undergo become less centered in an enclosed area of cultural experience and more entangled in the web of corrupting American influences. Stories like "Wake for Don Corsino," "The Lean Years," and "The Angel's New Wings" simultaneously examine internal cultural erosion and the disruptive external influences for which the railroad, Bishop Lamy's snobbish clergy, and Christmas tinsel are the chief metaphors. Finally, "The Colonel and the Santo," a story set after World War II, dramatizes some of the cultural misunderstandings that continue to strain Chicano and Anglo relations.

Although "Wake for Don Corsino" is a comic tale about a drunk who scares the wits out of his neighbors when he abruptly sits up during his own *velorio* (wake), it nevertheless provides a sharp satirical commentary upon the negative effects of American technology and the capitalistic impulse upon Hispano mores. Like a "faint trailing moan of a locomotive" (65), the American presence begins to resound throughout the territory, not through any direct interaction between Chicanos and gringos, but through subtle references to the railroad that quickly followed their arrival. The railroad, an early symptom of Yankee ingenuity in the West that has become a metaphor for social struggle in other Chicano narratives, is pictured as having "lately spun its threads of steel across San Miguel County" (65).[16] The spider image here is emblematic of Chavez's chagrin with a commercial enterprise that brought with it a poisonous reality.

Don Corsino, who has become the village drunk after the death of his wife, is described as having lost all of his cattle and horses "since he became a daily customer at the saloon, another institution that came with the railroad to Las Vegas and spawned little offshoots in scattered villages like El Piojo" (66). Ironically, the railroad has been double edged in its dealings with Don Corsino, for while he has been drinking himself into a stupor in the saloon brought by the railroad, his neighbors, one of whom hypocritically chants *alabados* (sacred ballads) at his wake, have been rustling his livestock piecemeal and peddling them at the "railroad stockyards in Las Vegas" (68). While no claim is made for pastoral innocence in these villagers, the railroad, and the material greed that fuels it, tears across the common grazing land, breaking a cooperative lifestyle for a handful of silver coins.

In another story set soon after the American occupation, Chavez's social perspective becomes sharper, even openly sarcastic. "The Lean Years" takes aim at the corrupting effects of railroad expansion, the wholesale land grabbing that dispossessed village people of their homes, and the American clergy's attempts to rid the Catholic Church in New Mexico of its "superstitious ways," as well as its native clergy. A story about a man's renewed love for his crippled wife, Chavez's tale may be read as an allegory in which an old, largely uninterrupted village culture is crippled under the weight of time and the invasion of a foreign culture intent upon establishing a new social and economic order.

Set in the period immediately after Jean Baptiste Lamy was named Bishop of Santa Fe, the story describes the annual trip a newly arrived French priest makes to a secluded village to say Mass. Not so much intolerant as condescendingly impatient with a people he regards as culturally primitive and theologically unsophisticated, the priest, a figure of Lamy himself, views a hand-carved *santo*, a statue of San José, that adorns the village chapel as an "ugly monster . . . with its stiff poise, its cheap tin coronet . . . and, worst of all, its unreal black beard that was nothing more than a patch of black smeared around thin drab lips" (80–81). As Chavez points out in *But Time and Chance*, it was precisely this snobbish attitude that led to Lamy's campaign to strip village chapels of their *santos*, a campaign carried out with such insulting efficiency that it almost killed the *santero* tradition altogether.[17]

Chavez's acerbic tone, here and elsewhere in the story, stabs deeply into the body of non-Hispanic clergy propagated by Bishop Lamy and his French and Irish successors to wring the backward, "superstitious," even "immoral" religious practices out of the native people. Bishop Lamy's program to "modernize" the Church little regarded the stabilizing worth of a people's religious traditions. Although a clergyman himself, Chavez's resentment of his people's treatment as an "inferior breed of pinto sheep in the Lord's fold" is unrestrained by his collar. In *My Penitente Land*, he amplifies the charge against the de-Hispanization of the Church:

> Lamy was chosen on the philistine assumption that French priests, for speaking a language derived from Latin, were ideally suited for a people who spoke a Latin-derived language of their own. This illogic has prevailed ever since, that a smattering of the language will supply for the grasp of a culture upon its native landscape. . . . The clash which occurred between the new and the native clergy was due to radical differences in outlook. . . . The resentment grew stronger when they [the native clergy] felt themselves regarded and treated as dust by the new broom. Chief among

> them was the famed Padre Martínez of Taos who, unlike his brethren who either left the ministry or exiled themselves to Mexico, stuck to his post and continued the good fight for his people against all abuses, whether civil or ecclesiastical.[18]

It is this bitter knowledge of the Church's abuses and what Chavez calls the French clergy's "insidious feeling of superiority" that informs stories like "The Lean Years," in which a European-born priest, convinced that the village primitives cannot understand "involved allegory," preaches the same sermon every year to the "simple folks who sat wide-eyed . . . like children" (78–79). Stripped of fellow Hispano clergy like their beloved Padre Martínez, who was summarily excommunicated without due process of canon law by Lamy, it is a wonder Hispanic New Mexicans have remained as steadfastly Catholic as they generally have. In fact, Lamy's "new broom" was so successful at sweeping away the native clergy that not until 1974 was a Hispano, Father Robert Sánchez, installed as Archbishop of Santa Fe—one hundred and twenty-four years of haughty contempt.[19] But such ecclesiastical policies have left scars, long lasting distrust, if quiet and brooding.

At the other edge of "The Lean Years" is an increasingly doomed sense that the landscape upon which José and his wife, Soledad, are playing out their drama of human love is straining under the influence of an encroaching American social and economic system. The new territorial railroad into Las Vegas brings with it not only the mercantile store, filled with frills people hardly need, but also the saloon and a brothel. At one point, José ventures into Las Vegas to sell his handmade furniture and to "see with his own eyes the strange and unbelievable things" of which he has begun to hear. Once in town, he is drawn into the saloon where he downs more and more sweet-tasting Muscatel and Tokay. Suddenly, two prostitutes, finely dressed and speaking a "strange language," enter the saloon. Drunk by this time, and tempted by these fair women, José stumbles off in the direction of the brothel. Along the way, however, he has a change of heart and decides to return to his village, appropriately named La Cunita (the cradle).

Even though this villager has gained a temporary victory over the American plague, the village itself is doomed to extinction. For the people of La Cunita, like people in numerous scattered land grant villages, have been ordered off the land. Soledad's gradual weakening and death is a metaphor for the gradual weakening of the village and the dissipation of its inhabitants. Chavez, however, does not settle for a symbolic gesture alone when he can be more direct:

> This past year some tall blond men with jowls like coxcombs had come with long worded papers from Santa Fe, saying that all the prairie around La Cunita now belonged to them. The inhabitants of La Cunita could no longer graze their cattle and sheep on the land. The sheriff of Las Vegas who came with them sheepishly said

> that they were right, and nothing could be done about it. After getting a pittance for the plots on which their houses stood, the men began taking their families to Las Vegas. They found steady work right away and began replacing the Chinese coolies in the railroad section gangs. (102)

The unmistakable reference to the legal maneuverings of the Santa Fe Ring, with its "long-worded papers" written by shyster lawyers, powerful bankers, and crooked politicians, is strikingly amplified by Chavez's description of the fat flesh hanging from these gringos' clownish faces. Clownish-looking and strange-sounding foreigners, but shrewd and manipulative enough to steal millions of acres in land grants and private ownings.[20] And as always, the victims of this complicity between the Anglo foreigners and the Hispanos in power, represented here by the sheriff from Las Vegas, were the common villagers who, deprived of their grazing rights, were forced to leave their homes for a tenuous existence in larger towns, embryonic cities.

José Vera himself is forced to move to Las Vegas, a booming railroad town in the late nineteenth century. Once there he trades his wood carving tools for a blacksmith's hammer and labors to keep the steam engines moving along the tracks of commerce. José, like most of the dispossessed, endures by strength of will, even makes a decent living for himself in the city, but life is never really the same. Having been removed from the land, the village folk are cut off from their historical essence. The old relationships are broken and people must reconcile their past with an irrevocably altered present.

Even villages that maintained a viable life show the debilitating effects of the Anglo presence. In "The Angel's New Wings" whiskery old Nabor remains the lone embodiment of pre-occupation values and mores. A *santero* who is largely reduced to repairing bultos, obviously the result of the Church's discouragement of the tradition, Nabor is dumbfounded when told that someone has stolen all of the *santos* from the church. "Who would want to steal them?" he asks the priest, but the answer is only too clear. "There are people in Santa Fe or Taos who buy them for good money" (7). Cruelly ironic, isn't it, that the same cultural philistines who, on the one hand, virtually outlaw a people's sacred images, should, on the other, offer "good money" (also ironic since Chavez knows they bought the *santos* for a "pittance") for the "quaint" if "crude" folk art they, to this day, so relish as Southwestern decor in their expensive adobe homes.

Yet, Chavez is critical of his own people as well. After all, the children who replace Nabor in setting up the Christmas *naciemiento* carelessly break the herald angel's wing, and on the eve of Christ's birth the villagers are having a raucous dance instead of watching quietly in the church. In fact, Nabor's allegorical, dreamlike wandering through the village in pursuit of the wooden angel that has magically come to life assumes the dimensions of a bewildering journey through a changing era he can little understand. People in the brightly lit dance hall push, make fun, and spin him around, their respect for their *ancianos* diminished. As he proceeds to the mercantile, where tinsel streamers and a mannequin Santa Claus have figuratively replaced the *santos* earlier stolen, it is clear that the shopkeeper, who is "weighing out some sugar with the added pressure of his thumb," is interested only in the flight of silver dollars into his till. However, while this fat shopkeeper is busy making love to his money, his wife lies in the goat-shed making love to another man. Later, of course, all of these characters attend Midnight Mass, but their worship is empty, hypocritical.

While Chavez the writer is careful not to sermonize in this and other stories, his implicit criticism of his own people's failure to watch over their own traditions and values is clear. Nevertheless, the corruptive influences of the American newcomers remain squarely indicted throughout Chavez's fiction that deals with post-1848 New Mexico. If Hispanos too willingly traded the traditions and rules of the old way for the material superficialities and self-indulgent pleasures of the modern American world, it may be because the bright tinsel, coupled with the American profit motive, a motive pictured as based primarily in greed, has been too coercive to resist with any sustained effort. Chavez's portrait of the Hispano's declining traditions and misdirected values are, to a great extent, seen as an extension of a money economy which diverts the human affections in favor of silver dollars.

In the end, it is apparent that Fray Angelico Chavez's fiction systematically examines the social, cultural, and even moral evolution of Hispano life in New Mexico as it moves from the stable, if troubled, culture of the eighteenth and early nineteenth centuries to a pronounced state of dislocation as the American presence made itself felt after 1848. Chavez's deceptively simple fiction may be read for its religious themes, since the stories do revolve around a village's religious matrix, but the tensions which test each character's faith are usually generated by events with clear social moorings. However simple Chavez's stories, it would be extremely reductive to assume, as some Chicano critics tend to do that his fiction ignores sociopolitical concerns or worse, as do his gringo reviewers, that he is a churchly hagiographer portraying what P. Albert Duhamel, in an early *New York Times Book Review* (1957), calls the "quiet lives of . . . a prayerful people."[21]

NOTES

1. In the Foreword to his *Selected Poems*, Chavez refers to a letter from T. S. Eliot, dated August 7, 1958, in which Eliot wrote: "I have read your poem with much interest and found it a very considerable achievement."

2. Some of Chavez's many titles include:
History:

Archives of the Archdiocese of Santa Fe, 1678–1900 (Washington, D.C.: The Academy of American Franciscan History, 1957), *Coronado's Friars* (Washington, D.C.: Academy of American Franciscan History, 1968), *My Penitente Land: Reflections on Spanish New Mexico* (Albuquerque: University of New Mexico Press, 1974), *Origins of New Mexico Families in the Spanish Colonial Period* (Santa Fe: Historical Society of New Mexico, 1954), *The Oroz Codex* (Washington, D.C.: Academy of American Franciscan History, 1972).
Poetry:

Clothed With the Sun (Santa Fe: Writer's Editions, 1939), *Eleven Lady Lyrics and Other Poems* (Paterson, N.J.: St. Anthony Guild, 1945), *Selected Poems with an Apologia* (Santa Fe: Press of the Territorian, 1969), *The Single Rose* (Santa Fe: Los Santos Bookshop, 1948), *The Virgin of Port Lligat* (Fresno: Academy Literary Guild, 1959; originally published in *Spirit* magazine, 1953).
Fiction:

From an Altar Screen; El Retablo: Tales from New Mexico (New York: Farrar, Straus & Cudahy, 1957), *The Lady From Toledo* (Fresno: Academy Guild Press, 1960) reprinted under the title, *When the Santos Talked* (Santa Fe: William Gannon, 1977), *New Mexico Triptych* (Paterson: St. Anthony Guild, 1940).

For an excellent and exhaustive listing of Chavez's publications, especially those articles that have appeared over some forty years in numerous magazines and journals, see Phyllis S. Morales' *Fray Angelico Chavez: A Bibliography of his Published Writings, 1925–1978* (Santa Fe: Lightning Tree Press, 1980).

3. "Notes on the Evolution of Chicano Prose Fiction," *Modern Chicano Writers: A Collection of Critical Essays*, Joseph Sommers, ed., (Englewood Cliffs: Prentice-Hall, 1979), p. 71.

4. (New York: Harper & Row, 1981), p. 48. Regrettably, Acuña's reference to Chavez seems haphazard, even out of context, relying as it does upon a newsclipping (*Albuquerque Journal*, 18 December 1970) rather than stemming from Chavez's actual historical scholarship.

5. *Selected Poems*, Foreword.

6. Commenting upon this scholarly hunch in his introduction to *Coronado's Friars*, Chavez writes:

> What occurred to me was the fact that some of these contemporary authors were writing identical, or else almost identical, phrases and paragraphs *at the same time and evidently without collusion*. Hence, they had to have a common source, at least for the biographical material we are treating here, even if such a previous source is not found in the bibliography of New Spain. Taking my cue from modern Biblical scholars in textual criticism, I postulated for myself a hypothetical first source. Such a hypothesis makes it possible for one to sift the different parallel texts and arrive at some plausible and even definite conclusions. This source I began to refer to as RB, because it seems to me beyond any doubt that it lies in certain lost writings of an early Franciscan in New Spain, one who delighted in taking down notes on his early brethren, a man by the name of Fray Rodrigo de Bienvenida. (p. xii)

I offer this extended passage as evidence of Chavez's careful and responsible methodology. More than a dreamy propagator of historical myths, he has here done much, as P. Morales in her *Bibliography* says, to correct "400 years of erroneous history" (p. 13).

7. *My Penitente Land*, Prologue, p. xiii.

8. *My Penitente Land*, p. 231.

9. *My Penitente Land*, p. 255.

10. In a most clever political use of biblical allusion, a use which makes his entire biblical framework seem sharply telegraphed toward that one sharp allusion, Chavez, relying on commonly assumed connotations of the term "philistine" and "Aryan," writes:

> . . . here we find a most apt [biblical] allusion in the invasion of Canaan by Goliath and the Philistines, a Hittite nation which was wholly unrelated to the "sons of Shem and Ham" in the

> Near East. A taller and more robust people, they likewise came from the European or Aryan "sons of Japheth." But here in this New World Canaan there was no David with his slingshot to stem the tide. The American Goliath conquered handily and, just as it happened that the Philistines left their name in "Palestine," so the new Hittites brought the name "American" to cover and saturate New Mexico in more ways than one. (p. 249)

11. For a full discussion of Martínez's alleged paternity, see Chapter 5. And for an entirely different view on this controversy, see Ray John de Aragon's *Padre Martínez and Bishop Lamy* (Las Vegas, N.M.: Pan American Publishing Co., 1978) in which Aragon writes:

> One writer says the priest was legitimately married to one Teodora Romero and that they had a rather large family. In fact, Teodora Romero was the wife of one of the padre's brothers and they did have a large family. But, the Martínez name was legion in the church records of Taos with similar name combinations; Antonio, José Antonio, or Antonio José. This may account for the stories that the priest had a harem and most of his descendents were proud to acknowledge his paternity. (p. 112)

12. *But Time and Chance*, p. 105.

13. In the Author's Note to *From an Altar Screen* Chavez defines the term *retablo* thusly:

> *Retablo* (ray-tah-blow), n. 1. A sacred picture crudely painted on a board. 2. A series of such paintings, also statues, set in panels or niches on a decorated frame to form a reredos or altar-screen.
>
> —Unwritten Dictionary of New Mexico Spanish

14. From the cover-leaf introduction to *From an Altar Screen*, this comment by Paul Horgan, a well-known Southwestern historian, is a typical reading of Chavez.

15. With the exception of "The Angel's New Wings," which appears in *New Mexico Triptych*, all of the stories to which I make reference appear in *From An Altar Screen*; all references to stories I discuss will be by page number only.

16. In Rudolfo A. Anaya's novel, *Heart of Aztlan* (Berkeley: Justa Publications, 1976), for example, the railroad system becomes the chief symbol of exploitation and oppression over an entire Hispanic community.

17. Unfortunately, as Chavez also points out, one part of this campaign was actually carried out by at least one clerical lackey, Padre Eulogio Ortiz, who was trying hard to please Bishop Lamy by "cleaning up" the Taos area.

18. *My Penitente Land*, pp. 258–59.

19. Father Robert Sánchez was installed as the Tenth Archbishop of Santa Fe on July 25, 1974 to the thunderous ovation of thousands of New Mexico Hispanos. The surnames of the preceding nine prelates read as follows: J. B. Lamy (1850–85), J. B. Salpoint (1885–1894), P. L. Chapelle (1894–1897), P. Bourgade (1899–1908), J. B. Pitaval (1909–1918), A. T. Daeger (1919–1932), R. A. Gerken (1933–1943), E. V. Byrne (1943–1963), J. P. Davis (1964–1974); see *The Official Catholic Directory* (New York: P. J. Kennedy, 1982).

Remarking on the anti-native attitude of these men of God, Chavez says: "It was his [Lamy's] successors, and the continuing flow of priests from France and elsewhere, who now regarded the "mexicans" as neither morally nor intellectually fit for the priesthood" (*My Penitente Land*, p. 259).

20. For a complete account of the dealings of this Santa Fe Ring, see Acuña's *Occupied America*, Chapter 3 or Carey McWilliams's *North From Mexico* (New York: Greenwood Press, 1968), Chapter 7.

21. December 15, 1957, p. 16.

PAST MEMORIES AND FUTURE VISIONS

The Contemporary Period

12

SABINE ULIBARRÍ
Another Look at a Chicano Literary Master

CHARLES TATUM

Poet, essayist, and prose writer, Sabine Ulibarrí holds an important place in contemporary Chicano literature. In addition to scholarly works, textbooks and thought-provoking essays, Sabine Ulibarrí has published two books of poetry, five collections of short stories, and he has edited another collection of his students' prose and poetry. All of his creative literature was originally written in Spanish although his short stories have also appeared in bilingual editions. When compared to other Chicano writers, his literary output is significant, particularly if one takes into account that he is one of a handful of contemporary Chicano writers who is completely comfortable with written literary Spanish. This fluency with written expression is a reflection of the writer's upbringing in a completely Spanish-speaking environment where Hispanics constituted the majority culture. In addition, literary Spanish was an important part of his childhood for his father would often read Spanish literature to his family. Ulibarrí's academic training and his rigorous study of the Spanish literary masters have undoubtedly reinforced his earlier language background and contributed significantly to his mastery of the language seen in his own creative works.

His two books of poetry, *Al cielo se sube a pie* and *Amor y Eduador*,[1] were both published in 1966 and are similar in content, language, and poetic expression although the first is perhaps broader in its subject matter. In *Al cielo se sube a pie*, using a language the Spanish poet Angel González describes as "pausado y preciso," (deliberate and precise) Ulibarrí includes poetry that deals with love, the woman, his native Tierra Amarilla, uprootedness, solitude, the tragic consequences of progress, life as a transitory state, and several other themes. His poetry is filled with color, finely rendered images, and language carefully selected and appropriate to the content. Dominant in this collection is poetry dealing with various aspects of love: the elusiveness of authentic love; the transitory nature of passion; deceit and disillusionment in the love relationship. In general, the woman/lover is idealized and exists in a more real state in his imagination than in true life. This concept seems to be in keeping with his vision of the illusory nature of love, especially physical love. The poet/male depicts himself, as, on one hand, privileged by her attention, favor, and affection yet, on the other, victimized by her distance and abandonment of him. A related love theme is his belief in the easy conquest of woman. Her willing submission is doomed not to last; only love after sacrifice and intentional effort on the part of both parties will endure. His view of woman in her role as a lover in this collection of poetry is best characterized as distrustful. She is beautiful—as he aptly describes in his series of *pie* poems—but mindless, affectionate and undependable. Her world is a limited one and her view of herself and others is shortsighted. In her relationship to the male she is the source of much of his pain and agony.

Another dominant theme in *Al cielo se sube a pie* is the poet's sense of uprootedness in an alien world in which a premium is placed on success and achievement. In the poem, "Fuego fatuo," he laments having left his native rural Northern New Mexico, having paid the price of loneliness and a feeling of abandonment for less authentic and ultimately less tangible rewards. The poet describes himself as the only member of his family who has left the mountain in pursuit of an elusive star, and while he has tasted success he is still searching for the "cima errante" (wandering summit). Although he is resigned to his self-chosen fate, the poet is saddened when he lets himself remember what he has sacrificed. In "Patria de retorno" (native land of my return) he recognizes the impossibility of returning to the comfort and security of his childhood home. Although he may be welcomed back by friends and family, nonetheless, he is still a "forastero en mi casa ancestral" (stranger in my ancestral home).

The poet is thus destined to wander the earth on a constant search, waiting for death, filled with hunger for permanence, plagued and saddened by his loss of roots and family. Poetry is his consolation, his vehicle to give expression to life's pain. Artistic expression provides a kind of salve for the poet's wounds and at the same time allows him to eternalize his pain.

As the title indicates, *Amor y Ecuador* has two major themes: poetry focusing on the poet's impressions and memories of Ecuador and poetry devoted to love. In the first section of the book on Ecuador, Ulibarrí shares with us the meaningfulness of his visit to the South American country in 1963. Always the keen and thoughtful observer, he records his visit in a way that allows us to share with him its personal significance. From the first poem, he draws us into the experience of passing time in the Andean country that is geographically so different from his native New Mexico yet has so much in common with it. They share a common heritage and the poet sees Albuquerque and Quito as two poles of the same Hispanic world. Ecuador in general and Quito in particular represent a positive element for the poet, something he has been out of touch with back home. He arrives in the Ecuadorian capital filled with hope and anticipation. He descends from his plane to find himself still in a world of clouds and sky and mystery. In one poem Quito is described as God's work and in another, the first line of each of a six-stanza poem devoted to Ecuador, he repeats: "Aquí todo me humaniza" (Here everything humanizes me).

The expected wonder and awe of Ecuador's rich Spanish-Indian history and its geographical splendor constitute only one aspect of his Ecuadorian poetry. In addition to this sensorial and cognitive awareness of geography and history, the poet is in touch with something deeply human that touches a sensitive chord in him. Perhaps he is at home here as he has not been since leaving his beloved mountainous Tierra Amarilla. The poet lets himself be touched by the people he passes on the streets and by the warmth and welcoming from Ecuadorian friends. He feels rejuvenated, joyful, excited and yet, profoundly saddened and angered by the misery and exploitation that surrounds him. In a poem titled "Indosincrasia" the poet reveals these conflicting feelings. The Indian is a reserve of dignity and strength, and at the same time the poet recognizes in his eyes the long history of frustrated hopes and suffering. The poet identifies with this experience and asks his brother, the inhabitant of the high and lonely Andes, to look into his New Mexican eyes where he will see reflected the same suffering of centuries. The poem ends on a note of solidarity and hope; together they can overcome their shared tragic history.

The poetry of the second part of *Amor y Ecuador* seems to have taken on a decidedly more melancholy tone than the love poems of *Al cielo se sube a pie*—this poetry has a bittersweet quality arising from the poet's belief that he cannot have what he wants; love, to him, is elusive, momentary, and even frightening. His own love overpowers him and he warns the beloved to flee lest she be destroyed by it. Images of abandonment, disillusionment after love making, and bitter memories of unrequited love abound. In one poem, he visits the birthplace of a past lover and is filled with the sadness of her absence. For the first time, we see references to sin and guilt associated with the poet's relationships with lovers. Tragically, the poet sees himself as destined to carry with him for life the burden of his guilt; he has altogether given up hope in salvation.

Ulibarrí's prose can best be characterized as a kind of intrahistory, a chronicling and recording of the values, sentiments, relationships, and texture of the daily lives of his friends and family, the Hispanic inhabitants of his beloved Tierra Amarilla. The writer himself has commented that with his short stories he has tried to document the history of the Hispanics of northern New Mexico, the history not yet recorded by the scholars who have written otherwise excellent studies of the region. Ulibarrí believes that these historians do not understand at a deep level the Hispanic heritage that predates by hundreds of years the arrival of the Anglo soldier and businessman in the mid-nineteenth century. He recognizes that the Hispanic world that he knew as a child is fast disappearing under the attack of the aggressive Anglo culture. His stories, then, constitute an attempt to document the *historia sentimental*, the essence of that culture before it completely disappears. In addition to this missionary zeal, his stories are just as importantly his attempt, as a personal objective, to regain his childhood experiences. As reflected in much of the poetry discussed earlier, he feels as though he has been uprooted from his culture and his family and in documenting his memories of a childhood and adolescence in Tierra Amarilla he is trying to resurrect for himself a repository of humanizing experiences. In answering the questions about his people—how they were (are); what it meant to live in an environment where Spanish was the dominant language; the significance of living daily the values and traditions of America's oldest non-Indian culture—he ultimately answers the questions about himself: Who am I? Where do I come from? What have I lost? How much of it can I regain?

Ulibarrí's short stories are more personal than documentary or social history. One looks in vain for explicitly social themes although they may be buried under a rich surface of local color, language, and family and community ties. He explains that he is different from many Chicano writers in that he was raised in a majority Hispanic culture and does not have an ax to grind in recreating the world of Tierra Amarilla. This is not to say, however, that he is not socially committed—this side of him is clearly evident in his essays and in his comments made before groups such as the 1967 Cabinet hearings in El Paso.

Most of his short narrations are about individual personalities: relatives and acquaintances, those he knew well and those around whom local legends had developed; those he loved and those he feared as a child. All seem to have affected him strongly and together they make up a whole community of Hispanos from Tierra Amarilla. It is apt to compare both of his collections of short stories to Spanish and Spanish American *costumbrismo*, the literary genre that is characterized by sketches of different regional customs, language, rituals, types, and values. Local color, legends, and personalities are the stuff of his stories as he methodically sets out to recreate this world for us. His stories are not sterile reproductions but rendered so that his poetic sensibility shows through and enhances the sense of excitement and mystery he associates with those memories.

The first story of the volume *Tierra Amarilla*[2] is an excellent example of how the author brings to bear his poetic sense upon his childhood memories. "Mi caballo blanco" reminds the reader of another poet, Juan Ramón Jiménez, who immortalized a little grey donkey in his memorable prose poem *Platero y yo*. Ulibarrí describes the magical qualities of a legendary horse that filled his childhood with poetry and fantasy. The young adolescent narrator tells us of the wonder with which he had heard of the marvelous feats, some real, some fictitious, of this unusual animal who roamed the high plateaus with his harem of mares. The horse symbolizes for the adolescent a world of masculine strength and sexuality, a world he is about to enter himself. He dreams of capturing this magnificent creature and parading him around the town plaza observed by lovely and awe-struck young women. He does capture the horse and goes to sleep believing that because of his feat he has finally entered the world of adulthood, yet the child in him remains; the inner excitement and laughter he feels betrays the exterior calm that for him is the proper demeanor for a real man. And when the horse escapes, not only does his fantasy world come tumbling down, but he recognizes that he's still very much a child at heart. He gratefully accepts his father's comforting words and decides that the glorious animal is better left an illusion in its freedom than being forced to enter the real world—the adult world—in captivity. Ulibarrí thus sensitively and skillfully reconstructs a pivotal moment in an adolescent's life—perhaps his own—where the battle between childhood and adulthood is fiercely waged.

The next three narrations of *Tierra Amarilla* are humorous accounts of personalities and the many stories, legends, and half-truths that developed in the community of which they were a part. The first is about Father Benito, a chubby angelic Franciscan friar who was assigned to the local parish. Although well-intentioned and loved by the parishioners he is described as somewhat naive. In addition, he was handicapped by knowing little Spanish. It was his ignorance of the language that was the source of much humor and mischief at his expense. Ulibarrí recounts that Sunday Mass was veritable torture for the parishioners who, anticipating that their dear Padre Benito was going to make a huge blunder during his sermon—he inevitably did when he gave it in his stumbling Spanish—would spend the entire mass desperately trying to keep from rolling in the aisles with laughter.

The third story of the volume is told from the perspective of a fifteen-year-old narrator who recalls how the local town drunk, Juan P., and his two spinster sisters got their name Perrodas. It seems one day many years before, the two sisters were attending a very solemn rosary for a dear friend who had passed away when one of them let pass a substantial amount of air. She fainted. The author speculates that this occurred either from embarrassment or because of the sheer amount of energy needed to contain the air. Only the dead person was not shaken by the explosion. The scandalous event was never fully discussed publicly but soon after it happened Juan and his sisters began to be called Perroda, a play on *pedorra* meaning flatulent. A more serious side of this story is the apparent delight with which the community labeled the family, thus destroying their reputation, turning Juan into a drunk, and dooming his two sisters to spinsterhood. The adolescent narrator is cognizant of this somewhat vicious side of his beloved community. The story also contains another serious sub-theme having to do with the narrator's conflict with his father who wanted him to abandon his books and his poetry to cultivate more virile and more worthwhile—in his father's view—pursuits. The narrator keenly feels this disapproval and goes to great lengths to please him by performing such manly activities as chopping wood.

"Sabélo" is a good illustration of how legends were created in Northern New Mexican communities. Once again, the story is presented by a young narrator—nine years old in this case—who filters reality through his child's imagination to give birth to another character endowed with fantastic powers. The story focuses on Don José Viejo, a sharp-tongued old man who was as ancient as hunger itself. After overcoming his fear of the old man, the young narrator develops a warm friendship with him and an almost religious respect. Don José is gifted with an innate talent for story telling, especially fantastic ones with himself as the central figure; for example, how he killed a huge bear after being badly scratched on the back. But the story that really captures the young boy's imagination has to do with Don José's ability to remove honey from a beehive without receiving so much as one sting. According to Don José, he is not bothered by the bees because, in fact, he is a bee or at least indirectly descended from bees. After swearing his young friend to secrecy, the old man tells him how this came about. His father was kind of a pied piper for bees who rescued them from captivity and liberated them in the forest. His mother was a queen bee who one day kissed her savior on the lips; he magically turned into a bee; they had a child—Don José—who was raised in the hive and then, inexplicably, took on a human form. Further, the scratches on his back are really bumblebee stripes and not wounds received at the hand of the fierce bear. The impressionable child concludes: "Yo me quedé temblando. Yo sabía que don José Viejo no mentía." ("I was left trembling. I knew that Don José Viego wasn't lying").

The last story of *Tierra Amarilla* differs in length, form and content from the author's other fiction. Dealing with a number of philosophical themes such as life as a dream, the father-son relationship, the development of the individual personality, the story, which is divided into six short chapters, seems to focus on the struggle of the narrator, an author of thirty years, to free himself from his dead father's image and domination to become an autonomous individual. Alejandro the narrator has returned to his birthplace, a small Hispanic town, to celebrate the completion of his biography of his father. Shortly into the visit he begins to notice that his friends and especially the family members are behaving strangely towards him, but it is not until he sees a reflection of his father's face in a raised wine glass that he is able to explain their behavior. Finally, random remarks made earlier about his resemblance to his father fall into place; somehow he has assumed his father's personality to the extent that others mistakenly are reacting as though he were him. In addition, an inner voice from his subconscious suddenly speaks to him—Alejandro believes he is hearing his own father, especially when the voice tells him, "Desde tu edad más tierna, yo te absorbí, y viví en ti" ("From your most tender years, I absorbed you and I lived in you"). Here the confusion between the two personalities is heightened. Are these voices real? Are they the result of the narrator's insecurity about his own identity? Is life a dream? Is he his father's dream? Is he not autonomous? What importance do his own life experiences have in defining and shaping his personality? All of these questions rush over Alejandro leaving him in a confused and vulnerable state. During the remainder of the story the narrator tries to answer these questions, all the while harrassed by what he believes to be his father's voice, which repeats that he wants to eternalize himself through his son. Alejandro falls into a troubled sleep and wakes up suffering from amnesia. He does not remember who he is or who the woman is who tenderly nurses and shows him affection. Although he does partially recover his memory, he remains at the end precariously balanced on the edge of confusion, not fully knowing who he is and not fully trusting that the woman who shows such love for him is really his wife.

With *Mi abuela fumaba puros y otros cuentos de Tierra Amarilla*,[3] Ulibarrí adds to his published work about his native northern New Mexico ten more sensitively rendered tales. In this attractive bilingual edition, beautifully illustrated by artist Dennis Martínez, Ulibarrí presents a tapestry of childhood memories of life among the hardy and proud Hispanos of Tierra Amarilla. His stories are a series of carefully drawn sketches of individuals—family, friends, acquaintances—who play an important role in a young boy's strides towards adulthood: the matriarchal grandmother, viewed with a combination of tenderness and fear; Uncle Cirilo of whose size and mighty voice the child lives in awe; the legendary Negro Aguilar whose feats as an indomitable *vaquero* and skilled horse-tamer are reputed in the furthest reaches of the county; the astute Elacio Sandoval, the biology teacher who talks himself out of marrying the woman he does not love; Roberto, who one day goes to town to buy more nails and does not return for four years.

With obvious enthusiasm, Ulibarrí shares with us the wide range of the young boy's feelings and experiences: his terror upon finding himself face-to-face with *la llorona* herself; the profound sadness upon learning of his father's sudden death; the proud response to his much admired childhood heroes when they deign to talk to him. The author draws on local legends and popular superstition and combines them with vivid details from his childhood to create a rich mixture of fact and fiction. His stories are tinged with hues of longing for a past that although he cannot relive, he has brought to life with deft and broad strokes of his pen. The book thus forms a composite of the memories of a writer sensitive to the child in him, who looks back nostalgically to a time of closeness and warmth among people who treated him with understanding and love.

As Rudolfo Anaya points out in his introduction to this attractive volume, what emerges in all of the stories is a strong sense of daily life and tradition among the Hispanos of Northern New Mexico as well as the bonds of their loving and sharing. Another important element is humor which, while present in his earlier stories, here is more ribald.

The title story is a sensitively created and tender description of the author's grandmother, a kind of silent matriarch who sustained the family for many decades through difficult periods and tragic events. In the narrator's memory her relationship to her husband, although somewhat tumultuous, was characterized by an underlying feeling of mutual respect and fear, "somewhere between tenderness and toughness." The narrator affectionately recalls that after his grandfather died, the grandmother would absent herself to her bedroom after the evening chores were done to smoke a cigar, symbol to the child of his grandfather's power over his family and ranch business and also of his grandmother's longing for her husband. As so many of the characters of his stories, the grandmother seems to represent for the author a graphic and vital connection with his past: his Hispano community, his family, his language, and his cultural roots.

The second story, "Brujerías o tonterías" (Sorcery or Foolishness) is a summary of local legends and characters (endowed with mysterious powers) who were prominent in Tierra Amarilla during the narrator's childhood: la Matilde de Ensenada who was reportedly a witch and go-between—*Trotaconventos*—between lovers; *el sanador* (the healer) another character whose knowledge of the supernatural properties of medicines and animals miraculously saves his uncle from certain death; and finally *la llorona* herself with whom the narrator has a terrifying encounter only to discover later that he had actually run into Atenencia, a mentally retarded woman who would relentlessly pursue her unfaithful husband and scare local inhabitants in the bargain.

The focus of the third story is the narrator's uncle by marriage, Cirilo, sheriff of Río Arriba County. He is described as big, fat, strong, and fearsome, especially from the point of view of the child who felt dwarfed in his presence. Not only did he capture and sometimes have to manhandle criminals, but he also kept the peace at the schoolhouse. On one occasion after the teacher could take no more harrassment from the young devils of students, Cirilo was called in. In a memorable scene, he quells the riot with merely his presence.

The next story is similar in that it also deals with another scandalously loved adventurer, who, most notably, wore no pants when he rode horseback and was punching cows. Other local characters central to other stories are: Elacio the astute biology teacher, who upon finding himself under pressure by her brothers to marry Erlinda Benavídez, arranges for his friend Jimmy Ortega to fall in love with her; Felix and Sally who found the restaurant La Casa KK—known locally as Casa CaCa—, prosper, and then split up; Mano Fashico, Don Cacahuate, Doña Cebolla, Pedro Urdemales, Bertoldo, all imaginary childhood friends from New Mexican folklore who in the words of the author "me endulzaron y enriquecieron la vida entonces y que ahora recuerdo con todo cariño" (They sweetened and enriched my life back then and I now remember them very tenderly).

In the final story of the collection, Ulibarrí describes the brotherhood of Penitentes, the secret religious organization of devout males of the community to whom, only in later years, he attributes their due and recognizes their importance in holding together the Hispano culture of northern New Mexico. It was they who filled the administrative religious and cultural vacuum of early New Mexico to give continuity and cohesiveness to the Hispano population. Ulibarrí cautions the reader not to believe all the exaggerated versions of the Penitentes' secret rituals—although in the story he does refer indirectly to some of their more extreme religious practices such as the ones that occurred during Lent.

As the title of Ulibarrí's third collection of short stories indicates, *Primeros encuentros, First Encounters*[4] focuses on the author's early experiences with Anglos and Anglo culture. While at least one of the selections—"Don Nicomedes"—deals with dominant culture racism in northern New Mexico, most present a sympathetic view of the complex process of cultural melding. As in the two previous collections of short stories, the author draws heavily on his memories of growing up Hispano in Tierra Amarilla. Tinged with sadness due to the loss of childhood innocence, his young protagonists struggle to come to grips with their emergence into adulthood. Leaving the haven of the family, they venture forth to find their way in a different, but not necessarily hostile, environment.

"Un oso y un amor" (A Bear and a Love) typifies this process. The narrator remembers tenderly the joyful and carefree times he spent as a teenager playing with his friends in the woods, his developing friendship with Shirley Cantel, an attractive Anglo girl, and then their separation as their paths divided as young adults.

Ulibarrí portrays Anglos not as flat sociological entities but as multi-dimensional characters with feelings as diverse as those of his Hispano characters. Because he remembers the two groups intermingling freely in Tierra Amarilla, their interrelationships—as in the above study—are portrayed as natural and without racial conflict. This is seen throughout the collection. In "El forastero gentil," for example, an Anglo cowboy—a Texan—is welcomed by a Hispano ranch family. Knowing little about his past, but sensing that he has suffered some deep disillusionment, Don Prudencio, the father, offers him his home and his family's companionship. The author deftly contrasts the stranger's rough exterior to his gentle response to the children. The Texan and the Hispanos develop a deep mutual respect.

This same respect is a characteristic found in other stories such as "La güera," "Adolfo Miller," "Don Nicomedes," Don Tomás Vernes," and "Mónico." Anglos, like Hispanos, are depicted as both good and bad, energetic and lazy, brutal and gentle. Although somewhat idealized, life in Tierra Amarilla is always interesting and varied as characters from the two cultures learn more about each other.

Pupurupú,[5] Ulibarrí's latest collection of short stories, shows two clear tendencies: a return to the nostalgic, memory-laden stories of *Tierra Amarilla* and *Mi abuela fumaba puros* and an incursion into fantasy. *Pupurupú* also contains stories that cannot neatly be classified as either predominantly nostalgic or fantastic, such as "El juez, mi rehén," and "Palomas negras."

Stories similar to these in Ulibarrí's first two collections need only be listed here, for they are of lesser interest than those that represent the author's experimentation with fantasy. They are: "Adios carnero," and "La niña que murió de amor."

Readers who have come to expect the simply told tales of growing up in and around Tierra Amarilla will be pleasantly surprised to find that Ulibarrí is equally comfortable exploring other literary veins. These stories are rich in tonality and psychological insight.

In "El gobernador Glu Glu," the author creates a mythical land ruled by a buffoonish character, Antonio Zonto Glu Glu, who has risen to his position of power thanks to one remarkable trait: he can not utter a single word against women without biting his tongue and saying "Glu glu." These absurd syllables are somehow irresistable to women who come to adore this nondescript little man.

Coached by his wife, Antonio launches his political career as a defender of women's rights, finally winning the gubernatorial election. Soon after, he dies a fulfilled and happy man. The author gently parodies the foibles of politicians and their tendency to seize upon current issues, using them for their own political gain.

"Monte Niko" is the finest example in *Pupurupú* of Ulibarrí's fantastic stories. He imbues the story's ambiance with qualities not found elsewhere in his writing. A fictitious people, the Nikoni, live harmoniously in the valley of Nikon blessed by nature and isolated from others' strife. They worship Talaniko, the god of love and peace, who has rewarded their loyalty and devotion by granting them fertile fields, spiritual tranquility, and leisure time to devote to the pursuit of art and philosophy. Niko, a young man of extraordinary sensitivity and intelligence, is chosen king to lead them. He defeats Peri Yodo, a terrible beast who is the incarnation of evil, gives his people commandments to live by, and dies soon after.

"El conejo pionero" and "Mamá guantes" are other stories in Ulibarrí's most recent collection that reflect the same mode as "Monte Niko." The first is a playful treatment of a man's friendship with a rabbit, the second is a somber consideration of interpersonal relationships.

As we have seen from the virtuosity and variety of his writings, Sabine Ulibarrí is a salient figure on the Chicano literary scene. In terms of New Mexico, he has spent a lifetime putting into words the essence of Hispano life as he lived and remembers it in Tierra Amarilla.

NOTES

1. *Al cielo se sube a pie*. (Madrid: Alfaguara, 1966); *Amor y Ecuador*. (Madrid: José Porrúa Editores, 1966).
2. *Tierra Amarilla: Stories of New Mexico. Cuentos de Nuevo México*. (Albuquerque: University of New Mexico Press, 1971).
3. *Mi abuela fumaba puros y otros cuentos de Tierra Amarilla*. (Berkeley: Quinto Sol Publications, 1977).
4. *Primeros encuentros. First Encounters*. (Ypsilanti, Michigan: Bilingual Press/Editorial Bilingüe, 1982).
5. *Pupurupú* (Mexico, D.F.: Sainz Luiselli Editores, 1987). *El governador Glu Glu y otros cuentos/Governor Glu Glu and Other Stories* (Tempe, Az.: Bilingual Press/Editorial Bilingüe, 1987).

13

THE DYNAMICS OF MYTH IN THE CREATIVE VISION OF RUDOLFO ANAYA

ENRIQUE LAMADRID

In the range and breadth of New Mexican literature there is no writer as deeply rooted in the native folkways and regional landscapes as Rudolfo Anaya. Yet, it is his prose that shows the greatest promise of transcending the limitations of narrow regionalism and ethnic literatures. The universal thrust of Anaya's creative vision is based in myth, which he defines impressionistically as "the truth in the heart." In the same discussion of myth he further elaborates his understanding of myth as it relates to harmony and alienation, the archaic and the modern, and the role of the unconscious as link to the universal:

> Our civilizing and socializing influence has made us not as unified, not as harmonious as archaic man. To go back and get in touch, and to become more harmonious, we go back to the unconscious and we bring out all of the symbols and archetypals that are available to all people.[1]

Anaya is a mythmaker, both intuitive and self-conscious, whose raw material is folklore, legends, and what might be termed native metaphysics. A creator rather than a collector, he transforms indigenous materials into a rich synthesis of symbol and archetype, new, yet "true to the heart." As mythmaker, Anaya is at his intuitive best when his conception of myth is guided by his unconscious as in *Bless*

Me, Ultima (1972), and again in *Tortuga* (1979).[2] *Heart of Aztlán* (1976) is a more deliberate and self-conscious if less effective effort at interweaving myth into a narrative. He uses myth according to archetypal definitions and formulae of Carl Jung, Joseph Campbell, or Mircea Eliade. Critics have been grappling with the dynamics of Anaya's mythopoetics ever since the appearance of *Ultima*. Yet, the critical analyses of myth has been as impressionistic as the author's. Thematic and archetypal analyses of myth have contributed much to elucidate the content of myth, but little to the understanding of its function as a system of cognition and communication. It is this latter aspect of myth that will be emphasized here to understand the achievements as well as the shortcomings of Anaya's mythopoetics.

As the first best seller novel of Chicano literature, it was impossible to dismiss *Ultima*'s introduction of compelling mythic themes into the disjunctive context of the combative and polemical ethnic literatures of the late sixties. *Ultima* was serene in the face of this turmoil, full of conflict, yet non combative, a portrait of the developing consciousness of the young protagonist, Antonio. The metaphysics of this emerging consciousness were so convincingly drawn that no reader doubted that the seeds of social conscience were deeply sown if yet untested in the character.

Myth was defined in *Ultima* as a way of knowing and making sense of the world. Myth as praxis, or a way of changing the world, was the next creative challenge Anaya faced in *Heart of Aztlán*. But the search for the juncture of the mythic and the revolutionary became overly self-conscious. The mythmaking flowed much less intuitively from Anaya's pen the more he pursued his stated purpose of "trying to touch the mythological roots."[3] Myth becomes epic archetype and narrative formula rather than a natural dialectical system of knowledge. However, as in *Ultima*, the net of symbols underlying the novel is compelling and coherent: on one side, the same sacred sense of redeeming telluric power that pervaded *Ultima* pitted against a dehumanized industrial capitalism symbolized by the infernal railroad shops with snakes of steel dominated by the SANTA FE tower, "The Holy Faith embedded in a faded cross, a perverted faith in steel" (*HA* 197). What weakens the novel and invalidates it politically speaking for many readers is a neo-classic scheme of mythmaking imposed on it by an author alluding to the classic heroic archetypes outlined by Jung, Campbell, and Eliade: the visionary quest of the hero, the descent into the collective subconscious, the ascent to the mountain, the return.[4] True, the overly familiar quest of Clemente Chávez has its analogues, even in history. A visionary Simón Bolivar climbed the mountain, the Aventine hill outside Rome, to utter his sacred oath vowing to change his world. But this is history mystefied (or "*myth*efied," to use the Spanish equivalent). Leaders emerge and to succeed must project a vision that their people share, but history continues to be forged by the masses. The myth of Aztlán developed in the novel is a collective vision skillfully evoked by Anaya in compelling imagery, the surging river of humanity, the pulsing heart of Aztlán. But it is ultimately incompatible with the deliberate imposition of classical heroic archetypes. Several critics attribute the novel's shortcomings to defects in craftsmanship, that Anaya does not allow his symbols to "accumulate enough power in themselves to exercise power in the text," in the words of Juan Bruce Novoa.[5] It is my contention that the symbolic scheme of Heart of Aztlán is impeccable. The defect lies in the overly scholastic conception and application of myth that obscures the juncture of the mythic and the revolutionary that Anaya was seeking.

Tortuga represents a return to the intuitive mythmaking of *Ultima* with a praxis that operates more in the individual soul than in the collective one. As Anaya has said, "just as the natural end of art is to make us well and to cure our souls, so is our relationship to the earth and its power. . . . I mean that there is an actual healing power which the epiphany of place provides."[6] The protagonist, nicknamed Tortuga is a boy imprisoned in his cast shell by a spinal injury. The disharmony in the boy's universe has physiological rather than social causes. Social institutions, in this case the hospital, are insensitive to the spiritual content of the healing process. The boy has to draw healing power directly from the earth itself in his rehabilitation.

Besides similarities in symbolism and the evocative if sometimes romanticized handling of poetic imagery, Anaya's three novels share an important structural element in mythmaking: the seer or spiritual guide whose role it is to mediate contradictions, the key function in myth as a system of communication. In *Bless Me, Ultima* the chief mediator is Ultima, the curandera, whose message is that conflict and contradiction are not dichotomous but rather dialectical oppositions in the ongoing cycles of the universe. In *Heart of Aztlán*, the seer is the blind Crispín, master of the blue guitar, adviser and guide to Clemente Chávez in his quest for the meaning of Aztlán. In *Tortuga*, the seer is Salomón, Tortuga's fellow patient who shows him the way of hope, "the path of the sun" (*T* 160). All three seers serve integrative functions, pointing out the oneness and sanctity of the universe and the meaning of human life and the healing power of the human heart.

The mythopoetics of Rudolfo Anaya pervade the entire body of his creative work including his numerous short stories. His most comprehensive insight into the workings and cognitive function of myth as an aspect of popular culture is contained in *Bless Me, Ultima*, the particular focus of this analysis. Anaya strikes a deep chord in portraying two primordial ways of relating to the earth, the pastoral and the agricultural. *Bless Me, Ultima* is not a quaint, ahistorical sketch of rural folkways, but rather a dialectical exploration of the contradictions between lifestyles and cultures. At the novel's heart is the process which generates social and historical consciousness. A Marxist Structuralist perspective defines this process as myth, the collective interpretation and mediation of the contradictions in the historical and ecological experience of a people.

In his account of the relationship between a *curandera* (folk healer) and her young apprentice, Anaya deeply penetrates the mythical conscience of the reader. Despite their enthusiasm for his novel, critics have thus far been unable to define the parameters of this response nor probe the reason for its depth. Contributing elements in the narrative include: the primordial quality of the rivalry of the Luna and Márez clans, the religious conflicts and rich dream life of the boy Antonio Márez, and the power of Ultima herself, which in the end is nothing more nor less than "the magical strength that resides in the human heart" (*BMU* 237). From the first reviews to later articles, an increasing body of vague but glowing commentary points to a rich "mythic" or "magical" dimension that underlies the novel.[7] To those who prioritize the social relevancy of Chicano literature, this psychic plunge seemed disturbing or even reactionary in its irrationality. Despite these claims, there appeared to be something exceptional about the emerging consciousness of the boy. It was mystically harmonious with nature, yet also incorporated a dynamic, even dialectical awareness of historical forces, from the colonization of Hispanic farmers and ranchers to the coming of the Anglos and World War II. These seeming contradictions invite a reexamination of the relation of myth and social consciousness, often defined as antithetical or incompatible categories that erode and undermine each other. Since the novel apparently transcends this impasse, we are obliged to consider a critical model comprehensive enough to explain this achievement. A review of commentary on the novel is the first step in this direction.

Bless Me, Ultima has undergone extensive dream and thematic analyses that include attempts to link its "mythic" elements to precolumbian roots.[8] The preponderance of interest in these "irrational" aspects plus the sometimes supernatural tone of the narrative has lead some politically progressive critics to characterize the novel as ahistorical, having only limited and passing value in depicting the "quaint" folkways of rural New Mexico.[9] Thematic analysis has enumerated various tendencies, especially the folkloric, but is unable to characterize the book as anything more than a local color or *costumbrista* piece.[10] Dream analysis has been more productive because of the consistency and symbolic unity of the many dream sequences.[11] Analysis of the mythic and religious systems, notably the "Legend of the Golden Carp" is unconvincing simply because Anaya's alleged allusions to Aztec or other precolumbian mythologies are not literal enough.[12] True, the idea of successive worlds, intervening apocalypses, and the exile of Gods is common in Native American religions. The suggestion of analogical patterns achieves credibility for the Golden Carp without having to invoke Huitzilopochtli or Quetzalcoatl as other Chicano writers have done. The political analysis, which deems the novel reactionary seems to be based on the assumption that Chicano novels should document only the most relevant social and political struggles. These diverse and fragmentary approaches have fallen short of estimating the overall impact and unity of the work and the structural integrity it has achieved on a number of levels.

Since the "mythic" dimension of *Bless Me, Ultima* is a point of confluence in the above commentaries, a definition of terms is necessary at this point. Thus far, the study of myth in Chicano literature is scholastic. The neoclassic allusions to Aztec and other precolumbian mythological and religious systems is fairly common in Chicano literature, especially in poetry and theatre. Critics have been quick to point this out, elaborating only superficially by tracing the origins of the myths and speculating on how they pertain to the sociocultural identity of the present day Chicano.[13] Freud was able to tap Greek mythology for insight into the European psyche and founded the basis for Western psychology. Inspired by the work of Octavio Paz and Carlos Fuentes on the Mexican national psyche, an analogous process has been initiated in Chicano literature and criticism, although it is doubtful that an institutionalized Chicano psychotherapy would result. The underlying assumption that would prevent this is that these mythic or collective psychological patterns supposedly lie outside time, eternally remanifesting themselves in different epochs.[14] This same danger plagues Chicano cultural studies in general, which often tend to analyze culture and its values as something eternal and independent of history, instead of the dynamic product or actual embodiment of history, conflict, and change.[15]

What I propose is a more dynamic critical approach to myth that goes beyond scholasticism and the tracing of classical mythologies. Myth is here considered to be an ongoing process of interpreting and mediating the contradictions in the everyday historical experience of the people. Such a structuralist approach to myth offers some analytical tools that can be applied in such a way as to avoid the ideological limitations of structuralism while opening the Chicano text to a dialectical analysis potentially much more penetrating and historically relevant than traditional thematic or culturalist approaches.

The reader of *Bless Me, Ultima* recognizes the elderly *curandera* as a kind of repository for the wisdom and knowledge invested in IndoHispanic culture. The novel functions well at this level, for Ultima is indeed in touch with the spirit that moves the land and is intent on conveying this knowledge to Antonio in her indirect and mysterious ways. Yet, the knowledge she commands and the role she plays go far beyond the herbs she knows, the stories she saves for the children, and her dabbling in "white" witchcraft. The crossed pins, the demon hairballs, the rocks falling from the sky, and the fireballs are "colorful" touches that are authentic enough in terms of folk legend. Anaya inserts the "witchery" only after having won the reader's trust in a clever conquest of their disbelief. However, the enumeration of the standard paraphernalia and the usual supernatural feats of a *curandera* are neither the reason for nor a barrier to the novel's success.

There is an ancient system of knowledge that Ultima exercises that in this novel does not happen to be in the herbs she uses. Any anthropologist is aware that taxonomies such as those of ethnobotany actually contain the philosophical roots and perceptual conventions of the culture.[16] However, herbs and related folk knowledge are not the ultimate focus of the novel, although it is understood that Ultima is intimately familiar with them. It is her role as a cultural mediator and Antonio's natural inclination towards a similar calling that link them to their real power, which is the ability to recognize and resolve the internal contradictions of their culture. These oppositions are clearly defined in both social and symbolic terms. The rivalry of the Lunas and the Márez, the struggle of good and evil, innocence and experience, Jehovah and the Golden Carp are not simply narrative devices. If they were, then they would be merely pretexts for a combination mystery story, morality play, and Hatfield-McCoy saga with a New Mexican flavor.

Something more profound is at work in *Bless Me, Ultima*, for the oppositions are dialectical, and they are mediated in a way that has counterparts in many different cultures around the earth. In his comparative studies of origin myths, Claude Levi-Strauss extracts the two most basic and primordial ones, which occurred either exclusively or in combination in every culture studied.[17] The "autochthonous" origin myth is exactly as the original meaning of the word implies: "one supposed to have risen or sprung from the ground of the region he inhabits." This version often has a vegetative model: man springs from the earth like a plant. The rival origin myth is more empirically based: man is born from woman. Then comes the task of finding the first woman. In *Bless Me, Ultima* the opposition between the agricultural Luna family and the pastoral Márez family has roots that go as deep as the very foundation of human consciousness as it moves from the paleolithic into the neolithic. Each lifestyle and the world view it is based on is as compelling, soul satisfying, and original as the other. The opposition as it occurs in the novel may be schematized as follows:

pastoral economy	agricultural economy
the Márez family	the Luna family
live in Las Pasturas on the open plains	live in El Puerto de la Luna in a fertile valley
people of the sun	people of the moon
descendents of conquistadors and seafarers	descendents of a priest

baptized in the salt water of the sea	baptized in the sweet water of the moon
speak with the wind	speak with their plants and fields
tempestuous, anarchic freethinkers	quiet, introspective pious people
live free upon the earth and roam over it	live tied to the earth and its cycles
the horse is their totem animal	corn is their totem plant

The earthshaking impact of the passage from hunting and gathering (paleolithic) into agricultural (neolithic) economies is recorded in mythologies the world over.[18] The crises and contradictions that history, economic change, and technological innovation bring are the chief motivating factors for the collective cognitive process called myth. The settling down of humankind into the sedentary ways of the neolithic brought with it the emergence of social classes and institutionalized religion and all the economic and social contradictions that accompany the birth of civilization. Likewise, the developments with agriculture of horticulture and animal husbandry are distinct enough to carry with them their own ideologies as evident above. Relating more specifically to the novel in question is the history of the colonization of New Mexico and the tremendous impact of the advent of large scale pastoralism. As grazing became more important, the communal egalitarianism of agrarian society began giving way to an emerging class system based on the partidario grazing system and the rise of *patrones* (bosses). However, such developments are not evident in the novel, perhaps because its locale, eastern New Mexico, was the last area to be settled before American annexation.[19] The anarchic freedom enjoyed by the Márez clan was ephemeral, the basic historical irony of the story. The coming of the Texas ranchers, the railroad, and the barbed wire destroyed the freedom of the plains. As the popular saying goes, "Cuando vino el alambre, vino el hambre" (When the barbed wire came, so did hunger). When an economic system is threatened, so is its ideology which starts filling with nostalgia as its dreams are broken.

These historical pressures intensified the oppositions listed above and made the birth of the boy Antonio Márez Luna especially portentious for both clans whose blood coursed through his veins. Each felt the importance of having their values dominate in the boy and both vied to establish their influence at the dream scene of Antonio's birth:

> This one will be a Luna, the old man said, he will be a farmer and keep our customs and traditions. Perhaps God will bless our family and make the baby a priest.
>
> And to show their hope they rubbed the dark earth of the river valley on the baby's forehead, and they surrounded the bed with the fruits of their harvest so the small

> room smelled of fresh green chile and corn, ripe apples and peaches, pumpkins and green beans.
>
> Then the silence was shattered with the thunder of hoof-beats; vaqueros surrounded the small house with shouts and gunshots, and when they entered the room they were laughing and singing and drinking.
>
> Gabriel, they shouted, you have a fine son! He will make a fine vaquero! And they smashed the fruits and vegetables that surrounded the bed and replaced them with a saddle, horse blankets, bottles of whiskey, a new rope, bridles, chapas, and an old guitar. And they rubbed the stain of earth from the baby's forehead because man was not to be tied to the earth but free upon it. (BMU, 5)

The disposal of the baby's umbilical cord and placenta was also a point of contention. The Lunas wanted it buried in their fields to add to their fertility and the Márez wanted it burned to scatter the ashes to the winds of the *llano* (plain). The intervention of Ultima to settle the feud illustrates her role of mediator and demonstrates the basic mechanism of myth. As in all cultures the thrust of mythical thought progresses from the awareness of oppositions towards their resolution.[20] Thus the importance in the mythic process of the mediator, which in many cultures assumes the form of powerful tricksters like coyote and raven in Native American mythology. In *Bless Me, Ultima*, both the *curandera* and the boy serve as mediators between the oppositions within their culture. Their intermediary functions can be traced throughout the text.

The middle ground that Ultima and Antonio occupy is evident even in spacial and geographic terms. Ultima has lived on the plain and in the valley, in Las Pasturas as well as El Puerto de la Luna, gaining the respect of the people in both places. Antonio's family lives in Guadalupe in a compromise location at mid point between Las Pasturas and El Puerto. Through the father's insistence, the house is built at the edge of the valley where the plain begins. Antonio mediates between father and mother, trying to please the latter by scraping a garden out of the rocky hillside:

> Every day I reclaimed from the rocky soil of the hill a few more feet of earth to cultivate. The land of the llano was not good for farming, the good land was along the river. But my mother wanted a garden and I worked to make her happy. (BMU, 9)

Even within the town Antonio occupies a centralized neutral position: "Since I was not from across the tracks or from town, I was caught in the middle." (BMU, 212). This positioning made it impossible to take sides in the territorial groupings of his peers.

Anaya explains the power of the *curandera* as the power of the human heart, but in fact demonstrates that it is derived from the knowledge of mythic thought processes, the awareness and resolution of contradictions within the culture. People turn to Ultima and Antonio at crucial moments in their lives because they are instinctively aware that mediators (*curanderos* and tricksters) possess an overview or power of synthesis that can help them resolve their problems. The multiple episodes of Antonio playing the role of priest are especially significant in this light. It is his mother's and her family's dream for Antonio to become a Luna priest and man of knowledge. In fact he performs the role seriously, administering last rights to Lupito, a war-crazed murderer and Narciso, an ally of Ultima and Antonio's family. The blessings he bestows on his brothers and his friends are real and invested with a power they never fully realize as they taunt him. In his spiritual searching, Antonio discovers the contradictions in Christianity and realizes that the scope of his mediations would include the "pagan", animistic forces implicit in the very landscape he inhabited. In his musings to himself, he feels the new synthesis that he will be a part of: " 'Take the llano and the river valley, the moon and the sea, God and the golden carp—and make something new.' . . . That is what Ultima meant by building strength from life" (BMU, 236).

The dynamism of mythic thought and its power of synthesis is poigniantly expressed in Antonio's description of the feelings and emotions that are aroused by contact with Ultima:

> She took my hand and I felt the power of a whirlwind sweep around me. Her eyes swept the surrounding hills and through them I saw for the first time the wild beauty of our hills and the magic of the green river. My nostrils quivered as I felt the song of the mockingbirds and the drone of the grasshoppers mingle with the pulse of the earth. The four directions of the llano met in me, and the white sun shone on my soul. The granules of sand at my feet and the sun and sky above me seemed to dissolve into one strange, complete being. (BMU, 11)

The power invested in the mythical process is the knowledge derived from seeing the world as a totality and understanding its contradictions in a dialectical manner. There are other characters in the novel who demonstrate differing degrees of awareness of this totality, proving that it is indeed a mechanism of popular culture rather than a mystery reserved for a privileged, visionary few. A good example is Narciso, a powerful man of the *llano* who nevertheless lives in the valley, having discovered its secrets. Ample evidence of this is his exuberant, drunken garden, the likes of which not many *llaneros* (plainsmen) could foster (BMU, 101).

In perhaps the most global or cosmic synthesis of the novel, Ultima in a dream reveals to Antonio the totality which subsumes the oppositions contained in his culture at the moment when they seemed about to split into a dichotomy and create another apocalypse:

> Cease! she cried to the raging powers, and the power from the heavens and the power from the earth obeyed her. The storm abated.
>
> Stand, Antonio, she commanded, and I stood. You both know, she spoke to my father and my mother, that the sweet water of the moon which falls as rain is the same water that gathers into rivers and flows to fill the seas. Without the waters of the moon to replenish the oceans there would be no oceans. And the same salt waters of the oceans are drawn by the sun to the heavens, and in turn become again the waters of the moon. Without the sun there would be no waters formed to slake the dark earth's thirst.
>
> The waters are one, Antonio. I looked into her bright, clear eyes and understood her truth.
>
> You have been seeing only parts, she finished, and not looking beyond into the great cycle that binds us all. (BMU, 113)

The implied definition of apocalypse in this system of thought is the destructive result of changes that are not assimilated, of oppositions that are not mediated. The awareness of the characters of the apocalyptic threat of the atomic bomb, first tested just to the southwest of their fertile valley, demonstrates a real and historical dimension of apocalypse. They sense the previous balance has been disturbed. The bomb seems to have changed the weather just as surely as World War II had twisted the souls of the men from the area who had fought. The need for a new synthesis is as urgent as ever in this new time of crisis. Ultima immediately involved herself in the healing of men who were suffering war sickness and it would be up to Antonio to continue the tradition of mediating contradictions both old and new.

In one sense the knowledge of Ultima may seem mystical because of the way it incorporates nature as well as culture, but when applied to society and history it is just as penetratingly comprehensive and its value just as valid. With Ultima's eventual death, her knowledge continues in Antonio and the reader feels sure that whatever his fate will be, he possesses the conceptual tools to continue to benefit his people and culture with their internal conflicts as well as with the oncoming struggle with a whole new set of oppositions stemming from the fast approaching and aggressive proximity of the Anglo culture and way of life.

In portraying power as the ability to think and understand in a dialectical way, Anaya demonstrates in *Bless Me, Ultima* the ancient collective cognitive process of mythical thought in Chicano culture and the importance of those individuals who take on the role of mediators (*curanderos*, tricksters, or activists) in pointing out and moving towards the resolution of the contradictions generated by human history and new technology. It is this dialectical conception of myth which underlies Anaya's most powerful and moving creative work. Only with the self-conscious application of heroic archetypes and a scholastic conception of myth can he be accused of mystifying his political and social concerns. In the former vision the magical qualities of Anaya's work become a form of knowledge while in the latter they run the risk of becoming little more than a quaint distraction or worse, an obfuscation of clear political thought.

NOTES

1. "Mitólogos y Mitómanos: Mesa Redonda con Alurista, R. Anaya, M. Herrera Sobeck, A. Morales y H. Viramontes," *Maize: Xicano Art and Literature Notebook*, 4:3–4 (Spring-Summer 1981), pp. 6–23.

2. Rudolfo A. Anaya, *Bless Me, Ultima* (Berkeley, California: Quinto Sol, 1972); *Heart of Aztlán* (Berkeley, California: Editorial Justa Publications, 1976); *Tortuga* (Berkeley, California: Editorial Justa Publications, 1979).

3. Richard S. Johnson, "Rudolfo Anaya: A Vision of the Heroic," *Empire Magazine Denver Post*, March 2, 1980, pp. 25–27.

4. Of special relevance on the topic of heroic archetypes see Joseph Campbell, *The Hero With a Thousand Faces*, (Cleveland: Meridian, World Publishing Company, 1969).

5. Bruce-Novoa, Review of *Heart of Aztlán*, *La Confluencia*, 1–2 (1976–78), pp. 61–62.

See also Antonio Márquez, "The Achievement of Rudolfo Anaya," in *The Magic of Words: Rudolfo Anaya and his Writings*, ed. Paul Vassallo, (Albuquerque: University of New Mexico Press, 1982), p. 40.

6. Rudolfo A. Anaya, "The Writer's Landscape: Epiphany in Landscape," *Latin American Literary Review*, 5–6 (1977–78), p. 101.

7. Among many others see Arnulfo Trejo, Review of *Bless Me, Ultima*, *Arizona Quarterly*, 29:2 (Spring 1973), pp. 95–96.

8. Vernon E. Lattin, "The Quest for Mythic Vision in Contemporary Native American and Chicano Fiction," *American Literature*, 50:4 (January 1979), pp. 625–40.

9. Juan Rodríguez, "La Búsqueda de Identidad y Sus Motivos en la Literatura Chicana," in *The Identification and Analysis of Chicano Literature*, ed. Francisco Jiménez (New York: Bilingual Press/Editorial Bilingüe, 1979), pp. 170–78.

10. Carlota Cárdenas Dwyer, "Myth and Folk Culture in Contemporary Chicano Literature," *La Luz*, (December 1974), pp. 28–29.

Carol Mitchell, "Rudolfo Anaya's *Bless Me, Ultima*: Folk Culture in Literature," *Critique* 22, No. 1 (1980), pp. 55–64.

Jane Rogers, "The Function of the La Llorona Motif in Rudolfo Anaya's *Bless Me, Ultima*," *Latin American Literary Review*, 5:10 (Spring-Summer 1977), pp. 64–69.

11. Roberto Cantú, "Estructura y Sentido de lo onírico en *Bless Me, Ultima*," *Mester*, 5:1 (Noviembre 1974), pp. 27–41.

Amy Waggoner, "Tony's Dreams—An Important Dimension in *Bless Me, Ultima*," *Southwestern American Literature*, Vol. 4 (1974), pp. 74–79.

12. Febe Portillo-Orozco, "Rudolfo Anaya's Use of History, Myth and Legend in His Novels: *Bless Me, Ultima* and *Heart of Aztlán*," M.A. thesis, San Francisco State University, 1981.

13. J. Karen Ray, "Cultural and Mythical Archetypes in Rudolfo Anaya's Bless Me, Ultima," *New Mexico Humanities Review*, 1:3 (September 1978), pp. 23–28.

14. Octavio Paz, *Posdata* (México: Siglo XXI, 1970).
Carlos Fuentes, *Tiempo Mexicano* (México: Joaquín Mortiz, 1971).

15. Joseph Sommers, "From the Critical Premise to the Product: Critical Modes and Their Application to a Chicano Literary Text," in *New Directions in Chicano Scholarship*, ed. Ricardo Romo and Raymund Paredes, Chicano Studies Monograph Series (La Jolla: University of California, 1978), pp. 51–80.

16. Claude Levi-Strauss, *The Savage Mind* (1962; rpt. Chicago: University of Chicago Press, 1970), pp. 1–34.

17. Claude Levi-Strauss, *Structural Anthropology* (New York: Basic Books, 1963), pp. 210–18.

18. Levi-Strauss, *Structural Anthropology*, pp. 206–231.

19. Marc Simmons, *New Mexico: A History* (New York: W. W. Norton, 1977), pp. 107–67.

20. Levi-Strauss, *Structural Anthropology*, pp. 224–25.

14

ALGO VIEJO Y ALGO NUEVO
Contemporary New Mexico Hispanic Fiction

ANTONIO C. MÁRQUEZ

It is a commonplace that the chief characteristics of New Mexican Hispanic literature are its pastoral and mystical affinities. For instance, José Armas's survey of New Mexico narrative fiction turns on this central point:

> If there is an area which is distinctive to Chicano literature in general and in particular to New Mexican writing, it is the naturalness and 'easiness' in which the mystical, spiritual, and magical world is interwoven with the literature. It is much more than a style. It is a form, a dimension of literature which captures an underground manifestation in the culture of Chicanos in *Nuevo Mexico*.[1]

This general view is attributable to the fact that much of New Mexican writing is rooted in a rich and inspiring folk base. Although this folk base and Hispanic cultural legacies have inspired valuable literature, the insistence on "the mythopoetic tradition" has often created misconceptions that New Mexican writing is restricted to quaint folkloric, pastoral, and mystical themes. This limited view has often been a disservice because it neglects the diversity of contemporary New Mexico Hispanic fiction.

Contemporaneity and diversity in the short story can be found, among others, in writers such as Robert Perea, Denise Chávez, Albert Lovato, Nash Candelaria,

Katherine Baca, and Kika Vargas. Perea's Vietnam stories, "Dragon Mountain" and "Small Arms Fire," are sparse, tough, skillfully executed works that forcefully depict the conditions of war and the participation of the Chicano in Vietnam. Chávez's "Baby Krishna's All Night Special," a surrealistic story about fear and paranoia, presents a nightmarish contemporary American scene. Lovato's "Agusa'o con los Velices" employs code-switching to create a unique medium for picaresque satire and to comically attack social conventions and attitudes. Candelaria's "Mano a Mano" is an acerbic, witty narrative aimed at the elitism of academe and the disparaging view of Chicano Studies in "traditional" university departments and curriculums. Baca's "Sterile Relationships" is a hilarious, sharply ironic story that dissects the exaggerations of male sexuality. Vargas's "The Corpse," a story reminiscent of Flannery O'Connor's grotesqueries, is a bizarre but well-wrought tale of death and madness.[2] What is notable about these representative writers is that they offer personal aesthetic visions and unique treatments of old and *new* themes in Chicano literature. In effect, their works cannot be easily categorized and these authors verify that there are new literary vistas being forged in New Mexican literature.

Emerging writers have also taken on the ambitious task of expanding the bearings of the New Mexican novel. Romero's *Nambe-Year One*, Torres-Metzgar's *Below The Summit*, Apodaca's *The Waxen Image*, and Candelaria's *Memories Of The Alhambra* and *Not By The Sword* demonstrate the variety, diversity, and in some exemplary cases the increasing sophistication of this genre.

Although a flawed novel, Orlando Romero's *Nambe-Year One* (1976) serves as an example of the increasing sophistication of New Mexican fiction.[3] Fray Angelico Chavez's perplexed admiration in his review of *Nambe-Year One* attests to the novel's departure from traditional forms:

> This novel, unlike Rudy Anaya's *Bless Me Ultima*, transcends time and space. Immediate and remote ancestry commingle with native landscape in kaleidoscopic doses that gave me an intellectual headache. While individual sections could not fail but elicit truest admiration for their vibrant qualities of ideas and expression, the work as a whole gave me that unpleasant hallucinogenic vertigo that I get from much abstract painting. . . . But the new Joycean literary set will rightfully acclaim the book as a minor masterpiece, and to them it is heartily recommended.[4]

By a Joycean or any other criterion *Nambe-Year One* is not "a minor masterpiece." But it is an ambitious work that experiments with fragmentary narrative structure, intricate point of view, and the fusion of mythic and psychological elements. Moreover, it is an engaging attempt at the literary mode called "magical realism." At one point, the narrator (ostensibly the author's persona) injects this telling comment: "Tonight I told her about a book in which a family had intermarried and had children with tails." The reference, of course, is to García Márquez's *One Hundred Years of Solitude*, and throughout Romero's novel there are marked influences of the magical realism practiced by contemporary Latin American writers. Although his eclecticism is not as imaginative as that of other contemporary Chicano writers who have appropriated this mode (e.g., Arias's *The Road to Tamazunchale*), Romero's juxtaposition of reality and fantasy gives the novel an interesting complexion.

Romero takes the general tack of magical realism that requires the reader to become an active participant in the reading of the fiction. The novel pivots on a passage where the patriarch of the family gently admonishes the narrator's youthful ignorance: "Understand, understand, don't be like the Americanos, they have to understand everything. It was a lesson, a miracle or a mystery. Just believe in mysteries, and you'll live a long time." The rite of passage that ensues (Mateo Romero's exploration of the mysteries of nature and man) includes ghost stories, legends, folklore, archetypal feminine forms, and a host of animistic figures and symbols. From these multifarious elements arise the novel's thematic issues: the life and death cycle, the mutability of existence, the pristine qualities of nature, the convergence of history and individual consciousness, and the retrieval of time past through memory and imagination. The thematic complexity of the novel is further complicated by the author's use of an "open structure" and poetic configurations to convey the narrator's psychological states and his search for a transcendent truth. Instead of chronological sequence and plotted narrative, the author seeks thematic unity through repeated images, metaphors, and impressionistic episodes that are left to both the narrator and the reader to connect. In effect, the novel's formlessness, disjunctures, and ellipses stylistically reinforce a central theme: reality is illusory and knowledge is elusive. Although this novelistic strategem is common in modernistic fiction, it is uncommon in the New Mexico novel and it accounts for the uniqueness of *Nambe-Year One*.

At the same time, its metaphysics and complex structure also account for the novel's failings. Precisely, Romero's attempts to merge lyricism and stream-of-consciousness create technical and thematic discrepancies. All too often the narrative is woolly and Romero injects passages laden with cryptic, baffling questions:

> If anything, you reflected natural life as I understood it. Was it because of the chill, or the anti-climactic release of the dreaded fear that you had for the black widow spider, that you were shivering? What inner truth I seemed to deny kept you from finding comfort in my arms? My thoughts were not alone because you asked me why I always seemed to penetrate your innermost parts and thoughts.

In contrast, Romero's story-telling competence and prose shine when he is more restrained. For example, "Bandido," the most interesting and effectively presented chapter in the novel, works because of the swift dramatic pacing, engaging story line, and the clear and succinct thematic point. Notably, the episode is less subjective and esoteric, and there is a distance between the narrator and the participants of the legend reenacted. The upshot is that *Nambe-Year One* springs from a poetic vision that is marred by novelistic shortcomings. These shortcomings and the mixed results of *Nambe-Year One* should be seen in the sympathetic light that it is a young writer's first novel and he cuts his teeth on tough literary matter. In this light, Romero's plucky novel deserves the critical and popular attention that it has been largely denied.

Diversity and further sophistication can be found in Joseph Torres-Metzgar's *Below the Summit* (1976), a work that surpasses *Nambe-Year One* in thematic import and novelistic accomplishment.[5] With minor reservations, I agree that "Joseph Torres-Metzgar has contributed a new dimension to Chicano literature with his novel *Below the Summit*. . . . The integration of the various narrative elements results in a novel which is valid as a work of literature and also contributes to the broadening of Chicano literature."[6] Specifically, Torres-Metzgar broadens Chicano literature by contributing the first full-blown psychological novel to the literature of New Mexico. Using interior monologue, Torres-Metzgar offers a convincing psychological portrait of a disturbed, repressed, and ultimately violent personality (Bobby Lee Cross). Cross's attitudes and actions are symbolically extended to capture the bigotry and injustice that Mexicans have historically suffered in Texas. The novel provides sharp insights into the sociocultural character of West Texas, and Torres-Metzgar's biting irony is especially effective when he focuses on the Texan's prejudice and hysterical rejection of "the Meskin." This is neatly dramatized when Cross marries a Mexican woman by the name of María Dolores and attempts to circumvent his family's racism:

> "She's of pure Spanish stock," Lee had said. "She isn't Anglo, but she's white as you are. Her ancestors were here in Texas long before your daddy and his daddy even thought of coming here. She's no mestizo, no half-breed, no indians thrown in somewhere to corrupt her blood. She's no Mexican, Daddy! She's white European like you and me."

Cross's self-deception moves him to insist that María Dolores's name be Frenchified to "Marie" and that she not speak Spanish, so as not "to ingrain any Mexican traits" in their son. In these incisive passages Torres-Metzgar aptly dramatizes the racist legacy of the United States and the extremes that it reached in places like West Texas.

The novel is less convincing and sags from psychoanalytical baggage when Torres-Metzgar resorts to hackneyed Freudian motifs. For instance, the hoary Oedipus Complex is attached to Cross's personality: "He couldn't imagine his mother opening her legs to any man, even his father, and slapping herself sensually upward against his hairy trunk. Her thighs would flare for no man. . . . She was someone apart, pure white lovely, and untainted." Of course, Cross's idealization of his mother will sharply conflict with reality, and Torres-Metzgar attempts a psychosexual etiology to explain Cross's hatred of women, specifically Mexican women. In a flashback it is revealed that when Cross was a teenager he had gone—"hungry for the flesh of a woman"—to a Juarez whorehouse. At this point, Torres-Metzgar works a ragged theme. The Mexican whore laughed at Cross's awkwardness and premature ejaculation, and the humiliation rankled him for years. From that day, women were all the same to him: "*The same stinking whores.*" One day returning home he sees a man fleeing from his house and in a frenzied state he thinks the man is his wife's "mexican lover." Actually, it had been a local "Texan American" by the name of Will Bushbee, who had just raped María Dolores. In a psychotic rage, Cross takes a butcher knife and hacks his wife to pieces. Forcing the psychosexual motif, the brutal murder is associated with the sexual act, and Cross feels "freed of all passion, completely satiated." In these passages there are too many echoes—from *Othello* to Mailer's *An American Dream*—that deny the novel originality and vitality. The only novelty in the treatment of this hackneyed theme is that Torres-Metzgar transports it to dramatize the violence and hate that reside deep in the heart of the Texas that he creates. However, the climax of the novel offers an acute point on legality and injustice. The concluding chapter, virtually an epilogue, intimates that Will Bushbee would not be convicted for rape and Cross would probably not be convicted either: "No jury made up of good Christian Texans is gonna send 'im downa river for some Mexican troubles."

Although it has its lapses, the characterization of Bobby Lee Cross is engaging; in the most effective passages, Torres-Metzgar manages to convey Cross's doubt, fear, hatred, and anxiety, and he makes Cross's actions and thoughts recognizably human. In contrast, the characterization of Tomás Serveto does not possess even partial verisimilitude, and here lies the novel's greatest weakness. Notably, Torres-Metzgar contributes an ironic chapter to the development of Chicano literature: the anglo characters in this "Chicano novel" are better developed and more convincing than the Chicano characters. The sagging plot line presents Dr. Serveto, a professor of history, as a noble and shining example of "Chicano consciousness," standing in sharp contrast to the abysmally ignorant rednecks that populate the novel. The grave problem is that Serveto is not developed as a character and functions simply as a mouthpiece. The strident messages attached to Serveto reduce the novel to a weary and simplistic polemic: racist, fascist Texas rednecks vs. honest, decent, oppressed Chicanos. Unquestionably, there is a real and ignoble reality that prompts Torres-Metzgar's passion. Chicanos have suffered and still endure great injustices in Texas. However, a novel that reduces this sociohistorical reality to stereotypical villains and heroes does not do justice to either history or literature. Such discrepancies are especially grating when one considers that there is much in the novel that is fresh and imaginative. The narrative is solid when Torres-Metzgar gives careful attention to individual characters and explores the deep-rooted influences that have defined their personalities. The excellent passages where he manages to unify theme and style merit praise and encouragement that he continue to refine his promising talents.

Rudy S. Apodaca's *The Waxen Image* (1977) is similar to *Below the Summit* in that it does not primarily deal with Chicano characters.[7] The similarity ends there. *Below the Summit* is a serious and ambitious novel; *The Waxen Image* is novelistic fluff. The publishers claim that "*The Waxen Image* combines the mystery narrative talents of the author with his keen knowledge of his native New Mexico." This is a false claim on both accounts. The assertion, if true, that *The Waxen Image* is the first mystery-suspense novel written by a Chicano only makes it an oddity. It has no distinction as a mystery novel. It simply reworks all the creaky mechanisms and cliches of the genre. The trappings of the potboiler are all there: exotic locales, adventure, beautiful and mysterious women, romance, and a contrived and implausible plot (a rather silly story of African witchcraft and the discovery of an elixir of life). All of this exercised in stock phrases and hackneyed prose. For example, this is the obligatory sex scene:

> His demands excited her; a tingling sensation ran up her spine every time she was aware of his animal desire for her. She wanted his demands. Her love for him was strong, and it was this love he demanded from her, as well as her body. And so she gave herself totally to him tonight.

The greater part of the novel lumbers along in such a manner.

The claim that the novel is enhanced by the author's knowledge of his native state also has no grounds. The information provided in the novel could be obtained from a tourist. In fact, that is the point of view of the novel. The central character is a San Francisco advertising executive that spends a few weeks in the Albuquerque–Santa Fe–Taos area. The novel's cardboard characterizations match the tourist view of New Mexico and the superficial narrative descriptions and explanations. Moreover, there is a curiosity in Apodaca's treatment of Chicano characters (the Native American populace is totally ignored). The two clearly identifiable Chicano characters are secondary characters that do not rise above stock figures of the mystery novel genre; one is the sheriff of a small town, the other is the "mad scientist's" faithful servant. As another reader has pointed out, the characters

> lack growth and seem in some measure unreal. Their dialogues by and large are patterned and homogeneous—using similar jargon, regardless of their social or educational backgrounds. This culminates in their speech being more pedantic than genuine, more stilted than informal. The reader may find this contrast bothersome.[8]

The stilted language is indeed bothersome. Apparently, Apodaca sought to avoid the stereotype of the dull-witted, rustic small town sheriff by dignifying Sheriff Domínguez with intelligence and eloquence. But stilted speech and extreme affectation make Domínguez an unintentional Nero Wolfe caricature:

> It's wiser to be sure about such things from the onset. . . . Later one might begin to think of what one would have found, and the thought is always up there in some corner of the mind creating worries because he failed to do something he later regrets not having done. Besides, the innocent man, I have always contended, has nothing to hide and therefore, it behooves him to cooperate with the authorities, lest they suspect he has something to hide.

In fairness one can consider that *The Waxen Image* does not aspire to "serious literature" and is simply meant as an entertainment, a goal suitable to its mystery-suspense format. In this respect, *The Waxen Image* proves that a Chicano can write a potboiler and target a commercial market. The merits of such literature and its avenues are arguable. However, it is less arguable that *The Waxen Image* is not a significant contribution to the literature of New Mexico. Apodaca's work is an example of the dilettantism in New Mexico literature and *The Waxen Image* regrettably confirms Sergio Elizondo's pointed criticism: "Its [Chicano literature] weakness is that there is a lot of literature that is more personal than anything, and it should not be published. There are many writers who do not write carefully; they have not yet learned to be discriminating."[9]

The only value of works such as *The Waxen Image* is that they create an appreciation for thoughtful and stylish novels like Nash Candelaria's *Memories Of The Alhambra* (1977) and *Not By The Sword* (1982).[10] The first and second parts of a trilogy of historical novels dealing with the pioneer families that founded Albuquerque, Candelaria's fiction is the most ambitious work by a contemporary New Mexican Hispanic writer. In *Memories Of The Alhambra*, Candelaria expertly combines sound historical research with storytelling to recreate a way of life and to richly detail the history of the Rafa family. The story is enriched by a series of flashbacks and memory fragments that connect generations of the Rafa family, and Candelaria juxtaposes present and past to create a trans-historical narrative with complexity and depth. Moreover, the narrative technique enhances the thematic crux of the novel: the convolution and confusion of history, and the specific complexity that it achieved in Hispanic America. Candelaria's provocative theme is the racist legacy that persists in New Mexico and he dissects the racial superiority of those who claim to be "pure Spanish" and disparage *mestisaje*, the product of the Spaniard commingling with Indian races. The psychological ravages of the racist legacy are centered on José Rafa. He, who had forbidden his son to marry because his intended bride was "a dirty Mexican," embodies the ignorance and false pride of racial superiority. After attending his father's funeral in Albuquerque he is seized by an obsession to trace his Spanish roots back to the heroic conquistadores that ventured to a new world, conquered and christianized heathens, and brought civilization to a savage land. José Rafa's attempt to reclaim his Spanish heritage is treated with pungent irony. The lineage of the intrepid conquistadores has been reduced to a weak-spirited, faltering middle-aged man trying to reclaim something that had long ago died and perhaps from the start had been simply an impulse of greed and ignominy. In the novel's climactic scene, José Rafa's subconsciousness touches the long denied truth. In a dream sequence he witnesses the massacre of an Indian camp by Spanish soldiers. Coming across the headless corpse of one of the Spanish soldiers, he raises the helmet visor and finds his roots in a nightmarish vision: "The still air gave lie to the wind, and he was certain he was not imagining. Not a Captain from Extremadura. A piercing shriek burst from his depths. The severed head that stared up at him was grinning. *And it was his own face!*" José Rafa dies shortly after this discovery and the realization that he, like the entire generations of Rafas, was a "Child of the Old World and The New. A new race. The New Mexican." José Rafa's illusory search for his roots leads to a thematic point couched in historical irony: those in search of conquest were absorbed into the passive but ultimately more conquering land that was the Americas, and the Spaniard became what he conquered.

With the exception of one chapter, *Memories Of The Alhambra* is an excellent historical novel. Candelaria dovetails the narrative to the phantasmagoric scene where José Rafa experiences the shock of recognition that his true roots lie in the New World, that the true "American experience" is *mestizaje*, and that he and his kind had deluded themselves with notions of racial purity. This crucial, climactic chapter is followed by a superfluous and strident chapter on Chicano history. The polemical thrust adds nothing to the novel; in fact, it weakens the narrative structure. In this respect, *Below the Summit* and *Memories Of The Alhambra* share a notable shortcoming. The resort to preachy voice and rhetoric indicates that the authors were not confident that the story and its characters could convey the thematic point. It is especially irksome in Candelaria's case because he possesses storytelling gifts and novelistic talent.

What is refreshing in *Memories Of The Alhambra* and moreso in *Not By The Sword* is the painstaking realistic details and the avoidance of romantic claptrap. Instead of the usual staples of this type of historical fiction—dashing *caballeros*, beautiful señoritas, and the pastoral serenity of pre-conquest New Mexico, Candelaria fleshes out the characters and informs his fiction with historical authenticity. One can quibble, though, that Candelaria's announced purpose—"Scenes with historical personages attempt to couple the essence of what the historical record shows with the imaginary roles the Rafas played"—yields mixed results. The attempt to capture the historical essence is workmanlike; the imaginative content is the major success of the novel. The recreation of Governor Manuel Armjio, Padre José Gallegos, Padre Antonio José Martínez, Archbishop Jean Lamy, Father Joseph Machebeouf and others who played prominent roles in the history of New Mexico is standard stuff. These historical figures have been extensively depicted, their treatment ranging from vilification to glorification, in the lore and literature of New Mexico. Although the historical background is accurate (more accurate than, say, Willa Cather's *Death Comes For The Archbishop*), Candelaria covers well-trodden ground and offers no new insights into these historical figures and the roles they played in New Mexico history. The novel is more interesting and engaging as historical fiction when it dramatizes little known historical facts. For example, Candelaria's use of the story of the St. Patrick Battalion is inspired. The St. Patrick Battalion, composed of Irish immigrants, gained both infamy and glory, depending on nationalistic point of view, when Irish soldiers deserted the invading American forces and fought on the Mexican side. Not surprising, this event is absent from the pages of American history and literature. Candelaria mines this historical fact to present a fascinating and tragic footnote to the Mexican War of 1846.

The larger merit of the novel lies in the vitality and rich detail that Candelaria brings to the imaginary characters, representatives of the common folk who endured these turbulent years. As the novel opens, the patriarch of the Rafa family reacts with indifference to the Anglo-American entry into New Mexico: "We have always been here, and the world keeps changing. It's lunacy. The Yankees are coming. Who cares? What difference does it make? It doesn't matter." But it did make a great difference; it opened a Pandora's Box. The novel delineates the cultural, religious, and political differences, and it focuses on the inevitable hostilities between Anglos and Hispanos in the American Southwest. The military conquest and subsequent annexation of New Mexico introduced new governmental systems and authorities. Attendant to the new systems was the ecclesiastical order and authority represented by Archbishop Lamy. The imposition of new authorities—usually arrogant, intolerant, and oppressive either in military or ecclesiastical form—led to the conflicts that are the thematic issues of the novel. The title alludes to historic conflict in New Mexico and the tools of conquest. The first two Rafas in New Mexico came from Extremadura; one was a soldier, the other a priest—the sword and the cross. The metaphor is restamped in the era covered by the novel, 1846–1854, as the bifurcated plot line focuses on two Rafa brothers: Carlos Rafa's armed resistance to the Anglo-American invasion (the sword), and Father José Antonio Rafa's dilemma as he is caught in the struggle between Archbishop Lamy and Padre Martínez for ecclesiastical power (the cross). There are no resolutions to these conflicts in the novel. Candelaria's story ends with the Treaty of Guadalupe Hidalgo. Foreshadowing devices in the novel make it clear that peace would not come with the treaty; it anticipates the infamous land-grabs and the disfranchisement of Hispanos. The novel closes with the demand made by the Surveyor General of The United States that Hispanos who chose to remain north of the Rio Grande show proof of land ownership. José Antonio Rafa's response is a plaint that echoed across the American Southwest: "We lived on this land for a hundred and fifty years. How can anyone dispute that we do not own it, even if we cannot find old papers?"

The sad story that follows this historical juncture is presumably the subject of the third part of Candelaria's trilogy, tentatively titled *The Inheritance Of Strangers*. One can hope that the third part is as good as *Memories Of The Alhambra* and *Not By The Sword*. These two novels admirably controvert the saw that "history is written by the victors." Candelaria excavates events, episodes, and moments of human dignity that were either erased from or never entered the historical record. His retrieval of that past, his imaginative recreation of daily life and personal struggles, and his smooth, crisp style make *Memories Of The Alhambra* and *Not By The Sword* two of the finest historical novels in the literature of New Mexico.

E. A. Mares, a poet and erudite cultural historian, has observed that New Mexican Hispanic writers are in the process of discovering "New Mexico, as a center from which creativity flows out to the nation and the world" and they are "utilizing all their personal, historic, and social resources to literally write their way into the American literature of the future."[11] With its reservations taken into account, this survey confirms the happy circumstance that New Mexico Hispanic writers are discovering a literary fountainhead. Indeed, the future of New Mexican Hispanic literature is very promising. Among the promises is the expectation that it will increasingly become a diverse and multifaceted literature.

NOTES

1. José Armas, "Chicano Writing: The New Mexico Narrative," *De Colores*, Vol. 5, Nos. 1–2 (1980), 69–81.

2. Robert Perea, "Dragon Mountain," *De Colores*, Vol. 4, Nos. 1–2 (1978), 33–41. Robert Perea, "Small Arms Fire," *Cuentos Chicanos* (Albuquerque: University of New Mexico Press, 1984), 119–24. Denise Chávez, "Baby Krishna's All Night Special," *Southwest: A Contemporary Anthology* (Albuquerque: Red Earth Press, 1977), 206–9. Albert Lovato, "Agusa'o con los Velices," *Cuentos Chicanos* (Albuquerque: University of New Mexico Press, 1980), 73–76. Nash Candelaria, "Mano a Mano," *Hispanics in the United States: An Anthology of Creative Literature*, Vol. 2 (Ypsilanti: Bilingual Press, 1982), 153–161. Kathleen Baca, "Sterile Relationships," *Cuentos Chicanos* (Albuquerque: University of New Mexico Press, 1984), 27–34. Kika Vargas, "The Corpse," *Cuentos Chicanos* (Albuquerque: University of New Mexico Press, 1984), 173–77.

3. Orlando Romero, *Nambe-Year One* (Berkeley: Tonatiuth International, 1976).

4. Fray Angelico Chavez, "Review of *Nambe-Year One*," *New Mexico Magazine*, Vol. 32, No. 4 (Fall, 1978), 246–47.

5. Joseph Torres-Metzgar, *Below The Summit* (Berkeley: Tonatiuth International, 1976).

6. Ricardo A. Valdez, "Review of *Below the Summit*," *Latin American Review*, Vol. 5, No. 10 (Spring-Summer, 1977), 156–62.

7. Rudy Apodaca, *The Waxen Image* (Mesilla, New Mexico: Titan Publishing Co., 1977).

8. Nasario García, "Review of *The Waxen Image*," *Rocky Mountain Review*, Vol. 32, No. 4 (Fall 1978), 246–47.

9. Bruce-Novoa, "Interview with Sergio Elizondo," *Chicano Authors: Inquiry By Interview* (Austin: University of Texas Press, 1980), 67–82. *The Waxen Image* is not a singular case. Other works that fall within this category: Robert C. Medina, *Two Ranges* (Las Cruces, New Mexico: Bilingüe Publications, 1974); Katherine Quintana Ranck, *Portrait of Doña Elena* (Berkeley: Tonatiuth International, 1982); Arturo García, *Schwammenauel Dam* (New York: Vantage Press, 1972); John E. Baca *Sound Retreat For The Conquistadores* (New York: Carlton Press, 1974).

10. Nash Candelaria, *Memories Of The Alhambra* (Palo Alto, California: Cíbola Press, 1977). *Not By The Sword* (Ypsilanti: Bilingual Press, 1982).

11. E. A. Mares, "The Center Is Everywhere: Hispanic Letters In New Mexico," *Century Magazine*, Vol. 2, No. 10 (February 1982), 9–11.

15

NEW MEXICAN CHICANO POETRY
The Contemporary Tradition

BRUCE-NOVOA

THROUGH THE MISSING LINK

Thinking back on the initial poetry of the Chicano Movement (1967–1973), no New Mexicans come to mind. Colorado had Rodolfo Gonzales and Abelardo Delgado (transplanted from El Paso); Texas had Ricardo Sánchez; and California produced Alurista in the south and José Montoya in the north. Although identified more with northern Californian Chicanismo, however, Montoya was born in the Sandía Mountains of New Mexico. Nevertheless, he is seldom listed as a New Mexican—for instance, his name did not appear among the poets recommended by the editors of this collection. Having moved to California in 1941 at age nine qualifies him as a West Coast writer, a classification supported by his poetry, sprinkled as it is with specific Californian references that anchor it in his adopted home state. Compared to New Mexican Chicano poets, differences emerge, especially in his urban themes and ties to a California based wing of the Chicano Movement, the Farm Workers Union. Yet this ex-New Mexican will serve us as a missing link.

One poem offers echoes of the New Mexican Montoya that can lead us into our topic. In "El sol y los de abajo," the title poem of his book, appears "El corrido de mi jefe," a brief elegy to his Father.

Acaballo iva el jinete	*[Riding went the horseman*
Se movía por los cerros	*Moving through the mountains*

Persiguido por los perros
Bien fajado su buen cuete.

Guerillero de la causa
Nobles fueron tus esfuerzos
No por gloria ni por versos
Fuiste a pelear por tu Raza.
(39)

Pursued by the dogs
Well buckled his trusty gun.

Soldier for the cause
Noble were your efforts
Not for glory nor for verses
You went to fight for your Race.]

Significant elements appear. Montoya utilizes the *corrido* or ballad form, considered the treasure trove of Chicano oral tradition and a convention associated with the popular, non-academic community. This effect is enhanced through archaic Spanish characteristics of the New Mexican popular dialect. The Spanish contrasts with Montoya's natural interlingual way of speaking, as the *corrido*'s set structure contrasts with his usual free verse. Appearing in the middle of a long poem written mostly in English and free form, the *corrido* stanzas evoke an older, more traditional cultural mind-set befitting the image evoked. Montoya then breaks off the nostalgic mode with a contemporary slang term, *Chale*, when he returns to the present time and to himself as subject of the verses.

Y ahora se encuentra tu hijo
En las mismas situaciones
Diferentes condiciones . . .

[And now your son finds himself
in the same situation
Different conditions

Chale!

No way!

My actions are not yet worthy
of the ballads . . . me faltan
los huevos de mi jefe and
the ability to throww off
the gava's llugo de
confución . . .
(39–40)

I lack
my dad's balls]

[gringo's yoke of
confusion . . .]

The distance separating Montoya from his grandfather reflects the difference between his usual poetry and that of the New Mexican poets, who perceive themselves as still within their tradition, because they still live in the midst of the culture. Yet they too prefer the free-verse form, predominantly in English, and feel the importance of recalling the oral tradition from the silence it could fall into if not captured in written poetry. Moreover, their poetry also reveals a sense of distance from an idealized past. While they evoke tradition, they also express the changes brought by modernity and alien cultural forces. And Montoya's nostalgic fragment gives us clues to both elements in the dialectic.

Centering the image cluster is the heroic figure of the outlaw on horseback fleeing over the mountains. The outlaw is a version of one of the most repeated figures in the New Mexican tradition, the outsider. This figure assumes different forms in varying contexts. Mountains and horses are repeated images, and taken together, they reveal an emphasis on the natural world dear to New Mexican Chicano poets. They often utilize it as a refuge from the oppressive presence of the Anglo-Americans with their supposedly alienated cultural ways. The use of dogs to allude to Anglo-Americans, while not an unusual trope in poetry, signals an emphasis on close animal/human relationship in New Mexican Chicano writing. Animals are often portrayed as agents or incarnations of human or divine will. The situation itself is highly significant in pitting a lone male against the onslaught of the other culture. Even though this figure is alone he symbolizes the community. Several elements stand out. Something threatens the protagonist, in this case the other culture. The male is the communal representative, protagonist of resistance activity: the group's survival is linked to his. The woman's absence represents the passive image male writers tend to give her, as a mere support and even as a threat—but most often, as here, she is not depicted at all. These elements can be seen as folk motifs. That Montoya sees history as a repetition of circumstances points to yet another characteristic of the New Mexican Chicano poets. They pursue history as a means, not just of self-understanding, but of self-realization within a tradition. Just as Montoya invokes a standard of values from the past that he wants to live up to, the New Mexican Chicano poets continually see themselves vis-à-vis the past as a defining spirit, present in particular figures and forms.

Montoya's poem ends, however, on a note of difference. "But Chilam Balam's prophetic/Chant has been realized—and the/Dust that darkened the air begins/To clear y se empiesa a ver el Sol (and one begins to see the sun)./I AM LEARNING TO SEE THE SUN" (40). The evocation of southern Mexican (Mayan) pre-Columbian literature, while typical of early Chicano Movement writing—references to high culture Mexican tribes, the linking to a pre-European prophetic tradition that lends an epic quality to the present political struggle, and the key image of the sun, borrowed from Native American religions, are quite close to Alurista and the Aztlán school of poets—it is atypical in New Mexico. Few such references surface in the poetry studied here, with the exceptions of Rudy Anaya's satiric poem, Antonio Mares' epic, and one poem by Baca. Entrenched New Mexican traditions appear vital enough to preclude the need to import a heritage in reality foreign to the culture of the region.

Finally, the situation of the man apparently alone, yet simultaneously among males alluded to through the animals, betrays a male-centered, chauvinistic vision. New Mexican Chicano poets, even when not indulging the romantic outsider image, are markedly adverse to concentrating on intimate heterosexual relationships. Women, if not absent entirely, are a peripheral or absent presence. Often they are depicted stereotypically. Exceptions are so few as to be striking in their mere existence. In this context the appearance of few women poets among them infuses a problematic dialectic. Much of what characterizes the surface of men's poetry is absent in the women's, and what the men lack in the way of personal experience will be found among the women. The thematic spaces they choose to inhabit appear so estranged that one wonders how they cohabit the same geographic region. They share the same history, but not the codes of expression, as if they spoke through distinct sets of imagery, seeing their experience from separate perspectives. As in Montoya's fragment, so in most New Mexican poetry women are absent from the core of male memory, relegated to the implicit wider sphere of their existence.

NEW MEXICAN CHICANO POETS

New Mexican Chicano poets form a small group, with relatively few publications. I discuss only those who have published at least one book. Demetria Martínez's manuscript is in press. One more caveat. The discussions of individuals will often occasion digressive ventures into related topics of interest. Beyond explication, I propose to contextualize the works within New Mexican Chicano poetry and, when appropriate, Chicano literature in general.

THE VILLAGE VOICE NEW MEXICAN STYLE

A desire to document the life of one's community is characteristic of Chicano writing. It responds directly to the absence, or falsification, of that life in the written record presented by the dominant culture. The dominant society's version of history is written from the East Coast perspective, attributing national origin to English ancestry. Literature follows suit, history and literature being handmaidens, two genres of cultural production designed by and for those who control society. Mass media pop culture reflects and reinforces high culture fictions. In this light Chicano literature can be seen as a rewriting of U.S. history to include the Chicanos, whose story has been passed down orally.

New Mexican Chicanos employ this strategy also. If anything, they have an even stronger sense of historical pride and the need to rewrite the record because they can rightfully claim a much longer continual presence in what is now the United States than any other group save Native Americans. Leo Romero could speak for an entire group of writers when he declares his task as that of historical recreation:

I search for a history of this valley
but no one wrote it down
so I look for anything
For a scrap of paper
with a few words
but I find nothing other
than some names and dates
written in family bibles
I am left to construct a history
where there are no written records (Agua Negra, 39)

For the written record to remain faithful to the oral tradition it intends to preserve, writers must focus on recording the voices of the community.

Leroy Quintana

Hijo del pueblo, New Mexico Poems (1976) declares openly an orientation that much of Chicano production has adopted. The author's primary identity derives from the community as its issue and heir. To this he adds, however, a subcategory of regional specificity: New Mexico. Nothing could symbolize more succinctly the position of the New Mexican Chicano poets. They relate to the essential program of Chicanismo, but always through the mediation of their particular experience. This could be said of other Chicano writers, but none of the major early poets chose to foreground their regional culture over their form of a generalized ideology of the movement. It is pertinent to recall that the first book from a New Mexican Chicano poet appeared in the mid 1970s when the ideological militantism of the Chicano Movement was rapidly erroding. In part, fragmentation was brought about by publications of Chicanos not involved in the centers that had defined Chicano literature: women, middle-class writers, and Chicanos from regional and cultural backgrounds that varied from that of the early writers. Thus, the appearance of a New Mexican style of poetry, prefigured by Rudy Anaya's fiction, figured in a general expansion of Chicano literature to represent more accurately the culture's many faceted reality.

At the same time, Quintana's book follows a general pattern of Chicano literature, as I explained it in *Chicano Poetry, A Response to Chaos*. *El hijo* starts with the death of community members, to which the book responds. What differs here is that the threat is immediately contextualized within existing communal rituals that interpret it as part of the normal life cycle. No sense of tradition disappearing is implied, as is often felt in Chicano poetry. The poet expresses no fear of impending cultural death. Members of the community pass away, but the community continues present and healthy.

In the small town
where I was raised
we always knew
when somebody on our side
had died

The bells
of the Iglesia de las Carmelitas
would ring
and the old ones would mention
don Ricardo or doña Martinez (no pagination)

Death casts no one into chaos here, rather the opposite. It is an occasion for reaffirming order. Note the emphasis on knowing, followed by concepts of time, "when," then place, "our side." This also conveys the division within the town: our side implies their side. More importantly, there is security in the system, thus making death an ordering instead of disorienting event. The control of death's menace is attributed to both church and community, symbolized in two ways of announcing the news. Together they turn the death into a repetition of established order, and thus not threatening. While the bells make each new death a repetition, the elders do likewise, but by remembering and naming the deceased, a form of elegizing. As long as this is possible, the community remains secure.

The rest of Quintana's book is a chorus of community voices, with the author almost disappearing into the role of recorder. Typical characters and motifs emerge: the village wiseman pronouncing popular truth (Don Ricardo), the town drunk, the outlaw, la Llorona, and the family members, especially the dead grandparents. Motifs include the sacredness of the mountains, the religious pilgrimage, witchcraft, buried treasure stories, corn planting, and folk healers. Character and motif combine in the story teller, Don Santos, who conveyed his tales mysteriously, silently, during his monthly visits, like some ritual of revelation that initiated the author into his culture's secrets.

This is possible because of the insulated, even isolated, quality of the "small town." Yet that same attribution cannot be read without a tinge of displacing nostalgia. Communal cohesion is temporally distanced, and between then and now the author introduces negative factors, like poverty, government intervention, labor exploitation, alcoholism, and racism. The sign of disruptive forces reaching in from outside is the soldier, taken away and returned changed. The war veteran has become a standard figure in New Mexico lore, with a characteristic disorientation caused by their military experiences. The war kills some, maims others, and unnerves the rest for life. The town misfit wears "khaki cap, shirt and pants." Ultimately, town order depends on family ties and generational links, yet the book ends on a version of the outlaw motif in which the father is known only through a photograph. Significantly, the man is "playing a *corrido*/on his quitar/in the state penitentiary." The oral tradition has been exiled to prison, in an echo of Montoya's image of his father. But here there is no romantic freedom, no triumph over the other, just incarcerated resistance by a lone man who should be home singing to his grandchild. This break in the oral tradition chain must be mended by the written test.

Before going on, it should be noted that Quintana does include several poems on women, notably his mother, grandmother, wife, and daughter. While sensitively portrayed, none is given a central role, and they are depicted in stereotypical roles. This may be the traditional way of handling them, difficult for men to alter while trying to retain any hold they can on the traditional culture.

Juan Estevan Arellano

Of the poets invested in the retention of the communal traditions by recording the voices of the people, Arrellano comes closest to straight anthropological documentation. *Palabras de la vista/retratos de la pluma, (memorias) [Words of sight/pictures of the pen, (memories)]*, a book of poetry and photographs the author presents as *fotoesía*, is written in characteristic New Mexican Spanish. Although the author claims to offer his memories, he starts with those of others, thus establishing that he and the community share a communal memory. In addition, Arrellano utilizes popular saying, riddles, songs, and folk motifs as material for poems. The collection is a catalogue of New Mexican folklore: personified animals ("Gallo blanco," a poem narrated by a dead rooster), skeletons and ghosts, the spirit of the moon, the horse, death personified as a woman (Doña Sebastiana), and the infamous coyote character. Several of his pieces have a picaresque quality, a mixture of folksy cleverness and down-and-out vulgar wit. The need to preserve these images is explained in the implicit threat represented by the rich, whom Arrellano attacks bitterly through satire.

While the language and content give the sense of being the closest rendering of the community's reality of any of the poets, the poems lack something. Like the photographs, they are too documentary and not mediated enough through lyric transformation. Their interest lies in the recording of voices as they speak, but poetry should be more. Missing is the artist's ability to edit raw material to draw out essential significance. Arrellano attempts to do it, but faithfulness to his sources holds him back. Moreover, since his purpose is to present those voices and images, perhaps we should not expect more. Even with its limitations, it is an interesting piece.

Robert Gallegos

A similar, but much less successful book is Gallegos's *Ambrosia Lake*. A well intentioned effort to write labor poetry about miners, a significant traditional occupation among New Mexican Chicanos, the poems bog down in mining terminology. Apparently motivated by the same desire to convey accurately the context of his group through their language, Gallegos burdens the poems with esoteric words, and then compounds the problem by adding numerous footnotes to define them. He conveys an underworld of incredibly difficult labor, matched by the efforts readers must exert to dig through the poems. Miners, working beneath the surface and isolated from general society, are yet another form of the outsider living in a situation with its own rules and codes of expression. Men become insensitive, and women are seen as sexual objects, even when they must work for the same economic reasons as the men. The book fails, however, because Gallegos, like Arrellano, remains too faithful to the documentary purpose. And since his group is even more distant from the reader than Arrellano's, Gallegos's poetry appeals only to a greatly reduced audience.

His erotic poems in *Carnero* are more accessible, but still lack quality. As one of the few attempts by Chicano poets anywhere to explore intimacy, they are of interest. However, the effort remains on the surface of the sexual, never delving into any greater significance. Worse, the poems are trite and unexciting. The subject deserves better treatment.

Leo Romero

While sharing with the above poets the desire to allow the community to speak through their poetry—as epitomized in his verses cited above—Romero gives the project a distinctive twist by creating a specific character/narrator who assumes the first person voice in both *During the Growing Season* (1978) and *Celso* (1985). The latter book even takes its title from the name of Romero's alter ego. This allows for the perspective, often scattered among several community members in the books seen above, to be centered, thus focusing the reader's interest in the development of a character while the information is conveyed. And that character comes from the heart of the mountain region of central New Mexico. He both lives in and personifies key elements of that rural cultural. That which he does not represent directly himself, he often re-presents through his function of oral tradition practitioners. Thus Romero's writing expands beyond the normal limits of poetry, invading both the realm of narrative fiction and drama. His poems are miniature stories garnered from the oral tradition; when read, especially if aloud, they may well evoke the mood of dramatic performance.

Romero's choice of perspective for the majority of his poetry is significant. From the general category of outsider, Romero has chosen the *pícaro*. Traditionally *pícaros* live off of society rather than for it, avoiding work at all costs, using their wits to skirt society's dictates. Since they refuse to follow the rules of order, they seldom marry, remaining loners. Their crimes, if any, are minor infractions necessary for survival or a minimum level of pleasure. Romero's Celso has, in addition, a New Mexican twist: he is the village trickster, the world-wise wino, the folk philosopher, and most significantly the curator of old tales, which he does not merely recount, but embodies as if having lived them.

In other words, Romero has created a character who lives, or imagines he lives, or simply claims to have experienced some of the most typical of the old folk tales of apparitions (the devil, ghosts, skeletons, witches), graveyards, death personified, or nature as a seductive woman. Celso even has, or pretends to have, an animal familar. Significantly, it is the coyote, whose position in the animal kingdom is the equivalent of the *pícaro's* in human society. At times these elements combine in long narratives that could be told almost as well in prose. Celso also branches out into the themes of the down-and-outer: an old bachelor who prefers wine to work, he dedicates himself to getting life's necessities and pleasures through deception (pretending to be dead so an old ex-nurse will give him mouth-to-mouth resucitation) or in exchange for his entertaining conversation. One gets the feeling that Celso is playing us for some reward that he will request at a strategic point in the narrative: to hear the ending we may have to invite him to stay for dinner, or at least another drink.

Next thing I remember
was waking up in the mountains
half frozen to death

Celso waits for someone
to refill his glass
before continuing his story (Celso, 26)

And we tolerate the subterfuge, as do other characters who listen to him in the poems, because the stories are at once familiar and new; also, because Celso is interesting, fascinating, even endearing.

The danger in Romero's Celso is that the line between cultural archetype and stereotype easily becomes a perilous tightrope when taken out of context, as publication is apt to do. For New Mexicans, the *pícaro* brings a set of culturally defined characteristics and an entire contextual knowledge that the writer can count on without bothering to recreate each time. The intertextual resonances are clear and specific for those who share the author's background. This is most apparent in the figure of Celso upon which Romero hinges much of his work. New Mexicans tolerate *pícaros*, at least in stories: in the traditional setting of a small community, even the town drunk is a member of society. Outside of that context, however, the character may be less appealing. In fact, Celso can resemble less the friendly village storyteller and more Spenser Tracy's offensive portrayal of a Steinbeck paisano in the film version of *Tortilla Flats*. This becomes painfully apparent in the stage version of *Celso*. Much ethnic literature faces this danger. Romero has bridged the distance between ethnic specificity and the greater audience because under the facade of the former lie universal themes of death, old age, nature, the free spirit, and, principally, desire.

Not all of Romero's writing is narrated by Celso. *Agua Negra* does not contain the character, and the first section is dedicated to poems about Romero's grandparents spoken in the author's voice. Yet Celso has become such a central figure in Romero's work that the rest of his poetry is now defined in relation to him. Other poems provide that necessary context for Celso, weaving the fabric of a traditional society capable of spawning and accepting the *pícaro*.

Romero stands well ahead of the poets mentioned above in that he has created a way to convey the reality of his regional tradition that sets up few barriers to general reading. Moreover, while accepting the task of recording the life of the community, he freely manipulates the material to fit his character. This is actually a traditional approach. Oral practitioners embellish the stories, molding them to fit the audience or the occasion. Romero surpasses his fellow poets because he is less of an anthropologist and more of an oral *cuentista*.

THE EPIC VOICE

A founding piece of contemporary Chicano poetry was Rodolfo Gonzales's *I Am Joaquín/Yo Soy Joaquín* (1967). It explained the Chicano community by tracing centuries of its evolution. As propagandistic historical rewriting intended to restore communal pride and purpose, *Joaquín* manipulated history according to ideological needs. Chicanos enthusiastically received *Joaquín* and even emulated it. Authors from different regions responded with their version of the epic of Chicano history. Alurista's *Flor y Canto en Aztlán* has a similar sweep and intent.

Miguel Méndez's *Los criaderos humanos (épica de los desamparados) y Sahuaros* is an allegorical epic with firm roots in the Arizona desert. Texans see *corridos* as their epic form, often citing Americo Paredes's *With a Pistol in His Hand* as historical rewriting from the Texas Mexican perspective. In New Mexico, two writers have produced epic poems in this mode.

The epic poets relate to the "village voice" group in that they also want to give the community its written history. The difference lies in that they do not seek that history in the collective popular voice. They are less anthropological and less specifically regional, preferring to give their poem the wider sweep of a voyage into time to encompass a wide panorama of events. Montoya alluded to this desire through reference to the *Chilam Balam*. Antonio Mares and Rudy Anaya offer New Mexicans epic poems written by two of their own.

Antonio Mares

The Unicorn Poem opens on a typical Chicano note, that of finding something omitted from official record.

On seeing a Detailed Map
I noticed the empty space
where there is no map,
only theater of man and myth,
the land of the unicorn
and less lovely beasts
trying to corral him. (5)

Mares will work a series of overlayed metaphors: the map, the myth, the search, and the struggle for survival and freedom. His poem fills empty space with the silenced history of the Chicanos of New Mexico.

What starts as a blank space on a map transmutes into the outline of houses on the map, and later into the silenced lives within squares of photographs of past generations, and even words that must be filled with meaning. He implies that they can be filled by myth because, contrary to its false popular interpretation as lie, myth is the symbolic representation of a group's version of universal truth. It relates a story of origins, of struggle and often wondering, and a popular culture history of how a people came to be what and where they are. This myth is to be played out, like a drama, a mythical allegory.

The choice of the unicorn as central metaphor of the myth, while eccentric, serves at least a triple purpose. First, the traditional symbolism of the unicorn becomes a metaphor for Chicanismo. It stands for beauty, purity, unity, love, and desire, as well as survival skills. A fierce fighter, impossible to catch or kill through violence, it would give itself to a pure maiden, becoming docile in her presence. It stood for Christ in Christian lore, the savior in the womb of a virgin. The single horn signified the unity of duality, the transcendence of otherness and separation. It was believed to possess healing power. On another level, its choice links Chicanos with a universal myth not usually associated with Mexican culture. Thus, Mares emphasizes the fundamental unity of peoples. And at yet another level, its blatant artificiality precludes simplistic historicism or realistic interpretation, forcing a reading in the realm of the symbolic. Thus Mares reminds readers that the poem is a created object with reality only in its own space of words. He underscores this by calling attention to the act of writing the poem and even to the words themselves and their ability to create realities. "Words become seeds of maize,/the healing herbs of the men./Words became mud villages/named with the flint edge/of cliff, wind and star,/Tiquex, Alcanfor, Isleta, Sandía" (11). His truth is symbolic, not documentary, but powerful.

Mares gives the Chicano origins myth of the blending of Native American and Spaniard some twists. For one, although naming the pre-Columbian gods, he insists "We are not Aztecs./We are the victims of Aztecs. . . . and we are far from Aztlán" (10), distinguishing himself from other Chicano writers who glorify the Aztecs. While we can read this simply as Mares's rejection of that particular tribe as origin, it also should be noted that it is factual. The Native Americans who came to New Mexico from central Mexico were not Aztec, but from tribes who had been surpressed by the Aztecs and later allied themselves with the Spaniards. In the same vein, in contrast to Gonzales's anti-Arabic stand in *I Am Joaquín*, Mares emphasizes the Arabic over the Castillian. Yet all of these evocations are, as the poet says, just a graveyard of words yearning for a life, "a song."

The song is New Mexico. It is in this space that the past takes on life, becoming a performance of dance and song, a sacred Native American/Christian ritual. Time accelerates forward into the recent past and eventually to the present, where the poet attempts to fill in the "tierra incognita" spaces left off the official map. The future is left uncertain, but with the promise of a new awakening.

Mares's epic is probably too esoteric and intellectually self-aware for a wide audience. It lacks the simplistic populism and harsh dualities of good and evil of *I Am Joaquín*. Mares proposes not a myth of bloodletting, but one of survival in love and goodness. His is an image of the unity of all peoples who would side with nature against the spoilers of the earth. To avoid fixation on the enemy, he prefers to concentrate on his own people, but always through the lens of the writer whose real material is language. And he explicitly states that he is the writer, the creator of those words, not simply the recorder of the communal voice. Hence, the level of diction is well above the common or popular level of speech. Unlike the writers of the previous category, Mares feels no need to keep his poetry at that level, preferring to let it soar to the heights of his well-trained mind.

Rudolfo A. Anaya

In his epic, Anaya takes the opposite tack, deliberately seeking a popular level of speech, filling his verses with colloquial slang and vulgarism. His two characters, comic versions of the Chicano barrio hero, remind one of Cheech Marin. Using marijuana they journey into the Mexican past in search of their origins. La Malinche guides them and they converse with historical and mythological figures about how the Mexican nation was formed. At the end they are sent back to instruct the Chicano of the north. The effect is one of satiric parody.

The comic tone undermines the entire effort. If we are to take it seriously, then we must question the diction and ridiculous effect it produces. Are we expected to give credence to characters called Juan Chicaspatas (John Smallpaws) and Al Penco (a play on words that evokes a picaresque folklore figure of dubious and untrustworthy character). If meant to satirize the epic pretentions of some Chicano writing, then too much space is dedicated to providing information on Mexican myths and history. Anaya simply has not handled the material well, perhaps not having decided what the intent was. The question arises as to why New Mexicans need to seek origins in Mexican myth at all, especially a version of it closely allied with Aztec history. As Mares says, "We are not Aztecs. . . . and we are far from Aztlán."

Lastly, Anaya claims, through the narrator/protagonist, that he sings to the women of Aztlán. However, the poem is not at all a song of praise to women and will probably offend many women by its general lack of senstivity in the treatment of female characters.

THE PERSONAL VOICE

The remaining poets differ from those studies above in that they neither turn their poetry entirely into a vehicle for communal voices nor do they offer a panoramic historical overview. If they speak for the people, then they do it within the tradition of the community speaking through the individual. They implicitly stand for the position that a community finds resonances in the personal experiences of each of its members, so it is better to explore the personal in depth. While Baca still attempts to bespeak the collective by echoing a multitude of voice in a portion of one book, in general these poets seek a distinctive personal style. As we would expect, this produces a poetry more intimate in character. If history is explored, it is the past of the persona and the immediate family. Since the developing personal expression is important to them, these poets shy away from the folkloric figures and motifs. After all, when the communal is no longer to be taken as a measure of value, then those figures and motifs go from well-known to well-worn. And the personal poet dreads cliché, even when it is called popular speech.

That the women poets would fall into this category might have been expected. Since men dominate the other forms of expression, it behooves women to seek an alternative. Also, it well could be that women have never been allowed to participate in that code of expression that forms the folkloric tradition of the other poets. Nor do the same mythic forms attract them. They are more concerned with surviving the real present in terms of individual experience and less pretentious than the men who assume they can speak for everyone else.

Jimmy Santiago Baca

The only man in this category marks the transition into the personal. Baca blends some features of the above groups into his strongly self-centered work. Like a response to Quintana's question as to identity of the prisoner in the photograph, Baca begins his career from prison, in the role of a key figure within the New Mexican tradition: the outlaw. It is as if Montoya's outlaw father spoke for himself, instead of remaining a silent idol. Echoes of Romero's project resonate in Baca: both begin in a personal search that channels itself into a character, in Baca's case Martín. The significance of that evolution is, nevertheless, different. Whereas Romero relinquishes the personal voice to a folkloric character, the pícaro outsider, Baca's personal *I* coincides with the figure of the outlaw and he moves away from it in his search for deeper personal understanding. Ironically, to do so he seems compelled to open a distance between himself and his persona by creating a character, Martín, who will take on an epic quality of historical searcher, although restricting himself to the immediate family. Martín recuperates, as Baca recreates, a reason for his situation, and then transcends it by finding a new common spirit and purpose. The poems of the second book are the record of his pilgrimage.

Immigrants in Our Own Land contains prison poems with almost no references to Baca's ethnicity. Clues can be found, but they are so subtle as to be more the reader's invention than the author's intention. The mention of "piñon trees" (23) stands out in its uniqueness among the many images that bear no ethnic specificity. The few references to Chicanos are not tied to the persona's identity, and in "So Mexicans are Taking Jobs from Americans," a pro-Mexican poem, the persona does not assume the identity of the accused, prefering to remain an ambiguous defender. Even the title poem, which one might expect to allude to Chicanos, is actually about how prisoners are treated. The essence of the collection lies not in ethnicity, but in individual self-knowledge and affirmation. "I Will Remain" offers the key.

I am after a path you cannot find by looking at green fields,
smelling high mountain air that is clear and sweetly
Odorous as when you fall in love again and again and again.
I am looking for a path that weaves through rock
and swims through dispair with fins of wisdom.
A wisdom to see me through this nightmare,

. . . .

I will take the strength I need from me,
not from field or new friends. With my old friends fighting!
Bleeding! Calling me crazy! And never getting the respect I desire

. . . .

I stay because I believe I will find something,

. . . .

Here on this island of death and violence,
I must find peace and love in myself, eventually freedom
And if I am blessed, then perhaps a little wisdom. (2)

Prison here fits into the ancient motif of the voyage into the wilderness, the descent into hell, from which the pilgrim emerges illuminated with truth. But it is not a voyage into a community, rather into the self. The book ends with no sign of the freedom he seeks and not much of the wisdom either.

While *Swords of Darkness* was published after *Immigrants*, the poems are dated two years earlier and are stylistically similar. Long verses dangerously close to prose, express the outsider's perspective, the prisoner's isolation from society. The last poem, "Walking Down to Town and Back," contains, however, childhood memories among which appear typical New Mexican motifs, to say nothing of specific place names like Belén and Sandía mountains. A horse-riding father takes the son to see a woman "who had seen our Virgin Mary" (no pagination). Suddenly the poem turns into a New Mexican folktale, with death, strange events involving malicious animals, the spirit of the deceased attempting to kill the spouse and causing a fire (a similar story appears in Romero's "His Sister" *Agua Negra*), and salvation coming in the form of divine intervention. The persona then claims to have also seen the Virgin and is marked for life by the apparition. The community treats him like a crazy drunk, resembling the pícaro. The poem is an origin myth of the outsider figure, an explanation of the category in which Baca finds himself in "Immigrants." And that situation is attributed to his father's intervention—in traditional guise of horse rider—a version of the cycle-of-history motif in which one generation inherits its destiny from the elders. Somehow that destiny is to speak of the dark unknown side of existence, to be the voice of "rude life" as the last poem states. In this context, *Immigrants* becomes a voyage into a wilderness to garner the wisdom necessary to live up to the destiny with which the young persona was marked.

Baca's recent book is a personal voyage into a dark personal past. Martín, the central character, orphaned—actually abandoned by his parents—in early childhood like a classic pícaro, goes in search of his parents' history. He begins with his memories—"My mind circles warm ashes of memories,/the dark edged images of my history" (3), adds what he can learn from others—"For some years I wandered cross country,/and those who had known my parents/came back to me again" (11), which in turn further provokes his own. He manages to reconstruct his parents' unhappy life and pathetic death. His arrival at the conclusion of their story releases him to begin his own search for a future, one with set goals that contrast sharply with his parents' experience: "I left Burque [Alburquerque] again, to buy a house,/a small piece of land, and marry a woman" (36). His mistake, however, is that he actually is repeating his parents' pattern of running away from a difficult home situation, and the result is equally unsettling: "Each city was filled/with children/like the child I had once been" (36). This encounter with his own past image sends him back to his origins where he discovers an identity even more basic than family ties: he is the "grit and sediment . . . mineral de Nuevo Mexico" (39), and specifically of the rural Manzano Mountain area. From this self-knowledge he draws strength and direction. Utilizing his mestizo heritage—"Apache words" plus "Spanish names of things"—he will work a plan that sounds simple.

I am ready to work
all I ask is that I don't starve,
that I don't fail at being a good man,
that things go good for me,
that I meet a woman who will love me deeply,
that I meet strong spiritual brothers and sisters,
and that I have healthy children. (39)

This commitment to region and basic values culminates in the rewards of revelation in the form of a vision of belonging, significantly stated in terms of New Mexican imagery: mountains, rocks, arrowheads, piñon nuts, pine cones, a red sun, and the brightly illuminated ruins of the Quaraí mission. Against this typical landscape, the poet projects archetypal images of a traditional mestizo family heritage:

I thought I saw the dark skinned ghost
of my grandfather, on his horse, with sombrero
waving to me from QUARAI,
and the gray haired ghost of my grandmother,
carding sheep fur
beneath the green teepee of a pine tree,
by the arroyo. (40)

Hispano male and Indian female set in a traditional ranching scene seen against the backdrop of the mission in the midst of nature; this is Baca's most nostalgic and idealistic moment.

The first half of the book culminates in an affirmation of success. Martín finds a mate, buys land, remodels a house, and has a child. Within this model of the nuclear family, the last poem ends on an apparently positive note.

I went inside
took Pablito from Gabriela
to let her sleep and rest,
then circled my arm around your body Pablo,
as we slept in the bed next to mama,
I promised you and all living things,
I would never abandon you. (49)

Martín declares a new life diametrically opposed to his experience of having been abandoned, left to live without home or parents.

In that context of fulfillment, the second half is remarkable. It opens with the burning of the house and with it, ten years worth of poems. Martín will eventually build another house on the same spot, thus transcending this set-back, but the ending, quite expected and anticlimatic, is less significant than the transformation Martín undergoes in the process.

The poems now become echoes of Chicano literature through the New Mexican motifs seen above. First, we have the threat of disappearance in the house burning, given particular significance of personal death of a sort by the loss of the poems. The wife then extends the circle of destruction to the family by stating, "'Oh, Martín, it's all gone'" (54). Then Martín goes into a form of exile, a stranger in a middle-class neighborhood, appropriately called the Heights to contrast with the South Valley where he lived before. The simbolic division of society into upper and lower, alienated and those still in touch with real life, is clichéd, but it is also Baca's entré into Chicano literature's superficial code. In this situation of impending loss of meaning, Martín begins recuperating the images of his source of orientation in the world. From his exile he recalls the barrio in which he has lived for an unspecified number of years—the ten years of writing is one hint, while later he mentions another son, now old enough to play on his own—and where he had become one of the people.

The poems enumerate characters, environments, and events, filling in that gap of years, bridging it as well as the new distance of exile. These memories are simultaneously an enumeration of New Mexican characters and motifs. Characters include outsider figures—drunks, lowriders, gang members, the barrio fool—the *curandera*, the witch, the elders, the veteran, and two figures evoked through allusion: Doña Sebastíana, death in the form of a woman, and the *santero* statue carver. The dominant motif is the closeness to the natural order in which trees are personified. Yet there is also a Chicano updating here noticeable in the inclusion of lowriders and gang members among the outsiders. In a distancing move, reminiscent of Montoya's breaking off of his nostalic memory with a *Chale* from the contemporary barrio idiom, Baca turns back to his own romantic image of the grandfather and rejects it in the form of a scene from a Western movie. Apparently he recognizes that his nostalgic ideals are no longer fit for the present. "My heart is an old post/dreams I tied to it years ago/yank against/to get free" (62). Martín turns off the television and immediately a contemporary form of the image appears to replace the old one: "A chavalo riding his bicycle/at dawn down Barcelona road,/clenching roses in his teeth,/in the handle-bar basket/are apples he took from random trees on the road." Note that the boy is a picaresque character involved in petty theft, but with a flare for the beauty of nature, a worthy successor of Romero's Celso, but urbanized.

It is this urbanizing up-dating Baca undertakes in the poems that follow, beginning with a parody of Montoya's famous elegy to a dead pachuco, "El Louie." (Bruce-Novoa, 14–25). The elegy to Eddie allows Baca to evoke common Chicano motifs of police oppression, gang graffiti as alternative to illiteracy, barrio slang, and the bitter cry of "stop it," all of which culminates in a typical plea for a place in the communal memory. "Your voiced whispered/in the dust and weeds,/a terrible silence/not to forget your death" (66). Martín's renewed pilgrimage takes him not back to the family past, a question he resolved in the first section of the book, but into the community. Perhaps more significantly, it takes him, for the first time, into an open intertextual dialogue with the specific code of contemporary Chicano literature. The second poem shifts focus, but continues this endeavor by first repeating the cycles-of-history motif, and then using another stock Chicano strategy: overlaying pre-Columbian figures onto contemporary barrio people, ending in an evocation of Alurista through citation when he calls a

Chicano "a distant relative/of Aztec warriors" (68). His wind-through-the-barrio poem also reminds one of Alurista. His bad-dude-turned-political-activist rings with an echo of Ricardo Sánchez, while another set of verses contain so many key references to Gary Soto that it is difficult not to read them as a tribute (86). The specifics of the intertextualities, however interesting, are less important than the general effect of weaving this poetry into the fabric of established Chicano literature that readers knowledgeable in that canon will recognize or at least sense.

Within this context Martín builds his new house, which we cannot avoid reading as a more authentic expression of his soul and art than the first. It is through this last image that we must reread the first section's culminating images to understand the meaning of the book. Martín portrays the new house as his child, and inversely, he is born from it. The symbol is of a self-generating circular flow of energy. Compared to the image of shared childbirth in section one, Baca here offers a disturbingly self-centered and even egotistical birthing, to say nothing of it being strictly male. When we recall that Pablo's birth, at which Martín was present as an assistant, was called a "Fertility dance of women" (48), we can read the building of the house as the fertility dance of men. What is disturbing, although typical of the poetry we have been studying, is that when Baca describes the ultimate act of creating origins—as opposed to tracing biological roots—women are conspicuously absent. If we extend the circle of that act, we find Martín in the company of men, who, in turn, are characterized as social loners and outsiders united in their willingness to help Martín. They are, in fact, representatives of the community that Martín had been recalling during his exile in the Heights, as if once beckoned from silence, the barrio community reciprocates by coming to Martín's rescue. At no point after the fire, however, does the wife or the first son reappear. Martín ventured into this new life alone and remains essentially solitary at the end, even among his peers.

Perhaps history is a cycle of repetitions in which fathers seal their son's fate. While Martín seems quite different from his self-destructive, alcoholic father, in the end he also has abandoned his family, prefering to live among men in a loose community of mavricks. His first son has been erased from his father's contexts, and another, Antonio, is recalled to allow Martín to fix him into a repetition of the motif of the macho horse rider escaping into the distance. Gone is the tight heterosexual intimacy of the closing of the first section. Gabriela, named repeatedly in the verses where she appears to love and reproduce for Martín, becomes the nameless "wife" in section two. The idyllic passion of first love has faded, replaced by the comradery of the all-male work crew. This should not be seen as progress, however, because Baca has Martín define his state before meeting Gabriela as "drifting" (42) and then has him return to it after the burning of the house and the last appearance of his wife. Her role, that of companion and collaborator in the project of home creation, is assumed by men friends. It is as though Martín, or Baca, has replanted a parody of the prison experience in the middle of his self-created utopia, an all-male bastion, but free of society's dictates. Perhaps we are to interpret this to mean that marriage and family are too restrictive. Tied as they are to the image of the first house, we could see them as a forced fitting of Martín's will to live outside the norms into an old mold. Despite the remolding, the shell still imposed conformity, as wife, marriage, and child apparently did also. He breaks with them to free himself from preestablished norms of living, just as he throws away the building plans and improvises the new house with the help of his friends. At the end we are expected to read this as an improvement: "create a better world, a better me, / out of love. I became a child of the house, / and it showed me/the freedom of a new beginning" (100).

The pattern is so traditional as to be archetypal: after the initial euphoria of love, come children, and the lover becomes just mother and wife. Nothing new here, just an old story in populist macho rhetoric. Even Baca's affirmation of freedom from social norms in the self-creating act among buddies is actually another, more insidious norm, that of the macho loner fleeing into his own world. In the end, Baca has replaced the grandfather's horse with Martín's lowrider, the mountain background with the vaulted livingroom, the great expanse of nature with his backyard: a Chicano version of the sublimated American Dream. Updated of course, because, although relegated to a static position, the grandmother was at least remembered.

In the end, Baca's poetry, while seeming to merge with the concerns of the groups discussed above, remains essentially self-centered, personal in an egotistical way. The community, women included, is there for his gratification, as almost everything else in the poetry we have reviewed here. The poetry is personal in that he focuses clearly on his intimate self, caring truly for almost no one else.

Cordelia Candelaria

Candelaria's title, *Ojo de la cueva* (literally *The Cave's Eye,* but in Spanish "eye" has a secoundary meaning of a spring, thus explaining the translation on the cover, "Cave Springs"), offers a microcosm of its contents, process, and main theme. Beginning with the latter, Candelaria searches for profound, hidden essences in the everyday reality, openings in the surface that can serve as epiphanies, and thus intensify experience intellectually, physically, and even spiritually. An eye that simultaneously looks out and opens inwards, that implies both light and darkness, and whose discovery quenches the body's thirst, while its existence traditionally centers space as a land marker from which orientation lines are drawn. This abstract axis mundi explanation assumes further reality when we learn that the title is also the name of Candelaria's home town, thus naming her own life center. As will be discussed below, the poems proceed like intense observations of the environment that seek to provoke an opening beyond the surface and a flow of revelation. Hence, they contain moments that are molded into potential reflections of the title metaphor. And in the last analysis, the book functions as search, discovery, exploration, and return from an Ojo de la cueva experience.

One cannot avoid the sexual symbolism of Candelaria's title, especially with the vaginal flower/cave cover illustration reminiscent of the super-realistic flowers of Georgia O'keeffe, another artist who focused intensely on the surface of reality around her, magnifying the commonplace into revelations of strange power and presence—and who made New Mexico both her home and subject matter. Even with this aside, there is a refreshing intimacy in the poetry itself, in which the female sex, in the various denotations and connotations of the word, is a center of focus. It is always from the author's *I*—a vaginal eye—that the world is viewed, and she continually reminds us that her I/eye is a She, giving the book its feminist quality, although only once shifting into strident aggressivity. Yet, sexual difference is explored, and in the context of the male dominated New Mexican poetry scene, with its encoded chauvinism, this difference is all the more evident. While the men offer male dominated communities and activities, Candelaria offers a female centering process and image.

The book begins slowly, as though searching for a catalyst, or an opening through which to enter into essential concerns. Life may consist of senseless existing on a surface of apparently insignificant events that prevent the fullness of being from revealing itself by stringing out time into a mere waiting for what may never appear until death puts an end to opportunity. This view is alluded to the first poem, "In Line"

I thought this lifetime
i could write a poem.
To my surprise
while at the check-out counter
clerk went seeking change
and i just wait. (9)

The triviality of the situation reinforces the effect: life can be lost in waiting for others to respond to what we have given. Once in this position, waiting seems the only alternative to losing a rightful return on our investment. But there is much more here. First, the mere act of creating a poem out of this trivial situation fulfills the expectations of the initial verses, while also turning passive waiting into a transcendent activity. The author wrests control over her life away from a distant other. Also, poetry's power is displayed in the molding of a common situation into a metaphor, in this case of the profound question of how one lives in the face of death, the ultimate check-out. The remedy lies in not allowing the other to control action and in finding a way to render time meaningful.

The poem is also subtly feminist. By alluding to a store, Candelaria raises the stereotypical image of the woman's duties. In this context, the woman fulfills her part in a transaction and then finds herself waiting for a response. The other, however, has left, presumably with her money, leaving her stranded, delayed, and dependent. The image of giving and receiving nothing in return, and yet continuing to wait for an absent other to respond in kind is another stereotype of the woman's life situation, unfortunately too often a reality. The challenge, then, is to transcend this impass, and the poetry does exactly that.

There is a Proustian sense to this view of life as a waiting on the surface for break in the routine, where something in the present opens us to a flood of memories—the philosopher Bergson stated it in terms of chronological Time being is interrupted by Duration, epiphanies into another sense of time as fullness and simultaneity. Candelaria even calls the poem "Crated" a "Proustian memory du temps perdu" (13). Significantly she applies the process here to a Chicano Movement motif, a farm labor demonstration, which then opens back in time to family picnics in the countryside. Like a Proustian epiphany, time closes back to the harsh present, with the nostalgic past disappearing under a suburban housing development. The juxtaposition of the labor-class movement and middle-class suburban consumerism, with a familial memory in between, creates a tension of contrasts that force us to consider how those two superficially opposed images have roots in the same family gathering and the desire to enjoy a better life in contact with nature. A similar process is found in "Graffiti Semiotics," although in place of time, the surface is language itself, and the setting man-made and intellectual. On a library wall, a woman encounters two words of graffiti—*Pussy* and *Cock*—producing a stark representation of desire, sex, separation, and even violation of the everyday surface of the environment, which in turn provokes an epiphany of comprehension: "The origin of signs" (10). Each of the first ten poems function in a similar manner, as if the author is testing different spots—motifs—in the surface of her world, searching for one that might prove more profound and lasting.

That opening appears in "You," a poem of sexual intimacy that treats the theme of duration, an appropriate synecdoche for the philosophical problem of Duration Candelaria has presented.

You lasted between my legs beyond the night.
Today your weight and movement yet strain
The muscles of each inner thigh, still press
Against my private nerves. But this soreness
Only hints at the tantilizing secrets
Playing out their quiet thrill inside,
Warming to an urgent pleasant ache
Where last I warmed you. And these secrets
Only echo something else within me still—
The substance—or matter—or realness
Of your caring every minute of one night.
Like love it lingers to compel a smile
Now and then and will long outlive the pain. (19)

The body retains sensations and the memory of a prolongued sexual encounter, an entire night of male ardor and firmness, perhaps, but she also states it as a "caring every minute." This could be the female version of a sexual fantasy. Yet it too disappears below the surface. The difference is that the surface is now her body, and she can delve into it for epiphanies, as she will do in the love poems that follow.

The love idyl, however, is as short lived as the reality of male ardor, and soon the poems shift to efforts to recapture the now lost initial feeling of joy. In a wonderfully female image for frustrated fulfillment, Candelaria describes the less than intense relationship of the established couple as "Bundles of bundles we stumble, looped tight/Like i u d coils spun ready to spring/We rummage inside ourselves" (23). Locked within the confines of what should be an intimate space, they waste themselves in useless activity, going nowhere and producing nothing. The passion phase of the persona's search for intense experience culminates in "Homely Burden," a poem about frustrated desire that Candelaria leaves ambiguous enough to allow readings on multiple levels, including the artistic and the sexual.

Longing is an agony of homely burden
the heart's dishwashing, private
unworthy of any show
not to be shared or
lingered over
or retold as truer fact
in fussy phrases from a poet's store.
Plain gut-longing
(from innermost rib and tenderest lining
of an urgent cavity)

defies conceit.
That raw pleasure of discomfort
presses muscle and mind toward center
tightly
steady
no abstractions
just press in
private and sure.

This agony of the ordinary
began with sculptor's struggle with his welder
(brilliant sun-tipped torch that once
killed even vision with its sparkler glow
or metal—they say it blinds you if you watch)
when mainline broke
torch shrunk to apology
adverted eyes
dull longing. (26)

The lover phase is replaced by the filial, with the son as the mother's central love object. However, as can be expected, the son eventually leaves home and the mother must face his absence. In Proustian fashion, the motif of absence introduces yet another male departure from the persona's life: a brother's death, which occupies the thematic center of four poems. The menace of death spreads into other forms of threats—nuclear war and crime—which in turn play themselves out in a poem of playful irony in which official efforts to protect society are misdirected into arresting, not criminals nor war mongers, but a mother of three for the possession of marijuana.

Seen as a unit, the poems have followed the movement of search, discovery, entrance, exploration of the depth of a revelation—that of the love with and for men. This, however, cannot sustain itself, and again in Proustian fashion, joy turns its other face of frustration, alienation, abandonment, motifs that finally focus sharply into their essence of death. Then the voyage starts to surface through more social expression of menace and destruction until returning once again to the trivial absurdity of societal relationships.

At this point in the book, with thirty-four of the fifty-four poems behind us, the center has been passed—somewhere in the transition from filial love to sybling death—both in terms of space and the intensity of the search. From here on the poetry plays itself out on that surface of delayed waiting for response from others who never prove capable of appropriate reciprocity. The best moments are when female images of self-appreciation or rebellion surface—and I do not use the term gratuitously, because unlike the delving below the surface to deep epiphanies, as in earlier sections, here the feeling is of emotion or rage bursting up through the repression of ordinary existence. It is as though the central metaphor has swung from the eye to the spring, from the exploring to the flowing function. And the inner stream, when restrained too long, explodes—yet a different form of epiphany.

Within this situation of waiting and accepting, death, as could be expected, hints at its impending arrival. Left to her own defense, the woman finds intimacy in nature—"Herself Portrait"—in a traditional formula for comprehending the death menace—two Llorona poems—or in outlets for frustration—smashing a cup—and produces at least one fiercely feminist attack on dominating males—"The Falcon Wife," the second to last poem in the book. It calls for violent revolt against male exploiters and culminates in an images of liberation.

> *Swooping falcon, disobey*
> *Dip down, tear his balls*
> *Deliver them*
> *b l e e e d i n g*
> *Into his ready grave.*
> *Wing toward open sky*
> *In the ether of your dreams.* (61)

No more waiting and serving, but revenge and free flight.

The last poem, "Faith," advises not to lose life in thought and seeking more than what it can offer, but to live it as it is and retain the best moment, which she chooses to specify as a baby's innocent, yet significant, reaching "for dusty flecks of air" (62). The image is yet another metaphor for desire and the attempt to grasp ephemeral illusions of beauty. Also, by centering this image, a coded reference to a nurturing poem "You Looked Up" (29), Candelaria shifts the center of the reading experience from abandonment and death to the intense love experience of a mother feeding her child, which in turn produces a centering epiphany superior to the pantheistic transcendence of nature. Once again, the poet takes control of her environment and molds it to her message.

Like the male poets, Candelaria has also gone on a search for origins and fulfillment. However, she finds it's not in the community, nor in political struggle, and certainly not in the traditional folk motifs nor in the new popular culture, urban ones. Her code seems at once more profound and more personal. She seeks fulfillment in terms of intensity—existentialistic terms we could say. Love is the key, but not the answer, because it fades like a man's ardor. There is a deep felt absence of duration in love and togetherness. In the end this absence becomes the essence of the life cycle itself, producing the situation of constant waiting. Candelaria's counterproposal to giving up and tolerating the lack of feeling and intensity is to turn the experience into poetry. It, like flecks of air, may be illusions, but they provoke movement, even desire, which in turn is expressed through an effort to touch and hold, metaphors for generative love.

Demetria Martínez

Turning, the manuscript of the first book by Martínez, the last and youngest of the poets studied here, contains a mixture of socially committed and personal poems. And in spite of the author's penchant for Manichean oppositions, the two main themes often interweave dialogically. A subtext of personal development, similar to what we found in Baca and Candelaria, binds them. Martínez presents aspects of her interests, focusing strongly on the Sanctuary Movement to aid Salvadoran refugees and on the interpersonal relationship of loving couples. The two themes link in poems about a love affair between a U.S. woman and a Salvadoran man. The themes also share a sense of fear and violence encountered in both realms of human interchange. Minor themes in the poems—such as family, U.S. society, problems of labor exploitation, abortion—also reflect the same concerns. Martínez is obsessed with the opposition of contradictory and conflicting forces, and within this world vision she delights in assuming the role of rebel. She sees life as a struggle between clearly drawn camps: those who set the lines of restriction and enforce the rules, and those who must cross those lines out of need. In the final analysis, however, without discounting the currently popular topic of Central America, the concern for women's right to personal freedom dominates the text, and in truth it is another case of crossing the restricting lines of definition in search of freedom.

From the start, the two main topics vie for preeminence. The author places on the dedication page an untitled poem not listed in the table of contents. It exists clandestinely, having slipped across the lines defining the sections of the book, invading a space traditionally reserved for communicating messages, not images, and even for requesting permission to speak from those who hold power. Appropriately, it is about refugees crossing the border undocumented.

Refugees at the border
of a century.
The Rio Grande, neck-high tonight.
Men, guns. Thunder.

The dangers are new but fear, familiar.
The old ones told us:
To find the eye of the storm
we must walk where lightning falls.

"Indocumentados."
Hunger, our one proof of origin.

Although we cry out,
we are not dying.

Too dark to see now.
Follow my voice.
(no pagination)

The "turn of the century" reference can project backward or forward, thus fusing the author's ancestors to the Salvadoran refugees today. The poem also introduces the motif of hunger as a mark of kinship, setting up the division of society into the haves and have-nots to appear in later poems. Violence is introduced as well, linking it to the attempt to guard borders. Taken together, violence characterizes efforts to maintain a social order of repressive divisions aimed at protecting the rich. By placing this poem under the enumeration of grandparents, it assumes the quality of origin piece, generating topics and a point of view—that of walking to the heart of a storm—with which the persona will identify.

However, the first poem listed in the table of contents, "Elena at Five Years," will strike the reader as radically different.

Elena warms a brown egg
Between her palms, close to her lips
Cold from a carton, Chosen from the dozen.

It is the center now of a sphere
Of kitchen towels in a drawer
Next to an amish cookbook,
Next to the oven's white side.

For three weeks at 3:15
Elena will breathe on that egg
Held between her lifelines
Against her grape-stained lips,
She anticipates the birth
Although brown eggs, her mother says,
Can't hatch.

But at 5, Elena
Has a good ear for heartbreaks.
Sidewalk cracks cry
When her tennis shoes touches them,
The lava chips that embroider

The yard have names,
And a brown egg is throbbing
In a the cup of her hand. (1)

The symbol of nurturing mixes with the old cliché of doing something with your own hands. Moreover, the child persists in spite of her mother's reasoned warning. The author sides with the child, closing the poem with a series of positive images. The result is a lighthearted poem of childlike naiveté, youthful determination, and sweet innocence, a world away from the dark images of the first poem. While the refugee poem is set outside, literally in the midst of opposing nations and questions of international law, the second is held within a kitchen, where mother and daughter converse intimately. Whereas one poem attributes origins to the family, the other places it in the girl herself and by herself.

The juxtaposition of differing types of poems reflects Martínez's already mentioned penchant for harsh oppositions. Yet, they form a dialogue in the space created by placing them together, as individual poems will force themes and images to interface. What they have in common is, first, the theme of origins. Both poems are about expecting a new beginning from a determined action carried out against great odds. In both, the protagonists move ahead in spite of restrictions. In both, a number of individuals will be delivered from darkness by a breaking out of repressing space; they will pass into life. As they end, both poems place the power of deliverance in the poet's traditional tools: voice and hands. Movement from one poem to the other also prefigures that of the text in which we are led through a series of socially oriented poems, to a focus on Salvador and refugees, then to the topic of love and nurturing, and eventually to the female persona's break from male dominance, ending with a joyful celebration of the young woman's rebellious freedom and creative potential. Along the way, the themes will be played out in specific settings and images, but the underlying emphasis is given to that of the creative and self-creative female, refusing to accept limitations and predefinitions. The brown eggs in Elena's hand will transmute into embryos in the persona's womb; the discouraging mother, into pressure to abort—"Brown eggs . . . can't hatch." And like Elena, the persona has faith in her ability to produce beautiful life from within herself through the power of her lone nurturing act.

While Martínez's work mixes the personal and the political, it does not contain any of the typical Chicano Movement retoric. Nor does it care to refute it. Candelaria at least briefly mentioned the farm workers' movement, if only to utilize it as a springboard into a family memory. Martínez, however, represents a new generation that demonstrates little attachment to the old code of Chicano literary expression. Certainly she is committed to political struggle, but not in the same terms. Absent as well is a sense of New Mexican imagery as encoded by the male poets. Like Candelaria, she ignores the folk motifs, but neither does she use Chicano motifs. This is not a criticism, simply an observation. In fact, the lack of those clichéd motifs is refreshing, contributing much to the sense of newness in both Martínez's and Candelaria's work. The latter, however, displays a stronger sense of regional identification. Martínez, of course, is still learning her craft—clearly apparent in the repeated use of simplistic rhymes, especially to close poems—so perhaps like Baca she will venture back into the specifics of her regional origins. Then again, she may not, signaling a new direction for New Mexican Chicano poetry.

From this survey of New Mexican Chicano poetry, it is clear that at least among the men there exist common goals and a common code of expression. That the women differ is a fact deserving of lengthy study to draw its profound implications, both for literature and the culture. We can say that if poetry needs new forms and language to progress, that catalyst is coming presently from the female poets, not all of whom have yet published books. Even Baca's breakthrough with a major mainstream house, must be balanced against the content, which, as shown above, reworks many well defined Chicano topics. Both his and Romero's works are skillful refinements of established forms and themes, the most recent high points in a familiar code of expression. The women seem fresher, more innovative in their thought, more stimulating and provocative in their imagery and concepts, exactly because they do not repeat the topics of that established expression. And since Chicanas have participated little in the published literature of the region, their books infuse different perspective and codes of expression into the context of their male comrades. I do not intend to pit men against women, but to note a difference and its effect on this reader. In the final analysis all these poets participate in the same project, that of creating and expanding New Mexican Chicano poetry. It is to their credit that, unlike the early Movement days, it is now impossible to speak of Chicano poetry without thinking of New Mexico.

WORKS CITED

Alurista. *Floricanto en Aztlán*. Los Angeles: Chicano Cultural Center, University of California, 1971.

Anaya, Rudolfo A. *Adventures of Juan Chicaspatas*. Houston: Arte Público Press, 1984.

Arrellano, Juan Estevan. *Palabras de la vista/retratos de la pluma (memorias)*. Albuquerque: Instituto del Río Grande, 1984.

Baca, Jimmy Santiago. *Immigrants in Our Own Land*. Baton Rouge: Louisiana State University Press, 1979.

———. *Martín & Meditations on the South Valley*. New York: New Directions, 1987.
———. *Swords of Darkness*. San José: Mango Publications, 1981.
Bruce-Novoa. *Chicano Poetry: A Response to Chaos*. Austin: University of Texas Press, 1982.
Candelaria, Cordelia. *Ojo de la cueva*. Colorado Springs: Maize Press, 1984.
Gallegos, Robert. *Ambrosia Lake*. Gallup: Southwestern Alternatives, 1982.
———. *Carnero*. Thoreau, N.M.: Carol Sayre Gallery, 1985.
Mares, E.A. *The Unicorn Poem*. Los Cerrillos: San Marcos Press, 1980.
Martínez, Demetria. *Turning*. Unpublished manuscript.
Méndez, Miguel. *Los criaderos humanos (épica de los desamparados) y Sahuaros*. Tucson: Editorial Peregrinos, 1975.
Montoya, José. *El Sol y Los de Abajo and Other* R.C.A.F. *Poems*. San Francisco: Ediciones Pocho-Che, 1972.
Paredes, Américo. *With a Pistol in His Hand: A Border Ballad and Its Hero*. Austin: University of Texas Press, 1958.
Quintana, Leroy. *Hijo Del Pueblo, New Mexico Poems*. Las Cruces: Puerto del Sol, 1976.
Romero, Leo. *Agua negra*. Boise: Boise State University, 1981.
———. *Celso*. Houston: Arte Público Press, 1985.
———. *During the Crowing Season*. Tucson: The Maguey Press, 1978.

A Selected Bibliography of New Mexican Hispanic Literature

MARÍA TERESA MÁRQUEZ

PRIMARY SOURCES: LITERATURE AND FOLKLORE

Ackerman, Marian Baca. "Vecino Vicente." *Las Mujeres Hablan: An Anthology of Nuevo Mexicana Writers*. Edited by Tey Diana Rebolledo, Erlinda Gonzales-Berry and Teresa Márquez. Albuquerque, N.M.: El Norte Publications, 1988. (Short story).

Aguilar-Henson, Marcela. *Figura Cristalina*. San Antonio, TX.: M & A Editions, 1983. (Poetry).

Alurista. "Myth, Identity and Struggle in Three Chicano Novels: Aztlán . . . Anaya, Méndez and Acosta." *European Perspectives on Hispanic Literature of the United States*. Edited by Genviève Fabre. Houston: Arte Publico Press, 1987.

Amador, Adela. "Tres cuentos de Placitas." *Cuentos Chicanos*. Edited by Rudolfo Anaya and Antonio Márquez. Albuquerque, N.M.: *New America*, American Studies Department, University of New Mexico, 1980. (Short story).

Anaya, Rudolfo A. "An American Chicano in King Arthur's Court." *Old Southwest, New Southwest: Essays on a Region and its Literature*. Edited by Judy Nolte Lensink. Tucson: The Tucson Public Library, 1987. (Essay).

Anaya, Rudolfo A. *Bless Me, Ultima*. Berkeley, CA.: Quinto Sol Publications, 1972. (Novel).

Anaya, Rudolfo A. *A Chicano in China*. Albuquerque, N.M.: University of New Mexico Press, 1986. (Travel Journal).

Anaya, Rudolfo A. "El paisaje de mi imaginación." *Dal Mito Al Mito: La Cultura di Espressione Chicana: Dal Mito Originario al Mito Rigeneratore*. Edited by Lia Tessarolo Bondalfi. Milano: Jaca Book, 1987. (Essay).

Anaya, Rudolfo A. *Heart of Aztlan*. Berkeley, CA.: Editorial Justa Publications, 1976. Reprint. University of New Mexico Press, 1988. (Novel).

Anaya, Rudolfo A. "Iliana of the Pleasure Dreams." *ZYZZYVA* I, no. 4 (Winter 1985):50–61. (Short story).

Anaya, Rudolfo A. "In Search of Epifaño." *Voces/Voices*. Edited by Rudolfo Anaya. Albuquerque: El Norte Publications, 1987. Reprint. University of New Mexico Press, 1988. (Short story).

Anaya, Rudolfo A. *Lord of the Dawn, the Legend of Quetzalcoatl*. Albuquerque, N.M.: University of New Mexico Press, 1987. (Novel).

Anaya, Rudolfo A. *Silence of the Llano, Short Stories*. Berkeley, CA.: Tonatiuh-Quinto Sol International Publishers, 1982.

Anaya, Rudolfo A. *The Adventures of Juan Chicaspatas*. Houston, TX.: Arte Público Press, 1984. (Narrative Poem).

Anaya, Rudolfo A. *The Legend of La Llorona: A Short Novel*. Berkeley, CA.: Tonatiuh-Quinto Sol International Publishers, 1984.

Anaya, Rudolfo A. *Tortuga*. Berkeley, CA.: Editorial Justa Publications, 1979. Reprint. University of New Mexico Press, 1988. (Novel).

Anaya, Rudolfo A., editor. *Voces/Voices: An Anthology of Nuevo Mexicano Writers*. Albuquerque, N.M.: El Norte Publications, 1987. Reprint. University of New Mexico Press, 1988. (Short stories and poetry).

Anaya, Rudolfo and Antonio Márquez, editors. *Cuentos Chicanos*. Albuquerque, N.M.: *New America*, Department of American Studies, University of New Mexico, 1980. Revised edition. University of New Mexico Press, 1984. (Short stories).

Anaya, Rudolfo and Simon Ortiz, editors. *Ceremony of Brotherhood, 1680–1980*. Albuquerque, N.M.: Academia Publications, 1981. (Poetry, fiction and artwork by Chicanos and Native Americans).

Apodaca, Rudy. *The Waxen Image*. Mesilla, N.M.: Titan Publishing, 1977. (Novel).

Aragon, Ray John De. *The Legend of La Llorona*. Las Vegas, N.M.: Pan American Publishing Company, 1980.

Aranda, Charles. *Dichos Nuevos/Collected From the Spanish*. Albuquerque, N.M.: Carlo Press Southwest, 1980. (Proverbs).

Aranda, Charles. *Dichos: Proverbs and Sayings from the Spanish*. Santa Fe, N.M.: Sunstone Press, 1977.

Aranda, Charles, *Dudes on Duds*. Albuquerque, N.M.: Carlo Press, 1984. (Novel).

Aranda, Charles. *New Mexico Folklore From the Spanish: Collected and Translated by Charles Aranda*. Albuquerque, N.M. n.p., 1977.

Aranda, Charles. *Special Collection of Dichos*. Albuquerque: Carlo Press, 1985. (Proverbs).

Arellano, Estevan. "Después de perdido volver a perder." *Flor y Canto II: An Anthology of Chicano Literature*. Edited by Arnold C. Vento, Alurista and Jose Flores Peregrino. Albuquerque, N.M.: Pajarito Publications, 1975. (Short story).

Arellano, Juan Estevan. *Entre Verde y Seco*. Dixon, N.M.: La Academia de la Nueva Raza, 1972. (Prose and poetry).

Arellano, Juan Estevan. *Inocencio . . .* , 1975. (Unpublished Novel).

Arellano, Estevan. "No es hablar de su vida, sino su muerte." *Voces/Voices*. Edited by Rudolfo Anaya. Albuquerque: El Norte Publications, 1987. Reprint. University of New Mexico Press, 1988. (Short story).

Arellano, Juan Estevan. *Palabras de la vista/Retratos de la pluma (Memorias)*. Albuquerque, N.M.: Academia Publications in cooperation with the Rio Grande Institute, 1984. (Poetry and photography).

Arellano, Manuel. "Poesía y baladas de Don Manuel Arellano (1861–1944)" *De Colores* 1, no. 3 (Summer, 1974):20–27. (Poetry).

Arellano, Romolo. "Las varas de San José." *Voces/Voices*. Edited by Rudolfo Anaya. Albuquerque, N.M.: El Norte Publications, 1987. Reprint. University of New Mexico Press, 1988. (Short story).

Armas, José. "El tonto del barrio." *Cuentos Chicanos*. Edited by Rudolfo Anaya and Antonio Márquez. Revised edition. Albuquerque, N.M.: University of New Mexico Press, 1984 (Short story).

Armas, José. "On the Day I Was Born." *De Colores* 2, no. 1 (1975):48–50. (Short story).

Armas, José. "The Woman on the Road (Folkstory)." *De Colores* 4, nos. 1–2 (1978):131–133.

Army, Mary Montaño. "The Chaos Chronicles (Excerpts)." *Las Mujeres Hablan*. Edited by Tey Diana Rebolledo, Erlinda Gonzales-Berry, and Teresa Márquez. Albuquerque, N.M.: El Norte Publications, 1988. (Sketch of the author's father).

Baca, Carlos C. de. *Vicente Silva: New Mexico's Vice King of the Nineties*. s.l., s.n., 1938. (Narrative).

Baca, Carlos C. de. *Vicente Silva, the Terror of the Las Vegas*. Truchas, N.M.: Tate Gallery, 1968. Reprint. Palmer Lake, CO.: Filter Press, 1978. (Narrative).

Baca, Elfego. *Here Comes Elfego; the Autobiography of Elfego Baca*. Albuquerque, N.M.: Vinegar Tom Press, 1970.

Baca, Fabiola Cabeza de. *We Fed Them Cactus*. Albuquerque, N.M.: University of New Mexico Press, 1954. Reprint. 1989. (Novel).

Baca, Fabiola Cabeza de. "The Women in New Mexico." *Chicano Voices*. Edited by Carlota Cardenas Dwyer. Boston: Houghton Mifflin Company, 1975. (Excerpt from *We Fed Them Cactus*).

Baca, Jimmy Santiago. *Immigrants in Our Own Land*. Baton Rouge, LA.: Louisiana State University Press, 1979. (Poetry).

Baca, Jimmy Santiago. *Jimmy Santiago Baca: Poems*. S.l., s.n. (Rockbook, no. 3, 1978).

Baca, Jimmy Santiago. *Martin & Meditations on the South Valley*. New York: New Directions, 1988. (Poetry).

Baca, Jimmy Santiago. *Poems Taken From My Yard*. Fulton, MO.: Timberline Press, 1986.

Baca, Jimmy Santiago. *Swords of Darkness*. San Jose, CA.: Mango Publications, 1981. (Poetry).

Baca, Jimmy Santiago. "The Escape." *The Americas Review* XIV, nos. 3–4 (Fall-Winter, 1986):30–47. (Short story).

Baca, Jimmy Santiago. *What's Happening?* Williamantic, CT.: Curbstone Press, 1982. (Poetry).

Baca, John E. *Sound Retreat for the Conquistadores*. New York: Carlton Press, 1974. (Novel).

Baca, Kathleen. "Sterile Relationship." *Cuentos Chicanos*. Edited by Rudolfo Anaya and Antonio Márquez. Revised edition. Albuquerque, N.M.: University of New Mexico Press, 1984. (Short story).

Baca, Manuel C. de. *Vicente Silva & His 40 Bandits*. Translated by Lane Kauffman. Washington, D.C.: Libros Escogidos, 1947.

Baca, Manuel C. de. *Historia de Vicente Silva, sus cuarenta bandidos, sus crimenes y retribuciones*. Las Vegas, N.M.: Imprenta La Voz del Pueblo, 1896. (Narrative).

Baca, Manuel C. de. *Historia de Vicente Silva: Sus cuarenta bandidos, sus crimenes y retribuciones; Corregida y aumentada por Francisco L. López*. Las Vegas, N.M., 1900. (Narrative).

Baca, Manuel C. de. *Vicente Silva y sus 40 bandidos*. ("A True Novel Written Over 100 Years Ago"). Translated by Charles Aranda. Albuquerque, N.M., n.d.

Baca, Nicolás. *Notebooks of Nicolás Baca: Poetry*. Encino, N.M., 1939. Spanish Text. Photocopy of holograph.

Baca, Prospero. *Coloquio de la pastorela*. Drama in verse. Introduction written by T. M. Pearce. Written in Bernalillo, New Mexico, 1935 (Microfilm of ms. (positive and negative) reel, 35 mm. Filmed with Los Pastores, 1926. Auto de los Reyes Magos, before 1912, Los Pastores, 1913, Pastoria, 19??, Coloquio del Nacimiento, Nacimiento de Niño Dios, 1902. University of New Mexico General Library).

Baca-Vaughn, Guadalupe. "The Souls in Purgatory," *Voces/Voices*. Edited by Rudolfo Anaya. Albuquerque: El Norte Publications, Inc., 1987. Reprint. University of New Mexico Press, 1988. (A short story).

Bernal, Vicente. *Las primicias*. Dubuque, IA: Dubuque Telegraph-Herald, 1916. (Poetry and prose).

Bilingual Review/Revista Bilingüe XII, nos. 1–2 (January-August, 1985):115–17. (Poetry by Jimmy Santiago Baca).

Brown, Lorin W., Charles L. Briggs and Marta Weigle. *Hispano Folklife of New Mexico: The Lorin W. Brown Federal Writers Project Manuscripts*. Albuquerque, N.M.: University of New Mexico Press, 1978.

Burbank, Jim and Sharon Neiderman, editors. *Tarasque I*. Albuquerque, N.M.: Tarasque, 1983. (Contains poetry by Leo Romero).

Campa, Arthur León. *Los Comanches: A New Mexican Folk Drama*. Albuquerque, N.M.: University of New Mexico (The University of New Mexico Bulletin, Language Series 7, no. 17, 1942).

Campa, Arthur León, "New Mexican Spanish Folktales." MA Thesis, University of New Mexico, 1930.

Campa, Arthur León. *Sayings and Riddles in New Mexico*. Albuquerque, N.M.: University of New Mexico (The University of New Mexico Bulletin, Language Series 6, no. 2, 1937).

Campa, Arthur León. *Spanish Folk Poetry in New Mexico*. Albuquerque, N.M.: University of New Mexico (The University of New Mexico Bulletin, Language Series 2, no. 3, 1930).

Campa, Arthur León. *Spanish Folk Poetry in New Mexico*. Albuquerque, N.M.:University of New Mexico Press, 1946.

Campa, Arthur León. *The Spanish Folksong in the Southwest*. Albuquerque, N.M.: University of New Mexico. (The University of New Mexico Bulletin, Modern Language Series 4, no. 1, 1933).

Campa, Arthur León. *Spanish Religious Folktheatre in the Spanish Southwest* (First cycle). Albuquerque, N.M.: University of New Mexico. (The University of New Mexico Bulletin, Language Series 5, no. 1, 1934).

Campa, Arthur León. *Spanish Religious Folktheatre in the Southwest*. (Second Cycle.) Albuquerque, N.M.: University of New Mexico (The University of New Mexico Bulletin, Language Series 5, no. 2, 1934).

Campa, Arthur León. *Treasure of the Sangre de Cristos: Tales and Traditions of the Spanish Southwest*. Norman, OK.: University of Oklahoma Press, 1963.

Candelaria, Nash. "Affirmative Action." *The Americas Review* XIV, nos. 3–4 (Fall-Winter, 1986):11–18. (Short story).

Candelaria, Nash. "Be-Bop Rock." *RiverSedge* (Chicano Collection) IV, no. 2 (1982):71–80. (Short story).

Candelaria, Nash. "Mano a mano." *Hispanics in the United States: An Anthology of Creative Literature*. II. Ypsilanti, MI.: Bilingual Press, 1982. (Short story).

Candelaria, Nash. *Inheritance of Strangers*. Binghamton, N.Y.: Bilingual Press/Editorial Bilingüe, 1985. (Novel).

Candelaria, Nash. *Memories of the Alhambra*. Palo Alto, CA.: Cibola Press, 1977 (Novel).

Candelaria, Nash. *Not by the Sword*. Ypsilanti, MI.: Bilingual Press, 1982. (Novel).

Candelaria, Nash. *The Day Cisco Kid Shot John Wayne*. Tempe, AZ.: Bilingual Press/Editorial Bilingüe, 1988. (Novel).

Cassidy, Elliot. *El hermitano* (Historical Drama). Santa Fe, N.M.: Federal Works Project, 1936.

Chacón, Eusebio. *El hijo de la tempestad. Tras la tormenta la calma*. Dos novelas originales escritas por Eusebio Chacón. Santa Fe, N.M.: Tipografía "El Boletin Popular," 1892. (Novellas).

Chacón, Felipe Maximiliano. *Obras de Felipe Maximiliano Chacón, "El cantor neomexicano:" Poesía y prosa*. Albuquerque, N.M.: Felipe M. Chacón, 1924. (Prose and Poetry).

Chacón, Felipe Maximiliano. *Short Stories*. Translated by Julian J. Vigil. Las Vegas, N.M.: Editorial Telaraña, 1980.

Chacón, Rafael. *Legacy of Honor: The Life of Rafael Chacón, a Nineteenth-Century New Mexican*. Edited by Jacqueline Dorgan Meketa. Albuquerque: University of New Mexico Press, 1986.

Chávez, Denise. "Baby Krishna's All Night Special." *Southwest: A Contemporary Anthology*. Edited by Geary Hobson. Albuquerque, N.M.: Red Earth Press, 1977. (Short story).

Chávez, Denise. *Hecho en México: A Bilingual Multimedia Performance Play*. Mounted November 28, 1982, Kimo Theater, Albuquerque, New Mexico. (Unpublished play).

Chávez, Denise. "The Closet." *The Americas Review* 14, no. 1 (Spring, 1986):7–18. (Short story).

Chávez, Denise. "The King and Queen of Comezón." *Las Mujeres Hablan*. Edited by Tey Diana Rebolledo, Erlinda Gonzales-Berry and Teresa Márquez. Albuquerque, N.M.: El Norte Publications, 1988. (Excerpt from a forthcoming novel, *Beatriz*).

Chávez, Denise. *The Last of the Menu Girls*. Houston, TX.: Arte Público Press, 1986. (Novel).

Chávez, Denise. "Novena narrativas y ofrendas nuevomexicanas." *Chicana Creativity and Criticism: Charting New Frontiers in American Literature.* Edited by María Hererra-Sobek and Helena María Viramontes. Houston: Arte Público Press, 1988. (Short play).

Chávez, Denise. "Willow Game." *Cuentos Chicanos.* Edited by Rudolfo Anaya and Antonio Márquez. Revised edition. Albuquerque, N.M.: University of New Mexico Press, 1984. (Short story).

Chávez, Ed. "Death March." *Voces/Voices.* Edited by Rudolfo A. Anaya. Albuquerque: El Norte Publications, Inc., 1987. Reprint. (Short story). University of New Mexico Press, 1988.

Chavez, Fray Angelico. *Clothed with the Sun.* Santa Fe, N.M.: Writers' Editions, 1939. (Poetry).

Chavez, Fray Angelico. *Eleven Lady-Lyrics and Other Poems.* Patterson, N.J.: St. Anthony Guild Press, 1945.

Chavez, Fray Angelico. *From an Altar Screen/El Retablo: Tales from New Mexico.* Illustrated by Peter Hurd. New York: Farrar, Straus and Cudahey, 1957. (Short stories).

Chavez, Fray Angelico. *The Lady from Toledo.* Fresno, CA.: Academy Guild Press, 1960. Reprint. *When The Santos Talked.* Santa Fe, N.M.: William Gannon, 1977. (Narrative).

Chavez, Fray Angelico. *New Mexico Triptych.* Santa Fe, N.M.: William Gannon Publisher, 1976. (Short stories).

Chavez, Fray Angelico. *Selected Poems With An Apologia.* Santa Fe, N.M.: Press of the Territorian, 1969.

Chavez, Fray Angelico. *The Single Rose: Poems of Divine Love.* Santa Fe, N.M.: Los Santos Bookshop, 1948.

Chavez, Fray Angelico. *The Virgin of Port Lligat.* Fresno, CA.: Academy Literary Guild, 1959. Originally published in *Spirit Magazine,* 1952. (Poetry).

Chavez, Fray Angelico. "A Romeo and Juliet Story." *Voces/Voices.* Edited by Rudolfo Anaya. Albuquerque: El Norte Publications, Inc., 1987. Reprint. University of New Mexico Press, 1988. (Short story).

Chávez, Margo. "Je Reviens." *Las Mujeres Hablan.* Edited by Tey Diana Rebolledo, Erlinda Gonzales-Berry and Teresa Márquez. Albuquerque, N.M.: El Norte Publications, 1988. (Short story).

Chávez, Margo. "Manina." *Las Mujeres Hablan.* Edited by Tey Diana Rebolledo, Erlinda Gonzales-Berry and Teresa Márquez. Albuquerque, N.M.: El Norte Publications, 1988. (Short story).

Chávez, Ronald P. "Man of Honor." *Voces/Voices.* Edited by Rudolfo Anaya. Albuquerque, N.M.: El Norte Publications, Inc., 1987. Reprint. University of New Mexico Press, 1988. (Short story).

Chávez, Tibo, Jr. *New Mexican Folklore of the Rio Abajo.* Portales, N.M.: Bishop Printing Company, 1972. (Includes prose and poetry by Sabine Ulibarrí, Leroy Quintana, Fray Angelico Chavez, and Fabiola Cabeza de Baca).

Chávez Lowe, Cosette. "A Lash for the Grace of God." *New Mexico Folklore Record* XI (1963–64):18–20. (Folk tale).

Cobos, Ruben. *Southwestern Spanish Proverbs/Refranes Espanoles del Suroeste.* Los Cerrillos, N.M.: San Marcos Press, 1973.

Comedy of Adam and Eve. Translated by Julián Josue Vigil. Las Vegas, N.M.: Editorial Telaraña, 1980. (Religious folkdrama).

Córdova, Gilberto Benito. *Abiquiu and Don Cacahuate, A Folk History of a New Mexican Village.* Los Cerrillos, N.M.: San Marcos Press, 1973. (Folklore).

Córdova, Josephine M. "Bruja Story." *Las Mujeres Hablan.* Edited by Tey Diana Rebolledo, Erlinda Gonzales-Berry and Teresa Márquez. Albuquerque, N.M.: El Norte Publications, 1988. (Personal recollections).

Córdova, Josephine M. "La bruja Alta Gracia." *Las Mujeres Hablan.* Edited by Tey Diana Rebolledo, Erlinda Gonzaless-Berry and Teresa Márquez. Albuquerque, N.M.: El Norte Publications, 1988 (Short story).

Córdova, Josephine M. *No lloro pero me acuerdo.* Dallas, TX.: Mockingbird Publishing Company, 1976. (Personal histories, prose and poetry).

Córdova, Josephone M. "The Heavy Cross." *Las Mujeres Hablan*. Edited by Tey Diana Rebolledo, Erlinda Gonzales-Berry and Teresa Márquez. Albuquerque, N.M.: El Norte Publications, 1988. (Family history).

Córdova, Kathryn M. "The Legacy of Rainbow." *Las Mujeres Hablan*. Edited by Tey Diana Rebolledo, Erlinda Gonzales-Berry, and Teresa Márquez. Albuquerque, N.M.: El Norte Publications, 1988. (Short story).

Córdova, Lorenzo de. *Echoes of the Flute*. Santa Fe, N.M.: Ancient City Press, 1972. (Narrative).

DeBaca, Elba C. "The Devil." *Las Mujeres Hablan*. Edited by Tey Diana Rebolledo, Erlinda Gonzales-Berry and Teresa Márquez. Albuquerque, N.M.: El Norte Publications, 1988. (Legend).

DeBaca, Elba C. "The Lady in Blue." *Las Mujeres Hablan*. Edited by Tey Diana Rebolledo, Erlinda Gonzales-Berry and Teresa Márquez. Albuquerque, N.M.: El Norte Publications, 1988. (Legend).

DeBaca, Elba C. "Witches." *Las Mujeres Hablan*. Edited by Tey Diana Rebolledo, Erlinda Gonzales-Berry and Teresa Márquez. Albuquerque, N.M.: El Norte Publications, 1988. (Legend).

De Baca, Elvera Adolfita. "Ben" *Las Mujeres Hablan*. Edited by Tey Diana Rebolledo, Erlinda Gonzales-Berry and Teresa Márquez. Albuquerque, N.M.: El Norte Publications, 1988. (Personal recollections).

De Dinkel, Reynalda Ortiz y Pino. "Peregrinación a la tierra del luminoso." *Las Mujeres Hablan*. Edited by Tey Diana Rebolledo, Erlinda Gonzales-Berry and Teresa Márquez. Albuquerque, N.M.: El Norte Publications, 1988. (Short story).

Delgado Espinosa, Frances. "Un chiste de un indio y su huerta." *New Mexico Folklore Record* 1 (1946–47):29. (Folk tale).

Espinosa, Aurelio Macedonio. *Los Comanches: A Spanish Heroic Play of the Year Seventeen Hundred and Eighty*. Albuquerque, N.M.: University of New Mexico. (The University of New Mexico Bulletin, Language Series 1, no. 1, 1907).

Espinosa, Carmen Gertrudis. *The Freeing of the Deer, and Other New Mexico Indian Myths/Se da libertad al venado y otras leyendas de los indios de Nuevo México*. Retold by Carmen Gertrudis Espinosa. Albuquerque, N.M.: University of New Mexico Press, 1985. (Stories in Spanish and English).

Espinosa, Gilberto. *Heroes, Hexes and Haunted Halls*. Albuquerque, N.M.: Calvin Horn Publishers, 1972. (Short stories).

Fernandez, David. "El hermano mayor." *Voces/Voices*. Edited by Rudolfo Anaya. Albuquerque, N.M.: El Norte Publications, 1987, Reprint. University of New Mexico Press, 1988. (Short story).

García, Arturo. *Schwammenauel Dam*. New York: Vantage Press, 1972. (Novel).

García, Marcella Lucinda. "Rosa Blanca, Rosa Negra, Rosa . . . Colorear. White Rose, Black Rose, Rose . . . Grow Red." *Las Mujeres Hablan*. Edited by Tey Diana Rebolledo, Erlinda Gonzales-Berry and Teresa Márquez. Albuquerque, N.M.: El Norte Publications, 1988. (Short story).

García, Nasario. *Recuerdos de los Vejietos/Tales of the Rio Puerco*. Albuquerque, N.M.: University of New Mexico Press, 1987.

García de Rivera, Clorinda. *Folklore Neomexicano*. Albuquerque, N.M.: Starline Press, 1982.

Gonzales, Gloria G. "The Woman Who Makes Belly Buttons." *Las Mujeres Hablan*. Edited by Tey Diana Rebolledo, Erlinda Gonzales-Berry and Teresa Márquez. Albuquerque, N.M.: El Norte Publications, 1988. (Short story).

Gonzales, James. "The Adventures of Salvador Domínguez." *Voces/Voices*. Edited by Rudolfo Anaya. Albuquerque, N.M.: El Norte Publications, Inc., 1987. Reprint. University of New Mexico Press, 1988. (Excerpt from a novel in progress).

Gonzales-Berry, Erlinda. "El tren de la ausencia." *Voces/Voices*. Edited by Rudolfo Anaya. Albuquerque, N.M.: El Norte Publications, Inc., 1987. Reprint. University of New Mexico Press, 1988. (Excerpt from a novel in progress).

Gonzales-Berry, Erlinda. "(Más) conversaciones con Sergio." *Las Mujeres Hablan*. Edited by Tey Diana Rebolledo, Erlinda Gonzales-Berry and Teresa Márquez. Albuquerque, N.M.: El Norte Publications, 1988. (Excerpt from a novel in progress).

Gonzales-Berry, Erlinda. "Rosebud." (Excerpts from a work in progress). *Las Mujeres Hablan*. Edited by Tey Diana Rebolledo, Erlinda Gonzales-Berry and Teresa Márquez. Albuquerque, N.M.: El Norte Publications, 1988. (Narrative sketch).

Gonzalez, Hirginia V. *Poem*, 1898. Special Collections, Zimmerman Library, University of New Mexico. Albuquerque, N.M.

Griego, Alfonso. *Good-bye, My Land of Enchantment: A True Story of Some of the First Spanish-speaking Natives and Early Settlers of San Miguel County*. Albuquerque, N.M. n.p., 1981. (Biography).

Griego, Alfonso. *Panchita: A Romantic Adventure of a Young Girl's Climb From Rags to Riches Through Honesty and Faith in God*. Albuquerque, N.M.: n.p., 1987. (Novel).

Griego, Alfonso. *Voices of the Territory of New Mexico: An Oral History of People of Spanish Descent and Early Settlers Born During the Territorial Days*. Albuquerque, N.M.: n.p., 1985.

Griego y Maestas, José. *Cuentos: Tales From the Hispanic Southwest*. (Based on Stories Originally Collected by Juan B. Rael; selected by and adapted into Spanish by José Griego y Maestas; retold in English by Rudolfo A. Anaya). Santa Fe, N.M.: Museum of New Mexico Press, 1980.

Griego y Maestas, José. "La comadre Sebastiana." *Cuentos Chicanos*. Edited by Rudolfo Anaya and Antonio Márquez. Albuquerque, N.M.: *New America*, American Studies Department, University of New Mexico, 1980. (Folktale).

Hispanic Folktales from New Mexico: Narratives from the R.D. Jameson Collection. Edited by Stanley L. Robe. Berkeley: University of California Press, 1977.

Jaramillo, Cleofas M. *Romance of a Little Village Girl*. San Antonio, TX.: The Naylor Company, 1955. (Autobiography. Sequel to *Shadows of the Past*).

Jaramillo, Cleofas M. *Shadows of the Past/Sombras del Pasado*. Santa Fe, N.M.: Ancient City Press, 1972. Reprint. New York: Arno Press, 1974. (Autobiography).

Jaramillo Lavadie, Juanita. "Gramita on the Road." *Las Mujeres Hablan*. Edited by Tey Diana Rebolledo, Erlinda Gonzales-Berry and Teresa Márquez. Albuquerque, N.M.: El Norte Publications, 1988. (Narrative sketch).

Kopp, Jane and Karl. *Southwest: A Contemporary Anthology*. Albuquerque, N.M.: Red Earth Press, 1977. (Includes fiction and poetry by Rudolfo Anaya, Leo Romero, E. A. Mares, Denise Chávez, Orlando Romero, and Leroy Quintana).

Lamadrid, Enrique R. "Enemy Way." *Bilingual Review/Revista Bilingüe* XII, nos. 1–2 (January-August, 1985):92–96. Reprinted in *Voces/Voices*. Edited by Rudolfo Anaya. Albuquerque, N.M.: El Norte Publications, 1987. Reprint. University of New Mexico Press, 1988. (Short story).

Lamadrid, Enrique R. "White Woman's Burden." *Bilingual Review/Revista Bilingüe* XII, nos. 1–2 (January-August, 1985):90–91. (Short story).

Lechuga, Elida. "Bitter Dreams." *Voces/Voices*. Edited by Rudolfo Anaya. Albuquerque, N.M.: El Norte Publications, 1987. Reprint. University of New Mexico Press, 1988. (Short story).

Lechuga, Elida A. "Remembrances." *Las Mujeres Hablan*. Edited by Tey Diana Rebolledo, Erlinda Gonzales-Berry and Teresa Márquez. Albuquerque, N.M.: El Norte Publications, 1988. (Excerpt from a novel in progress).

López de Padilla, María Esperanza. "Autobiography." *Los pobladores Nuevo Mexicanos y su poesía, 1889–1950*. Edited by Anselmo Arellano. Albuquerque, N.M.: Pajarito Press, 1976.

"Los americanos." Recited to Aurelio Espinosa by Juan Cháves y García de Puerto de Luna, New Mexico. *Literatura Chicana*. Edited by Antonio Castañeda Shular, Tomas Ybarra-Frausto and Joseph Sommers. Englewood Cliffs, N.J.: Prentice-Hall, Inc., 1972.

Los moros y cristianos. Videorecording. Santa Fe, N.M.: New Mexico State Library, 1979. ("Mounted drama, medieval warriors on horseback battle for the Holy Cross.").

Lovato, Albert. "Augusa'o con los velices." *Cuentos Chicanos*. Edited by Rudolfo Anaya and Antonio

Márquez. Albuquerque, N.M.: *New America*, American Studies Department, University of New Mexico, 1980. (Short story).

Lucero-White Lea, Aurora. *Literary Folklore of the Hispanic Southwest*. San Antonio, TX.: The Naylor Company, 1953.

Lucero White-Lea, Aurora. "The Impartiality of Death." Collected by Aurora Lucero White-Lea. *Literature Chicana*. Edited by Carlota Castañeda Dwyer, Tomas Ybarra-Frausto and Joseph Sommers. Englewood, N.J.: Prentice-Hall, Inc., 1972. (Folktale).

Mares, E. A. "Florinto." *Cuentos Chicanos*. Edited by Rudolfo Anaya and Antonio Márquez. Revised edition. Albuquerque, N.M.: University of New Mexico Press, 1984. (Short story).

Mares, E. A. *Lola's Last Dance*. (Unpublished play).

Mares, E. A. *The Unicorn Poem*. Los Cerrillos, N.M.: San Marcos Press, 1980.

Martínez, Demetria. *Turning*. Tucson: Bilingual Press, Forthcoming, 1989. (Poetry).

Martínez, Paul E. "Don Teodoro." *Cuentos Chicanos*. Edited by Rudolfo Anaya and Antonio Márquez. Albuquerque, N.M.: *New America*, American Studies Department, University of New Mexico, 1980. (Short story).

Medina, Roberto C. *Fabian Doesn't Die*. Las Cruces, N.M.: Bilingüe Publications, 1981. (Novel).

Medina, Roberto C. *Fabián no se muere: Novela de amor*. Las Cruces, N.M.: Bilingüe Publications, 1978. (Spanish translation of *Fabian Doesn't Die*).

Medina, Roberto C. *Two Ranges*. Las Cruces, N.M.: Bilingüe Publications, 1974. (Novel).

Meléndez, A. Gabriel. "The Scars of Old Sabers." *Writers Forum* 11 (Fall, 1985): 157–62. (Short story).

Meléndez, A. Gabriel. "Visiones otoñales/Autumn Visions." *Voces/Voices*. Edited by Rudolfo Anaya. Albuquerque, N.M.: El Norte Publications, 1987. Reprint. University of New Mexico Press, 1988. (Short story).

Metzgar, Joseph Torres. *Below the Summit*. Berkeley, CA.: Tonatiuth International, 1976. (Novel).

Montoya, Ciria S. "Dichos de José María Sánchez (My Father)". *Las Mujeres Hablan*. Edited by Tey Diana Rebolledo, Erlinda Gonzales-Berry, and Teresa Márquez. Albuquerque, N.M.: El Norte Publications, 1988. (Proverbs).

Olonia, Joseph M. "The Last Walk." *Voces/Voices*. Edited by Rudolfo Anaya. Albuquerque: El Norte Publications, 1987. Reprint. University of New Mexico Press, 1988. (Short story).

Ortiz, Virginia. "Chistes." *Voces/Voices*. Edited by Rudolfo Anaya. Albuquerque, N.M.: El Norte Publications, 1987. Reprint. University of New Mexico Press, 1988. (Collection of riddles and jokes).

Otero, Miguel Antonio. *My Life on the Frontier, 1864–1882*. Press of the Pioneers, 1935. Reprint. Albuquerque, N.M.: University of New Mexico Press, 1987.

Otero, Miguel Antonio. *My Nine Years as Governor of the Territory of New Mexico, 1897–1906*. Albuquerque, N.M.: University of New Mexico Press, 1940.

Otero, Miguel Antonio. *The Real Billy the Kid; With a New Light on the Lincoln County War*. New York: R. R. Wilson, 1936.

Otero, Miguel Antonio. *Otero: An Autobiographical Trilogy*. Reprint. New York: Arno Press, 1974.

Otero Nina. "Clown of San Cristobal and Two Other Living Tales of the Spanish Colonials in New Mexico as Told to the Author." *Survey Graphics* 24 (January, 1935): 16–18.

Otero, Adelina. "My People." *Survey* 66 (May 1, 1931):149–51. (Personal histories).

Otero, Nina. "Count La Cerda's Treasure." *We Are Chicanos*. Edited by Philip D. Ortego. New York: Washington Square Press Pocket Books, 1973. (Legend).

Otero, Rosalie. "Amelia." *Voces/Voices*. Edited by Rudolfo Anaya. Albuquerque, N.M.: El Norte Publications, Inc., 1987. Reprint. University of New Mexico Press, 1988. (Short story).

Otero, Rosalie. "The Closet." *Las Mujeres Hablan*. Edited by Tey Diana Rebolledo, Erlinda Gonzales-Berry and Teresa Márquez. Albuquerque, N.M.: El Norte Publications, 1988. (Short story).

Otero-Peralta, Rosalie. "Angelina." *Cuentos Chicanos*. Edited by Rudolfo Anaya and Antonio Márquez. Albuquerque, N.M.: *New America*, American Studies Department, University of New Mexico, 1980.

Otero-Peralta, Rosalie. "Las Dos Hermanas." *De Colores* 2, no. 3 (1975):66–73. (Short story).

Otero-Warren, Nina. *Old Spain in Our Southwest*. New York: Harcourt Brace, 1936. (Narrative sketches).

Padilla, Genaro M., editor. *The Short Stories of Fray Angelico Chavez*. By Fray Angelico Chavez. Albuquerque: University of New Mexico Press, 1987.

Pearce, Thomas Matthews. *The New Mexican "Shepherds" Play*. Berkeley: University of California Press, 1956.

Perea, Robert. "Dragon Mountain." *De Colores* 4, nos. 1–2 (1978): 33–41. (Short story).

Perea, Robert. "Small Arms Fire." *Cuentos Chicanos*. Edited by Rudolfo Anaya and Antonio Márquez. Revised edition. Albuquerque, N.M.: University of New Mexico Press, 1984. (Short story).

Perea, Robert. "The Battle of Engineer Hill." *The Americas Review* XIV, no. 2 (Summer, 1986):15–20. (Short story).

Perea, Robert L. "Trip to Da Nang." *Bilingual Review/Revista Bilingüe* XII, nos. 1–2 (January-August, 1985):97–102. (Short story).

Puerto del Sol 12, no. 1 (March, 1972):9–10. (Poetry by Leo Romero).

Puerto del Sol 12, no. 2 (March, 1973):5–7. (Poetry by Leroy Quintana).

Puerto del Sol 13, no. 1 (April, 1974):50–52, 78–79. (Fiction and poetry by Orlando Romero and Joseph Somoza).

Puerto del Sol 13, no. 2 (Fall, 1974):93–94. (Poetry by Leroy Quintana).

Puerto del Sol 15, no. 1 (Fall, 1978):1–6, 14, 49–51. (Poetry by Leo Romero, Leroy Quintana and Joseph Somoza).

Puerto del Sol 16 (Spring, 1981):3–9. (Poetry by Leo Romero).

Puerto del Sol 17 (Summer, 1982):1–2, 114–20, 122–24, 128–29. (Poetry by Leo Romero and Romolo Arellano).

Puerto del Sol 18 (Spring, 1983):21–22, 135–36. (Poetry by Leo Romero and Romolo Arellano).

Quintana, Leroy V. *Hijo del pueblo: New Mexico Poems*. Las Cruces, N.M.: Puerto del Sol Press, 1976.

Quintana, Leroy V. *Sangre*. Las Cruces, N.M.: Prima Agua Press, 1981. (Poetry).

Quintana, Leroy V. "The Reason People Don't Like Mexicans." *Five Poets of Aztlán*. Edited by Santiago Daydi-Tolson. New York: Bilingual Press/Editorial Bilingüe, 1985. (Poetry).

Rael, Juan B. *Cuentos españoles de Colorado y Nuevo Mexico*. Stanford: Stanford University Press, 1957. 2nd revised edition. Santa Fe, N.M.: Museum of New Mexico Press, 1977.

Rebolledo, Tey Diana, Erlinda Gonzales-Berry and Teresa Márquez, editors. *Las Mujeres Hablan: An Anthology of Nuevo Mexicana Writers*. Albuquerque, N.M.: El Norte Publications, 1988.

Revista Chicano-Riqueña Año VIII, no. 4 (Otoño, 1980):11–12. (Poetry by Jimmy Santiago Baca).

Romero, Leo. *Agua negra*. Boise, ID.: Ahsahta Press, 1981. (Poetry).

Romero, Leo. *Celso*. Berkeley, CA.: Tonatiuh-Quinto Sol International, 1980. *Grito del Sol Quarterly Books*, Year five-Book four. Reprint. Houston, TX.: Arte Público Press, 1985. (Poetry).

Romero, Leo. *During the Growing Season*. Tucson, AZ.: Maguey Press, 1978. (Poetry).

Romero, Leo. "Owl." *Cuentos Chicanos*. Edited by Rudolfo Anaya and Antonio Márquez. Albuquerque, N.M.: *New America*, American Studies Department, University of New Mexico, 1980. (Short story).

Romero, Orlando. "Augustine Primavera." *Southwest, A Contemporary Anthology*. Edited by Karl and Jane Kopp. Albuquerque, N.M.: Red Earth Press, 1977. (Short story).

Romero, Orlando. "La lluvia." *Voces/Voices*. Edited by Rudolfo Anaya. Albuquerque: El Norte Publications, 1987. Reprint. University of New Mexico Press, 1988. (Excerpt from *Nambe-Year One*).

Romero, Orlando. "María Mueller. María & Domingo Machote. (Two Short Stories)." *De Colores* 4, nos. 1–2 (1978):75–79.

Romero, Orlando. "Nambe-Year One." *Grito del Sol* Year One, Book One (January-March, 1976):39–61. (Excerpt from novel by same title).
Romero, Orlando. *Nambe-Year One*. Berkeley, CA.: Tonatiuth International Press, 1976. (Novel).
Sálaz-Márquez, Ruben. "White Mice." *Voces/Voices*. Edited by Rudolfo Anaya. Albuquerque, N.M.: El Norte Publications, Inc., 1987. Reprint. University of New Mexico Press, 1988. (Short story).
Sánchez, Irene Barraza. "Memorias de Tomé." *Las Mujeres Hablan*. Edited by Tey Diana Rebolledo, Erlinda Gonzales-Berry and Teresa Márquez. Albuquerque, N.M.: El Norte Publications, 1988. (Personal recollections).
Sandoval, Arturo. "El Correo." *Voces/Voices*. Edited by Rudolfo Anaya. Albuquerque, N.M.: El Norte Publications, 1987. Reprint. University of New Mexico Press, 1988. (Short story).
Sandoval, Linda. "A Short Trip Home." *Las Mujeres Hablan*. Edited by Tey Diana Rebolledo, Erlinda Gonzales-Berry and Teresa Márquez. Albuquerque, N.M.: El Norte Publications, 1988. (Short story).
San Marcos Review 1, no. 2 (Spring, 1978). (Poetry by Leo Romero).
San Marcos Review (Featuring Spanish and Latin American Contemporary Poetry) 2, no. 2 (Autumn, 1979). (Poetry by Joseph Somoza).
San Marcos Review 1, no. 1 (n.d.). (Poetry by Leo Romero and Leroy Quintana).
San Marcos Review (Spring, 1983):13, 46–47, 49. (Poetry by Erlinda Gonzales-Berry, June Jaramillo and Francisca Tenorio).
Sedillo, Michele. "The Birthday Party." *Voces/Voices*. Edited by Rudolfo Anaya. Albuquerque, N.M.: El Norte Publications, 1987. Reprint. University of New Mexico Press, 1988. (Short story).
Sehestedt, Nell Soto. "A Rose for Alicia." *The Americas Review* XIV, no. 2 (Summer, 1986):21–37. (Short story).
Sehestedt, Nell Soto. "Private Views." *Las Mujeres Hablan*. Edited by Tey Diana Rebolledo, Erlinda Gonzales-Berry and Teresa Márquez. Albuquerque, N.M.: El Norte Publications, 1988. (Short story).
Sena, Marie Isabel. "The Little Stone Hat" (A True Miracle Story). *New Mexico Folklore Record* 1, (1946–47):30–36. (Folk tale).
Somoza, Joseph. *Greyhound: A Poem Sequence*. Sacramento, CA.: Grande Ronde Press, 1968.
Somoza, Joseph. *Olive Women: Poems*. Los Cerrillos, N.M.: San Marcos Press, 1976.
Tenorio, Francisca. "Old Dogs, New Tricks." *Voces/Voices*. Edited by Rudolfo Anaya. Albuquerque, N.M.: El Norte Publications, 1987. Reprint. University of New Mexico Press, 1988. (Short story).
The Americas Review XV, no. 1 (Spring, 1987):48–61. (Poetry by Denise Chávez).
The Americas Review 15, nos. 3–4 (1987):65–84. (Poetry by Denise Chávez).
The Journal of Ethnic Studies 15, no. 1 (Spring, 1987):48–67. (Poetry by Denise Chávez).
Tijerina, Reis López. *Mi lucha por la tierra*. Mexico, D.F.: Fondo de Cultura Económica, 1978. (Autobiography).
Torres, Lorraine. "Ojalá que no!" *Las Mujeres Hablan*. Edited by Tey Diana Rebolledo, Erlinda Gonzales-Berry and Teresa Márquez. Albuquerque, N.M.: El Norte Publications, 1988. (Short story).
Ulibarrí, Sabine Reyes. *Al cielo se sube a pie*. Mexico: Impresora Medina, 1961. Reprint. Madrid: Ediciones Alfguara, 1966. (Poetry).
Ulibarrí, Sabine Reyes. *Amor y Ecuador*. Madrid: Ediciones J. Porrua Turanzas, 1966. (Poetry).
Ulibarrí, Sabine Reyes. "Don Nicomedes." *Ceremony of Brotherhood*. Edited by Rudolfo Anaya and Simon J. Ortiz. Albuquerque, N.M.: Academia, 1981. (Short story).
Ulibarrí, Sabine Reyes. *El gobernador Glu Glu y otras historias/Governor Glu Glu and Other Stories*. Tempe, AZ.: Bilingual Press, 1988.
Ulibarrí, Sabine Reyes. "El hombre sin nombre." *Mosaico de la vida: Prosa Chicana, Cubana, y Puertorriqueña*. Edited by Francisco Jiménez. New York: Harcourt Brace Jovanovich, 1981. (Novella).

Ulibarrí, Sabine Reyes, editor and translator. *La fragua sin fuego/No Fire for the Forge*. Los Cerrillos, N.M.: San Marcos Press, 1971. (Short stories and poetry).

Ulibarrí, Sabine Reyes. "Mi abuela fumaba puros/My Grandmother Smoked Cigars." *Grito del Sol* Year Two-Book One (April-June, 1977):9–31. (Short story).

Ulibarrí, Sabine Reyes. *Mi abuela fumaba puros y otros cuentos de Tierra Amarilla/My Grandmother Smoked Cigars and Other Stories of Tierra Amarilla*. Berkeley, CA.: Quinto Sol Publications, 1977.

Ulibarrí, Sabine Reyes. "My Wonder Horse." *Voces/Voices*. Edited by Rudolfo Anaya. Albuquerque: El Norte Publications, 1987. Reprint. University of New Mexico Press, 1988. (Short story).

Ulibarrí, Sabine Reyes. *Primeros encuentros/First Encounters*. Ypsilanti, MI.: Bilingual Press/Editorial Bilingüe, 1982. (Short stories).

Ulibarrí, Sabine Reyes. *Pupurupú, cuentos de niños/Children's Stories*. Mexico: Sainz Luiselli Editores, 1987. (Stories in English and Spanish).

Ulibarrí, Sabine Reyes. *The Condor and Other Stories/El condor y otros cuentos*. Houston: Arte Publico Press, 1988. (Short stories in Spanish and English).

Ulibarrí, Sabine Reyes. "The Heavenly Horse." (Children's Story) *De Colores* 4, nos. 1–2 (1978):116–20. (Short story).

Ulibarrí, Sabine. "The Stuffing of the Lord." *Chicano Voices*. Edited by Carlota Cardeñas Dwyer. Boston: Houghton Mifflin, 1975. (Short story).

Ulibarrí, Sabine Reyes. *Tierra Amarilla, cuentos de Nueva México*. Quito, Ecuador: Editorial Casa de la Cultura Ecuatoriana, 1964.

Ulibarrí, Sabine Reyes. *Tierra Amarilla: Stories of New Mexico/Tierra Amarilla: Cuentos de Nuevo México*. Translated into English by Thelma Campbell Nason. Albuquerque, N.M.: University of New Mexico Press, 1971.

Unser, Carol. "Tesoros escondidos." *Las Mujeres Hablan*. Edited by Tey Diana Rebolledo, Erlinda Gonzales-Berry and Teresa Márquez. Albuquerque, N.M.: El Norte Publications, 1988. (Oral history).

Valdes-Fallis, Guadalupe. "Recuerdo." *De Colores* 2, no. 3 (1975):60–65. (Short story).

Vargas, Kika. "The Corpse." *Cuentos Chicanos*. Edited by Rudolfo Anaya and Antonio Márquez. Revised edition. Albuquerque, N.M.: University of New Mexico Press, 1984. (Short story).

Velez, Daniel Roll. "24 Kilates." *Cuentos Chicanos*. Edited by Rudolfo Anaya and Antonio Márquez. Albuquerque, N.M.: *New America*, American Studies Department, University of New Mexico, 1980. (Short story).

Vergara, Lautaro. "Historia de un minero." *Cuentos Chicanos*. Edited by Rudolfo Anaya and Antonio Márquez. Albuquerque, N.M.: *New America*, American Studies Department, University of New Mexico, 1980. (Short story).

Vigil, Cleofes. "El fletero y el ranchero." *El Cuaderno* 2, no. 1 (1972):41–43. (Short story).

Vigil, Julián Josue. *Arse Poetica*. Las Vegas, N.M.: Editorial Telaraña, 1980. (Poetry).

Villagrá, Capitan Gaspar Pérez de. *Historia de la Nueva México*. 2 Vols. México: Imprenta del Museo Nacional, 1900.

Villagra, Gaspar Perez de. *History of New Mexico*, by Gaspar Perez de Villagra, Alcalá, 1610. Translated by Gilberto Espinosa; introduction and notes by F. W. Hodge. Los Angeles: The Quivira Society, 1933.

SECONDARY SOURCES

Adams, Eleanor B. "Two Colonial New Mexico Libraries, 1704, 1776." *New Mexico Historical Review* 19 (1944):139.

Anaya, Rudolfo A. "The Writer's Landscape: Epiphany in Landscape." *Latin American Literary Review* nos. 5–6 (1977–78):101. (Essay).

Anaya, Rudolfo and John Nichols. "A Dialogue." *Puerto del Sol* 17 (Summer, 1982):61–87.

Arellano, Anselmo. "La Poesía Nuevomexicana, su Desarrollo y transición durante los fines del siglo diez y nueve." Paper presented at Paso Por Aquí Symposium, January 9, 1985. Albuquerque, New Mexico. (Discusses the development of poetry in New Mexico).

Arellano, Anselmo F. *Las Vegas Grandes on the Gallinas 1935–1985*. Las Vegas, N.M.: Editorial Telaraña, 1985. (Historical sketches, prose and poetry).

Arellano, Anselmo F. *Los pobladores nuevo mexicanos y su poesía, 1889–1950*. Albuquerque, N.M.: Pajarito Publications, 1976.

Arellano, Estevan. "*La historia de un caminante or sea Gervacio y Aurora*." *La Palaba* 2, no. 1 (Primavera 1980):57–66. (*La Historia* written in 1881; considered one of the earliest unpublished Chicano novels).

Armas, José. "Chicano Writing: The New Mexican Narrative." *De Colores* 5, nos. 1–2 (1980):69–81. Reprinted in *Contemporary Chicano Fiction, A Critical Survey*. Edited by Vernon E. Lattin. Binghamton, N.Y.: Bilingual Press/Editoral Bilingüe, 1986.

Arthur L. Campa. Edited by Anselmo F. Arellano and Julian Josue Vigil. Las Vegas, N.M.: Editorial Telaraña, 1980. (Collected essays).

Austin, Mary. *Auto sacramental-Los pastores, Collected by Mary Austin*. Santa Fe, N.M.: n.d., n.p.

Austin, Mary. "Folk Plays of the Southwest." *Theatre Arts* XVII (August, 1933):299–606.

Bauder, Thomas A. "The Triumph of White Magic in Rudolfo Anaya's *Bless Me, Ultima*." *Mester* 14, no. 1 (1985):41–54.

Benson, Douglas K. "A Conversation with Leroy V. Quintana." *Bilingual Review/Revista Bilingüe* XII, no. 3 (September-December, 1985):218–29. (Interview).

Benson, Douglas K. "Intuitions of a World in Transition: The New Mexican Poetry of Leroy V. Quintana." *Bilingual Review/Revista Bilingüe* XII, nos. 1–2 (January-August, 1985):62–80.

Binder, Wolfgang. *Partial Autobiographies: Interviews with Twenty Chicano Poets*. Erlangen: Verlag Palm, 1985. (Includes an interview with Jimmy Santiago Baca).

Branch, Louis León. *Los Bilitos: The Story of Billy the Kid and His Gang*. New York: Carlton Press Inc., 1980.

Brito, Aristeo, Jr. "*Paraiso, caída y regeneración en tres novelas chicanas*." Ph.D. Diss. University of Arizona, 1978. (Analyzes *Bless Me, Ultima, Pocho* and *Peregrinos de Aztlán*).

Bruce-Novoa. "Canonical and Noncanonical Texts." *The Americas Review* XIV, nos. 3–4 (Fall-Winter, 1986):119–35. (Includes references to Rudolfo Anaya's *Bless Me, Ultima* and to *El hijo de la tempestad* by Eusebio Chacón).

Bruce-Novoa. *Chicano Authors: Inquiry by Interviews*. Austin & London: University of Texas Press, 1980. (Includes an interview with Rudolfo A. Anaya).

Bruce-Novoa. "Chicano Poetry: An Overview." *A Gift of Tongues, Critical Challenges in Contemporary American Poetry*. Edited by Marie Harris and Kathleen Agüero. Athens and London: University of Georgia Press, 1987. (Mentions a New Mexican play celebrating the crossing of the Rio Grande, Gaspar Pérez de Villagrá's epic poem chronicling Oñate's expedition, and Father Martínez's publishing efforts in early New Mexico).

Bruce-Novoa. *La literature chicana a través de sus autores*. Mexico,D.F.: Siglo Veintiuno Editores, S.A., 1983. (Spanish translation of *Chicano Authors: Inquiry by Interviews*).

Bruce-Novoa. "Portrait of the Chicano Artist as a Young Man: The Making of the Author in Three Chicano Novels." *Flor y Canto II: An Anthology of Chicano Literature*. Edited by Arnold C. Vento, Alurista and José Flores Peregrino. Albuquerque, N.M.: Pajarito Publications, 1975. (Analyzes *Bless Me, Ultima, Pocho* and . . . *Y ño se lo tragó la tierra*).

Bruce-Novoa. Review of *Heart of Aztlán*. *La confluencia*, nos. 1–2 (1976–1978):61–62.

Calderón, Hector. "Rudolfo Anaya's *Bless Me, Ultima*. A Chicano Romance of the Southwest." *Crítica* 1, no. 3 (Fall, 1986):21–47.

Campa, Arthur León. *A Bibliography of Spanish Folklore in New Mexico*. Albuquerque, N.M.: University of New Mexico. (The University of New Mexico Bulletin, Language Series, vol. 2, no. 3, 1930).

Campa, Arthur León. *Arthur L. Campa*. Edited by Anselmo F. Arellano and Julian Josue Vigil. Las Vegas, N.M.: Editorial Telaraña, 1980.

Campa, Arthur León. *Hispanic Culture in the Southwest*. Norman, OK.: University of Oklahoma, 1979.

Campa, Arthur León. *Hispanic Folklore Studies of Arthur Campa*. New York: Arno Press, 1976.

Campa, Arthur León. "The New Mexican Spanish Folktheatre." *Southern Folklore Quarterly* (June 1941):127–31.

Campa, Arthur León. "Religious Spanish Folk Drama." *The New Mexico Quarterly* (February 8, 1932).

Campa, Arthur León. *Religious Spanish Folkdrama in New Mexico*. n.p.,n.d. Reprinted from the *New Mexico Quarterly* 2, no. 1 (February, 1932):3–13.

Candelaria, Cordelia. *Chicano Poetry, A Critical Introduction*. Westport, Conn.: Greenwood Press, 1986. (Analyzes poetry by Leo Romero; makes references to works by Rudolfo Anaya and Felipe Maximiliano Chacón).

Cantú, Roberto. "Degradación y regeneración en *Bless Me, Ultima*: el chicano y la vida nueva." *The Identification and Analysis of Chicano Literature*. Edited by Francisco Jiménez. New York: Bilingual Press/Editorial Bilingüe, 1979.

Cantú, Roberto. "Estructura y sentido de lo onírico en *Bless Me, Ultima*. *Mester* 5, no. 1 (November, 1974):27–41.

Cárdenas Dwyer, Carlota. "Myth and Folk Culture in Contemporary Chicano Literature." *La Luz* (December, 1974):28–29. (Briefly discusses myth and folk culture in *Bless Me, Ultima*).

Carpenter, Lorene Hyde. *Maps for the Journey: Shamanic Patterns in Anaya, Asturias, and Castañeda*. Ph.D. diss. University of Colorado at Boulder, 1981. (Analyzes *Bless Me, Ultima*).

Carrasco, David. "A Perspective for a Study of Religious Dimensions in Chicano Experience: *Bless Me, Ultima* as a Religious Text." *Aztlán* 13, nos. 1–2 (Spring-Fall, 1982):195–221.

Carrillo, Loretta. "The Search for Selfhood and Order in Contemporary Chicano Fiction." Ph.D. diss. Michigan State University, 1979. (Discusses *Bless Me, Ultima*).

Castro, Donald. "Chicano Literature: A Bibliographical Essay." *English in Texas* 7, no. 4 (Summer, 1976):14–19. (Makes references to *Bless Me, Ultima*).

Cazemajou, Jean. "Mediators and Mediation in Rudolfo Anaya's Trilogy: *Bless Me, Ultima*, *Heart of Aztlán* and *Tortuga*." *European Perspectives on Hispanic Literature of the United States*. Edited by Genvieve Fabre. Houston: Arte Público Press, 1988.

Chacón, Eusebio. "Elocuente discurso." Reproduced by Anselmo F. Arellano. *De Colores* 2, no. 1 (1975):39–46. Also published in *La voz del pueblo*, 1901.

Chávez, Denise. "Words of Wisdom: Writers Seek to Define Distinctive Southwest Identity." *New Mexico Magazine* 65, no. 12 (December, 1987):72–78. (Discusses the literary environment in New Mexico; mentions several Hispanic writers).

Chavez, Fray Angelico. "The Mad Poet of Santa Cruz." *New Mexico Folklore Record* no. 3 (1948–1949):10.

Chavez, Fray Angelico. Review of *Nambe-Year One*. *New Mexico Magazine* 32, no. 4 (Fall, 1978):246–47.

Córdova, Gilberto Benito. *Bibliography of Unpublished Materials Pertaining to Hispanic Culture*. Los Cerrillos, N.M.: San Marcos Press, 1973.

Dasenbrock, Reed Way. "Intelligibility and Meaningfulness in Multicultural Literature in English." *PMLA* 102, no. 1 (January, 1987):10–19. (Discusses *Bless Me, Ultima*).

Dobie, J. Frank. *Guide to Life and Literature of the Southwest*. Austin, TX.: University of Texas Press, 1942. (Mentions selected early New Mexico Hispanic writers).

Dolan, Maureen. "Aspects of Chicano Reality With Reference to the Novels of Rudolfo A. Anaya." Ph.D. diss. Glasgow, Scotland, 1984.

Donnelly, Dyan. "Finding a Home In The World." *Bilingual Review/Revista Bilingüe* 1, no. 1 (January-April, 1974):113–18. (Review of *Bless Me, Ultima*).

Eckley, Grace. "The Process of Maturation in Anaya's *Bless Me, Ultima*." *English in Texas* 9, no. 1 (Fall, 1977):8–10.

Elias, Edward. "*Tortuga*: A Novel of Archetypal Structure." *Bilingual Review/Revista Bilingüe* IX, no. 1 (January-April, 1982):82–87.

Englekirk, J. E. "Notes on the Repertoire of the New Mexico Spanish Folk Theatre." *Southern Folklore Quarterly* 4 (1940):227.

Englekirk, J. E. "The Source and Dating of New Mexico Spanish Folk Plays." *Western Folklore* 16 (1957):232–55.

Espinosa, Aurelio M. "Romancero nuevomejicano." *Revue Hispanique* 33, no. 84 (1915):446–560. (Examines traditional New Mexican poetry).

Espinosa, Aurelio Macedonio. *The Folklore of Spain in the American Southwest*. Edited by J. Manuel Espinosa. Norman, OK.: University of Oklahoma, 1985.

Espinosa, Gilberto. "Spanish Folklore in New Mexico." New Mexico *Historical Review* 1 (1926):135–55.

Espinosa, J. Manuel. "Additional Hispanic Versions of the Spanish Religious Ballad 'Por el rastro de la sangre.'" *New Mexico Historical Review* 56, no. 4 (October 1981):349–67.

Espinosa, J. Manuel, "The Virgin of the Reconquest of New Mexico." *Mid-America* 18, New Series 7, no. 2 (1936):79–87. (Narrative).

Espinosa, José Manuel. *Spanish Folk-Tales From New Mexico*. New York: Kraus Reprint, 1969.

Fernandez, José B. *Alvar Nuñez Cabeza de Vaca: The Forgotten Chronicler*. Miami, Fl.: Universal, 1975.

García, Nasario. "The Concept of Time in *Nambe-Year One*." *Contemporary Chicano Fiction, A Critical Survey*. Edited by Vernon E. Lattin. Binghamton, N.Y.: Bilingual Press, 1986.

Gaston, Edwin W. Jr. Review of *The Waxen Image*. *Rocky Mountain Review* 32, no. 4 (Fall, 1978):246–47.

Gerdes, Dick. "Cultural Values in Three Novels of New Mexico." *The Bilingual Review/La Revista Bilingüe* 7, no. 3 (1980):239–48. (Discusses *Nambe-Year One* by Orlando Romero, *Heart of Aztlán* by Rudolfo Anaya and *Below the Summit* by Joseph V. Torres-Metzgar.

Gerdes, Dick and Sabine Ulibarrí. "Una misma cultura, dos distintas literaturas: La mexicana y la chicana." *Grito del Sol*, Year Three-Book Four (October-December, 1978):91–115. (Discusses, from a literary perspective, the relationship between Mexicans and Chicanos. Uses *Bless Me, Ultima* as an example of Chicano literature with universal themes).

Gingerich, Willard. "Aspects of Prose Style in Three Chicano Novels: *Pocho, Bless Me, Ultima* and *The Road to Tamazunchale*." *Form and Function in English*. Edited by Jacob Ornstein-Galicia. Rowley, Mass.: Newbury House Publishing, 1984.

Gish, Robert. "Curanderismo and Witchery in the Fiction of Rudolfo A. Anaya: The Novel as Magic." *New Mexico Humanities Review* 2, no. 2 (Summer, 1979):5–12.

Gonzales-Berry, Erlinda. *Chicano Literature in Spanish Roots and Content*. Ph.D. Diss. University of New Mexico, 1979. (Contains a chapter on Sabine Ulibarrí).

Gonzales-Berry, Erlinda. Review of *The Two Guadalupes:Hispanic Legends and Magic Tales from Northern New Mexico*. Edited by Marta Weigle. *The Americas Review*. Forthcoming.

Gonzales-Berry, Erlinda. "Vicente Bernal." *Dictionary of Literary Biography*. Edited by Carl Shirley and Francisco Lomelí. Forthcoming, 1989.

Gutiérrez, Armando. "Politics in the Chicano Novel: A Critique." *Understanding the Chicano Experience Through Literature*. Mexican American Studies Monograph Series no. 2 (April, 1981): 7–14. (Analyzes *Heart of Aztlán*).

Heard, Martha E. "The Theatre of Denise Chávez: Interior Landscapes with Sabor Nuevomexicano." *The Americas Review* 16, no. 2 (Summer, 1988):83–91.

Heisley, Michael. *An Annotated Bibliography of Chicano Folklore from the Southwestern United States*. Los Angeles: Center for the Study of Comparative Folklore and Mythology, University of California, Los Angeles, 1977.

Hernández-Gutíerrez, Manuel de Jesús. *The Barrio, The Anti-Barrio and The Exterior: Semiotic*

Textualization of "Internal Colonialism" in Chicano Narrative. (Spanish Text). Ph.D. diss. Stanford University, 1984. (Mentions works by Rudolfo Anaya, Orlando Romero, and Roberto C. Medina).

Hoffman, María López. "Myth and Reality in *Heart of Aztlán*" *De Colores* 5, nos. 1–2 (1980):111–114.

Johnson, Elaine Dorough. "A Thematic Study of Three Chicano Narratives: *Estampas del valle y otras obras, Bless Me, Ultima* and *Peregrinos de Aztlán*." Ph.D. diss. University of Wisconsin, Madison, 1978.

Johnson, Richard S. "Rudolfo Anaya: A vision of the Heroic." *Empire Magazine, Denver Post* (March 2, 1980):25–27.

Jung, Alfred. "Regionalist Motifs in Rudolfo A. Anaya's Fiction (1972–82)." *Missions in Conflict: Essays on U.S.-Mexican Relations and Chicano Culture*. Edited by Renate von Bardeleben, Dietrich Briesemeister, and Juan Bruce-Novoa. Tubingen: Gunter Narr Verlag, 1986.

Lattin, Vernon E. "Ethnicity and Identity in the Contemporary Chicano Novel." *Minority Voices* 2, no. 2 (Fall, 1978):37–44. (Briefly discusses *Bless Me, Ultima*).

Lattin, Vernon E. "The Horror of Darkness: Meaning and Structure in Anaya's *Bless Me, Ultima*." *Revista Chicano-Riqueña* VI, no. 2 (Spring, 1978):51–57.

Lattin, Vernon E. "The Quest for Mythic Vision in Contemporary Native American and Chicano Fiction." *American Literature* 50, no. 4 (January, 1979):625–40.

Lattin, Vernon E. "Time and History in Candelaria's *Memories of the Alhambra*." *Contemporary Chicano Fiction, A Critical Survey*. Edited by Vernon E. Lattin. Binghamton, N.Y.: Bilingual Press, 1986.

Leal, Luis. "Chicano Literature: An Overview." *Three American Literatures*. Edited by Houston A. Baker. New York: Modern Language Association of America, 1982. (Mentions *Historia de la Nueva México*, Miguel A. Otero's *My Life on the Frontier*, Fray Angelico Chavez's collections of poetry, Rudolfo Anaya's novel, *Bless Me, Ultima* and Sabine Ulibarrí's creative works).

Leal, Luis. "Cuatro Siglos de Prosa Aztlanese." *La Palabra* 2, no. 1 (Spring, 1980):2–12.

Leal, Luis. "Mexican American Literature: A Historical Perspective." *Revista Chicano-Requeña* 1, no. 1 (Primavera, 1973):32–44. (Mentions works by Gaspar Pérez de Villagrá, Miguel A. Otero, Vicente Bernal, Fray Angelico Chavez and Rudolfo Anaya).

Leal, Luis. "Hispanic-Mexican Literature in the Southwest, 1521–1848." *Chicano Literature: A Reference Guide*. Edited by Julio A. Martínez and Francisco A. Lomelí. Westport, Conn.: Greenwood Press, 1985. (Briefly discusses *Historia de la Nueva México*).

Leal, Luis. "In Search of Aztlán." *Denver Quarterly* 16, no. 3 (Fall, 1981):16–22. (Briefly compares *Heart of Aztlán* with *En el nuevo Aztlán*).

Leal, Luis. "Mexican American Literature, 1848–1942." *Chicano Literature: A Reference Guide*. Edited by Julio A. Martínez and Francisco A. Lomelí. Westport, Conn.: Greenwood Press, 1985. (Mentions early New Mexico writers).

Leal, Luis and Pepe Barron. "Chicano Literature: An Overview." *Three American Literatures*. Edited by Houston A. Baker. New York: The Modern Language Association of America, 1982.

Lewis, Marvin A. "New Mexico: The Real, The Marvelous, The Fantastic." *Introduction to the Chicano Novel* by Marvin A. Lewis. Milwaukee: University of Wisconsin-Milwaukee, 1982. (*Focuses on Bless Me, Ultima, Heart of Aztlán* and *Nambe-Year One*).

Lewis, Marvin A. "The Urban Experience in Selected Chicano Fiction." *Contemporary Chicano Fiction, A Critical Survey*. Edited by Vernon E. Lattin. Binghamton, N.Y.: Bilingual Press, 1986. (Discusses *Memories of the Alhambra* by Nash Candelaria).

Lomelí, Francisco. "Chicana Novelists in the Process of Creating Fictive Voices." *Beyond Stereotypes, The Critical Analysis of Chicana Literature*. Edited by María Herrera-Sobeck. Binghamton, N.Y.: Bilingual Press/Editorial Bilingüe, 1985. (Contains some discussion of New Mexico's Hispanic women writers, Fabiola Cabeza de Vaca and Nina Otero-Warren).

Lomelí, Francisco. "Eusebio Chacón." Chicano Literature: A Reference *Guide*. Edited by Julio A. Martínez and Francisco A. Lomelí. Westport, Conn.: Greenwood Press, 1985.

Lomelí, Francisco. "Novel." A *Decade of Chicano Literature (1970–1979): Critical Essays and Bibliography*. Edited by Luis Leal, et al. Santa Barbara, CA.: Editorial La Causa, 1982. (Describes works by Rudolfo Anaya, Eusebio Chacón, Manuel C. de Baca, Felipe M. Chacón, Nash Candelaria, Rudy Apodaca, Robert Medina and Joseph Torres-Metzgar).

Lomelí, Francisco, and Clark Calahan. "Miguel de Quintana, poeta nuevomexicano ante la inquisición." *Revista Chicano-Riqueña* 12, no. 2 (Summer, 1984):51–68.

Lomelí, Francisco A. and Donaldo W. Urioste. *Chicano Perspectives in Literature: A Critical and Annotated Bibliography*. Albuquerque, N.M.: Pajarito Publishing, 1976. (Contains annotated entries of novels by Rudolfo Anaya and other Chicano writers).

Lopez, José Timoteo, Edgardo Nuñez and Robert Lara Vialpando. *Breve resena de la literatura hispaña de Nuevo México y Colorado*. Juárez, Chihuahua, Mexico: Imprenta Comercial, 1959.

Lyon, Ted. "'Loss of Innocence' in Chicano Prose." *The Identification and Analysis of Chicano Literature*. Edited by Francisco Jiménez. New York: Bilingual Press/Editorial Bilingüe, 1979. (Includes discussion of Rudolfo Anaya's *Bless Me, Ultima*).

Malpezzi, Frances. "A Study of the Female Protagonist in Frank Waters' *People of the Valley* and Rudolfo Anaya's *Bless Me, Ultima*." *South Dakota Review* 14, no. 2 (Spring, 1976):102–110.

Mares, E. A. "The Center is Everywhere: Hispanic Letters in New Mexico." *Century Magazine* 2, no. 10 (February, 1982):9–11. (Essay).

Márquez, Antonio. "Algo viejo y algo nuevo: Contemporary New Mexican Hispanic Fiction." *New Mexico Humanities Review* 8, no. 3 (Fall, 1985):65–74. (Analyzes *Nambe-Year One, Below the Summit, The Waxen Image*, and *Memories of the Alhambra*).

Márquez, Antonio. "Into the Mainstream: Sabine R. Ulibarrí's 'Hombre sin nombre'" Unpublished study, 1988.

Márquez, Antonio. "The Achievement of Rudolfo Anaya." *The Magic of Words: Rudolfo Anaya and His Writings*. Edited by Paul Vassallo. Albuquerque, N.M.: University of New Mexico Press, 1982.

Meyer, Doris L. "Anonymous Poetry in Spanish-Language New Mexico Newspapers, 1880–1900." *The Bilingual Review/La Revista Bilingüe* 2 (1975):259–75.

Meyer, Doris L. "Early Mexican-American Response to Negative Stereotyping." *The New Mexico Historical Review* 53, no. 1 (1978):75–91.

Meyer, Doris L. "Felipe Maximiliano Chacón: A Forgotten Mexican-American Author." *New Directions in Chicano Scholarship*. Edited by Ricardo Romo and Raymund Paredes. San Diego, CA.: Chicano Studies, University of California, San Diego, 1978.

Meyer, Doris L. "The Language Issue in New Mexico: 1880–1900: Mexican-American Resistance Against Cultural Erosion." *The Bilingual Review/La Revista Bilingüe* 2, no. 3 (1977):99–106.

Meyer, Doris L. "The Poetry of José Escobar: Mexican Emigre in New Mexico." *Hispania* 61 (1978):24–34.

Mitchell, Carol. "Rudolfo Anaya's *Bless Me, Ultima*: Folk Culture in Literature." *Critique* 22, no. 1 (1980):55–64.

"Mitólogos y mitómanos: Mesa redonda con Alurista, R. Anaya, M. Herrera-Sobeck, A. Morales y H. Viramontes." *Maize: Xicano Art and Literature Notebook* 4, nos. 3–4 (Spring-Summer, 1981):6–23.

Moesser, Alba Irene. *La literatura méjicoamericana del suroeste de los Estados Unidos*. Ph.D. diss. University of Southern California, 1971. (One chapter discusses Fray Angelico Chavez's prose and poetry; another Sabine Ulibarrí's poetry and short stories).

Mondin, Sandra. "The Depiction of the Chicana in *Bless Me, Ultima* and *The Milagro Beanfield War*: A Study in Contrasts." *Mexico and the United States: Intercultural Relations in the Humanities*. Edited by Juanita Lawn, et. al. San Antonio, TX.: San Antonio College, 1984.

Monleón, José. "Ilusion y realidad en la obra de Rudolfo Anaya." *Contemporary Chicano Fiction*, A *Critical Survey*. Edited by Vernon E. Lattin. Binghamton, New York: Bilingual Press, 1986.

Morales, Alejandro Dennis. *Visión panorámica de la literatura méxico americana hasta el boom de 1966*. Ph.D. diss. Rutgers University, State University of New Jersey, 1975. (Examines Gaspar

Pérez de Villagrá's *Historia de la Nueva México* and Sabine Ulibarrí's *Al cielo se sube a pie*. Also discusses Nina Otero's "Count La Cerda's Treasure" and Fray Angelico Chavez's cuentos).

Morales, Phyllis S. *Fray Angelico Chavez: A Bibliography of His Published Writings, 1925–1978*. Santa Fe, N.M.: Lightning Tree Press, 1980.

"Notes on the Evolution of Chicano Prose Fiction." *Modern Chicano Writers: A Collection of Critical Essays*. Edited by Joseph Sommers. Englewood Cliffs, N.J.: Prentice Hall, 1979.

Ortego, Philip D. "Chicano Poetry: Roots and Writers" *New Voices in Literature: The Mexican Americans*. Edinburg, Tx.: Department of English, Pan American University, 1971. (Analyzes Fray Angelico Chavez's poetry in *Eleven Lady-Lyrics* and *The Single Rose*).

Padilla, Genaro M. "A Reassessment of Fray Angelico Chavez's Fiction." *MELUS* 11, no. 4 (1984):31–45.

Padilla, Genaro M. "The Anti-Romantic City in Chicano Fiction." *Puerto del Sol* 23, no. 1 (1987):159–79. (Examines *Heart of Aztlán, Pocho, Bless Me, Ultima, The Autobiography of a Brown Buffalo* and *The Revolt of the Cockroach People*).

Padilla, Genaro M. "The Recovery of Nineteenth Century Chicano Autobiography." *European Perspectives of Hispanic Literature of the United States*. Edited by Genvieve Fabre. Houston: Arte Público Press, 1987. (Identifies Padre Antonio José Martínez's "Relación" and Raphael Chácon's "Memorias" as autobiographical documents).

Paredes, Américo. "The Folk Base of Chicano Literature." *Modern Chicano Writers, A Collection of Critical Essays*. Edited by Joseph Sommers and Tomás Ybarra-Frausto. Englewood Cliffs, N.J.: Prentice Hall, 1979. (Briefly mentions Aurelio M. Espinosa, Arthur L. Campa and the study of folklore in New Mexico).

Paredes, Raymond A. "The Evolution of Chicano Literature." *Three American Literatures*. Edited by Houston A. Baker. New York: Modern Language Association, 1982. (Mentions Captain Marcos Farfan's play describing "la entrada" into New Mexico and Gaspar Pérez de Villagrá's *Historia de la Nueva México*. Includes a short discussion of New Mexico's early Hispanic writers and a brief analysis of *Bless Me, Ultima*).

Pearce, T. M. "The Bad Son (El Mal Hijo) in Southwestern Spanish Folklore." *Western Folklore* 9, no. 4 (October, 1950):295–301.

Pearce, T. M. "What is a Folk Poet." *Western Folklore* 12 (1953):242–48. (Examines Prospero Baca's *Book of Personal Versos*).

Portillo-Orozco, Febe. *Rudolfo Anaya's Use of History, Myth and Legend in His Novels: Bless Me, Ultima* and *Heart of Aztlan*. M.A. Thesis. San Francisco State University, 1981.

Quintana, Inez. "El norte de Nuevo Mexico visto por Sabine R. Ullibarrí." *El Hispano* (Septiembre 9, 1988):3. (Review of *Pupurupu*).

Rael, Juan B. *The New Mexican Alabado*. Stanford University Publications, University Series, Language and Literature 9, no. 3. Stanford, CA.: Stanford University Press, 1951.

Rael, Juan B. *The Source and Diffusion of the Mexican Shepherd's Plays*. Guadalajara: Libreria La Joyita, 1965.

Ray, J. Karen. "Cultural and Mythical Archetypes in Rudolfo Anaya's *Bless Me, Ultima*." *New Mexico Humanities Review* 1, no. 3 (September, 1978):23–28.

Rebolledo, Tey Diana. "Hispanic Women Writers of the Southwest: Tradition and Innovation." *Old Southwest, New Southwest: Essays on a Region and Its Literature*. Edited by Judy Nolte Lensink. Tucson: The Tucson Public Library, 1987. (Discusses contemporary Chicana writers and early Hispanic women writers).

Rebolledo, Tey Diana. "The Maturing of Chicana Poetry: The Quiet Revolution of the 1980's." *For Alma Mater: Theory and Practice in Feminist Scholarship*. Edited by Paula A. Treichler, Cheris Kramarae, and Beth Stafford. Urbana and Chicago: University of Illinois Press, 1985. (Mentions Denise Chávez's work and her use of la virgen de Guadalupe as "an integrating figure").

Rebolledo, Tey Diana. "Tradition and Mythology: Signatures of Landscape in Chicana Literature." *The Desert Is No Lady: Southwestern Landscapes in Women's Writing and Art*. Edited by Vera

Norwood and Janice Monk. New Haven and London: Yale University Press, 1987. (Discusses early New Mexican Hispanic women writers and their creative works).

Rivera, Rowena A. "A Fifteenth-Century Spanish Romance in New Mexico." *The New Mexico Folklore Record* XV, (1980–1981):8–12.

Robinson, Cecil. "Rudolfo Anaya: An Overview." *Puerto del Sol* 19, (Fall, 1983):125–33.

Rocard, Marciene. "The Chicano: A Minority in Search of a Proper Literary Medium for Self-affirmation." *Missions in Conflict, Essays on U.S.-Mexican Relations and Chicano Culture*. Edited by Renate von Bardeleben, Dietrich Briesemeister and Juan Bruce-Novoa. Tubingen: Gunter Narr Verlag, 1986. (Makes references to Miguel Otero's works).

Rocard, Marciene. "The Remembering Voice in Chicana Literature." *The Americas Review* XIV, nos. 3–4 (Fall-Winter, 1986):150–59. (Quotes Enriqueta Vásquez, a Nuevo Mexicana writer, on Chicana literature).

Rodríguez, Juan. "El desarrollo del cuento chicano: Del folklore al tenebroso mundo del yo." *The Identification and Analysis of Chicano Literature*. Edited by Francisco Jiménez. New York: Bilingual Press/Editorial Bilingüe, 1979. (Contains a short discussion of Nina Otero's "Count La Cerda's Treasure" and briefly mentions Sabine Ulibarrí's *Tierra Amarilla*).

Rodríguez, Juan. "La busqueda de identidad y sus motivos en la literatura chicana." *The Identification and Analysis of Chicano Literature*. Edited by Francisco Jiménez. New York: Bilingual Press/Editorial Bilingüe, 1979. (Mentions *Bless Me, Ultima*).

Rodríguez, Juan. "Notes on the Evolution of Chicano Prose Fiction." *Modern Chicano Writers: A Collection of Critical Essays*. Edited by Joseph Sommers and Tomás Ybarra-Frausto. Englewood Cliffs, N.J.: Prentice-Hall, 1979. (Contains references to Nina Otero and Fray Angelico Chavez).

Rodríguez, Juan. "Short Story." *A Decade of Chicano Literature (1970–1979), Critical Essays and Bibliography*. Edited by Luis Leal, et. al. Santa Barbara, CA.: Editorial La Causa, 1982. (Mentions short story writers, Denise Chávez, E. A. Mares and Estevan Arellano).

Rodríguez, Juan. "Temas y motivos de la literatura chicana." *Festival Flor y Canto II: An Anthology of Chicano Literature*. Edited by Arnold C. Vento, Alurista, and José Flores Peregrino. Albuquerque, N.M.: Pajarito Publications, 1975. (Discusses *Bless Me, Ultima*, . . . *No Se Lo Trago La Tierra*, *Peregrinos de Aztlán*, and the *Autobiography of a Brown Buffalo*).

Rodríguez del Pino, Salvador. "La novela chicana de los setenta comentada por sus escritores y críticos." *The Identification and Analysis of Chicano Literature*. Edited by Francisco Jiménez. New York: Bilingual Press/Editorial Bilingüe, 1979. (Gives the perspectives of Chicano writers and critics on the literary works published in the 1970's; includes Rudolfo Anaya's views).

Rodríguez del Pino, Salvador. "Una poesía chicana: Una nueva trayectoria." *The Identification and Analysis of Chicano Literature*. Edited by Francisco Jiménez. New York: Bilingual Press/Editorial Bilingüe, 1979. (Mentions Gaspar Perez de Villagrá's *Historia de la Nueva Mexico*).

Roeder, Beatrice A. "Los Comanches: A Bicentennial Folk Play." *Bilingual Review/Revista Bilingüe* 3 (1976):213–20.

Rogers, Jane. "The Function of the La Llorona Motif in Anaya's *Bless Me, Ultima*." *Latin American Literary Review* 5, no. 10 (Spring-Summer, 1977):64–69. Reprint. *Contemporary Chicano Fiction, A Critical Survey*. Edited by Vernon E. Lattin. Binghamton, N.Y.: Bilingual Press, 1986.

Salazar Parr, Carmen. "Current Trends in Chicano Literary Criticism." *The Identification and Analysis of Chicano Literature*. Edited by Francisco Jiménez. New York: Bilingual Press/Editorial Bilingüe, 1979. (Summarizes several literary critical approaches; includes critical studies of *Bless Me, Ultima*, . . . *Y no se lo Tragó la Tierra* and *Pocho*).

Sánchez, John B. "Vicente Bernal." *LULAC News* 5, no. 6 (September, 1938):7–8.

Sánchez, Pedro. *Memoria sobre la vida del presbitero Antonio José Martínez*. Santa Fe, N.M.: Compañía Impresora del Nuevo México, 1903. (Biography).

Schiavone, Sister James David. "Distinct Voices in the Chicano Short Story: Anaya's Outreach, Portillo Trambley's Outcry, Rosaura Sanchez's Outrage." *The Americas Review* 16, no. 2 Summer, 1988:68–82. (Discusses Rudolfo Anaya's *Silence of the Llano*).

Shea, John Gilmary. "The First Epic of Our Country. By the Poet Conquistador of New Mexico, Captain Gaspar de Villagrá." *United States Catholic Historical Magazine* (April, 1887):4.

Sommers, Joseph. "Critical Approaches to Chicano Literature." *Modern Chicano Writers: A Collection of Critical Essays*. Edited by Joseph Sommers and Tomás Ybarra-Frausto. Englewood Cliffs, N.J.: Prentice-Hall, 1979. (Makes references to *Bless Me, Ultima*).

Sommers, Joseph. "From the Critical Literary Text." *New Directions in Chicano Scholarship*. Edited by Ricardo Romo and Raymund Paredes. Chicano Studies Monograph Series. La Jolla, CA.: University of California, 1978.

Somoza, Oscar Urquidez. *Visión axiológica en la narrativa chicana*. Ph.D. Diss. University of Arizona, 1977. (Discusses el curanderismo, religion, and the family in *Bless Me, Ultima. Nambe-Year One*, and in other Chicano novels).

Tatum, Charles M. *Chicano Literature*. Boston: Twayne Publishers, 1982. (Discusses early New Mexico Hispanic writers and their works, and Rudolfo Anaya's *Bless Me, Ultima, Heart of Aztlán*, and *Tortuga*).

Tatum, Charles M. "Contemporary Chicano Prose Fiction: Its Ties to Mexican Literature." *The Identification and Analysis of Chicano Literature*. Edited by Francisco Jiménez. New York: Bilingual Press/Editorial Bilingüe, 1979. (Mentions the literary works by Miguel Otero, Fray Angelico Chavez and Rudolfo Anaya).

Tatum, Charles M. "Some Examples of Chicano Prose Fiction of the Nineteenth and Early Twentieth Century." *Revista Chicano-Riqueña* Ano IX, no. 1 (Invierno, 1981):58–76. (Discusses New Mexico Hispanic writers, Manual M. Salazar, Eusebio Chácon, Felipe Maximiliano Chácon, and Miguel Otero).

Testa, Daniel. "Extensive/Intensive Dimensionality in Anaya's *Bless Me, Ultima*." *Latin American Review* 5, no. 10 (Spring-Summer, 1977):70–78.

Trejo, Arnulfo. Review of *Bless Me, Ultima*. *Arizona Quarterly* 29, no. 2 (Spring, 1973):95–96.

Trujillo, David F. Review of *Memories of The Alhambra* by Nash Candelaria. *De Colores* 5, nos. 1–2 (1980):130–32.

Tully, Marjorie F. *Annotated Bibliography of Spanish Folklore in New Mexico and Southern Colorado*. New York: Arno Press, 1977.

Ulibarrí, Sabine. "Cultural Heritage of the Southwest." *We Are Chicanos, An Anthology of Mexican-American Literature*. Edited by Philip Ortego. New York: Washington Square Press, 1973. (Essay).

Urioste, Donaldo, W. *The Child Protagonist in Chicano Fiction*. Ph.D. Diss., University of New Mexico, 1985. (Chapter 4 discusses *Bless Me, Ultima* by Rudolfo Anaya. Chapter 5 examines Ulibarrí's *Tierra Amarilla: Cuentos de Nuevo Mexico*).

Urioste, Donaldo W. "Costumbrismo in Sabine R. Ulibarrí's Tierra Amarilla: Cuentos de Nuevo Mexico." *Missions in Conflict: Essays on U.S.–Mexican Relations and Chicano Culture*. Edited by Renate von Bardeleben, Dietrich Briesemeister, and Juan Bruce-Novoa. Tubingen: Gunter Narr Verlag, 1986.

Urtiaga, Alfonso. "Epic Poem by New Mexico Explorer Tells Country's First Historical Saga." *New Mexico Magazine* 66, no. 4 (April, 1988):75–80.

Valdes-Fallis, Guadalupe. "Metaphysical Anxiety and the Existence of God in Contemporary Chicano Fiction." *Revista Chicano-Riquena* 3, no. 1 (Winter, 1974):26–33. (Discusses *Bless Me, Ultima*).

Valdez, Ricardo A. Review of *Below the Summit*. *Latin American Review* 5, no. 10 (Spring-Summer, 1977):156–62.

Vallejos, Thomas. *Mestizaje: The Transformations of Ancient Indian Religious Thought in Contemporary Chicano Fiction*. Ph.D. Diss. University of Colorado, Boulder, 1980. (Examines transformation of Indian myth, ritual, and ethics in *Bless Me, Ultima* and *Heart of Aztlán* by Rudolfo Anaya, *El Hombre sin Nombre* by Sabine Ulibarrí and *Nambe-Year One* by Orlando Romero).

Vassallo, Paul, ed. *The Magic of Words: Rudolfo Anaya and His Writings*. Albuquerque, N.M.: University of New Mexico Press, 1982.

Vigil, Cleofes. "Hay un dicho que dice." (Parable) *De Colores* 4, nos. 1–2 (1978):125–26.

Waggoner, Amy. "Tony's Dreams-An Important Dimension in *Bless Me, Ultima*." *Southwestern American Literature* 4 (1974):74–79.

Weigle, Marta. "Guadalupe Baca de Gallegos' 'Las tres preciosidas (The Three Treasures)' Notes on the Tale, Its Narrator and Collector." *New Mexico Folklore Record* XV (1980–81):31–35. (Folk tale).

Contributors

Reed Anderson is professor and chair of the Department of Spanish and Portuguese at Miami University in Oxford, Ohio. He has written on modern Peninsular Spanish novel and theater, and has a book on Federico García Lorca.

Juan Bruce-Novoa is professor at Trinity University in San Antonio, Texas. He has published extensively on Chicano literature and has been instrumental in fomenting interest in Chicano literature in European Universities. His two major publications are *Chicano Authors: Inquiry by Interview*, and *Chicano Poetry: A Response to Chaos*.

Clark Colahan is associate professor at Whitman College in Walla Walla, Washington. He received his Ph.D. in Spanish literature at the University of New Mexico. His publications include an edited translation of Cervantes's *Persiles y Segismunda* and articles on Southwest Colonial literature.

Erlinda Gonzales-Berry is associate professor in the Department of Modern and Classical languages at the University of New Mexico where she teaches Chicano and Latin American literatures. Her research covers Chicano culture, language, and literature, and she is coeditor of *Las Mujeres Hablan: An Anthology of Nuevo Mexicana Writers.*

Enrique Lamadrid is assistant professor in the Department of Modern and Classical languages at the University of New Mexico. His publications include work on Chicano literature and New Mexican folklore.

Luis Leal is professor emeritus from the University of Illinois at Champaigne Urbana. An internationally reknowned scholar of Mexican and Chicano literatures, Professor Leal is currently Assistant Director of the Chicano Studies Program at the University of California, Santa Barbara.

Francisco Lomeli is professor at the University of California, Santa Barbara, in the Spanish and Portuguese and Chicano Studies departments. With Donaldo W. Urioste, he wrote *Chicano Perspectives in Literature: A Critical and Annotated Bibliography*, and he is coeditor of *Chicano Literature: A Reference Guide* and *A Decade of Chicano Literature (1970–1979).*

E. A. Mares is a writer from Albuquerque. He holds a Ph.D. in European history and has published extensively in the fields of creative writing, literature, and history.

Antonio Márquez is associate professor at the University of New Mexico where he teaches in the English department. His publications are in the area of Chicano narrative and American literature.

María Teresa Márquez is a librarian at Zimmerman Library at the University of New Mexico. She has done extensive bibliographical work on Rudolfo Anaya and is coeditor of *Las Mujeres Hablan: An Anthology of Nuevo Mexicana Writers.*

Genaro Padilla is associate professor in the English department at the University of California, Berkeley where he teaches Chicano Literature. He is currently working on Chicano autobiographies and is editor of *The Short Stories of Fray Angelico Chavez.*

Tey Diana Rebolledo is associate professor in the Department of Modern and Classical Languages at the University of New Mexico where she teaches Latin American literature. She has published articles on criticism, Chicana writers, and Hispanic women writers of New Mexico. She is coeditor of *Las Mujeres Hablan: An Anthology of Nuevo Mexicana Writers.*

Rowena A. Rivera, associate professor of Spanish at the University of New Mexico, received a Ph.D. in Latin American Literature from the University of Colorado. She is the coauthor, with Thomas J. Steele, of *Penitente Self-Government: Brotherhoods and Councils 1797–1947*.

Charles Tatum is chair of the Department of Spanish and Portuguese at the University of Arizona. He received his Ph.D. in Latin American Literature at the University of New Mexico. He is editor of the *Journal of Latin American Popular Culture* and is author of *Chicano Literature*.